Snapshots
On A
Journey
HOME AT LAST

IAN F.M. SAINT-YVES

Snapshots On
A Journey

Snapshots On
A Journey

Home At Last

an authobiography

By:

IAN F.M. SAINT-YVES

authorHOUSE®

AuthorHouse™
1663 Liberty Drive
Bloomington, IN 47403
www.authorhouse.com
Phone: 1-800-839-8640

First published by AuthorHouse   05/11/2011

ISBN: 978-1-4567-7885-9 (sc)
ISBN: 978-1-4567-7886-6 (ebk)

Printed in the United States of America

Any people depicted in stock imagery provided by Thinkstock are models, and such images are being used for illustrative purposes only.
Certain stock imagery © Thinkstock.

This book is printed on acid-free paper.

Contents

Chapter One

In the land of my birth, India 1936-1944

I was born on Palm Sunday, 5 April 1936, in the Park Nursing Home, Calcutta, by Caesarean section, the only child of Eric and Catherine Saint-Yves. My Father, a naturalised British citizen of French extraction came from a family whose ancestor first arrived in India in the early 1800s from Landerneau, in Brittany. By profession, he was a Chief Marine Engineer, specialising in dredging, who worked for the Calcutta Port Commissioners. By necessity, his job kept him away from home for some weeks at a time. During one of these spells away, his father registered me as a French citizen, an act which slightly complicated my life. It was through his wish to be an engineer that he met my Mother, he came to Glasgow to study for his "steam ticket". He met my Mother through a friendship with her elder brothers, who were also studying for their "tickets". At the time of my birth, my Father was 35 years of age and my Mother was 31.

My Mother was a Glaswegian, a Fleming (a group of people who had fled persecution in the Low Countries many generations before and had largely settled in the south-west of Scotland). In many respects, she was a typical Glaswegian, exactly five feet tall, with deep red hair and a short temper to match, allied to a sharp mind and tongue. There were no shades of grey as far as she was concerned. From a moderately large, Protestant family, she was the only girl in a family of six brothers, and was consequently spoiled (by her own admission). My Father doted on her and freely admitted that he kept her "wrapped in cotton wool", unnecessarily so as she was more than capable of looking after herself.

My earliest memory is of our house on Hastings Road, Calcutta. This was a large house with barred windows on the ground floor; perhaps this was originally to prevent burglary while allowing the breezes to percolate throughout the house, but I have a suspicion that its real purpose was to prevent the semi-wild monkeys which abounded in the area, (Monkey Row was nearby), from entering the house. I distinctly remember that there was a table upon which there was a bowl containing bananas and other fruit, against the wall under a window. One day, much to my surprise and delight, I saw a long, hairy arm reaching in through the bars to pinch the bananas.

Our next house was a town flat in Park Mansions, 11 Middleton Row, also in Calcutta. My most clear recollection of this flat was of the marble floors. At this time, I began to realise that my Father was not continuously at home and that I was almost totally in the care of an Indian lady, my Ayah, whom I adored. We also employed a cook and a jemahdar, both of whom lived close by. I know this because I used to visit their homes and drink the distinctly flavoured "chi" (tea) which they gave me to drink. In these very early years, Hindi was my first language and it was to remain so until I was about five years of age.

My memories of Park Mansions are very pleasant indeed, as life appeared to be one of perpetual enjoyment. Whether they were of my birthdays or Christmasses I cannot remember, but I do recall two or three parties with my friends most vividly. These memorable recollections were due, in large part, to the great care my Dad took in making "Kohi Bags"; these consisted of fairly large, paper covered, cane frames in the shape of an aeroplane or ship, filled with popcorn, small toys and a variety of sweets, which were then suspended from the ceiling. At a given moment, which was the highlight of the party, Dad would enter the room, stand under the model surrounded by all the expectant children, and then poke a large hole in its under-belly so that the contents deluged the children standing underneath and scattered all over the floor, to be followed quickly by the expectant, prospecting children. It was very exciting.

My Father came from a large family, with brothers, sisters and many aunts, uncles and cousins. On many Sunday afternoons, our small family would join and be engulfed by this larger one. Again, my memories of these Sunday "tiffins" are happy as they always included games for the many children running around the house and garden. However, I have one unpleasant memory which my Dad dealt with adequately. One of the older boys present had found one or two cigars and, presumably as a joke, had given me, (at about the age of three), a lit cigar to smoke and then placed me on a low table as an exhibit. I had just started to puff on the cigar when my Father entered the scene, was obviously upset by what he saw but instead of spanking my bottom, he made me puff it three or four times with the expected result—I turned a nasty shade of green and was violently sick, a remaining memory to this day. Now, I am a non-smoker although, perversely, I did enjoy the occasional "social" cigar.

On the occasions my Dad was at home, we enjoyed a very close relationship. I remember him as a gentle man, always very caring and considerate and with the welfare of the family uppermost in his mind. When involved in do-it-yourself home decorating and repairs, he always included me; we were a team. On one occasion I did let him down, however. While rummaging through his wardrobe in the bedroom unknown to him, I found a box of matches and proceeded to light them. The burning smell attracted Dad and brought him through to the bedroom and, after removing the matches, he gave me a good spanking, the only time he ever laid a hand on me in anger in my whole life.

The Morris 8 saloon car was my Dad's baby and he spent many happy hours tinkering with it. On some week-ends, the three of us would go to "Firpo's", the in-place in Calcutta at that time, for drinks and lunch. I still have a vague memory of driving down Chowringhee, the main thoroughfare, after lunch with Mum and Dad in the front seats and me standing upright behind and between them looking out of the car window and saying, "She's a fashion plate, Dad." every time we passed a well dressed woman.

During these early, care-free years, I also made my first tentative steps up the educational ladder by going to kindergarten. My first girl-friend was from these days; she was called Mary Poll Parrot (surely fictitious?)

and was an incessant chatterbox and my constant shadow both at and away from school.

Somewhere around my second birthday, I know that my family went back to Glasgow to attend a double wedding—Mum's two brothers, (one of whom trained with Dad), were marrying two sisters, and Dad was to be best-man. I do not remember the wedding but I remember seeing a wedding group photograph in which Dad's bow tie was the only one crooked although it had been a tea-total wedding; this always struck me as amusing. For the wedding, I was the page-boy, dressed in my Erracht Cameron kilt and frilled blouse crowned by my curly, blond head of hair (although I had been born a red-head). My cousin, Morag, the daughter of my Mum's eldest brother, was the page-girl.

At that time, my Mum's family lived at 314 Mossspark Drive, Glasgow. It was also the time of the Empire Exhibition which was held in Bellahouston Park. One main feature was the Empire Tower, which stood on a hill and which could apparently be seen when floodlit at night from the back door of the house. I have been told that I used to say "Good night Ian's Tower" every night before going to bed.

On our return to Calcutta after the wedding, my Grandfather Fleming accompanied us. His name was John MacIntyre Fleming and he lived with us during my early years. He was a Glaswegian and had been employed as a storeman in the Queen Street, Glasgow, store of the Singer Sewing Machine Company. He was a kindly man but very fond of his national beverage, and he and I were the best of friends. One of our regular routines was for us to go for an afternoon walk to the "maidan", the large park in Calcutta dominated by the white Victoria Memorial building. Of course, Grandpa encouraged me in all of my daft, childish whims; one of these was owning a pet white duck which was not only kept in one of the bathrooms (yes, the bathtub was filled with water for the duck's pleasure) but which also accompanied the two of us on our walks, waddling and quacking behind me attached to a long length of string. We became quite well known personalities as a result of these meanderings.

As we lived in a mosquito-infested area, each of our beds was draped in a mosquito net under which we lay on going to bed for the night. One incident which befell Grandpa provided us with considerable amusement, although not to him, and also proved that he did not sleep under his net. One night, we were all awakened by sneezing and the clatter of some object as it hit the marble floor of his bedroom. Hurriedly, Mum, Dad and I rushed through to his room only to see Grandpa down on his knees, in his pyjamas, gingerly picking up the smashed pieces of his false teeth off the floor. If he had been using the net, his teeth would not have been smashed on the floor. This episode provided us with much amusement for a long time after.

At about this time, I developed a severe attack of scalp ringworm. In those days the remedy was to shave off all the hair and to rub the patches of ringworm with sulphur soaked in some kerosine. As a result of the treatment, I lost my golden head of hair because when it grew back in it was light brown.

The second World War was not long started and there was much uncertainty in India at this time as the Japanese had begun their westward push into Burma and Assam and, in some instances, were said to be within one hundred miles of Calcutta. One of the results was that it was decided that Grandpa should return home to Glasgow, which he did by sea returning via South Africa. It would be another three years before I would see him again. At about the same time, my parents decided that I should be registered as a British colonial citizen, which I duly was.

I must have heard this when I was a bit older but I do remember my Dad saying that rather than permit Mum and me from falling into the hands of the Japanese as prisoners of war, he would seriously consider cutting our throats before killing himself. Fortunately for all of us, the need never arose. I think that my Dad's decision was based on his experiences as an Engineer Officer in Essential Services. Just prior to the fall of Singapore, he and other officers in the Calcutta Port Commissioners were seconded to the war service, ferrying men and military equipment from Calcutta to Singapore. I have heard him speak of the incompetence of the military planners. Apparently they sent shiploads of unarmed troops by convoy to Singapore where they were taken prisoners by the Japanese almost as soon as they had disembarked. The military equipment for the troops arrived in later ships and was also delivered to the Japanese.

It may have been because of the Japanese threat or because Dad was away from home for long periods or, more likely, because the best schools tended to be Catholic ones, that I first found myself being sent away to boarding school at the age of five. I really have no recollection of my first boarding school in Mussouri. I may even be confusing the geography. I only know that Mum must have accompanied me, but whether I am recalling this journey or the one to my next school in Darjeeling, I know not although I believe it to be the latter. I can only recall that we travelled by train to a place called Derra Dun. Here we changed to a mountain-gauge railway; I can vaguely remember seeing the last of the carriages running almost parallel to the engine as the train wound its way round sharp mountain curves. Eventually we disembarked and piled into buses for the final part of the journey.

This episode must have happened about 1941-42; these years also marked the peak of civil disobedience against British rule in India, led by Mahatma Gandhi. In later years, I remember Mum saying that my journey to school occurred at the very peak of the protests. While in the train travelling north from Calcutta, I vaguely remember seeing the burnt-out railway stations, and later being told by Mum that the train had been side-tracked for hours at a time, to avoid conflict along the way. My lasting impression of this obviously frightening journey (to Mum, I found it quite exciting) occurred in the final stage when we were all in the buses after leaving the train. This also happened to be the day that Gandhi had been jailed by the British.

Our particular bus was full and among its passengers were two Sikh army men, both armed with revolvers. To reach our destination, we had to pass through a few villages the inhabitants of which were fervent Gandhi supporters. At one of the villages, the small bus convoy was surrounded by a large group of excited and angry villagers who eventually managed to bring the bus to a halt; the crowd became more angry, stones were thrown and windows broken. At this stage, the two Sikhs took charge and told us to lie down on the floor of the bus and, at the same time, informed us that should the need arise, they would not hesitate to shoot the attackers. Once again, we were lucky; no shots were fired and the bus convoy was allowed to pass safely to reach its eventual destination.

St. Joseph's College, Darjeeling, I do remember quite clearly. Staffed by Jesuits, it had established an enviable academic reputation. The building itself was imposing—grey, monolithic, fronted by banked playing-fields, with Kanchenjunga, the world's third highest mountain covered in eternal snow, as a backdrop. The motto of the school was "SURSUM CORDA".

Dad had also attended this school, so there was a good reason for my being there. Although I was attending a Catholic school, my upbringing was non-sectarian but Christian. That I was not brought up a Catholic (although my Dad's family were Catholics) was due to two facts. The first involved a vital episode in my parents' early life together. They were married in a Church of Scotland ceremony in Glasgow on Boxing Day, 1934. Shortly after the marriage, the Catholic parish priest on a home visit apparently stated that my parents were living in sin as they had not been married (that is, in a Catholic ceremony). Quite correctly, my Dad physically ejected this bigoted man from their home. The second fact was that Mum was a Presbyterian and was very proud of her Covenanting antecedents. I must confess that I was never burdened with religion at home; neither Mum nor Dad were church-goers, although Dad tried to go to the annual Christmas midnight Mass and later in life as a teenager, I accompanied him. The only teacher whom I can remember from those far off days was Father Coutts, although I cannot recall what subjects he taught me. He could have been my house-master. The memories I have of him are good ones.

My recall of school activities is also very sketchy. Pets, of course, were not permitted; however, we did keep pets—pet insects. The playing fields fronting the school were surrounded by a bank of earth, saucer-like, and many of the boys, including me, made small holes in the earth bank into which we placed our insect pets (beetles and praying mantis were the most popular), closing the hole with a plug of moss to imprison the poor creatures.

Inevitably, religion played a large part in the Jesuit school life and I well recall being crocodiled off to chapel two or three times a day. Eventually, I took my first communion and adopted the communion name of St. Andrew, Scotland's patron saint. This enforced religiosity must have left

7

its mark because my wife, Margot, many years later, accused me of being a Jesuit by nature and upbringing, presumably because I tend to be idealistic, almost missionary in my actions, allied to a strong self-discipline.

It is possible that I spent two scholastic years there, although I cannot remember. I do remember, on the odd occasion Mum visited me from Calcutta, walking with her through the narrow, crowded streets of the hill-station perched precariously on the hillside, to a small restaurant where we would sit at a small table and enjoy ice cold, fresh milk which tasted like nectar to me. I also remember that, prior to the arrival of winter at which time Darjeeling was totally snow-bound and isolated, our trunks containing our belongings would be packed on to the buses, and then the trains, accompanied by the excited pupils and many staff members, for the long journey to the hot southern plains, and myself to Calcutta.

Occasionally, on a late Saturday morning in Calcutta, Mum and I would go to the Lighthouse Cinema. On one of our visits, the air raid siren sounded and so we were evacuated from the cinema, but instead of going to an air raid shelter, we trooped out into the street and looked skyward. Very high up in the clear blue sky, we could just make out a tiny Japanese 'plane glistening like a drop of rain on a pane of glass. We later learned that it had been a sole straggler. That was my only encounter with the Japanese threat to our peace.

There is one other lasting memory of my life in Calcutta. Occasionally when I was home from school, I was left with an elderly Scot called Roy Wright, while Mum went to work as a departmental head at Whiteway Laidlaw, a large department store. He lived in a block of flats around the upper storey of which ran a verandah. One of my friends, an older boy, also lived there and, in the afternoons, the two of us would fly our kites from the verandah. The sky at this time of the day was full of kites, most of them at a considerable height. The object of kite flying was not just to fly it but to engage it in aerial combat, the express intention of manoeuvering your kite into such a position with respect to another kite, so as to be able to cut through the string of the opposing kite and cast it adrift, thus registering a kill. This was a most fascinating way of spending an afternoon.

In 1944, just after my eighth birthday, it was decided that Mum and I should return home to Glasgow so that I could go to school in Scotland. Dad, still on essential service, was not allowed leave of absence.

The day came for our departure from Howrah station and my Dad came to see us off. I was not to see Dad for another three years. The train compartments appeared to be for families as Mum and I shared a square-shaped compartment in which the beds folded up against the walls when not in use. I realise now that this was very practical as the journey from Calcutta to Bombay, across the Deccan, took a few days days, and the compartment became our home. There were no restaurant cars or cooking facilities; instead, meals were ordered in advance at each station, the order telegraphed ahead of the train so that the prepared meal would be available at the next station stop. Bed linen and towels were also changed at designated stations. This good organisation did not stop me from buying Indian sweetmeats from the sellers at the station stops. To this day, I love the sickly sweetness of jilabees, russigolahs and goulamjambs. Eventually, we arrived in Bombay and transferred to the ship which would take us home safely, but not without some excitement.

Chapter Two

The Voyage Home to Scotland:
a new School 1944

Boarding the ship which was to take us home is only a very vague memory, suffice to say that it was a British India Steam Navigation ship called the "Modasa" and that it was not a particularly large ship, but painted grey from bow to stern.

There was one particularly notable thing about our voyage home—at that time, we were part of the largest convoy to leave India for the United Kingdom. The number of ships in the convoy was a war-time secret, but I do remember the aircraft carrier "Courageous", the corvette "Delphinium" and an un-named submarine being part of it, as they regularly sailed past us on a parallel course for short periods of time during the voyage.

The voyage was uneventful and, to a child, exciting. A great deal of effort was made to entertain the many children on board. One activity was to learn how to knit; I clearly remember sitting on a hatch in the late afternoons trying to knit a scarf, but by the time I had finished it, it looked more like a truncated, triangular pennant.

The convoy was on constant alert and one of the daily chores of the crew on board the Modasa was to raise and lower the barrage balloons, the gas-filled blimps which provided a degree of protection against relatively low-flying enemy aircraft. One of my regular duties was to "assist" the soldier (one of a small army contingent on board to man the gun) responsible for this task and I did so with considerable enthusiasm and without fail, watching the wire gradually unwind from the winch, allowing the blimp to rise to a predetermined height.

It was also the first time that I began to pay attention to music, probably due to the fact that the off-duty crew would sit on the hatches and play their 78-records on wind-up gramophones and sing to them. The tunes that I clearly remember are: "You are my sunshine", "I've got sixpence" and "Daisy, Daisy".

There were always activities for the children on deck. Easily the highlight of the voyage for us was the "Fancy Dress Party". I recall that Mum and I made a cardboard hat in the shape of a ship and called it "Modasa". At the height of the party, the Delphinium moved alongside and arranged a Breeches-buoy between the two ships; this was not to transfer anyone but to provide the hungry kids with doughnuts. I can still visualise everyone lining the ship's rails to watch the doughnuts, safely enclosed in a waterproofed, naval kitbag, being slung across the subdued, grey waves from a warship to a passenger ship full of mothers and children. After the Delphinium and the submarine moved alongside for a short while. In the late afternoon, after the festivities, I solemnly launched my Modasa over the ship's rails into the darkening, restless sea.

It was not all fun and games on the voyage. The Modasa was armed with a small gun set on a bow platform, plus a small primitive rocket-launcher and a couple of Oerlikon anti-aircraft guns. A shipboard detachment of soldiers serviced these weapons. Apart from practice alerts, during which we collected our life-jackets and moved quickly to our pre-allocated lifeboats, we also had one or two air raids. The main one occurred while we were heading for Aden. In this raid, we sadly lost a pilot and his aircraft from the accompanying carrier.

However, conflict was not confined to war-time action alone. Many mothers ran into opposition from their children in the dining room where, for the first time, we were meeting the wonders of war-time cuisine, which we found distasteful and difficult to consume. The first delight was the dried banana which looked like something you should never touch and certainly not eat. If this object was soaked in water for a while, it swelled to produce a bloated, cardboard tasting banana. The next treat in store was powdered egg. This had a really strange taste and together with the fact that it never appeared to be cooked properly, I am sure were the main reasons for my dislike of eggs for years to come. Spam, the great American meat, also made its appearance, but my taste buds considered it to have a most unusual flavour and I was really never hooked on it. However, it was to margarine, in its initial primitive form, that I must give my "totally disgusting award". I am only now appreciating the currently available margarines, which are also good for your health. However, I did not dislike all of these "new" foods—I quite enjoyed eating Pom made from a dehydrated potato powder.

Eventually and to our great delight, we arrived unexpectedly at the Tail of the Bank in the Firth of Clyde, (our port of arrival was also a secret in these times), one grey, damp morning, 5th June 1944, the day before D-Day. Our ship and cargo were pretty small fry on that particular day, so we were quickly disembarked on to a very congested, bustling wharf where we were met by Mum's brother, Cameron, and his wife, Margaret. On the water, there was an armada of boats and ships of all shapes and sizes, all very active. At this time we did not appreciate that the invasion of Europe was due to start the next day and that this would soon empty the Firth of men, ships and material as they moved south.

Although we initially stayed at 314 Mosspark Drive, Glasgow, (my Grandmother's home originally but now the home of my Aunt and Uncle), Mum soon rented a small, old-fashioned flat in Largs, Ayrshire (a seaside town famous for the battle in which the Scots under Alexander III defeated the Vikings under Haakon IV of Norway in 1263, and which is now commemorated by the Pencil monument) in Gogoburn Road, at the back of the town. The flat had a hole-in-the—wall bed and was wholly served by gas. My memory is of my Mother lighting the gas mantles, one on each side of the fire place, as the night came down, and then turning them off before going to bed. I watched this evening ritual from the bed recess, well tucked up in my sheets and blankets. It was a happy house for us, only slightly marred for me by a long spell of boils on my legs.

Mum and I would go for walks along the beach road to the Pencil, to the boating pond where I would sail my model boat, then buy ice-creams from an Italian cafe, Nardini's, on the sea-front; occasionally, we would even climb the Haylie Brae. On Saturday evenings, we would go to the pictures at the Viking cinema; this building was fronted by a model of the bow section of a Viking long-boat, set in a small concrete pool. On the one Easter we spent in Largs, my cousins Morag and John Fleming came to visit us. We made hard-boiled eggs, painted them with gay designs before setting off for the Haylie Brae, where we rolled them down the hillside.

Mum only rented the flat long enough to arrange my admission as a boarder to Glasgow Academy, one of the oldest public (private) schools in Scotland, situated at Kelvinbridge, as she was soon to return to India to rejoin Dad.

I entered the Boarding House at 12 Belmont Crescent in September 1944 and was to stay there, except for school holidays, for four and a half years. I entered the Academy in the Junior school and remember that the name of my first form mistress was Miss MacEwan.

The Boarding House was a relatively happy place for about thirty boys whose parents were abroad, largely in the Colonial Service. The boys' ages ranged from about seven to eighteen years, and there was a quite strict hierarchy. We were very fortunate to have excellent House Parents, Captain Jack and Mrs. Ethel Coleman-Smith, an equally delightful housekeeper, Mrs. Wilson, and an excellent cook, Miss Thomson.

Jack Coleman-Smith had been in the Indian army and, according to an apocryphal story, had lost one testicle there in some engagement best left unrelated. His nicknames were "Coley" or "Colebags", and apart from being the House Parent, was a celebrity in his own right. Every morning at 6.30 am, he gave a live radio broadcast from the BBC studios in Queen Margaret Drive on physical education, his theme song being: "Jump, jump, jump little frog. Why don't you jump right over the log?" which he would sing at the start and end of each session, in his baritone voice. He was also bald, but that did not occasion any cruel schoolboy barbs. During school hours, he was the principal Physical Education Instructor and, together with his colleague, Mr. Henry U'ren ("Pissy" to the boys), put us through many hours of torture.

Ethel must have been a very beautiful woman in her youth as she was still very attractive in middle age. She was devoted to Jack, and being childless, to "her" boys. Kindness with firmness was what she practised, to which was added a very keen perception of house undercurrents. You felt that you were able to approach her at any time. She was affectionately called "Ethel" or "Mrs. C".

Mrs. Wilson was a typical Glaswegian, small, grey-haired and full of fun. All the boys loved her. The smooth, harmonious running of the House was in no small measure due to this dynamic women. On the other hand, Miss Thomson was a large, jovial woman who did wonders in the kitchen. I can honestly say that the food we received was as good as any home cooking, no small feat in those days of late rationing. Oddly, I cannot recall that either of these two ladies ever received nicknames from the boys.

The boys were split into sections: the Juniors, Middle and Senior pupils. The largest dormitory contained seven beds, but most only contained about four beds, with an occasional two bed room for the senior boys. The whole house was carpeted. The studies were divided as for the dormitories in sections, each boy having his own desk. Each grade of student was expected to study for set periods both before (for the youngsters) and after high tea, which was at 6pm. (This habit of having my meal at 6pm has remained with me to this day.) Then, before going to bed, we would have our baths, sometimes two in a bath—they were always good fun.

In the long summer evenings, when it stays light until about 10.30 pm, we would be allowed to go out either into Belmont Crescent, where we would race around the gravel verge or else play King-ball, or go down to the school playground, just down the road, where we would play football before returning for our baths and bed. Once in bed, we would do all the forbidden things like whispering after lights-out, having midnight feasts, reading under the sheets by torchlight, all the while keeping a weather eye open for the duty senior or even Coley himself.

The meals in the Boarding House were always formal and every meal was preceded by the saying of Grace, which was usually delivered by the Head boy. The unchanging Grace was "For what we are about to receive may the Lord make us truly thankful." There were two long tables in the dining room; at the top table sat the senior boys with Coley, and at the lower table sat Mrs. C with the juniors. The middle and junior boys were rostered to set and clear the tables for all meals; this included drying but not washing the dishes. During the week, we had breakfast and high tea in the Boarding House with lunch at school, while at the week-ends all meals were eaten at the House. We always had a glass of milk and a biscuit before going to bed.

Although we had Prefects in the House, the juniors did not act as "Fags" for them, although occasionally we were asked to clean their shoes and rugby boots as a punishment. However, the Head boy was allowed to use the slipper across your bottom for any serious misdemeanour, although they were always accountable to Coley for their decisions and actions. I only received the slipper once from the School Captain, who was also a boarder, and the strap once from Coley—I can't remember what they were for. In reality, it was a home from home.

In 1948, while I was still a boarder, I developed appendicitis. Lying uncomfortably in bed, I awaited the arrival of the Consultant Surgeon, Mr. Eric Gerstenberg; he was also a former pupil of the school. When he arrived, I found him to be very immaculately dressed, small in stature with dark, slicked back, black hair and a rather brusque, business-like manner; I suppose that he was a dapper man. Anyway, he quickly decided that I needed an operation and I was whisked away to a private Nursing Home called the "Park Nursing Home" in Park Circus (coincidence, as I was also born in the Park Nursing Home, but in Calcutta). The operation was successfully and quickly over and I can still remember my convalescence because I experienced the sensation of bubbles seemingly bursting under my stitch line. My recovery was otherwise uneventful. About eight years later, I again met Mr. Gerstenberg but under slightly different circumstances.

The boarders always tended to stick together at school and we tended to consider ourselves an elite group as we always appeared to have a large number of prefects, Ist. XV (rugby union), and Ist. XI (cricket) members among us. Scholastically, we were probably not quite as elite as we imagined ourselves to be.

When not at the books, how did I fill in my time? During the week, after school, two or three afternoons were taken up with rugby training in the winter and cricket in the summer. On these occasions, we would take the tram out along Great Western Road to Anniesland where the Academical playing fields were. After our exertions, we always enjoyed the hot, communal baths, especially if we had been playing rugby in sleet and snow. I played for the school in the under 11 1/2 and under 12 1/2 years rugby teams.

On a Saturday morning, a group of us not caught up in playing rugby or cricket for the school at Anniesland or elsewhere would catch the tram or bus to go to the Vogue cinema at Anniesland Cross, after which we would rush back for lunch. After lunch, if we were not honour-bound to watch the Academicals (former pupils) playing rugby or cricket at home, we would grab our bathers and rush along Great Western Road, sometimes catching a tram if handy, to the Western Baths in Cranworth Street. This was a private club in which the Boarding House had a block membership. The whole afternoon was spent there and the time just flew past, under the watchful but stern eye of Mr. Jamieson, the Baths Master. I learned to swim there. Many years later I was to return to Cranworth Street, Hillhead. After leaving the Baths in the late afternoon, we would invade Byres Road and one fish and chip shop in particular, each to buy a shilling bag of fresh chips which we would eat while chattering our way back to Belmont Crescent. In the evenings, it was either the crescent or the school playground for us.

Sunday mornings saw us in a crocodile line, dressed in our kilts, tweed jackets, hose and brogues, crossing Kelvin Bridge in the charge of a senior boy, on our way to Lansdowne Church, which had the most slender and tallest steeple in Glasgow, where we endured a Presbyterian service for a period just in excess of one hour. After leaving church, we had two alternatives. The first, our favourite, was to walk past Hubbards Bakery in Otago Street, because the baking tins would have just been emptied and often contained "heels" of loaves which would still be warm and soft. We just loved eating these. Our second alternative was to go to the Botanic Gardens, at the corner of Queen Margaret Drive and Great Western Road, enter the beautifully kept and warm greenhouses, largely to escape from the wild weather outside. In the afternoon, we usually went to the school playground where we would play football or explore a large, concrete lined, open tank half-filled with debris and water and which contained dozens of frogs. When that palled, we would climb the fence and clamber down the bank of the Kelvin River to the weir, where we would taunt and throw stones at less fortunate youths, called "Glesca Keelies", on the other bank of the river. So much for the sons of gentlemen. We were given an evening off study on a Sunday. During the long summer evenings, I loved to look out the dormitory window towards Park Circus (high on a hill overlooking Kelvingrove Park) and the twin towers of Trinity College.

There were other activities such as ice-skating at Crossmyloof (which we only did very occasionally), tobogganing in Kelvingrove Park (when there was enough snow) and having morning tea in Hubbards Tearooms at Kelvinbridge (when we had enough money) which filled our hours and left us with many happy memories.

All my efforts were not physical, however. Once a week, under the long-suffering gaze of Miss Blackburn, I undertook a gruelling one hour of pianoforte tuition; I even practised every night of the week for about twenty minutes during the study period. She must have thought me one of her better pupils but I cannot understand why, looking back on it, for she took me to hear the visiting Russian pianist Moisiewitch playing at Green's Playhouse. Unfortunately, my piano playing lapsed after leaving the house. One last memory, which was an annual event, was the Boarding House Christmas Show, in which we all participated, both on and back stage, and to which we invited friends and relatives. This was great fun. I remember being in the chorus line on one occasion. This escapade influenced me for I was to continue my thespian activities for a short while at a later stage and in a different country.

There was one Sunday chore which I had almost forgotten about, but which has stood me in good stead over the years. Every Sunday morning, between having breakfast and setting off for church, we sat down to write our letters to our relatives and friends. I still write very regularly to my wife and children whenever I am separated from them, although it is no longer a chore but an act of love in which I feel very close to them.

Chapter Three

The Middle School Years, 1945-1949

As in all Public schools, the pupils were required to wear a distinctive uniform. Our uniform consisted of a grey shirt with the Academy light/ dark blue striped tie, grey long or short trousers and a navy blue blazer emblazoned with the school badge and motto "SERVA FIDEM" on the breast pocket, topped off with the grey, navy blue quartered school cap. The cap was compulsory wearing once off the school grounds; it was a source of constant strife as the prefects tried to enforce the rest of the pupils to wear it. It was a silly adornment.

I quickly moved through the Junior school and into Transitus, the half-way stage between the Senior and Junior schools, although the classes themselves were held in the main school building.

The school building was in the classical Greek style and dominated the northern aspect of Kelvin Bridge. It was tall, of grey stone, square in shape and girded with windows all round. Inside the building, there was a central courtyard at ground level, the space so created continuing up through the building. For two storeys, the classrooms were arranged around this central space, each storey being fronted by a verandah. Every week-day morning an Assembly was held before the start of classes, at which the Junior and Middle school pupils gathered in the courtyard, while the senior boys lined the verandahs outside their classrooms. The school choir stood at the back of the stage, which was sited to one side of the courtyard. A hand-pumped organ (this chore was carried out by one of the middle school pupils) was to the right side (facing), while the teachers sat at the front of the stage, fronted by the Rector standing at a movable lectern.

The format of the morning assembly never varied. The Rector would start off with a short prayer, which would then be followed by a hymn. At this stage, one of the prefects would read a selected passage from the Bible, and this in turn would be followed by another hymn, after which the Lord's Prayer would bring the religious part to a close. The Rector would conclude the assembly by making the school announcements outlining the activities for the day. Even to this day, there are still quite a few hymns to which I can put most of the words.

I suppose that I must have been an above-average pupil as I remained largely in the A-stream and regularly collected prizes at the annual School Prize Giving ceremonies. My bent was towards French and Latin, although I also did reasonably well in Geography, History and Biology. At this particular period, the Academy had excellent teachers. The Rector, F. Roydon Richards, was a classicist and only rarely taught, confining himself to the senior classicists. The ones whom I can remember now exerted great influence on me. In French, I was very fortunate to be taught by a tall, black-haired, middle-aged man with a slight stoop called Chris Varley. He was a friend of the Coleys and was frequently at the Boarding House. His patience and gentleness were extraordinary. Kenneth Miles, an English Cambridge graduate, was both my English and Latin teacher, and although we were not the greatest of buddies, he certainly gave me a solid grounding in both these languages. At a later date, "Baggy" Aston and "Bruiser" Engledow were also to briefly teach me English and French respectively. I did not spend all of my time on languages but also dabbled in Chemistry under Jock Carruthers, (he was also CO of the Cadet Corps), Geography under Bill Ogilvie, basic Mathematics under Hugh Skilling and yet more French with "Basher" Ainslie (he had been a paratrooper at Arnhem in that ill-fated episode of the war) who also participated in the Cadet Corps. Basher was quite a formidable sight on Corps afternoons as he came in battle-dress uniform and, with his broken nose, squat, powerful frame, did not brook any cheek. Yet, he was well liked.

Sometime in the late 1940s, Mum returned to Glasgow and rented a small flat off an old spinster called Jessie Lawson, a Church of Scotland Deaconness; the flat was at 107 Otago Street, Hillhead, at the Kelvingrove Park end as opposed to the Red Hackle whisky end. This was grand as I was able to skip along illegally after school and have some light refreshments, usually buns and Barr's Irn-Bru, while chatting to Mum. It also allowed me to keep white mice in a specially built, glass-fronted, two-storeyed cage. Also, I did not have to travel far on my week-ends off.

My Dad also came home for a short spell one summer. I remember this for two reasons. The first was about the same time as I was in Transitus A. My examination marks must have shown signs of deterioration due to my increasing non-academic activities. One summer evening, when Dad and I were out strolling after our high tea, he gradually steered the conversation around to school work and examinations, pointing out to me gently but firmly that although it was nice to have friends, they would not support me in later life, this being entirely my own responsibility through my own efforts. It was a chat that I have never forgotten.

The second reason was more pleasurable. During my summer holidays, Dad used to take me to Bingham's Pond, in front of Gartnavel Hospital, off Great Western road. Here, we would hire a rowing boat and Dad would teach me the rudiments of water-craft and rowing. Many a happy hour was spent in this way. In later years, when I was at Glasgow University and very active in the Boat Club, (rowing), he would say that I first learned the rudiments on those summer afternoons with him.

During those holidays in which my parents were abroad, I went either to my Aunt Violet's in Ibrox, (almost next door to the Rangers Football Club grounds), or to Aunt Margaret and Uncle Cameron in Mosspark. Usually, I spent the longer holidays with Aunt Violet as she had more freedom in her job as a collection agent and her home atmosphere was much more carefree.

Aunt Violet was Mum's Aunt but was not much older than Mum. She had led a hard life and now worked as an agent for a credit society, the Provident, which required her to to be out at all hours and in all weather so that she could be sure of finding her clients at home to make her collections, as her salary was solely dependent on commission. Her elder brother, Peter, was also an agent and they both worked from her ground floor flat at 10 Whitefield Road, which was fairly handy as their collection area covered Govan and Ibrox. Aunt was about five feet two inches tall and overweight but nothing was too much bother for her, and although her house was not spotlessly clean, I always enjoyed myself there. Her mother stayed with her and they both slept together in a large double bed in the hole-in-the-wall. Her mother was still physically active although she suffered from some degree of amnesia, which was not surprising as she was well over ninety years of age when I first came in close contact with her. When I was twelve, she once grabbed a poker from the blackened, cast-iron fire range and chased me out of the house and around the Anderson shelter, a war-time relic still standing in the back garden, shouting, "Ye little bugger, ye." as she thought I had been cheeky to her.

The Ibrox flat had two large bedrooms and a large lounge, together with a large kitchen and toilet. The front room was rented to a permanent male, invalid lodger who acted like one of the family. On my holidays, I occupied the back bedroom. Aunt Violet also had a young, male relative, Peter Stoddart, who returned to Ibrox after war service in the Far East with the RAF. I was never sure of Dinky's relationship, as that was his nickname, to Aunt, and no one ever mentioned the subject. He and I were very good friends; however, at this stage in his life, he was too busy chasing his various lady friends to bother too much about me. His favourite was Jenny Justice who lived in the flat above; he never married her in the end.

However, he did enjoy another passion, motor bike racing, the Speedway, which took place at the White City on Paisley Road West, not far from the Rangers ground. Whenever I was on holiday, he would take me with him to the Speedway where I was enthralled not so much by the racing as by the different characters representing all strata of Glasgow life whom I saw there. Occasionally, we also attended the greyhound racing, which was also held at the same venue but on different evenings.

Mum bought me a Cairn terrier which I called "Shoona". This little dog eventually bossed everyone in the house and even had time to have one or two litters. It stayed at Whitefield Road, and I was able to see it on my holidays and when I sneaked away from the Academy on the subway, alighting at Copland Road.

Uncle Peter had been a sailor in his earlier years and had sailed the world. It was said that, after one of his trips, he had brought home a marmoset for Aunt Violet. On the colder nights, when the grate fire had died down but the oven was still warm, the marmoset would climb in and sleep there, with the door open. Unfortunately for the poor beast, one day it was forgotten about, and the oven door was closed on it. The grate fire was lit and the marmoset roasted to death, its cries remaining unheard. At another time, Uncle Peter brought home an African parrot. This lived in a large cage which hung high at the kitchen window, overlooking the back garden. It was a non-stop talker, loved eating cooked pigs' trotters and lived with the family for over thirty years. Its favourite pastime was annoying Shoona by "barking" at it.

Aunt Violet and Uncle Peter had one activity which I did not appreciate. Every so often, Uncle Peter would buy uncleaned sheeps' stomachs along with pigs' trotters. He would dump them in the sink and start to clean them himself. However, my problem began when these "delicacies" started to boil; the smell was unbelievable and I was often close to sickness as the obnoxious odour permeated the whole house very quickly. Worse was to follow, however, when they would offer me this awful offal to eat. It was many years later before I was able to face properly bleach—cleaned tripe; indeed, it is now one of my favourite dishes.

It would have been sacriligeous if, after living almost next door to the Rangers ground, I had never visited it to watch the mighty Glasgow Rangers play. It was George, my Aunt's long-term lodger, who occasionally took me to the home matches. We always stood securely at the Rangers end of the stadium and although the whisky and beer flowed freely and the crowd very partisan, I do not recall any violence to mar these outings on a Saturday afternoon. In those days, the conditions for spectators were very primitive and adequate toilet facilities were non-existent, leading to the fascinating but disgusting spectacle of seeing dozens of men facing the outside walls of the stadium and urinating, with the steam rising from the streams and puddles at their feet, before leaving the grounds and pouring out on to Copland Road.

Uncle Cameron, Mum's younger brother, and his wife, Margaret, lived in Mosspark on the south—west side of Glasgow. I liked Uncle Cameron as he was a kind but rather ineffectual man who worked as an Insurance agent. I was rather less fond of Aunt Margaret, who was cold, distant and house-proud. Mum's older brother, John, had married Margaret's older sister, Mary. They were quite the opposite, warm-hearted, generous and cheerful at all times. Uncle John was an engineer and both had spent a considerable time in Iraq before returning home to a nice flat on Paisley Road West, at the corner of Jura Street facing Bellahouston Park, which had been the site of the Empire Exhibition. Neither couple had had any children.

On my Grandfather's return home from India, he had stayed with Uncle Cameron and Aunt Margaret at Mosspark. However, he was unhappy there as Aunt did not like looking after him, especially as he was a pipe smoker; she also worked in town, so I suppose that she really did not have too much spare time on her hands. Eventually, she forced him to smoke his pipe outside the house. In those days, we thought this was rather inhuman but it now makes good sense, especially on cold, wet, windy days when the windows and doors would have been tightly sealed and the coal fire blazing and fuming.

In 1947, Uncle Cameron and Aunt Margaret took me along with them on their summer holidays. I remember spending a day in London visiting Trafalgar Square, St. Paul's Cathedral (I was fascinated by the Whispering Gallery) and the Tower of London. We sailed across the Channel and then caught a train to Basel. Here, in the Railway Restaurant, I was overcome by the great variety of cakes and pastries, rich in cream, icing and fresh fruit; I can remember stuffing myself with strawberry gateau. This gastronomical hedonism was new to me as Britain was still under food-rationing. Moving on by train, we stopped at Lucerne which became our base for the holiday. We stayed in a small, private hotel the owner of which was also the chef. He made us feel very welcome and tried his best to overfeed us. I enjoyed the holiday as it was very varied. On the days we stayed in Lucerne, we sported on the Lake (swimming and pedalling furiously in two-person water-cabs), visited museums, attended the casino in the evenings (where Uncle played roulette) and enjoyed our first flag-waving demonstrations and Alpine horn solos, which alternated with yodelling.

On our excursions, we visited Altdorf, (the home of William Tell), the Rhone glacier, (walking through the shimmering pale blue tunnels cut into the slowly moving glacier), and Engleberg, apparently the venue for the 1936 Winter Olympic Games). Was it at Altdorf that we also saw our first St. Bernard mountain rescue dogs? On one lovely, tranquil evening, the paddle steamer took us to Schaffhausen on the other side of the Lake. Mt. Pilatius, close to Lucerne, was there for us to conquer and this we did reaching the summit by cable-railway, reputedly the steepest in the world. From the summit, the Black Forest was clearly visible well below us in Germany, as was a restaurant where we sat down to a good meal. On another day, we made for the Black Forest. An ever lingering memory of Switzerland is the sight of cows wandering through the narrow streets in the afternoons, presumably on their way to be milked, with their large, tinkling cow bells dangling from their necks. When the time came for us to return home to Glasgow, Uncle bought himself an expensive watch which he tried to slip past the Customs officer; unfortunately for him, he was caught and ended up paying duty on it although he was allowed to keep the watch.

One Christmas holiday, I stayed with Uncle John and Aunt Mary. Aunt was a great baker and, because it was the Festive Season, she was very busy baking away, although she encouraged me to "help" her. I was allowed to make doughnuts and especially enjoyed punching out the holes, and licking clean the almost empty baking bowls. All this activity was for a good reason, the Christmas Party. It was a family party to which I was asked to invite some of my friends. Grandpa always played "Santa Claus" but his large "roman" nose was hard to hide and always betrayed his true identity. Apart from the lovely food, the highlight of the party was "Mungi". Mungi was a composite Glasgow character who stood in front of the lounge window and did a song and dance act for the children. In reality, Mungi consisted of Uncle Cameron as the top-half, with Uncle John as the feet (using his hands) hidden from view by a draped table, doing coordinated acts. It was really very clever and funny. These parties were always a great success.

World War II ended in 1945 with victory in Europe before victory in Japan. I must have been staying with Uncle John and Aunt Mary in Jura Street at this time because I can recall them taking me to the large open air gathering which was held in George Square to celebrate the victory. It wasn't even raining. The crowds were huge and everyone appeared to be in the best of spirits, probably in more ways than one. The celebrations went on for hours but eventually we made our way homewards by means of a corporation, double-decker bus. We sat up stairs, in the smoking section although neither Aunt nor Uncle smoked; this was purely for us to watch the public joy, both on and off the bus, as we made our way slowly home. In 1996, Aunt Mary, (now a widow and over 90 years old), told me that she had specially asked Uncle to take us as her parents had done the same for her at the end of the first World War and she had always remembered the experience.

My cousins, John and Morag Fleming, (the children of Mum's oldest brother, Dod), lived in the small Perthshire village of Doune, in a small flat above some shops in the village square, in the centre of which was the old Celtic Cross. Doune was famous for its Castle, which once belonged to the Bonnie Earl of Moray, and for its pistol making in days gone by. Formerly, the market was held in the square but this had long ceased. However, once a year, they still held the Doune Fair, and on the Saturday of this event, there was always a Children's Fancy Dress parade. Of course, we entered the parade. Morag entered as an Indian lady, (she was slightly older than me, while I was slightly older than John), dressed in a sari and looked very authentic, perhaps too authentic as she failed to win a prize. I cannot recall my costume but I do remember winning a prize. John did not win either. John wasn't upset but Morag was very annoyed. I always enjoyed my stays at Doune as John and I appeared to spend all our time in the fields trying to snare rabbits and, when that palled, return home to beautiful home baking. Aunt Marion always looked after us very well. One very important legal act took place before I left Glasgow in 1949. At my birth, as Dad was away most of the time on dredging duties, my Grandfather, Jules, took over and had me registered as French. After a great deal of inconvenience, I was eventually made a British colonial citizen.

Early in 1949, Dad resigned from the Calcutta Port Commissioners and spent a short holiday with Mum and I in Glasgow before taking up a post as Chief Engineer on the "Islander", a small 1100 ton ship owned by the British Phosphate Commission. He was to be based in Fremantle, Western Australia. And so, later in the year, I left Glasgow Academy and Glasgow with Mum and Grandpa, to sail to Fremantle on the P & O liner, "Strathaird".

The voyage out lasted about three weeks and it was a very pleasant and relaxed one. I was fortunate to be befriended by the Master-at-Arms, a giant of a man called "Tiny" Storey. He took me around with him every day and allowed me to help him organise the deck chairs, games equipment and other shipboard activities. I did have one unpleasant incident as the ship was passing through the Red Sea. Presumably due to youthful exuberance, I developed heat stroke and suffered salt/fluid deprivation, which confined me to the cabin for a couple of days. However, my recovery was complete and I was soon active again. There was a Fancy Dress party for the children. With Tiny's help—he made me long flowing, golden locks out of hemp—Mum dressed me up as Nell Gwynne, complete with basket and oranges. Much to my surprise and indignation, I was awarded the first prize for girls and it took quite a bit of persuasion to convince the judges that I was a boy. The trip out was very enjoyable and it was an excellent prelude to our new life in Australia.

Chapter Four

A new land, Australia,
and a new life, 1949-1953

We landed at Fremantle at a most dismal and inauspicious time. Australia was in the throes of one of its periodical, crippling, industrial strikes. This time the miners were on strike and electricity usage was strictly limited.

In 1949, Fremantle was a most disappointing port town. It reminded us of an American, mid-west, frontier town and there were indeed still hitching-rails for tying horses outside some of the buildings, although the horses had long since disappeared. The High Street was dominated by the old, convict-built gaol at one end, while each side of the road was lined with large, single storeyed buildings, with the occasional covered pavement formed by overhanging verandahs.

Our first residence was in one of the taller buildings on the High Street, which went under the name of the Orient Hotel. It was owned by two elderly spinsters, the Misses Parry. The hotel was supposed to be one of the better ones in town but it was dingy, not too comfortable and had obviously seen better days. Mum and I shared a fairly large room which was comfortable enough while Grandpa had a single, adjacent room. There were no tea and coffee facilities in those days and although any form of cooking was banned in the rooms, Mum and I bought a wee solid fuel stove for ourselves upon which we brewed tea for the three of us. Apart from the breakfasts, we ate all our meals outside. In this respect, we were most fortunate for almost next door to the hotel there was a very good, small delicatessen/restaurant owned by an Ulsterman, Mr. Turner, where we ate most of our evening meals. I will always remember Mr. Turner and his small restaurant because it was in there that I first came across the T-bone steak. These steaks were an absolute joy to me as we had just come from Scotland where the meat was still rationed and the choice was strictly limited. I ate T-bone steaks night after night until they were literally coming out of my ears. Mr. Turner befriended me and, after closing up for the night, he would often take me down to the harbour wharf, lend me a handline and together we would fish contentedly for a couple of hours, from the edge of the wharf with our legs dangling over the water, the mouth of the Swan River.

The evenings were difficult for us in those early days and we found time passing very slowly. In the late afternoon, we would buy a newspaper from a bare-footed boy of about my own age called "Snowy". At first, we did not understand what he was trying to sell as he appeared to be shouting "Poiper". We also thought that Australians were very poor because, apart from Snowy, there were many children running about bare-footed. In Scotland, nobody ran about without wearing some form of footwear. After reading the paper and having our dinner, the evenings were spent either walking the streets window-shopping or occasionally going to the pictures. Again, we did not understand the name of the picture house because Snowy told us it was "Oits" when, in fact, it turned out to be Hoyts. There was no electricity due to a strike and the elder Miss Parry gave us two candles to burn in our rooms when we first arrived. After a day or two, when we asked for new ones, she asked if we were eating them.

One of our co-residents at the hotel was Sir Frank Gibson, a former Mayor of Fremantle, who resided there permanently. He was a tall, silver-haired, imposing man who, during our sojourn, showed considerable kindness to us. On our departure, he gave me a signed copy of "Gateway to Australia", a book on Fremantle, published while he was in office.

Such were our introduction and initial impressions of Australia, a few good but the majority uninspiring.

Meanwhile, Dad was sailing the Indian Ocean, travelling between Fremantle, Christmas and Cocos Islands and Singapore, on the "Islander", an 1100 ton ship belonging to the British Phosphate Commission. He was the Chief Engineer and took great pride in exerting it to its maximum speed of 10 knots per hour. I was very fortunate as I was able to spend quite a lot of time on board with Dad and the Chinese crew. On most occasions when the Islander returned to Fremantle, she would be forced to anchor out in Gage Roads for a few days until a berth became available. During these visits, I would be taken on board, sometimes with Mum, and then spend most of the daylight hours fishing over the stern with a handline, in the company of the off-duty crew, for kingfish and the occasional small shark. These were excellent days.

On one very special occasion, I joined Dad on the Islander for a trip to Christmas Island. As far as I can remember, the return trip took about three weeks. For the first day or two I was not only violently sea-sick but became sun-burned. The whole ship was my kingdom, following Dad to the engine-room, the skipper to the bridge, and "Chippy", the carpenter, on his rounds. Arriving at Christmas Island, the Islander anchored in a beautiful little, deep bay with very clear water, into which the flimsy-looking jetty protruded like badly joined bits of spaghetti. I believe that a cyclone had recently struck the island. I will always remember the first time I went ashore—in an outrigger, dug-out canoe; it leaked and before we reached the shore, the canoe was half submerged, only the outriggers keeping us afloat. Still, it was fun and we did arrive on shore safely. I found the little township quite fascinating, crowded as it was with Islanders, Chinese, Malays, Indians and a smattering of Europeans. The small, run-down, low-slung houses and shops also exerted a seedy charm. I was also very fortunate to observe the famous red crabs in their annual mass migration to the sea. Still, it was the bay which I found most interesting, with the Islander, the fishing, the bustling shore-line and the loading of the Danish charter ships, Stensby and Vensby, at the jetty.

There were four other officers aboard. The captain was a large, jovial Englishman called Mr. Barley while the Chief Officer was an old grizzeled, Australian known as Pop Seager. His favourite off-duty pastime was drinking a mixture of milk and whisky; when he went to the toilet (situated at the stern), he would leave the door open and when anyone approached, he would call out, "The minister's in". The second engineer was a very nice, quiet Eurasian whom Dad thought a great deal of, called Bulow. The radio officer was another Aussie, but one in his early thirties; when ashore, he would take me to the outdoor swimming pool. Dad always said that the Islander was a happy ship. I know that I always enjoyed myself on it.

However, my life was not all fishing, eating T-bone steaks and candles. Mum soon enrolled me at Scotch College, which was and still is situated on Shenton Road, Swanbourne, a seaside suburb between Fremantle and Perth. The main railway line runs along the lower end of the school property. I enjoyed Scotch, which was then under the Headmastership of a New Zealander, Mr. Geoffrey Maxwell Keys, or "Bunchy" to the boys. He was later to earn a doctorate for an educational thesis. He also had a less polite nickname, "Greasy". During my four years at this school, I only had one small complaint to lay against him; this related to the fact that although I participated fully in the school activities and held some senior posts in school societies and teams, I was never made a prefect but only a "Senior".

Initially, going to school meant that I had to catch the train at Fremantle every morning for the half-hour run into Swanbourne. The journey was never boring as we had a good crowd of "Freo" boys on board. (This was my first introduction to the Aussie diminutive "o" at the end of nouns). They included Bryce and Peter Butterworth, (their Father, Peter, was a Scottish engineer from Greenock), who actually lived very close to me eventually in Swanbourne after we had all moved, and Clyde "Chookie" Bant (from Beaconsfield, a Fremantle suburb, who had won a scholarship to Scotch and was later to become Dux of the school). Except for Peter, who was a few years younger, we were all about 13 and finished up in the same class, Form 4, and also played Rugby Union throughout, together.

After a while, Mum managed to rent part of a bungalow at Melville, an area of East Fremantle. The address was 3 Prinsep Road, and the bungalow was owned by a retired Geordie engineer called Bill Davidson. He was a nice old man and allowed us full use of the house and garden, in which he cultivated a wide selection of fruits, including two or three varieties of grapes. Grandpa happily spent most of the day dozing under a tree. We were quite happy there although Mr. Davidson did have one very strange and annoying habit; every morning as were having breakfast, (I had to rise early to catch the bus to the station outside the chemist's shop), he would walk through from his bedroom, dressed in his pyjamas and dressing gown with a urine-filled china chamber pot held obtrusively out in front of him, into the kitchen then stop for a moment or two to talk to us before walking out into the garden where he would empty the contents of the pot into a ten-gallon drum, the contents of which he said he used for his grapes. We had to admit that his grapes were absolutely delicious.

At the foot of his garden, there was an old corrugated iron shed. When I asked him if I could keep chickens, he readily agreed, and so it was that I bought 30 day-old chickens, six pullets and the remainder cockerels. Unfortunately, I lost about ten to some viral disease but not one of them was a pullet. I had to buy bran and pollard, feed them daily, make sure that the brooder was filled with oil in order to keep them warm at night while they were small, and keep the shed clean and secure. As they matured, they were allowed to roam about the garden and quite soon we were gathering a few eggs. However, we had too many cockerels and gradually their numbers were reduced after many chases around the garden trying to catch the next victim for the chopping block. It was my job to chop off the head and then pluck and clean the carcass. Of course, I had a favourite cockerel, but eventually and inevitably his turn came and he seemed to know it. When his day arrived, he led me a really merry chase for quite a while all around the garden, cackling as loudly as he could while flapping his wings before I eventually caught him and put him out of his misery. That meal did not appear to taste quite so delicious. The pullets stayed alive and I eventually left them with Mr. Davidson.

The morning train journey took us over the Swan River, past the industrial suburb of Leighton, with its lovely white beach, then inland a little to Mosman Park, Cottesloe and finally Swanbourne, where we all poured off the train. When I first started to make this journey, one of the sights which intrigued me was the continuous row, suburb after suburb, of small wooden sheds standing at the bottom of each garden; I was to learn that these were outside toilets and that most Australian houses did not have inside toilets as that was considered to be unhygienic.

We did not see Dad for many weeks at a time as he was at sea on the Islander and only rarely called at Fremantle. It was left largely to Mum to obtain our own home in Australia. After a considerable amount of searching, Mum managed to rent a nice semi-detached house from Jim and Kath James, who were the tenants of Mrs. Ellemore, an elderly lady who still lived in the other part of the house. We were very happy at 14b, North Street, Swanbourne, as not only was it a nice, modern, compact, easily managed house with a small garden front and back, but was also within a few minutes of Scotch and Swanbourne beach, Kath and Jim became my parents' best friends in Australia, and their son, John, and his wife, Maureen, are our good friends to this day.

It was while we were at North Street that Dad changed jobs and joined the Western Australian Government Service as Chief Dredging Engineer on the "Sir James Mitchell". Originally intended to be posted to Kwinana, south of Fremantle, to prepare the approach to a proposed new oil refinery, the Sir James was instead posted to Albany in the south-west of the state, to keep open the harbour in King George's Sound, reputed to be an even better harbour than that of Sydney. Although we were disappointed, it was still better than Dad being at sea, as he was now able to drive the 400 miles each way to see us two or three times a month.

Occasionally, when I was on holiday, I would accompany Dad down to Albany. He had bought an old but well-maintained, 1936 Chevrolet, and although he never went above 60 mph, I never found the 400 miles long and boring. Albany, in the early 1950s, was a sleepy hollow of a place situated at the south-west tip of the Australian mainland. The harbour was magnificent with only the long, narrow jetty jutting out into the water. When not out dredging, the Sir James tied up alongside the jetty. I would spend two or three days on board, fishing mainly, but occasionally sightseeing in the surrounding agricultural land and taking innumerable photos of the "Dog Rock", a natural formation just outside the town.

It was at North Street that I also started to take an interest in gardening as I was now solely responsible for our two small plots. The back garden was fenced off and this allowed me to keep an aviary, a rabbit, a cat and a lovely Scotch terrier called "Whisky", who actually looked after the rabbit when it was allowed out of its hutch to run around the garden. Whisky knew when

I was due to return from school and he would wait for me patiently, sitting at the gate. When we left Australia in 1953, we gave Whisky to John James and we were all deeply saddened when the dog was accidentally knocked over and killed in its own garden by a car whose driver had swerved to avoid an Alsatian chasing another dog out on the street.

Shortly after our arrival, Mum and I went into Perth to do some shopping. On that particular occasion, I was wearing my Hunting MacLean kilt and balmoral. While waiting for Mum outside Boan's, a large department store, I was stopped by a lady radio reporter who then proceeded to interview me. Neither of us heard the programme, so I am unable to comment on it and do not even know if it was aired.

Between 1949 and 1953, Scotch made great strides in all fields of activity, the most obvious of which was the rebuilding programme. I always found Mr. Keys quite approachable but it was well known that he curried favour with the farming or "cocky" faction of school parents as they, according to his view, held the money and the power. This showed itself most obviously in the weighted appointments of boarders, (mainly sons of pastoralists), to the ranks of prefects and seniors, on a regular basis. Probably as a result of this bias, he was also known in the school as "Greasy Keys".

At that time, Scotch College had an excellent group of teachers, greatly appreciated by the boys. The Deputy was "Bull" Campbell, a veteran of World War I. He was a great teacher and provided us with an excellent grounding in Latin and English; he was also a good friend to all of us. During my first year the Governor of Western Australia was due to retire, so a competition was held in school for the best hand-writer to pen a "Farewell" on behalf of all the pupils in the Public Schools of WA as Scotch had been chosen as the representative school. Prior to this, Mr. Campbell, acting as Head, had chosen me as a public speaker to make the presenting speech to the retiring Governor at a special public meeting to be held in a city hall. Well, I entered the writing competition and happened to win it. However, as I had already be chosen to make the speech, it was decided that I should not also write the "Farewell"; the runner-up, Mickey Hearman, wrote it, which I later presented to the Governor, Sir James Mitchell, making the Farewell Speech at the same time.

Mo Cowan was a later English teacher who gave us a good grounding in modern English and American literature. This concentration on modernity with a relative neglect of the classics led me into some difficulty when I had to sit my Scottish Leaving Certificate on my return home a year or two later. He was also the guiding light behind the Scotch College "Reporter", the school magazine. Soon after my arrival, I joined the Reporter Committee and eventually, in my final year, I became the joint editor with Bryce Butterworth.

"Ticks" Jenkinson was our mathematics teacher and, a few years later when I was back in Scotland, he came to visit me. A strict disciplinarian, I now realise that this facade was for our own good. Biology was a very popular subject due in no small measure to the enthusiasm of "Ally" Thomas, the teacher. A small man with piercing eyes, he needed to wear thick spectacles. This resulted in him receiving the nickname "Beady eyes". Biology was never boring.

Mathematics was never one of my favourite subjects but all this changed when "Jazz" Dancer came to Scotch. Jazz was an elderly man who, it was said, had once been a professor of mathematics at Singapore University at the outbreak of World War II. At the fall of Singapore, he had been taken prisoner and jailed at Changi, his health suffering as a result. Teaching uninterested, young pupils was a new experience for him and he could not understand why we were unable to follow his explanations in which he would jump three or four steps at one time. During his classes, my friend David Forman and I eventually gave up try to understand him and would, at the start of his class, lie along the bench and read books. However, this soon palled and I could stand it no longer. So, during one period, I stood up in class and told Jazz that he was wasting our time and his as we did not understand him. For a short while, there was a total silence and then Jazz carried on as if nothing had happened. Next day, we took our usual places in class. Jazz entered and launched straight into a criticism of myself and my fellow students which lasted for the full 40 minutes of the period. Needless to say, we were all suitably chastened. However, Jazz changed his teaching style to suit his erstwhile pupils and became a much appreciated teacher. He even became very helpful and supportive to me.

What was happening to my scholastic attainment? Well, that was progressing satisfactorily. In the Junior Leaving Certificate I passed in eight subjects, a result which pleased me greatly. Next year, when the time came for me to sit my Higher Leaving Certificate, I do not recall being unduly worried by the thought. The only outstanding memory I can think of concerned my French exam. As the exams were held in early summer, most of us spent our spare time down at the beach, and I was no exception. This particular exam was to be held immediately after lunch; unfortunately, I had rushed off to the beach and quite forgot about the time, so that when I returned to sit the exam, I discovered that I was half an hour late. However, I was allowed in, and fortunately I passed the exam. In fact, I managed to gain seven subjects. This result gave me entrance requirements to any University in Australia to study Medicine. For the few remaining months of my Australian schooling, after the summer holidays, I moved into the sixth form where we did such interesting subjects as Civics, which included the study of government and political systems.

As a rugby player, I joined the small group of enthusiasts who were trained by Mr. Patmore, an ex-Royal Navy man. Rugby was not recognised as the main school sport, (Australian Rules football was), but nevertheless our numbers grew and we acquitted ourselves well in open competition over the years. Bryce Butterworth, Chooky Bant and Dalz Sadleir, my best friends, were also members of this select group. In 1952, I was not only voted "Best and Fairest" and presented with a cup by Neville Nankerville, a former captain, but also awarded my "colours". In 1953, I was rewarded my colours and was also elected team captain. It was rumoured that had I stayed, I would have been chosen to captain the State Schoolboys Team. My positions in the team were initially scrum-half and later, stand-off.

Military cadets, army and air force, were also an integral part of the school scene. Although I never rose above the rank of private, I did win a place in the school Shooting Team, firing 0.303 rifles at Swanbourne Rifle Range, and gaining my "crossed rifles" in the process. I took up rowing and managed to learn the rudiments of this demanding sport. Most of my time was spent in "fours". I never did represent the school in this sport. I also tried my hand at hockey and Aussie Rules; I only managed to fracture my left wrist playing the latter sport.

However, life at school was not all sport. I also threw myself into the intellectual side of life. I participated in the Debating Society and was in the school Debating Team. This may have been due to the fact that we also debated against our sister Public Schools; the debates were quite social occasions. Scotch was also blessed with having a very talented language teacher, Miss Joan Secombe, although she was usually called "Ma", who not only continued to instruct me most ably in Latin and French but also directed the annual school Dramatic Society plays. Largely through her influence, I joined the society and took part in two consecutive plays, the first being R.C. Sheriff's "Badger's Green" and the second, Bernard Shaw's "You Never Can Tell", in both of which I played the leading lady. In the former play, I was wearing a plaster cast for my broken wrist. The latter play was entered in the open State Drama competition and we came second in the metropolitan area in 1951. The support from the Mothers' Committee, the members of which were responsible for making the costumes, was exceptional, due in no small measure to the guidance and leadership of Mrs. Toop.

It can be seen that I led a very full life at Scotch, but I did not look for glory. I was only appointed to the rank of "Senior" and not prefect. I believe this was due to the fact that I was not an Australian and that I did not belong to an influential family. Maybe my perceptions were wrong but I came across this during the whole of my Australian professional life at a later stage.

Barrie Newman. a boarder, was one of my best friends. His home was a wee hamlet called Loudon, near Donnybrook, in the south-west of the state, where his parents ran the local store and post office. On a couple of school holidays, I was invited down to his home where I spent some of my happiest, youthful days in Australia. His parents were warm, welcoming and friendly, and his sister, Betty, was an added attraction although she tended to treat us with total disdain. It was on these visits that I learned to ride, the first episode being the most frightening as I lost my footing in the stirrups and the horse galloped off with me hanging on for dear life. It was here too that I shot my first, and last, emus and kangaroos, actually eating their meat later on. They were really fun days, and the evenings too were interesting as we would sit and talk with his parents for ages, mainly about science. Back in Swanbourne, Barrie would be a frequent visitor to North

Street, but I always felt that I had the better of the deal as my experiences in the bush were so different from my routine ones. Once, I also visited the sheep farm of another school friend, David McCowan, another rugby player, at Wagin. These all created lasting and wonderful memories.

I had some good friends in my class. Apart from Bryce, Chooky, Dalz and David, there were also Ross Fimister and John Brind. Most of our spare time, during the summer months, was spent on the beach. If I was with Bryce and his brother, Peter, we usually went to Swanbourne; however, if I went with David, Ross or Dalz, we would cycle to North Cottesloe which was a much more social beach, with many more girls to chat up.

I did not neglect my social graces at school. Dancing classes were held in the old wooden gymnasium, so I joined the class. Unfortunately, there were no girls, so I learned the basic steps dancing with the other boys. Still, it was quite an amusing pastime.

As for girl friends, I only enjoyed the company of two nice young ladies, both pupils at the Presbyterian Ladies College (PLC). The first one was called June Morgan. Strangely enough, when I first met her I did not know that she was the daughter of my Dad's new boss in the WA Dredging section. On our first date, in which we went to a film, I took her a small bunch of flowers—I don't think that she ever experienced that before. June was a blonde, quite a big girl with a very easy nature and we got on very well together. In my last few months, I met a very attractive brunette, slim and of average height and build. Her name was Jenny Raison; she was a boarder at PLC. She came from Bencubbin and her parents' home was called "Jeeda Mia". For the first time, I really felt that I was in love. However, one of our first dates was a bit of a disaster. We had arranged to meet on St. George's Terrace in order to watch the parade to commemorate the coronation of Queen Elizabeth. Well, I turned up at the appointed time and place but for some reason which I never discovered, Jenny did not; I waited for over two hours in vain. Still, things improved after that. She used to come and watch us play Rugby. Just before I left for Scotland, we went to the School Dance. She wore a simple, white, long dress and I thought that she looked lovely. When I left for home, I was very sad indeed to leave her and said that I would return as soon as possible. I was not surprised that Bryce took over for a while after I left. Such is life.

Mum was left very much on her own for long spells although I must admit that the James family looked after her, and indeed all of us, very well. She did not find herself a job so she must have found time lying a bit heavily on her hands, although she did have Grandpa with her for a year or two before he returned home. He spent most of his time snoozing in the garden. For a few months, we had Peggy Saunders staying with us. I think she was more a friend of Dad's. Her easy going nature did not upset the domestic tranquility.

For a variety of reasons, I was really sad to learn that my parents had decided to return to Scotland and that I was to return with them, to re-enter Glasgow Academy in order to sit my Scottish Leaving Certificate as the Australian one was only considered to be equivalent to the Scottish Lower Certificate.

Before leaving Australia, Mum and Dad gave me a wonderful farewell party. We hired a small hall and a band. I invited all my friends and their girl friends. It was a lovely evening and a great way to leave. Bryce presented me with a nice pen and pencil set during his short farewell speech; I still have it, unused. When the day came for us to leave, I vowed to my friends that I would be back one day. The day of our departure was an internationally auspicious one as it was the day on which the Korean Armistice was signed, 31 October 1953. Oddly enough, I cannot recall the name of the boat upon which we sailed away from Fremantle. A psychological block, perhaps?

Chapter Five

The Return to Scotland, 1953

The trip home was quite uneventful and I remember that I seemed to spend most of my time swimming. Mum had a cabin to herself but I shared one with Grandpa; this was not constricting for me as I only saw them at meal times.

On board, I made friends with three people with whom I spent most of my time. The first was an English girl of my own age called Pamela Blaikie who was returning to Salford with her parents. She was my girl friend for the trip home. The other two were Gudde Binder and her son, Nils, returning to Copenhagen. Nils was about 13 years of age, blond and big for his age. He spoke good English although his mother only spoken broken English.

Our first port of call was Colombo. Grandpa and I went off by ourselves and hired a rickshaw to do some sightseeing around the city. One of our stops was at the Botanical Gardens where I was really impressed by the Orchid display and which has left me a fervent orchid fan ever since. I have a photograph of Grandpa and me sitting in the rickshaw, with me wearing a wide brimmed, floppy, white cotton hat. Overall, I found Colombo a sticky, uninviting city.

Malta was a different world. The ship anchored in the Grand Harbour of Valetta, a magnificent setting, made more interesting by the fact that there were many ships anchored there, British warships among them. I remember going ashore with Grandpa, Gudde and Nils. To reach the city approaches, we went up on a lift which ascended from sea-level and went straight up the mediaeval wall to the street level. Valetta had still not recovered from the Nazi bombing of the war approximately ten years previously and there were still many bombed-out, derelict sites lining the streets. It was an interesting place. I recall that we took a small, local bus, at the entrance of which was a wee, lit-up, crucifix, to Sliema, a nearby beach resort, where we spent a couple of hours bathing in the blue Mediterranean, and sun-bathing on the warm sand and rocks. Returning to Valetta, we went to the Phoenicia Hotel for refreshments, then a very posh hotel. As the ship's departure was not until about 11pm, we stayed ashore and enjoyed participating in the late evening socialising and shopping, in which the whole population of Valetta appeared to be out walking the streets or sitting in road-side cafes drinking. It was a whole new world to be absorbed.

After saying cheerio to our friends, we spent a day or two in London seeing the sights. While walking down one of the main streets, wearing light grey trousers with my maroon Scotch blazer, I was stopped by a young man, who turned out to be an Old Scotch Collegian. It felt as if I was being welcomed back.

Travelling up by train from London, we were met in Glasgow by Uncle Cameron and Aunt Margaret. Uncle did not recognise me at first as I was now full grown at 5ft. 8ins., weighed 10st. 7lbs. and sported a crew-cut hair style. I suppose that we must have stayed with them initially at their new bungalow in Cardonald, in the south-west of the city. However, I do know that Mum did not stay long in Scotland because, after settling me into Glasgow Academy as a day pupil, arranging for me to stay with Aunt Violet at 10, Whitefield Road, Ibrox, and fixing Grandpa up in a nice boarding house nearby, she went off to Narayanganj, in Bengal, to join Dad, who was working there as the Chief Engineer in a large jute mill. Grandpa was able to walk around to see us every day and come for his main meal.

I had stayed at Whitefield Road before leaving for Australia and had, in fact, left my Cairn terrier, Shoona, with Aunt Violet; so, it was very familiar territory for me. When I first got off the bus, I could see Aunt waiting for me, with the dog in her arms, as she had been expecting our arrival. When I shouted out "Shoona", the dog jumped out of my aunt's arms and raced down the road towards me, jumped into my arms and licked my face. She had not forgotten me after four years.

My stay with Aunt Violet while I was studying for my Scottish Higher Certificate was a happy one. Aunt was a spinster, about 5ft. 2ins. in height and rotund, with dark but grey-flecked hair and a generally untidy appearance. Her appearance reflected her home; it was warm, friendly and untidy. By this time her Mother had died at 94 years of age. Aunt still worked alongside her brother in Govan. Life had not been easy for her but Uncle Peter and Dinky gave her every support.

Aunt's flat was in a "wally" close, on the left hand side of the ground floor. I moved into the large double bedroom but did nearly all my homework in the large lounge, gazing out of the window looking out onto the road, during the long summer evenings.

While at school, my daily travel routine was the same. I walked through Ibrox Terrace, up Copland Road to the subway, (underground train station), caught the train to Kelvin Bridge, walked up the steep flight of stairs, and crossed Great Western Road to reach Belmont Street, on which the school was situated. I made the same journey in reverse on returning home.

I thought it was quite ridiculous that my Australian School Certificate had not been given full recognition and consequently I was not particularly pleased to be back at school. I did not participate in any of the school activities and refused to join the Cadet Corps. Even Rugby did not receive my whole attention and I only played for the second XV in a desultory fashion, I was also in the second XI for cricket, a game which I had never played before, even in Australia. At the school sports, I gained two second places in "throwing the cricket ball" and the "hop, step and jump". Scholastically, I concentrated on English, Mathematics A and B, Physics, Chemistry and Biology. English I found particularly difficult as it was back to Shakespeare, which I had not studied at all in Australia. Mr. "Bing" Crosbie offered me great assistance and I passed it without any trouble. Mathematics B was my stumbling block and I had to resit it in the University Preliminary Examinations.

Life was not all concerned with school. My Aunt's immediate neighbours were a Belfast family. Their older daughter was called Joan, about the same age as myself and also sitting the Leaving Certificate. Much to my delight she found Biology difficult to assimilate and so I was only too happy to study along with her, assisting her as required, most often in the absence of both my Aunt and her family. I enjoyed these "study" sessions. However, the relationship did not last very long as she soon realised that she could hook bigger fish with fast cars and more money at their disposal.

My next girl friend, while I was at Ibrox, was Irene. She was a small, sharp, blonde from Clouston Street. I cannot say that I was really interested in her but we did spend a lot of time together over a few months. This relationship came to an end when I was accepted for Glasgow University and moved into "digs" in Hillhead, right next door.

While at the Academy, I became good friends with a pair of twins called Allan and Roger Cannon, and with their friend Ronnie MacLean. So it was, at the end of our school years, that the four of us decided to hitch-hike to the South of France. Wearing kilts and laden down with our rucksacks, we set off for the Mediterranean. Our first stop was London and, travelling in pairs, I with Ronnie, we moved south along the main road to London, making for the home of Ronnie's Uncle who lived in an inner London suburb. After numerous stops at road-side cafes along the old A1, we arrived first after almost 24 hours of non-stop travelling. It was lovely to have a good hot bath and a rest, while waiting for the twins, who arrived about three hours later. After a large meal, we then settled down to a long, sound sleep.

Ronnie's Uncle very kindly offered to drive us down to Folkestone the next evening. After packing the car, we set off eagerly. The drive down was quite uneventful and with £15 in my pocket, I boarded the cross channel ferry with my three friends. For once, the Channel was not rough and I was not seasick.

Arriving in Dunkirk, I remember that we went into a roadside cafe at about 6.30am. Even ten years after the war, the town still showed many signs of the conflict. Again, we decided to travel in pairs, and again I teamed up with Ronnie. However, it was not long before we decided to travel singly, meeting up at our pre-designated Youth Hostel in Marseille, we hoped. I recall moving through Lille and Amiens and being invited in for lunch by a general practitioner in Armentiere. He was a Breton and was intigued by my French ancestry, being also Breton. However, I had a deadline to meet and moved progressively south down the Rhone valley, but not before meeting up with my three friends in Paris. Needless to say, we spent most of our time in Pigalle and Montmartre, more viewing than participating, but we still enjoyed ourselves. We did make a special trip to St. Maurice-sur-Seine, where we sat at a riverside cafe eating our first plate of moules-mariniere, washed down with vin rouge. It was a happy afternoon and we felt as if we were really living.

Moving south, we leap-frogged each other on the way to Marseille. I appeared to move quite rapidly and just south of Lyon, I was given a lift by the Weill family, on their way back home to Dijon. Although the car was fairly full with Mother, Father, teenage son and daughter, they somehow managed to squeeze me and my rucksack in. They were an exceedingly friendly and generous family. It turned out that Mrs. Weill was a Paediatrician, while Mr. Weill was a University Professor and, much more interestingly, I think they said that they were Communists. I stayed overnight and had a very enjoyable stay.

Moving on from Dijon, I had a stroke of extremely good luck as my next driver was an English business man on his way to Spain, in his Rolls Royce. I felt like Lord Muck sitting in the front seat of the Rolls. He was also very generous and I recall being taken to a five star restaurant, run by the second best chef in France, for lunch. As evening came, we stopped at a town, the name of which I cannot recall, although it could have been Orange, as I can still visualise the ruined Roman amphitheatre; here, we overnighted but he went to a posh hotel while I went to the Youth Hostel. Next morning, true to his word, he collected me and we continued our luxurious journey. It was not too long, however, before we reached Avignon and here we parted, as his road lay towards Spain and mine towards Marseille. It was a memorable leg of the journey.

There are only a couple of things which I remember about Avignon. The first, at which I had a superficial look, was the Pope's Palace and the second was a large roadside sign advertising the "Hotel Saint-Yves". It gave me quite a thrill. I was equally lucky with my next lift as I was picked up in town and taken to Marseille, where my host again invited me to his home, where I met his family and joined them in another lovely meal. After the meal, he dropped me off at the Youth Hostel, where once again, I was the first to arrive.

When we were all together again, we decided that we would make for the Hostel at Six-Fours, near Toulons, so we piled into the local bus and made off. At the back of the bus, seated close to us, we noticed a blond, bearded, bespectacled man and a striking, dark-haired, young woman. It was not long before we were in conversation; they introduced themselves as Chris Gede and Lise, his girl-friend. They were Danes and were also making for the same Youth Hostel. It turned out to be a very fortuitous meeting for me.

In 1954, Six-Fours was a lovely little, sea-side village, dominated by a Foreign Legion barracks on a nearby hill. We did very little apart from eating, drinking, sunbathing and swimming, nearly always in the company of Chris and Lise. We found Lise quite fascinating as she would quite freely change into her bathing costume on the beach, exposing her rather full breasts to four pairs of disbelieving eyes. Our stay there passed all too quickly and it was not long before we were back in Folkstone, late at night. It was raining quite heavily, and I was standing quite disconsolately in a shop doorway hopefully waiting for a lift. A small, heavily wrapped figure swayed unsteadily towards me and finished up in the doorway beside me. It turned out that he too was a Scot and was returning home to his bed-sit after a small, celebratory evening with friends. I accepted his offer to join him and followed him back to his small, cramped but clean room where I slept uncomfortably but thankfully on an old armchair. He even provided me with a ham and eggs breakfast before setting out on the road north.

My wait was quite a short one as a large bus pulled up alongside me and out stepped a man who spoke to me in good but accented English. It turned out that the bus contained the members of the Czechoslovakian Jawa Motorcycle Team, just starting out on a tour of Britain. I was offered a lift to just north of London, which I accepted. It was not long before I was back in Glasgow after a very memorable holiday and in which I had made a life-long friend in Chris.

My schoolboy French and French ancestry had stood me in very good stead, as had the French bread and Camembert cheese, which I bought, and the ripening grapes which I pinched from the vines en route.

Chapter Six

The Adult World: Glasgow University, 1954

I suppose that my return from Six-Fours marked the end of my carefree schooldays and the beginning of my adult life, although I did not think of it in that light at the time.

My first few days after my return were concerned with University affairs and my preparation for entry. I had been offered a place in the Medical Faculty at Glasgow University provided that I was accepted by the members of the Interview Committee. My whole attitude to a medical career had always been ambivalent. From ever since I can remember, my Mother had said that I was to be a doctor. Apparently Dr. Choudhury, the Obstetrician who had delivered me by Caesarean section, had said to Mum that I had the hands of a surgeon. Forever after, there was no consideration given to any other career for me by my parents, although I suspect that the decision was Mum's. I suppose that I fell in with the idea because I never really gave it too much thought, never found that I had to exert myself unduly and found that the path to Medicine at Glasgow University was smoothened by the fact that I wore the "old school tie". Nevertheless, I still find it very interesting that I considered Journalism as a second choice had I not been accepted. Ever since, I have been a frustrated journalist and have many articles, booklets and books (so far) on medicine, medical politics, politics, poetry and now this autobiography, some of which have been published.

Needless to say, I was accepted for Medicine. Those were the days in which I wore the Academical tie to all important events. There is no doubt whatsoever that the "old school tie" played an important part in many young lives. Now, I never wear it and am rather against all forms of elitism.

One of my first acts after acceptance was to enrol for the Freshers' Camp at Duck Bay on Loch Lomond side. The new students stayed for a week in a large converted, country house called Auchendennan, which was later to become a Youth Hostel. Apart from the visiting senior students who arrived intermittently to give us insights into various aspects of University life, most of us appeared to spend our time eating, drinking and chasing members of the opposite sex. Time passed very quickly and I was soon back preparing myself for entry to my new career and the start of a six years under-graduate course.

One of my more immediate concerns was to find accommodation near the University as I wished to be independent during my student years. I was very fortunate to find a good landlady in Mrs. Wall, an elderly Geordie, who owned a large house at 20 Sutherland Street, just off University Avenue. The house was on two levels, ground and semi-basement. I shared a large room at the semi-basemant level, with Adam Williams, a tall English, naval architect student. It was a bright and cheerful room facing onto the street, and one in which the two single beds were scarcely noticeable. Adam was a Roman Catholic and insisted on pinning a reed cross to the wall above the head of his bed. The other lodgers consisted of an older school teacher called Christine Barclay, (who appeared to have an interest in Adam), a Norwegian engineering student called Freddy Martinsen, a railway junior executive called Alex McCulloch and an elderly English, medical student drop-out called John McGifney. We were a relatively happy gang, and every evening when we gathered around the large dining table for our dinner, the room would be filled with laughter, usually resulting from our good natured teasing of Christine. Mrs. Wall was a good cook and I received breakfast and an evening meal seven days a week for £3; I had my clothes laundered separately each week. Mrs. Wall did not lay down any rules and I do not recall any excesses by the lodgers, apart from John, who was fond of the drink but who would retire quietly to his room on returning home. I spent three and a half years there and, in the last year,

Mrs. Wall's son, Fred, and his wife, Maisie, took over the running of the house. From then onwards, the accommodation gradually deteriorated as they were an untidy couple and did not appear to be too interested in the lodgers. The house was excellent for me as it was next to the University and the Western Infirmary, where I was to do most of my training.

During my years there, my parents were in East Pakistan, now Bangla Desh. Dad had a post as the Chief Engineer in a large jute mill. It was not a particularly well paid job, and it took him all his time to send me £5 per week (as he had to pay £10 on the Black Market due to stringent currency restrictions). Fortunately, I also received a small grant from the Scottish Education Trust which enabled me to pay my University fees and some of my books. To supplement my allowance, I worked at Christmas and part of every summer holiday ; the Christmas job was with the Post Office sorting and delivering mail, while I worked as barman in the Maitland Bar, in Howard Street, just off St. Enoch's Square, during the summer breaks.

Occasionally I would spend all Christmas in the main sorting office in, I think, Wellington Street, at other times out in the vans servicing the Hillington Industrial Estate and, at one Christmas break, delivering mail in the Cowcaddens. This latter area was a complete eye-opener to me. I had never been aware of such squalor and poverty before, and I think that I have only seen worse in the shanty towns of Manila during my travels around the world. These were tenement buildings, and entry to the flats was through a "close", (a common entrance to a group of flats). Every close I visited was in a shocking state of disrepair, with a shared toilet between landings for four flats ; almost without exception, the toilet bowl would be broken and the effluent would be seeping through the cracks in the bowl and trickling slowly down the stairs. It goes without saying that the smell was atrocious. To try to deliver mail to a household in such a tenement close was also an effort as the occupants almost always refused to answer the door knock until they were sure that it was indeed the postman calling. Most "homes" were almost devoid of any creature comforts, including linoleum on the floors; however, almost without exception, situated in the middle of the main room, and perched on a wooden fruit box, would be a very large TV set, which was a very important status symbol even then. I never ever forgot my brief, but conscience-forming, sojourn in the Cowcaddens.

The Maitland Bar was owned by a Chartered Accountant called Mr. Maitland, who had inherited it from his father. This small bar enjoyed a very varied clientele. During the week, from opening time until closing time at about 2.30 pm, it was frequented by the owner, his business friends and associates and a few of the local bookmakers. Each class of customer automatically gravitated to their own area of the bar, which was almost semi-circular in shape. The Maitland cronies would move to the far end, the bookmakers to the end nearer the entrance, the casuals to the centre, and those wishing a degree of privacy, to the three or four dark-stained, wooden cubicles lining the central wall area, where they would receive waiter service. Mr. Maitland usually appeared before lunch to check the accounts and the stock, after which he would have a drink or two with his associates. Otherwise, the bar was the domain of Willie Calder, a Highlander, in his late fifties, who had started in the bar during the time of the elder Mr. Maitland. We were all entitled to a half-day off during the week, as we worked until about 11 pm each evening, and on Willie's half-day, the bar was in the care of big Vincent MacKenzie. The working hours were long. We were all in the bar by 9.30 am in order to prepare the bar for opening at 11 am, continuing through until about 2.30 pm, but we had to be back by 4.30 pm in order to be ready for the 5 pm opening. Closing time was 10 pm, I think, and if we were fortunate, we would be all cleaned up and on our way home by about 10.15 pm. However, on a Saturday night, we were lucky if we had everything cleared by 10.45 pm, after which we had our weekly drink "on the house". However, it was on Glasgow Fair Fridays in the month of July that I really saw heavy drinking. It started about lunch-time with the workers having received their holiday pay; they just drank and drank as if alcohol was going out of fashion, and then, just before closing time, they would start buying their carry-outs, bags and bags of spirits and beer. Leaving the pub after work was a disgusting experience as there were men lying drunk on the pavement, men staggering along the road, with vomit and the smell of vomit everywhere. This social behaviour was repeated at the evening session but even more so. I do not believe that that I have ever seen such drunkenness anywhere else in the world; fortunately, it does not appear to be so blatant in public anymore.

My first day at the University, I remember quite vividly as I seemed to spend most of my time in one queue or another trying to enrol in one class or another. Between queues, I was constantly harassed by various Club members touting for new blood from the Freshers. Only one club attracted my attention and that was the University Boat Club (a rowing club, GUBC). Maybe it was because I had rowed at Scotch College, or maybe it was because the club had been awarded the most "Blues", or maybe it was because it was a semi-autonomous body outside the total control of the University Athletic Club and received its funding directly from the University Court. It also happened to be the oldest sporting and second oldest club in the University. Maybe for all of these reasons I joined it and never regretted one moment I spent with my fellow rowers and friends down at the Boat Club, below King's Bridge on Glasgow Green.

I do not recall much of my first academic year as the studying did not interest me too much, being concerned with Physics, Botany, Chemistry and Zoology, all of which I had done for my Australian and Scottish Higher Leaving Certificates. Although I tended to go to the classes, I cannot say that I studied seriously, leaving the intense work to the few weeks before the Final examinations at the end of the year. Physics, however, nearly proved my undoing. Our lecturer was Seamus MacNeill, a Gaelic speaker and a famous piper who eventually became Principal of the Piping College in Otago Street, Glasgow. He was a tall, thin, forbidding-looking man who wore unframed spectacles. During a practical lesson in which we were using weights and pulleys, I tripped over a wire and brought the whole contraption clattering to the floor. It also brought Mr. MacNeill hurrying over to me, but I escaped lightly with a telling off. Along came the Finals, and when the Physics exam was over, I realised that I was very much a borderline case, and so it was no surprise to me when I was asked to go and see him. After giving me the routine dressing-down, he said that he would pass me if I promised to read the textbook again. He knew and I knew that I would never open that textbook again. I did win a First Class Certificate of Merit in Chemistry though. And so I passed onto the second year without resitting any subjects.

Life was not all study, however. I threw myself into Boat Club activities. On two week-day afternoons and for most of the daylight hours on Saturdays, and occasionally on Sundays, I would wend my way from the top of Byres Road, Hillhead, and catch a number 10 tram all the way to Bridgeton, alighting at Templeton's gaudy carpet factory, (modelled on the Doge's Palace in Venice, it was said), before walking across Glasgow Green to the Boat Club. I suppose that it was in this environment that I began to experience my first empathy with things Scottish, for it was on Glasgow Green that the Highland Army of Bonnie Prince Charlie encamped on its march into England.

There were about eight new or novice oarsmen in that first year of 1954 and we were put in the coaching hands of Charles Pilkington. Charles was a character, and had won a Cambridge "Blue" in the 1941-1942 era; he never went anywhere without his very faded, pink Leander scarf. I believe he was an heir to the Pilkington Glass family, and indeed the members of the University eight, of which I was the stroke, on our way down to the Thames Head of the River a year or two later, visited his parents at their family home. Charles was a fanatic and he would spend hours with us on the bare, wooden floor, dressed in long grey trousers, old shirt worn always with a tie, a well worn sweater, heavy stockings and old shoes, putting us through our paces with floor exercises, in an effort to coordinate our shoulders with the movements of our arms. After this, Charles and four novices would pile into a rowing tub, one seated on the bow planking, with two rowing, and Charles with the fourth novice seated at the stern, from where he tried to steer the craft. The tub could barely cope with the load but this was immaterial and we would push off from the steps and disappear into the gloom, under King's Bridge and up towards Dalmarnock Bridge and far beyond to where there were no houses on the banks and where there was little or no sign of human influence. This ritual scarcely altered throughout the year, although we gradually were allowed to progress to clinker fours. When in the fours, Charles would sometimes act as the cox and coach us at the same time, but most often he would follow us along the bank path on a bicycle, shouting at us through a megaphone held in one hand and trying to steer a safe course with the other Occasionally our torture would be relieved by hearing Charles utter a yell as he fell off his bike on hitting an unseen obstacle on the path. Nevertheless, we admired Charles greatly and he did teach us a great deal about rowing. Not infrequently, we would have a day's outing on the Forth and Clyde canal; these episodes involved two fours and their crews, embarking at Maryhill and rowing to Dullatur and back, a distance of approximately twenty-five miles. Needless to say, we were quite exhausted after these outings although we were harangued all the way there and back again by Charles. Strangely, I understand that he had studied Theology at Cambridge with the intention of joining the Anglican clergy. At this stage, he had not married but I learned later that he did so and returned to England.

It was about this time that I began to take a keener interest in the Fair Sex. In my first year, my girl friend was Fiona Dickson; I had, in fact, met her before she had left school. She was still in her final year at Hutcheson Girls' Grammar School. We stayed together for about two years. She believed in the old adage that the way to a man's heart is through his stomach. Consequently, every Saturday evening after the rowing, I would meander across to her home in Crosshill for a meal which she would prepare while I looked on, in an interfering way. She was of Highland stock and would spend some of her holidays in Wester Ross. Usually, after the meal, we would go either to the pictures or to the Men's Union Dance at the University. After leaving school, she decided to do nursing and enrolled at the Western Infirmary. Perhaps I had something to do with that decision.

My next girl-friend was Jeanette, a lovely blonde nurse who lived in Thornliebank, but who usually stayed, when off-duty from the Victoria Infirmary at Langside, at her brother's flat along Argyle Street. I thought she was very beautiful but I never felt comfortable with her, perhaps because I knew that there was an older chap after her, and I believe that they eventually married. After a quiet evening at the flat, we would catch the last public transport out to the Victoria Infirmary where I would leave her at the back entrance, before starting my long walk all the way back to Hillhead through the centre of the city, not reaching home until about 1 am on Sunday morning. This was a distance of about six miles or more. I must have been in love, or mad or both.

The Boat Club was almost my whole extra-curricula life apart from the girls. Charles made us enthusiasts. After our first year, we were put into an old "fine eight", (smooth hulled), quite a different experience from rowing in clinker fours. I was made the stroke of this "eight". About ten of us were drilled meticulously as we had been entered for the Tideway Head of the River race on the Thames. On our way down, we paid a visit to Charles' parents, a delightful old couple who made us all feel very welcome.

Arriving at Windsor, we found that Charles had arranged for us to make our camp in the grounds of Eton College; so, for about ten days, this group of "Glesca Keelies" were at Eton. The management of Eton College Boat Club very kindly lent us their training eight, which we also used in the Head of the River race. We really enjoyed our training on the Thames and the setting was idyllic, Windsor Castle dominating everything.

The weather must have been good as training continued without a hitch. For some obscure reason, I was made camp cook and, I am pleased to say, nobody appeared to suffer as a result of my culinary efforts. In the evenings, as I was one of the few with a driving licence, Charles allowed me to drive his Hillman Husky station wagon. A few of the lads would pile in and we would then set off on a tour of the quaint pubs in the area. This was 1955 and drinking and driving were standard practice. Oddly, I had my small accident with the car when I was dead sober. One morning, while driving, I misjudged the width of one of Windsor's narrow streets and scraped the side of a van. Charles made no comment and I was allowed to continue driving.

We soon discovered that Windsor Great Park, along the banks of the Thames, was one large public, fornicatorium. In the long summer evenings, it was not uncommon to witness fornicating couples. We puritanical Scots thought this to be a bit immoral and decadent but interesting nevertheless. As for the "Head" itself, we did our best and finished 185th, gaining twenty places from our starting position. In our spare time, we were also into pinching road signs. We had our eye on the main one, a large, white, wooden sign with black lettering saying "MAIDENHEAD" on it; this was sited on a park railing at the corner of the main road. One evening, about 11 pm, four of us, armed with screw driver and pliers, entered the park and hid in the bushes just behind the sign. No sooner had we hidden ourselves than two ladies also entered the park, hid behind some other, nearby bushes and started to urinate. We were almost washed away but did manage to remain quiet and hidden, eventually extricating the sign and carrying it back triumphantly to camp and eventually to the Boat House on Glasgow Green, where it joined other similar trophies.

Every year, GUBC held its Annual Supper in the Men's Union. This was an eagerly awaited and enjoyable event, organised by the Committee members. As many of the former members and Old Blues as were available were sent invitations, and their presence guaranteed a very convivial evening. For all of my years there, George Johnston, a 1936 Blue, had been club President and also of the Scottish Amateur Rowing Association. He was an institution in his own lifetime, both in the serious business of rowing and in the Club's social milieu. At the Supper, dress was "formal" in that the Blues wore their Blue blazers, while the lesser mortals wore their GUBC blazers, (with the crossed oars emblazoned on the breast pocket), and bow ties in club colours. After the eating phase had been completed, those present replete with alcoholic libations were entertained by very serious and witty speeches, fortunately kept reasonably short. The speeches were made by the Captain, George and one or two guest speakers, after which the trophies won during the year were presented to the winning crews. Undoubtedly, however, the highlight of the evening was the "Punch", prepared by the Captain and George according to a secret recipe, a very potent one, in two large, silver trophy bowls. There was a ritual attached to this passage of the Punch. George would ask for silence and then stand facing the diners before lifting the right hand bowl of Punch from the table in both hands, and then bowed to the guests before sipping the concoction, then bow again and turn to face the Captain on his right. He would then bow to the Captain, who would return the bow, before sipping again, after which they would both bow to each other. After accepting the bowl, the Captain then turned to the guest on his right and started again. In the meantime, George had started off the same ceremony with the second bowl but this time on his left. In this manner, the Punch travelled around all the diners and continued to do so until the bowls were almost empty, at which stage they were returned to George by the current imbibers, ritual being observed. After this, George made the final toast to the Club, the guests and the Captain. Thereafter, we all adjourned and congregated around the piano for the singsong, for which GUBC was justly famous. Once again, George was the leader voicing such ditties as Eskimo Nell, the Wheel and other such classics. Everyone participated; these songs were a relic from the demobbed, mature students, a few of whom were still in and around the University. The beer flowed freely and, in an intoxicated state, we performed such feats as Cossack Dancing, (at which I happened to be the Club champion), and the Muffin Man. About midnight, the few stalwarts still capable would somehow make for the Boathouse and continue the festivities for as long as they were able.

Many years later, on a return visit to the Club, I found that George was still going strong.

I did move on to higher office in GUBC, never won a blue but did gain colours for coaching the junior crews, the first to do so. I successfully coached a novice four, the only successful crew in that particular year. In that crew was a large Norwegian called Jon Haffner who later left my crew and moved into the first four where he went on to gain his Blue, and also to captain the Club shortly after I left. I was Treasurer in 1956/57, Vice captain in 1957/1958 and Captain in my final year of Medicine, 1959/1960. I had a very good relationship with the University registrar, Mr. Hutcheson, and was quite adept at obtaining equipment, new Fours and Tubs from the University Court through his good offices. Every crew tried to bring back a Trophy after attending regattas in other parts of the country; these were usually road-signs. As a result, the Boathouse Committee Room had a large collection of trophies on the walls. They were highly prized and guarded. In my year as the Captain, I also instituted the "GUBC Diary", but I understand that this was only continued for a year or two after my departure. Before leaving, I donated two trophies, a Quaich for the Best Four and a Cup for the Best Eight. The Boathouse was also used by a few senior members who possessed keys for their amorous adventures. The site appeared to appeal to young ladies; maybe because of the obviously masculine, smelly, dirty feel of the place, but they were always keen to savour its delights.

Repairs to the Clubhouse and Boats were carried out by club members and when we weren't actually rowing, we would be busy repairing. One or two of the members were excellent with their hands, the most notable being Stan Struthers, who also rowed with me in the same four. One major undertaking was "doing up" the floor of the changing room. For this we asked members to collect all the spare linoleum from their homes and, when we had sufficient, we got down to laying this hotch-potch on the floor—it truly was a coat of many colours. I made two or three good friends at the club. I coached Brian Neville and Iain Ramsay when they first joined two years after I arrived. Brian was the best man at my Wedding. He, Iain and Stan are very good friends to this day. Another close friend was Jack Hamill, a few years older than us, and a very amusing red-head. He was Vice Captain or, as we called him, Captain of Vice as he was always chasing girls. We still keep in touch.

From my third year onwards, the fortunes of the club declined and we were not very successful in the rowing field. However, the Committee decided that we would build up an esprit de corps, and in this we were most successful. There was a terrific sense of cameraderie, which was aided by the wearing of the GUBC blazer and a six-foot long, woollen scarf, draped around the neck and allowed to hang over the shoulders. To improve our spirits, we also held small dances at the Boathouse occasionally. As I was now in contact with radiographers and nurses at the Western Infirmary, I was always able to bring a few young ladies with me to these events. They seemed to enjoy themselves as they always came when asked. Although the Boathouse was in Glasgow Green, at the edge of a rough neighbourhood, we did not suffer much inconvenience apart from the very occasional burglary. In fact, one Saturday morning, as I walked from the High Court in the Saltmarket, through the Green to the Boathouse, I skirted around the edge of a gang fight, in which about twenty youths were involved. I was not molested and, in fact, they did not even glance at me. I obviously did not "belong". Foolhardy of me, perhaps.

In my Vice Captain's year, we sent another eight down to the Tideway Head. We procured an old St. Andrew's Association Humber ambulance for our trip south. The members sat along the sides of the cabin, while the roof rack was piled with our goods, chattels and oars. Things were going well until we reached Lesmahagow; we noted a slight unsteadiness which caused the driver to slow down. Looking out of the right window, we saw the back wheel roll past us. The Humber was carefully brought to a halt. Piling out, we made a good inspection and proved to our satisfaction that nothing was amiss and replaced the retrieved wheel securely. We continued our trip south without any further escapades. This time the eight did a lot better, perhaps because I was now the cox and not the stroke. We gained 84 places and finished at 101.

Apart from GUBC, I was also peripherally involved with the Men's Union, then under the management of Mr. Renwick. For a couple of years, (medical students took a minimum of six years to graduate), I was on the Entertainments Committee. This entailed being on occasional duty collecting tickets at the Friday and Saturday night dances, but it also allowed one to admit friends in unofficially without tickets when these were sold out. Due to being discovered, I was banned for life from the Union—I have never found out if the ban is still in force. The Union also held an annual social event towards the end of the first term of the academic year called "Black Friday". This was supposedly a formal event to which one invited the young lady of your choice, or more likely a choice young lady. Usually, you would go out to dinner and then arrive at the Union, where there were two Balls in progress simultaneously, upstairs with Jazz and downstairs with more sedate music; there were also three bars. However, the affair owed its notoriety to the "Squeezy" which, in the workaday world, was the reading room. This room contained many armchairs which, during Black Friday, were arranged in many combinations to accommodate smooching couples, the room being in total darkness. It has been said that, on more than one occasion, the cleaners refused to clean the room out following Black Friday because of the number of condoms they found lying about. It is nice to know that the students were considerate even then. If you lasted to the Saturday morning after a night of debauchery, you could both enjoy a cooked breakfast of sausage, ham and egg before staggering out into the cold light of day. The Squeezy was also in operation during the normal Friday and Saturday night dances. Many a young lady went astray there. I attended Black Friday in the first three years of my University life, each time with a respectable young lady, and each time we enjoyed ourselves.

The Glasgow Union was also noted for its debating and political involvement. Many debates took place in which a few of the recent and current politicians honed their debating skills. Two who spring readily to mind are Donald Dewar, a school colleague who was later the first Chief Minister after devolution, and the recently deceased John Smith, both of the Labour Party, the latter being the former Leader. Although not at Glasgow University, Robert MacLennan, the Liberal Democrat member for Caithness and President, was at school with me. In fact, his father, Sir Hector, a former President of the Royal College of Obstetricians and Gynaecologists, was my tutor in my final year of Medicine. Similarly, Professor Stanley Alstead's son, Alan, was a school classmate, although he joined the Army, was promoted to Brigadier and commanded a Scottish regiment.

At the end of the third term of the first academic year, we prepared ourselves for the basic medical sciences of Anatomy, Physiology, Botany and Biochemistry in the second year. "Wee George" Wyburn was Professor of Anatomy. Much of the anatomy dissection time was in the last session of the afternoon and it was really a great temptation to forego anatomy and disappear elsewhere, especially on warm, sunny, summer afternoons. I must admit that we all did this on many occasions. In fact, we ran a rota system on each dissection table to ensure that work proceeded according to schedule. There were five of us at our table—Bisi Senbanjo from Nigeria, (with whom I tried to keep in touch), Fraser Scorgie, Gordon Smith, Robert Russell and myself. It was a good table and we enjoyed many a laugh. At regular intervals during the terms, we would be given "vivas", which consisted of an oral test combined with a practical anatomical examination on the cadavre, carried out by one of the demonstrators, who were themselves studying anatomy for the primary examination of the FRCS or FRFPSG. We were also quite a bright group and we all sailed through medicine without too much trouble. The Physiology, Botany and Biochemistry sessions are now almost a total blank to me although I think that the Professors of Physiology and Biochemistry were called Garvin and Davidson respectively. During this period, and indeed throughout my studies, I followed my usual "study plan" of doing a minimum of work during most of the term, followed by a short spell of intense study two or three weeks before the degree exams.

Not all the fraternising with the opposite sex took place at the Men's Union. The Queen Margaret Ladies' Union and Westerlands, (the University Athletic Club's clubhouse out at Anniesland), were also venues for dances on occasion, the latter being used by the sporting clubs to bolster their finances. There was one venue which had a far more notorious reputation and that was the Glasgow School of Art in Garnethill, based in a Charles Rennie Mackintosh building. Even the ordinary week-end dances enjoyed a "bad" reputation but it approximated Sodom and Gomorrah on the evening of the Annual Art School Ball. Tickets to this event were very highly prized and almost impossible to obtain if you were an outsider. At the Ball, little or no attempt was made to maintain a semblance of propriety, and the participants arrived in the spirit both literally and figuratively, as the Ball was held in Fancy Dress. They were really abandoned affairs and lasted all night. I went to two of them and thoroughly enjoyed them.

Around about 1957/58, at one of the regular week-end Art School dances, I met Nancy Anderson. She was a very charming and intelligent young woman of my own age and, at that time, working as a secretary. Her parents had a large villa called Ard-an-Tigh, off Corrour Road in Giffnock. They always made me very welcome. She had a slightly younger sister called Jean and a much younger brother called Jim. Nancy and I went together for almost three years, and during this period, she gave up her secretarial work and entered nursing at the Victoria Infirmary. We got on very well together. Along with my good friend, Graham Robertson, another medic, who partnered Nancy's friend Ann Poule, the four of us went to the Lacrosse Ball and had a great night out, not arriving back home until the wee small hours of the morning. I seriously considered marrying Nancy but we started to drift apart, and it all came to naught. A few years later, and after I was married, I visited Nancy on one of our trips home.

In 1956, during the last term of our pre-clinical period, the Suez and Hungarian uprisings took place. These events had quite a profound effect on many of us. Some of my colleagues in the class decided to mount an emergency ambulance/drugs expedition to Hungary and naturally, I offered my services. Dad was not too happy with this idea. In any event, the final team chosen was a small one, just enough to man the ambulance. I believe that they only managed to reach Vienna where they handed the ambulance over to the Red Cross.

So time passed by and it soon dawned on us, the medical students, that the 2nd. Professional Examinations would be upon us at the end of the second term of the third year. These were considered to be the most difficult of all the medical examinations, largely due to the stiff anatomy papers which were set. Once again, a spurt of study at the end saw me through into my clinical years.

Chapter Seven

Torridon, Wester Ross 1956

The year 1956 was quite an eventful one for me in one way or another. In the summer holidays, after completing all our pre-clinical examinations, Graham Robertson, my friend and fellow medical student, and I hitch-hiked up through Perthshire into Inverness-shire looking for work on the Hydro-electric schemes, but without any luck. It was a beautiful summer and the countryside looked stunning. In desperation, we sought work at the Inverness Labour Exchange where we were offered jobs as estate labourers on Lord Lovelace's Torridon estate, on the far north-west coast. As we had no money and had never been there before, we accepted the post quickly and, by mid-afternoon, we had been collected by the foreman of the estate, Donnie MacKenzie, in a Land Rover. The drive back to Torridon was beautiful. Torridon, to my mind, is the most beautiful place I have seen anywhere in the world. I loved the scenery and the atmosphere instantly. The estate occupied the south side of the upper part of Loch Torridon, which is a sea loch, and included Loch and Ben Damh, the Loch and Ben of the Stags. The Lovelaces lived in the "big house" which had the head of the loch on its right, with Ben Alligin and Liathach immediately in front across the loch. A finer site could not be imagined. Graham and I were given a double "bothy", staff accommodation, facing onto the court-yard, tractor and hay storage area of the outhouses. We were to provide our own food and cook for ourselves. The bothy was spartan but comfortable with an upstairs bedroom and a downstairs living room, kichen, and small toilet. The living room had a wood-burning fire place. I did the cooking.

There were two shops in the area, one on our side of the loch in the clachan of Annat, and the other on the far side in Fassaig. The Fassaig store was owned by a former London policeman who had been reared in Torridon. His name was Donnie MacDonald and he was married to a charming Welsh lady. This couple had a son who was slightly younger than us, called Young Donnie, who also worked on the estate as a labourer, and who eventually showed us most of the ropes on the estate and the places of local entertainment. In addition, there was a grocer's van delivery from Kinlochewe, eleven miles away along a winding mountain road, once a week. From this grocer, we obtained our necessities which included two dozen bottles of Carlsberg Special beer for our weekly fluid intake.

As many of the local men were called Donnie, they had evolved a system of identification which made use of either their occupation or their place of residence. Donnie, the estate foreman, was known as "Donnie Bayview" after his cottage, Donnie MacDonald was known as "Donnie London", while the owner of the Annat shop, another Donnie MacKenzie, was known as "Donnie Shop".

Occasionally Graham and I would pinch the Land Rover which was routinely parked outside the bothy. We would run it to the top of the hill above Colin MacRae's house, switch off the engine and then coast quietly downhill past his house, not turning the engine on until we were near the first house in Annat. On these occasions we would drive to Fassaig and occasionally to Alligin. Once when we were driving back from Alligin in the gloaming, I bounced the side of the Land Rover off the rock face and almost landed up in the loch. Next day, we had to own up to the fact that we had taken it as the damage, although not extensive, was quite visible.

On rare occasions, we would leave Torridon on a Friday afternoon and travel across to Inverness, where we would book into the same "bed-and-breakfast" for the week-end. On the Saturday night, we would go to the dance held at the Caledonian Hotel and whoop it up. It was on one of these week-ends that we met Andy Stewart; the singer of popular Scottish songs; he introduced himself in the hotel lobby. It was only after a period of a few years that I realised who he was as I had not been impressed by him.

We started work about 8 am., all of us meeting in the tractor shed opposite the bothy. We were a strange crew. There was old Colin MacRae, the previous estate foreman, but now over 80 years old, dressed in well worn harris tweed plus-fours, with a pipe stuck firmly in his mouth. His favourite English expression, for he was a native Gaelic speaker and English was a foreign language to him and to most of the older folk, was "They'll be havin' rain in the HE-brides". Next was Finlay MacKenzie, the gille or gamekeeper, with his two cairn terriers; he was also dressed in the almost mandatory harris tweed plus-fours, but also wore a deer-stalker hat. Finlay's wife was called Minnie, a wee, wisp of a woman. Occasionally we would be joined by Farquhar Finlayson but he was considered an outsider as he came from the neighbouring area around Loch Carron. Graham and I were never very sure what Farquhar did, although I think he was officially the gardener. Finally, apart from ourselves, there was Young Donnie, who either walked or cycled to work every morning.

Colin lived in the estate gate house at the foot of the small incline leading up into the estate proper. He was looked after by his daughter, Annie, who was the chief maid in the Big House. Finlay and Donnie Bayview lived in Annat. Finlay's house was traditional but the thatch and turf had been replaced, although the house was still lit by kerosene lamps, while the cooking was done on an open peat fire, the peat for which he cut himself from his plot up the glen. Donnie Bayview's house had been an original cottage but had been modernised and now had all the modern conveniences, and was tastefully furnished by his wife, Alice.

It was hard to imagine that, of the older members of the village, Finlay had only been out of the glen once in his life on a very short visit to London twenty years before, while Colin, Donnie Shop, (the owner of the local shop), and Farquhar had never ever been out of the immediate area. Donnie Bayview, having been in the Lovat Scouts, the original commando group during the war, was relatively widely travelled. Young Donnie had done his National Service in the Scots Guards at Windsor, spending all his time in the Officers' Mess; he returned to Torridon as fast as he was able and in later life very rarely ever left except to go to Inverness on business as he took over his Father's shop and became "Donnie Shop".

Once we had all gathered in the tractor shed, the older members would discuss the local events in Gaelic; this unfortunately excluded the three youngest members, as Young Donnie only had a smattering of the Gaelic. Eventually, Donnie Bayview would tell what chores he wanted us to do for the day. Most of the work was concerned with timber clearance, sheep gathering, shearing, harvesting and converting former shepherds' cottages for rental to fishermen and hunters during the approaching Game season. Time passed quickly, and the work although very strenuous was also very varied and gave us city-slickers a fresh approach to life. Donnie Bayview was a big, strong man in his late forties, dressed in his blue bibbed dungarees, and always wearing a "bunnet", he was always available and willing to give us advice and assistance.

One afternoon, Graham and I were asked to put the cut hay into small stacks down in one of the lower fields near the village cemetery at the entrance to Annat. Well, it was the "midgie season" and they were flying around in their thousands, dense black clouds hovering about. We started our task but after about fifteen minutes, I had to stop because I had been bitten so badly that I had developed an allergic reaction which caused me severe facial oedema, severe enough to almost close my eyes.

Apart from our Carlsberg Special diet, we ate very well. Alice MacKenzie was always inviting us over for afternoon teas and for the occasional evening meal, after which Donnie would bring out the mandatory bottle of whisky and place it on the table. Young Donnie's parents also invited us across for meals from time to time. As it was the salmon and hunting season, we were also well supplied with fresh salmon and trout, together with hung venison, by the people who had rented the estate cottages at, what appeared to us to be, exorbitant rates. We ate very well and Highland Hospitality was certainly not found wanting.

Our leisure time at Torridon was also very varied. On the Saturday morning of our first week-end there, Graham and I went into the shop of Donnie MacKenzie, Donnie Shop, where the locals were all gathered, blethering away in Gaelic while they smoked. It was very easy to see that very little business was ever transacted there as it was small and dingy, with very few items of merchandise for sale; however, it served a far more useful purpose as a meeting place for the men folk. As we entered the store, there was a break in the Gaelic, then we were asked by Donnie Bayview what we wanted. I said that we would like to go fishing the next day, Sunday. There was a shocked silence for a few moments, then old Colin said, very deliberately, "There'll be no fishin' on the Sabbath.". That was the end of that conversation as Graham and I trooped out sheepishly. We had forgotten that this was the stronghold of the "Wee Frees", a very strict Presbyterian sect. Instead, the next day, we lay on one of the rocks beside the loch, sunbathing, dozing, eating and drinking—all very civilised.

On Sundays, especially if there were fishermen at the cottages, we would hitch a lift into the Kinlochewe Hotel, where we would spend the afternoon drinking as bona-fide travellers. About once a month, the Highlands and Islands Mobile Film Unit would appear at Kinlochewe and everyone from miles around would troop into the village hall to see the picture. It was one of the highlights of the social calendar.

We also went to church one Sunday morning; it was a traditional small, stone-built church situated on a hillock at the side of the loch and surrounded by trees. I think we must have accompanied Alice and Donnie but we did not sit beside them. In this part of Wester Ross, the local inhabitants were largely "Wee Frees", members of the Free Presbyterian Church of Scotland. We entered the church and sat behind a large, tweed-suited gentleman with two young children, aged about eight and six years. This particular service was in English. When the first hymn was announced, the Presenter rose from the front pew, faced the congregation, lifted a tuning-fork which he struck hard on the table in front of him and sang a note which corresponded to the tuning-fork frequency, after which the congregation joined in the hymn singing. The Wee Frees do not believe in the use of any other musical instrument in church. However, the highlight of the service was due to a musical note of a different variety and quality. At a quiet point of the service, there was a sudden loud "fart" from one of the children sitting immediately in front of us. Of course, they burst out laughing as did Graham and I, and the mirth continued for a considerable time despite the best efforts of a very embarrassed father to quieten them.

Every so often, a small Ceilidh would be held at the village school in Fassaig. On one of the occasions, we caught up with young Donnie; we also met two young ladies, one dark and sultry Swiss, the other an English blonde. Both were working as au-pairs during the holidays for Lord Lovelace's nephew up at the big house. The Swiss girl could not speak much English; as I was the only one able to speak French, we hit it off together. Young Donnie charmed the English girl. After an early finish to the Ceilidh, the four of us returned to the big house, Graham returning to the bothy, where we held our own wee party into the small hours.

Torridon is one of the great Scottish meccas for mountaineers and not infrequently we would put up one or two English climbers overnight if the Youth Hostel was full. Most of them, appeared to be totally ill-equipped for the Scottish mountains. One evening, two climbers arrived unexpectedly at our front door, so we invited them in and offered them traditional Highland Hospitality—a large bottle of Queen Anne whisky. During our festivities, and not unexpectedly, my girl friend arrived as I had arranged to meet her. So I excused myself, collected a tartan rug and another bottle of whisky before taking her up into the hay-loft next door, where we spent a very memorable few hours. The two girls were at Torridon for about ten days; the time flew in and I really missed her after she had left.

Looking back on it now, I realise that it was the overall Torridon experience which totally converted me to Scottishness and awakened in me an interest in the Gaelic culture and language. Many years later, I took my wife, Margot, then my teenage daughter, Michèle, and finally a Danish friend, Mette Kirketerp, to Torridon; they all found it enchanting, the Dane going as far as to say that she preferred it to the Norwegian fjords. Many years later, I even considered a single-handed general practice there; however, Margot, my future wife, put an end to that as she considered it to be far too isolated although very beautiful.

Chapter Eight

The Budding Doctor, 1957-1960

The studies really started in the middle of our third year, 1957. Most of our lectures were still held at the University but more and more of our time was spent in the Pathology Department and Clinical Units within the many hospitals scattered around Glasgow. Wherever possible, I tried to arrange my classes so that I did not have to stray far from the University and the Western Infirmary, both of which were almost at my front door.

I was quite interested in Pathology, particularly histology. I studied this subject, along with Bacteriology/Virology at the Western Infirmary Department of Pathology. At that time, the Professor was D.F. Cappell, the author of our standard textbook of Pathology. He was very ably assisted by Bernard Lennox and John Anderson, both of whom became Professors later, I believe. The latter two made the subject very interesting and alive. During this period, we were introduced to the delights of the Post-mortem room, where a small number of us would sit on benches watching an autopsy at the same time as the salient pathological features were being explained to us. It was never a boring subject.

In the medical field, I was attached at various times to Dr. Olav Kerr's Unit in the Western. He was also a Glasgow Academical and he undoubtedly favoured the select few. A tall, austere man, he nevertheless was well respected and had a sense of humour. A few medical attachments were also spent in Professor Wayne's Unit, where we came in most contact with Dr. Abe Goldberg, who later became the Professor of Medicine. I also undertook attachments at the Southern General Hospital in Govan, where I came under the tutorship of Dr. Gavin Shaw; he was a very good lecturer and demonstrator who managed to teach me quite an appreciable amount of theoretical and clinical medicine. For my Infectious Diseases, I travelled to Ruchill Hospital, just north of the Western. Here I came under the strict attention of Dr. Tom Anderson, another Academical. Dermatology lectures were given at the old Anderson College, near the entrance to the Western. It wasn't a very appealing subject as far as I was concerned. However, there was one branch of Medicine which failed to excite me at all; this was Public Health which was presented very boringly and badly, at least I thought so. One of the highlights of our course was the specialty of Forensic Medicine. For this subject, we were very fortunate to have Professor John Glaister, ably assisted by Dr. Robertson, to lecture to us and keep us interested, for it was an enthralling subject. One of the basic subjects of medicine was Pharmacology and in this we were lectured almost wholly by Professor Stanley Alstead, although he was a fairly "dry" lecturer. However, he was co-author, along with Professors Dunlop and Davidson, of our textbook on Medicine. In the surgical field, I also tried to remain fairly close to home. Most of our lecturing was carried out by Professor Charles Illingworth, Professor of Surgery, in the Western Infirmary, ably assisted by "Paddy" Forrest and William Burnett, both of whom were later to become Professors, the latter in Australia. Our Orthopaedics lectures were provided by Professor Roland Barnes and his staff, the most notable being Mr. Howat, Mr. Parkes, (the Hand surgeon) and Mr. "Tommy" Gardner, the latter being the most approachable and helpful. For "Ear, Nose and Throat", I travelled to the Victoria Infirmary at Langside, to the Unit of Mr. Strang, if I remember correctly. It wasn't one of my favourite subjects and didn't inspire me very much. Most of my "clinical" surgery was undertaken in Mr. Gerstenberg's Unit at the Western, where he was very ably helped by Mr. Henry Wapshaw and Mr. Neil MacLean. Mr. Wapshaw was a slow, methodical man but always gave the impression of being unsure, while Mr. McLean was decisive and dynamic. They were both very good lecturers. This was also the Unit in which I did most off my general surgery locums as a student.

No medical course would be complete without Psychiatry. Again, I found the lectures to be confusing and was not very enamoured of the subject. However, it had its interesting moments as we occasionally went across to Gartnavel Mental Hospital in the evenings to be shown clinical cases of interesting patients. At that time, Gartnavel was under the direction of Dr. Angus MacNiven, a tall, austere-looking man who had a habit of riding around the grounds on a white horse. The evening sessions were always interesting and therefore well attended. One of the most dynamic and progressive Units at that time was The Department of Obstetrics and Gynaecology, for which there were two Professors, Dr. Anderson at the Glasgow Royal Infirmary and Dr. Ian Donald at the Western. As far as I can recall, most of my Gynaecology I learned from Professor Anderson and his lucid lectures, while the Obstetrics was the province of Professor Donald. At that time, Professor Donald and his staff were pioneering the use of Ultrasound in Obstetrics. Obsterics/Gynaecology did not appeal to me very much either.

Having run the whole gamut of subjects and lecturers, I decided that I should eventually like to become a surgeon. This was because the subjects appeared to be more interesting, (or were they just presented better ?), and the surgeons more stimulating that the physicians. But, as Rabbie Burns said, "The best laid schemes of mice and men gang aft agley."

Students were also required to do an attachment with a general practitioner towards the end of the course and my attachment was with a Dr. Scobie, another Academical, whose practice was in the Govan area, on the south side. I would sit in on his surgeries and listen to his words of wisdom and observe his approach to patients and his clinical skills. I do not know if it did me much good but it was better than sitting in at lectures. If I remember correctly, he was considerably involved with the British Medical Association. I must not give you the impression that my life was all work and no play, for that would have made Ian a very dull boy.

At the end of the 1958 summer term, Graham, Eric Osborne,(a fellow, tall, languid medic), and I decided that we would catch up with Chris Gede, the Dane whom I had met in Six-Fours a couple of years before. I had kept up with him and he had offered me his flat in Valby, Copenhagen, should I ever want it. So, laden down with our rucksacks, we set off and managed to cross the Channel together, but thereafter, travelling together became impossible. In a field, somewhere in northern

France, we said our farewells and headed off independently for Denmark. Eric looked most unhappy to be going off on his own, but Graham and I were wanting to get started right away. I had an interesting trip across the northeren parts of France, Belgium, Holland and Germany. I called in at a Gendarmerie in Valencienne in the evening to enquire about a Youth Hostel, but there wasn't one and I was just beginning to wonder what I should do next when an elderly lady approached me and offered me accommodation for the night at her home. This I gratefully accepted for it was a very comfortable but old-fashioned home; the lady was also very kind to me. Travelling across Holland, I met a young Dutchman from Breda who joined up with me, and together we moved across into Germany and found a place in a Youth Hostel. You cannot visit Hamburg without going to the Reperbahn in the "Red Light" district, but I cannot say that it left much impression on me.

Then it was up along the Jutland peninsula where I called in to see Chris who was. However, I soon dumped him after he more or less forced himself into an elderly couple's home and demanded that they not only fed us but also put us up for the night. It was the most arrogant episode I think I have ever encountered. Eventually, I reached Hamburg staying for a while with his Mother in her home village. Before crossing to Fyn island, I accepted a lift from a man who invited me to his home in Odense where there was to be a party that evening. I attended the party and it was a good one. My major recollection is of about a dozen people, myself included, seated around a long table before the dinner was served. Our host, my driver, seated at the head of the table, arose and said a few words in Danish, picked up his glass of Akvavit and said, "Skol" before downing the liqueur in one gulp, everyone following suit. The others rose in turn, repeating the ritual. After about half a dozen toasts, and a modicum of food, I was unable to take any more, so I excused myself from the table and lay down on a bed, falling asleep for two hours. On awakening, I rejoined the party. Somehow or other, I managed to start hitch-hiking again next morning and reached Chris's flat without any further interesting diversions. Graham was already there, having had a very quick trip up Jutland and across the islands. Eric did not appear until the next day, having gone right across northern Germany and entering Denmark by bridge. He really looked exhausted.

Chris had not yet separated from Lise. His flat was quite small and we must have caused tham a great deal of inconvenience, but they looked after us very well. We visited the Karlsberg Brewery, where we partook liberally of the various beverages on offer and looked at Rodin's statue of "Le Penseur" in the gardens. On one or two evenings, we visited Nyhavn, specifically No. 17, in which an excellent Jazz Band was in residence; we also visited the famous Tivoli Gardens, the War Museum and made a point of seeing the "Little Mermaid" statue and the "Gefion" water fountain. I have one outstanding recollection. One evening, Chris took us to a party. All I can remember about it is sitting on a floor in a fairly small room, the walls of which were painted a deep red. On one wall of the room, there was a large, black relief of Queen Nefertiti. After a very potent combination of dense smoke and Carlsberg Specials, I soon felt the room closing in on me. Fortunately, my three colleagues must have felt the same as we left soon after. On leaving, I recall all of us singing in the street, "I belong to Glasgow". But we did not go home immediately. We entered a wine bar where there were singing waiters, who sang as they served their customers. When they became tired, they invited the customers to sing. After being egged on by my friends, I arose and once again started to sing, "I belong to Glasgow" but it was not appreciated and I gradually sank down into my chair. We eventually went home, drunk but tired and happy.

Chris also wanted us to sail a yacht for him from Copenhagen to Aarhus, but as none of us had done any serious sailing, we declined the offer. Nevertheless, we did leave Chris, and wound our way back to Aarhus on Jutland where we visited the University and the model old town. At the University, we were interviewed and photographed as we were wearing our kilts. The article and photograpgh eventually appeared in the University magazine. This was a very fortunate occurrence as will be explained later. We did not stay long in Aarhus as we were heading for the International Students' Centre at Hald in the heart of Jutland.

Graham, Eric and I had chosen the time for our stay at Hald most fortuitously. Unknown to us before our arrival, the first week-end was the one in which the Scandinavian Airlines Service (SAS) had chosen to hold their annual convention and they had taken the centre over. The reason for our admittance remains a mystery. Nevertheless, we were made to feel very welcome and we struck up a particular friendship with a slightly older man called Sven. I suppose the SAS staff must have done some business but it certainly did not intrude into the social life. The whole week-end appeared to be taken up with eating, drinking and partying. The one thing that amazed me about the Danes was the fact that they appeared to become happier the more they drank; this was quite the opposite to the Scots and was a new experience for me. Eric and I met two delightful young Danish ladies who were our constant companions during the orgiastic week-end and for the few days we stayed thereafter. My friend's name was Hanne, a student nurse from a small village south of Copenhagen. Eric and I, together with our two lady friends, spent a lot of time at an old ruined Viking fort situated on a hill overlooking a lake; occasionally, we would see Graham, far below, single-handedly, sailing a dinghy up and down the lake. We were sorry to leave Hald.

Not many months after our return from Denmark, Graham was thrown out of his parents' home for personal reasons. As he had nowhere to stay at short notice, my parents took him in with us for a few weeks so that his studies would not be interrupted too much and to give him time to sort out his personal problems. He married Doris, a very nice woman from Inverness, and after graduation, he spent a very frustrating time as a Glasgow GP before taking my advice and migrating to Albury, New South Wales, Australia.

Roger Cannon and Kerr Chatfield, two medical students and school friends, joined me one summer on another trip to Denmark. We must have flown across from Glasgow and stayed in Chris's flat in Valby. It was a hot summer and we did very little but lie on the beach at Klampenborg as far as I can remember.

Another close friend, Irwin Thompson, and I spent a glorious week-end in a tent on an open hillside above Crianlarich, under the shoulder of Ben More, reaching there after an enjoyable ride on his Lambretta, loaded with our gear. We both thoroughly enjoyed the solitude, the weather and the whole outing. Ever since this time, I have never felt truly free until I reach Crianlarich on the many trips to my favourite part of the country, Torridon and Sutherland.

For parties, we would frequently go to other hospitals outside the city boundaries. On one occasion, two classmates and I caught the bus to Stonehouse Hospital and took part in a very wild party indeed, which lasted all night. One paired up with a nurse and disappeared quite early in the evening with her; the other was not so lucky and decided to leave about midnight.

After our Obstetrics/Gynaecology lectures, the students were required to witness a prescribed number of Caesarean sections; this I did at Rotten Row Maternity Hospital. We were also required to do a set number of normal deliveries and witness a few abnormal ones. Eric and I did these during out vacations and we chose Raigmore Hospital in Inverness, under the charge of Dr. Hay. We duly arrived at Inverness, and surprise, surprise, we discovered that there was a hectic social scene here also, as Inverness also had the Royal Infirmary, sited in the town itself. Consequently, there was an excess of nurses of the opposite sex with considerable time on their hands. Eric and I threw ourselves wholeheartedly into the social scene and even managed to accomplish our obstetric chores with a minimum of effort and interest. We made friends with two nurses from the Royal who shared a lovely stone villa on the banks of the River Ness. My friend's name was Olga and we spent much of our time very enjoyably on the Ness Islands during the long summer evenings. On one occasion, the four of us had an evening picnic in the shadows of Urquhart Castle, at Drumnadrochit. I can recall Olga and I leaving this romantic spot about 2am, not having sighted "Nessie", but then, we were not really looking for the monster. On the night before our departure from Raigmore there was a final, exceedingly wild party. As I was going on to Loch Morlich the next day to meet my friend Jack to do some climbing in the Cairngorms, I arranged to meet her there too in the early afternoon. I recognised Jack easily enough on my arrival but the only way I recognised this nurse was by her lovely legs. I excused myself from Jack to entertain her for a couple of hours. I was really amazed that she came all the way from Inverness by public transport; she must have enjoyed the previous night's entertainment very much indeed.

This little dalliance delayed our departure that afternoon quite considerably and it was quite late in the afternoon before we started out for Loch Avon and the Shelter Stone. The climb took us a few hours and by the time we reached the hills overlooking the lochan of Loch Avon, it was very dark. Occasionally, we would see the moon's reflection on the loch surface as we slithered down the steep, scree slope to the loch's edge, after which we walked along it, up a slight slope to the Shelter Stone, set back from the head of the loch. Entering the shelter, we tried not to disturb the few climbers already there asleep, before crawling into our sleeping bags exhausted. We enjoyed beautiful weather and Loch Avon was a little gem, with a golden beach, small but exquisite, reflecting the strong sun, at the head of the loch. The hills rose almost sheer from the lochside and many of them were clad in purple heather. It was truly beautiful. We spent the days in the neighbourhood, walking the hills and in the evenings, we would return to the Shelter Stone for another chilly but unforgettable night.

Later in the same year, some newly graduated Glasgow doctors came to Inverness to complete their residential requirements. As can be imagined, life was not all work. Apparently during another wild party, the Hospital matron appeared on the scene to complain about the noise. The "happy" doctors, however, were not overawed by her, but manhandled her into a storage cupboard where they kept her locked up all night. Therefore, it was not surprising to learn that Glasgow students and residents were henceforth banned from seeking appointments in Inverness for many years.

Glasgow students have always had a reputation for wild behaviour, especially during the 1960s. These episodes frequently reached the world headlines, especially during University Rectorial Installations. This event was held in the old St. Andrew's Halls, later burned down. Quite honestly, the students went just to let off steam, make mock and have a time of absolute abandon. The stalls and balconies were packed to overflowing and it was quite obvious from the number of small paper bags and other containers being carried into the hall that the event was going to be a particularly wild one, even although it was being held in the late morning before the pubs had opened. Right from the moment the official party had stepped up on to the stage, all hell broke loose. It was not possible to hear anything apart from the horrendous noise from the student body. Almost as quickly, the airspace of the hall was obliterated with flying objects of all descriptions. It was not long before the official party was in total disarray. Mr. R.A. Butler, a very senior figure in the Conservative

Party, on attempting to address the gathering, was showered with rolls of toilet paper, and his suit ruined with pounds of flour and many eggs. The meeting was brought to a rapid close and as the students poured out of the Hall into the surrounding streets, the police present found that they were unable to cope. All roads were blocked, cars were stopped and two or three lorries delivering beer to local pubs were relieved of their goods. It had been a great day for student anarchy but done without any malicious intent. Changed days!

There is an annual student event in Glasgow which is generally welcomed, always provides light relief and is the means for obtaining much needed additional funds for worthy causes—this is the Students' Charities Day. All student Colleges participate and the Glasgow City Council permits collectors free use of transport throughout the city centre. It starts about 9am, with the students all in fancy dress, gathering at strategic points scattered throughout the city centre, picking up their collection cans. Thereafter, either singly, in pairs or in groups, they harass the Glasgow citizens on buses, in the subways, shops, cars and anywhere handy. It continues without stop until about 5pm when the collection activities slow down and the collection cans handed in. There is then a period of about two or three hours in which the students recuperate and prepare themselves for the next part of the day's activities. This consists of dances held in the various student unions scattered around the city and which continue until midnight and beyond. In conjunction with the actual collection, a Charities' Queen is also chosen. The Charities' Day basic motto is "YGORRA", a Glaswegian corruption of "you have got to". It leaves itself open to many interpretations and each successive Charities' Day uses a variation. There are many: two for example are, "Ygorra dob a bob in" and "Ygorra Phil McCann". These events are always fairly successful and do manage to raise many thousands of pounds for Charities.

Shortly after our return from the week-end above Crianlarich, Irwin asked me to be his best-man at his wedding. I gladly accepted as Irwin and Margaret Robertson, his fiancee, were among my best friends. It was a formal wedding. On the day of the wedding, our hired grey, morning suits were delivered to my home address. Irwin arrived up about an hour and a half before the event allowing us ample time to get ourselves ready. In the last half hour preceding the wedding, we each had a good stiff whisky. It was a nice, straightforward Church of Scotland wedding service and I managed to act with decorum, not dropping the ring at the crucial moment. The reception followed at which there was dancing. It was a good wedding. After graduation and residencies, they migrated to the USA and I have never heard from them since.

Apart from the graduation ceremony, there was one event which attracted a fair amount of our time, effort and money. This was the Final Year Dinner. At the beginning of our studies in 1954, our intake of students formed the Delta Club, and elected its first Committee members; the members were changed every so often. They were charged with raising funds for both the Dinner and the Final Year Book during the six years of our studies. In those days, the Ladies held a separate Dinner from the Gentlemen. Somewhere in the last part of our studies, the Committee members informed us that we would have to pay additional sums towards the Dinner. Although many objected, I believe that I was the only one who did not pay and who did not attend the Dinner in the end. Maybe that was childish. I did, however, receive my copy of the Year Book, a much more worthwhile memento containing, as it did, photographs with apt quotations of every student in the class. My photo was adorned with two quotations. The first, from Burns, was "There's ae faut the whiles lay tae me, I lo'e the lasses, Gude forgie me", while the second one was "All I know I learned at my Mother's knee and other low joints". I found the latter very apt as my Mother was only five feet in height. Ever since, I have never attended any reunions and do not intend to do so.

My Final examinations did not really worry me unduly but there was one facet of them which will always remain in my mind. Each student was required to examine a major case patient and a minor case patient in the clinical examination. When my time arrived to examine the minor case patient, I approached the screened-off area, entered it to find Sir Derrick Dunlop standing at the foot of the bed in which there was a middle-aged man lying flat in bed, slightly short of breath. Sir Derrick said that I was to proceed. After introducing myself to the patient, and requesting his permission to examine him and perhaps suggest a treatment schedule later, I could readily see that he was becoming progressively more breathless the longer he lay flat. Without saying anything else, I moved up to the head of the bed, helped the patient to sit up and rearranged his pillows accordingly. Sir Derrick then interrupted me, thanked me for my actions on behalf of the patient, and then said I could leave. It had purely been an exercise in bedside manner, observation and simple remedial measures.

It was not too long before the final results were displayed on the Medical Faculty notice board at the University. I had passed.

Chapter Nine

Graduation and Residencies, 1960-1961

After six years of study, good comradeship, laughter and social activity, the 1954 intake of medical students eventually completed their course and graduated. It was freely admitted by our teachers and lecturers that we had been one of the best intakes for many years, very few of us being left along the way.

The Graduation was in June 1960 in the Great Hall of Glasgow University. Mum and Dad, as proud parents, received their tickets to attend and, on the day managed to obtain two reasonable seats, three quarters of the way down the hall. They were very proud indeed as I was the first member of the family, on either side, to complete a University education. The hall was packed to capacity as this was a multi-faculty graduation. As the University dignitaries entered, the congregation rose from their seats. When everyone was comfortably re-seated, the Chancellor walked to the centre of the dais and made a speech of welcome, congratulations and encouragement. I think that the medical faculty graduated first. I did not think it a very impressive ceremony as I felt as if we were passing along a conveyor belt, as indeed we were, even to the extent that I was wearing a "skin", the hired academic, black gown and mortar-board which I carried and which I had collected from a store representative in the cloakroom below, immediately before the start of the ceremony. The undergraduate, on hearing their name read out in Latin, mounted the steps on the right, walked across the front of the dais, shook hands with the Chancellor, was tapped on the head by him with a graduate mortar-board, and then handed the graduate scroll which was rolled up inside a black, University badge emblazoned, black, tubular container, after which the graduate descended the stairs on the left to return to their seat. The whole "graduation" probably took about a minute although the ceremony lasted about two and a half hours as there were many graduates to process. After the formal ceremony, most gathered in the University cloisters and courtyards where graduation photos were taken. Mum and Dad took me out to a nice lunch before we returned home. It was a pleasant and important, but somehow unimportant, day for the three of us.

One of the few not to graduate was my close friend Graham, due to his personal problems. He was now married and was also having to work as a barman to make ends meet. Fortunately, he graduated at the second sitting held later in the year. In my final student year, my steady girl friend was a blonde called Moira. She was good fun. And although not a student herself, she had close connections with the University as her mother was a senior secretary in the Administration. They lived on Crow Road, not too far from Anniesland Cross, in a ground floor tenement flat. She was my girl friend when I graduated, and she may have thought that she had "hooked" me as she became a bit demanding and, as I had no intention of settling down in the immediate future, we separated. I heard that not too long afterwards, she married a Church of Scotland minister and went to live somewhere in the Western Isles.

A bit before we graduated, Eric and I had arranged to do a clinical clerkship at Aalborg Hospital on Jutland, Denmark, although we did not speak a word of Danish. In the six weeks or so between graduation and the start of the hospital residencies at the beginning of August, Eric and I arrived in Aalborg, where we were met by a tall, slim, fair-haired doctor, slightly older than ourselves, who introduced himself as Mogens Kirketerp. The amazing thing was that he said he knew us. We were quite intrigued by this statement and, after much discussion, it transpired that he had been a student at Aarhus University in the same year in which we had had our photos taken for the university magazine. He had recognised us from that photo. He was a very quiet, gentle and kind person and was married to a lovely Norwegian called Anna, and also the proud father of twin girls, Mette and Bente. Many years later, they met my wife, Margot, and we became good friends and have remained in touch ever since.

Mogens took us to our flat in a modern apartment block. It was lovely, with everything provided for us, our meals being taken at the hospital canteen, if need be. We were very comfortable and contented here. At 9am every week-day morning, we reported to Dr. Christiansen in the Medical ward. When all the doctors had arrived, a small clinical meeting was held at which we discussed therapy and the latest laboratory and X'ray results. Then we followed Dr. Christiansen on his ward round, which lasted for about an hour, after which we were finished for the day, as we were unable to communicate in Danish. But time did not lie heavily on our hands as we were well cared for by Mogens and Anna, and by Dr. and Mrs. Michelsen, who frequently invited us to their homes for meals. On one or two occasions, we went for picnics. I particularly remember visiting a Danish Schloss set in a moat; this was with Mogens and Anna.

Mogens wanted us to join the local scene so one evening, leaving Anna at home, he took us to the "Ambassador". This was a night club with a large, convivial beer-garden type room on the first floor, and a sophisticated night club on the floor above. One of them was called the "Pulter Kammeret". Thereafter, we spent many an evening there. It was particularly enjoyable to be sitting among a happy crowd of people, drinking Tuborg or Carlsberg beer, swaying from side to side with arms linked, singing at the top of one's voice. Quite a few of the young men were obviously students as they were wearing the white, flat-topped, peaked cap common then in European student circles. Again, I was impressed by how friendly the Danes became the more alcohol they consumed. It was also in the "Ambassador" that we saw our first strip-show, performed by a delectable young lady assisted by a moderately sized python.

It was not long before Eric and I made the acquaintance of two very nice young ladies from the hospital. Eric's friend, Judith Krogsgaard, was a medical secretary, brunette and quite tall. Over the length of our stay, she became quite besotted with Big Eck (as his friends called him). My friend was a blonde, attractive, quiet, laboratory technician called Kirsten Pedersen, who had her own flat nearby. The four of us had a great time together.

However, there were two other young ladies who also interested me. Through Judith, Eric and I were invited to a Skagen beach-house for a week-end. Here I met Inge Larsen, a well-built, blonde student, to whom I felt quite attracted. However, there was an older Dane interested in her and I did not have much success in this venture. The more interesting part was the fact that her brother was a Chess Grand Master.

Through a contact at the hospital, I met Jill Jensen, another blonde but more delicate. We met towards the end of our stay in Aalborg. She affected me considerably and before leaving, I arranged to meet her in Copenhagen on our way home. We did meet and, in the quietness of the flat, I proposed to her but sensibly she suggested that we should think about it for a while. On returning home, I told Dad. He told me two things: the first, do not marry until you can afford two wives and the second, it is difficult to marry someone from a different culture, even if it is European. Jill and I wrote to each other for a while but gradually the correspondence ceased.

During our stay in Aalborg, we had also arranged for Chris to visit us for a day or two. He duly came, unchanged, pipe still clamped in his jaws, but this time with a little blonde, beautiful daughter called Annelise hanging on to his hand. Lise had left him. Our friends in Aalborg made him feel most welcome. He still had his flat in Valby, which he offered to us again and in which we stayed for our last few days in Denmark.

We had also arranged to meet Judith and Kirsten in Copenhagen and I can recall spending a very pleasant morning sitting at the Frascati pavement cafe on the Radhus Plaz talking away and sipping coffee. Oddly enough, quite by chance one evening, we also bumped into Inge in the Students' Union while we were inquiring about reciprocal university arrangements, but we just acknowledged each other.

Returning to Glasgow through Bridgeton, I was depressed after having spent such a great time in a fresh and clean country among friends and to return to a dirty, smoky, industrial city, but this was home and the low spirits did not last for long.

It was almost time for me to take up my first post as a Resident on 1 Aug 60. I had arranged to do my first six months in the Medical Unit of Dr. Basil Rennie at Stobhill Hospital, on the north-eastern outskirts of Glasgow and, at that time one of the biggest hospitals in Europe. Although I had not realised it at the time, Dr. Rennie was also an Academical. On the appointed day, the new residents arrived and were duly allocated their individual rooms in a block, which shared a common lounge. My co-resident in Dr. Rennie's unit was my friend Eric, with whom I had just been to Denmark on holiday; he also had the room next to mine.

At work, we were rarely graced by the presence of Dr. Rennie and the unit was run by Dr. Markson, a nice, quiet, unassuming man, Dr. Jim Nielson, the senior Registrar, Dr. Alasdair MacDougall, the Registrar and Dr. John Morrow, the Senior House Officer, who was trying to study for his MRCP. Our team was responsible for a male and a female ward. For the first half, I looked after the male ward and than changed over for the second half with Eric to look after the female ward. Of course, during time off and holidays, the remaining resident looked after both wards. The work was not too demanding and we soon settled down to a steady routine. It was a happy unit.

Dr. Rennie wore spectacles on the end of his nose and walked with a pronounced limp. Only once did I experience any friction with him. He had admitted a private, female patient to the ward but he had forgotten to inform me accordingly. When she arrived, I naturally started the routine investigations after taking the history and carrying out the clinical examination. She was quite obviously suffering from a lack of thyroid hormone, a condition called myxoedema, and so, after removing blood for the appropriate tests, I started her on the correct therapy. When Dr. Rennie arrived, he was horrified and almost speechless when he learned what I had done for his private patient. After pacing agitatedly up and down the ward floor for a few moments, he turned to me and said, "You are quite right. It was really quite obvious." That was the end of the matter.

In addition, each ward was ruled by a Sister. The male ward was in the charge of a dark-haired sister, slightly older than ourselves, and the female ward by a blonde, English sister. They were both very efficient and friendly. One sister always conveyed to me a sense of having "hidden passion" and so I decided to cultivate her. She was a change from my usual type of girl friend as she was quite slim and a brunette. Nevertheless, I persevered and she eventually succumbed. We spent many a pleasant evening in "I Spy's" room after she had finished her evening shift. She always called me "I Spy" because I initialled my written reports with "I St-Y".

Again, Stobhill was a great place for social activity and John Morrow, our SHO, had a grudging respect for Eric and me in this demanding field of human endeavour. It was a very hectic time, both with wild parties and private engagements.

The Festive Season was upon us. Houghmagandie is an euphemism introduced by Rabbie Burns for sexual intercourse. On Christmas morning, I rang up the hospital switchboard operator and asked him to announce over the public address system that a Dr. Houghmagandie, a visiting doctor, was required in a certain ward. After a bit of good natured bantering, the call duly floated over the air waves causing quite a little mirth.

For the patients' Christmas festivities, Eric and I were chosen to be the principals in the drama, Eric as Santa Claus and me as the Christmas fairy. After the serious business of the ward rounds had been completed, and we were off duty, Eric changed into the traditional red costume, stuffed a pillow under his jacket and prepared his bag of gifts. My costume was quite ridiculous as I was dressed in a ballerina's tutu and bodice, thick stockings and heavy boots, all the while running around waving my magic wand. My own hair was shrouded in a blond, flowing wig and my face was plastered with make-up, with pronounced lipstick around the mouth. In these appealing costumes, Eric and I started on our ward rounds about 10.30 am, shaking hands with the males and kissing the females, including the sisters and staff nurses, before handing them their presents. We did this for all of the wards, at each of which, after handing out the presents, we joined the staff members in the staff room for a drop or two of Christmas cheer. This hectic procession continued until about 2pm, after which time Eric and I were very merry indeed, and gracefully retired to our rooms to recuperate in time for the evening party.

During this cavorting, we both met many nurses whom we had not previously encountered. My attention was drawn to a very cuddly blonde, who turned out to be a mid-European. She soon proved to be very friendly. However, one of her less endearing traits was her ability to exaggerate and it was not long before I began to hear rumours about how rich I was, how I had a Lagonda sports car and other similar but quite untrue tales. Although our liaison was relatively short, it was very enjoyable.

If it were possible, the social life became even more frantic at this time of year. There was both a Christmas Party and a New Year Party given by the residents, with festivities also running during the days in between. They were both memorable in their own ways. To the Christmas Party, I invited my girl friend from the Western Infirmary, (perhaps like carrying coals to Newcastle), and soon we retired to my room, both very merry, where we continued with our jollifications, during the course of which she passed out. However, it was still only about midnight, and I could hear that the party was still in full swing judging from the noise drifting upwards, so I girded my loins, so to speak, and rejoined the fray leaving my friend asleep in my room. It was not long before the dark-haired sister and I were in conversation and, after a drink or two, we moved across to the library in another building, closed the door and amused ourselves until the dawn broke through. I then returned to my room, awakened my sleeping beauty from the Western, sobered her up and took her back to her own hospital.

The Hogmanay Party was a very amusing affair. A few of my Australian friends, then staying in Kangaroo Valley in London, had contacted me and I had invited them up for the party. About 10pm on New Year's Eve, three or four Australian couples suddenly appeared at the door. Among them were Ross Fimister from Scotch College, my old school, and Ian Steele. Well, they were made very welcome and soon everyone was very merry indeed. Among our resident doctors was a female who was very straight-laced, did not drink alcohol and who thought the celebrations sordid. As the night passed into morning, Ian, now very much the worse for wear, decided that he just had to lie down, so he stumbled and fumbled his way upstairs to the bedrooms, opened the door of the first room he came across and, without switching on the light, fell flat onto the bed quite oblivious to the fact that there was another person lying on it trying to sleep. Shortly after, the apparition of a dishevelled woman in a woollen dressing gown appeared in the lounge doorway, stood surveying the scene and then said in a loud voice, "One of your drunken Australian friends has just thrown himself on top of me as I was trying to sleep." after which, she turned and went back upstairs. The rest of us burst into laughter, but I quickly collected Ross, took him up to the unwanted body and manhandled Ian into a spare room where we dumped him unceremoniously onto an empty bed before returning to the party, which continued well into the dawn.

At the Nurses' Christmas Party, I met another two young ladies who provided me with more than a passing interest. One was a resident doctor who approached me fairly early in the course of the party and invited me to her room. How could I resist such an invitation from a colleague? Nevertheless, it was not one of my more memorable escapades, and it was not long before I was back at the party as she had to go back on duty. Much later in the evening and after finishing duty, a petite, blonde nurse appeared and we soon sensed a mutual attraction. She had spent a part of her life in Southern Rhodesia, (now Zimbabwe), and intended to return there after training. She was very enthusiastic in her social activities and it was not too long before we were up in her room. Our liaison continued for a month or two after my spell at Stobhill had ended. I can still recall making long trips on the bus from Hillhead to Stobhill to visit her in the evenings when she was off-duty and we were not going out. Before leaving the hospital, she gave me a Swiss Army knife—maybe she should not have as there is an old saying that a gift of a knife cuts the friendship.

It was with some regret that I left Stobhill. I had learned quite a bit of medicine and had also enjoyed a very hectic and simple social life. On leaving, my nickname was "The Sex Symbol of Stobhill", a considerable exaggeration I would say.

From Stobhill, I returned to the Western Infirmary on 1 Jan 1961 to complete my residency in Casualty, with an occasional stint on the Orthopaedics wards during holidays. As well as being close to home, I also had a room in the doctors' residence, which was on the ground floor, off a main hall of the hospital. The residence consisted of a long corridor, off which were about six or seven rooms on each side, leading to the ablution and toilet block at the end. My room was third one down from the entrance on the right and it was well placed for me to hear the entrance door opening and shutting; it was a basic room nevertheless.

My co-residents were Joe Barretto, a Goan with a great sense of fun and mischief, married to a Scottish girl, Gordon Forrest, a bit more serious and a former Boat Club member, and Sandy Martin, tall, pale and serious who kept very much to himself. Gordon and Sandy belonged to the previous year's intake but had graduated with me. Our Senior House Officer was Alasdair Cochrane, a thick-set, red-head, whose passions were Janie, (a medical secretary), the bagpipes which he played and whisky, more or less in that order. There was little interference from the Registrars and the Consultants kept a loose but watchful eye over all our activities. Jimmy Robertson, the plasterer, and Sister McKnight were still there from my student locum days, as were the trainee radiographers, junior nurses and a new staff nurse.

Casualty was a busy department and time passed very quickly. It was the clearing station for most of the orthopaedic and accident emergencies and it was not too long before we became proficient in fracture diagnosis and treatment, plaster of paris application, suturing and the cajoling of drunks. My previous undergraduate, locum experience proved to be a great help to me. We were a happy team and we worked in with each other. On occasion, when the SHO in the Orthopaedics ward was off on holiday, I would move upstairs to the wards and take care of the inpatients.

The new staff nurse was an engaging personality: petite, blonde, sharp in mind and tongue but very efficient and amusing most of the time. Close association at work almost inevitably brings close social contact and it was not long before she and I were fairly constant companions. She had a little flat not far from the Infirmary and we spent quite a lot of time together there. I always found her fascinating but she too was a consummate tease. Finally, she became very possessive and we gradually drifted apart. Perhaps because she was a staff nurse, she tended to avoid all the doctor parties; she had obviously seen it all before.

About the middle of my spell in Casualty, a hockey match was arranged between the doctors and the nursing staff, to be played one afternoon on the playing fields of Kelvinside Academy at Balshagray. This proved to be a very fateful occasion for me. I was in the team and finished up on the right wing. I noticed that one of the opposition was a fairly tall, attractive brunette, dressed in a grey skirt and brown V-necked sweater. Apart from tackling her once or twice during the course of the game, I had no further contact with her that afternoon, but I had noticed her and deep down a spark was kindled.

A week or two later, at a party given by an Indian doctor at a flat near Charing Cross, I noticed that this hockey-playing brunette was also present, but again, I paid no undue attention to her. As the party progressed, it became a bit wild—I learned later that the host had been "spiking" the already alcoholic punch—and somehow I finished up in the middle of a "drinks" fight between this nurse and another man. Quite unexpectedly, a glassful of alcohol engulfed my face. I arose, dried my face with my handkerchief, grabbed this nurse by the arm and dragged her off to the bathroom where I doused her under the cold water tap. In this state of dampness, I kissed her full on the lips and immediately asked her if I could walk her back to her quarters at the Western. I think now, probably to both our surprise, she was amazed that she said yes. And so this was how I became involved with Marguerite (Margot) Stewart who, about two and a half years later became my wife and best friend. On the walk home, I asked her if she would like to go out with me the following week but she said that she would think about it as she had heard about my reputation from her friends. Just to be on the safe side, I gave her my home telephone number. Later, when she had told her friends that she was considering going out with me, the standard retort was, "You're not going out with Him, are you?" However, the next week, I 'phoned Margot to ask her out. I could sense by her hesitation that she would refuse, so I immediately said I will meet you outside the Hillhead cinema 7PM on Friday. Later, Margot told me that she had had every intention of not going out with me before I had 'phoned but I had not given her a chance to refuse. And so our life-long love affair started very patchily at first. Just to give lie to the stories concerning my reputation, I did not attempt to kiss her for the first six weeks we went out together. This was contrary to all she had heard about me. But so much was to happen before our marriage on 5 Nov 1963, Guy Fawkes Day.

Not long after Margot and I started our relationship, I introduced her to my Mum and Dad. Dad thought that she was a lovely girl and told me that I was very lucky to have met her. Sadly, shortly after this, he suffered a mild heart attack and was a advised to rest, so he took to his bed about lunch time until late afternoon, but he was asked to be kept under supervision. Margot at this time was on night duty and so I asked her if she would mind coming home to look after Dad when she came off duty; she agreed to this. So, when she came off duty, she came home about lunchtime and crawled into the double bed along with Dad, who then began to regale her with true stories of his life; unfortunately, after a relatively short time, she fell asleep but she still managed to hear more of Dad's life than he ever told me. He was very, very fond of Margot and she of him

The Casualty Department was quite social and Tommy Gardner, a Consultant, took an interest in the staff. One evening in June, he arranged a bus trip to Loch Lomond for a picnic. My friend, the blonde staff nurse finished up sitting beside me all the way to the loch and beside me during the picnic itself. This annoyed Margot a great deal but I sensed this late in the picnic stage, so I sneaked off to join Margot. The two of us went for a quick dip in the chilly loch. However, some of our colleagues saw us and ran off with our clothes which they hid in nearby bushes. Chilled, we spent about twenty minutes looking for them. Eventually, we all piled back into the bus for the trip back to the Western. It had been a beautiful outing in all respects. At this stage, Margot and I were not serious but had started going out with each other.

There were also parties held in the Residence at the Western, in the lounge area. These were not as wild and as noisy as those I had attended at Stobhill. Apart from occasionally seeing Margot, I was also juggling my social life to accommodate two trainee nurses at the same time. Before I had actually met Margot, one of her friends, a trainee nurse was frequently on night duty and I always knew her nights on call. The system was that the nurse would come down to the doctor's door and knock on it to waken him and call him to the ward. On her nights, I would listen for her distinctive walk and allow her to waken the doctor on call, and then wait for her to pass my door, at which time I reached out and pulled her, unprotesting, into my room where we spent a very pleasant ten minutes or so before she would return to the ward, quite dishevelled and with her hair awry. Margot would say to her, "I see you have been with Saint-Yves again", to which she would just shrug her shoulders and smile.

While I was in residence, the junior doctors continually complained about the quality of the food being supplied to them. So I led a mini-strike and complained to the Hospital Superintendent, Dr. MacQueen, about it. However, not all of the doctors agreed, one saying to me, "It's just about as good as my mother makes." I made a face and said, "Really!" However, my efforts did lead to an improvement. Coincidentally, and quite unknown to me, Margot was also leading a nursing protest about the food at the same time.

Looking back at that first year, it is quite amazing to recall that our total salary was £420 per annum, for unlimited hours on duty and that, after deductions for taxation, national insurance and accommodation, we actually received the princely sum of £20 per month. Changed days!

And so a very important part of my life drew to a close. I had finished my compulsory year in hospital and, most important of all, I had met my future wife but had not yet realised it.

Chapter Ten

The In-Between Years, 1961-1963

My residential year in hospitals ended on 31 Jul 1961 but in those days I had been seduced by the so-called glamour of surgery and had decided on following a surgical career. Consequently, I had arranged to do a surgical locum in the unit of Mr. J. Longland at the Glasgow Royal Infirmary, near Glasgow Cathedral. Mr. Longland was a relatively famous personality as he had been a surgeon in some war-time situation and had been mentioned in a book which I believe was called the "White Rabbit".

His unit was a busy one and although I was now a Senior House Officer, the position did not lessen my work load. I was called upon to do quite a lot of assisting in theatre and, I have to admit now, it strengthened my resolve to do surgery. We had a vascular surgeon called Mr. Watt who asked me to assist him in by-pass surgery of the lower limb. The exact technical details are not important now but it involved by-passing the diseased artery with a teflon graft. With the graft in place, and the blood transfusion running freely, Mr. Watt released all the necessary clamps. Well, I have never seen so much blood appear so quickly—within seconds, the abdominal cavity was full to overflowing even though the suction apparatus was running at full capacity, the blood volume being maintained by pumped blood transfusions. However, all was not lost and very gradually the level of blood fell, slowly parts of the intestines, instruments and surgical packs began to surface like islands in a receding flood. It was very disturbing. Gradually, everything was brought under control. The operation was considered to be a success and the patient did well.

The worst part of the duty was when the unit was on call for the hospital. A week-day night was not too bad as most of the patients were genuinely requiring prompt surgical attention. However, when the unit covered the week-end, it was a whole new ball game. In this situation, I spent almost my whole day, from 9am to 2am the next morning in the Receiving area of the Infirmary. This was situated on the ground floor, was very old fashioned and totally inadequate but readily accessible to patients walking in off the street. In those days there was a small ward attached to the Receiving area which was used to retain patients for a maximum period of 24 hours observation; it was a very valuable and busy ward. The Casualty/Receiving area was reputed to be the busiest such unit in Britain and I quite believe it. It was Go, Go, Go. However, if I thought that the day-time shift was busy, the evening proved to be sheer hell, especially if there had been a big football match in the afternoon, the most notorious being the Rangers/ Celtic derby. On such occasions, the hordes poured in, mostly drunk, most having been involved in fights and most very abusive. Although I treated them to the best of my ability, I had little or no sympathy for them and, whenever possible, I sutured up their lacerations without local anaesthesia and used the largest needle consistent with the size of the wound. It was in such situations, where every alternate patient sported a head injury, that the small observation ward proved its worth. Although each unit stopped receiving patients at midnight, the work for the unit staff continued until about 2am, as all patients seen up until midnight had to be fully processed and treated by the receiving unit. On these early mornings, as I did not have a car and lived a few miles away, the hospital provided me with a taxi. However, we were expected to be back on the wards by 9am for the routine ward rounds. Fortunately, at mid-day, we were allowed off for the rest of the day. It was a very tiring and demanding schedule.

Nevertheless, it did not interfere totally with my social life although it did slow it down slightly. At this time, I was becoming more involved with Margot but was also still dating other young ladies. There was one blonde and very beautiful, staff nurse in Casualty at the Royal in whom I was very interested. I was still coaching at the Boat Club and had a key to the place. After an evening out with her, we would go back to the deserted Boat Club, where I would turn on the gas fire, which also provided the only light, and then we would settle down comfortably on a dilapidated old couch. In my efforts to entertain her and Margot at the same time, I ran into problems, so I started to tell Margot I was busy or away out with the lads. Well, the whole thing came to a head one evening at a dance I was attending with Margot out at the Rob Roy Motel near Aberfoyle. A senior Registrar from the Royal was also present and, as the whisky flowed, he became more garrulous and it wasn't too long before he began telling Margot about this lovely blonde whom I was seeing. Needless to say, Margot was most upset and so I decided to give up my blonde, a good and fateful decision.

Margot and I, now going "steady", spent almost all of our spare time together. However, I did take a break with my two friends, Jack from the Boat Club and Eric. We had decided on a holiday in Rimini on the Italian Adriatic coast. Flying from Gatwick on a charter flight, we landed at some country airport only to discover that we had to take a long bus journey of several hours to reach Rimini. Once we reached there however, we found that we had been booked into a nice modern hotel with friendly staff. During the days, we spent most of our time on the beach and, in the evenings, eating and drinking in the various night-spots. We did, however, spend a few days in Rome, travelling there, across the spine of Italy, by bus. In Rome, we visited all the usual tourist attractions but I most clearly remember all the lovely pastry shops in which I tended to over indulge myself. We chatted up the two tourist guides, one of whom was a Swedish blonde, but without much joy. On another trip, we travelled to San Marino. I found this a fascinating enclave, and one in which we appreciated the sweet, chilled wine to a considerable extent. It was a good holiday and also the last time that we would all be together.

While at the Royal, I continued to stay with Mum and Dad at home. They were, at this time, going through a very difficult stage financially. Dad had had difficulty in obtaining a job on his return from abroad, but eventually obtained one as a draughtsman with Babcock-Wilcox in Renfrew. This meant that he had to make two long and tiring journeys by public transport every working day and this soon took its toll. Mum had a job as a book-keeper with Brechin Brothers, butchers, in Renfield Street, which she quite enjoyed. It was not surprising that Dad gave up his job, but what was surprising was his decision to buy a small grocery store in Elderpark Street, Govan, opposite the Elder Park. It was a tiny little shop in a very depressed area. His customers were largely unemployed and Dad, too humane and generous, was not business man enough to refuse credit, with the result that he had a continual battle to meet the deadlines of his creditors. Over and above this, the hours were very long, leaving home at 9am in time to travel across Glasgow on the subway and open the shop by 10am. He kept the shop open until 10.30 pm, catching the last subway back, not reaching home until about 11.15pm. This happened six days a week, only Sunday being a rest day going in late and leaving early for home. On reaching home, he straightened up the day's accounts before falling into bed after midnight, exhausted and worried.

Fortunately, Mum kept her job at Brechins. She would rush home from work, have a quick meal before joining Dad in the shop. Whenever possible, I would also go to the shop in the evenings to give them moral support. As can be imagined, the shop was not profitable. To feed us, Mum and Dad only took as much food from the shop as we needed. It was a soul-destroying time which lasted for about a year and a half. I am convinced that this continual worry was responsible for the exacerbation of Dad's angina, which he first developed in East Pakistan (Bangla Desh). In any event, inevitably, Dad suffered a heart attack, not too severe, which was successfully treated at home. Margot, on her off-duty, came to our flat during the day to look after him and provide company while we were at work. They became very close friends, Dad regaling her with stories of his younger days in the Merchant Marine sailing around the world. After recovery and the sale of the shop, Dad, much against his will, signed on at the Unemployment Bureau. He came to accept this philosophically and used to say that he now belonged to the best "club" in Britain. However, he was still not happy with this state of life and felt that he had let his family down. We were not worried so long as he remained well.

After my locum at the Royal Infirmary, I arranged a locum post with a group General Practice on Glasgow Road, Paisley, opposite Paisley Grammar School. This Practice was then headed by a Dr. Hay and also included Drs. Bannatyne, MacLaren, MacGregor and Gibson, the latter being very kind to me in my trials. The Medical secretary and general factotum was a lady called Lena, who lived above the surgery with her elderly mother. I enjoyed my two spells with the practice but I did not feel that general practice was my vocation.

I had always wanted to work overseas; I suppose that you could say it was in my blood as I came from an old French, colonial family. So, I decided that I should gain wide training and experience to fit me for this task. Along with Joe Barretto and Madan "Budgie" Sharma, the three of us, all Glasgow graduates, enrolled at the Liverpool School of Tropical Medicine and Hygiene. Accommodation was a problem but I was very fortunate to be offered a room in the home of Joe and Pilar Brady and their two children, Peter and Katherine. Joe was the School's medical photographer. Their home was a true "home from home" for me and I was immediately accepted by them as one of the family. I was doubly fortunate for Joe always drove me to the School every morning.

In those days of 1962, Professor Brian Maegraith, an Australian, was in charge of the School; he was a clinician. Professor Tom Wilson, an Ulsterman, was on the Public Health side. In addition, we received lectures from Dr. Leithhead, a Scot, Dr. Kershaw and Dr. William MacDonald, another Scot, who taught us Entomology. They were ably assisted by an excellent laboratory staff headed by Mr. Dagnall. The lectures on Malaria given by Professor Maegraith, both clinical and preventive, awakened my interest in this major health problem which has remained with me ever since. The practical application of anti-malarial methods which I was to employ later formed the complete basis for almost all other preventive medicine which I have since undertaken in my professional life. Malaria is a great, and perhaps the best, teacher.

My spare time at the week-ends was usually spent with Joe and Budgie. On these occasions, we either headed north for Glasgow and our separate ways, flat out in Joe's VW Beetle, or for north Wales. I loved north Wales, which I rated close to Scotland in my interest largely because of the magnificent castles scattered along the coast. My own preference was for Conwy Castle. It was also lovely to hear Welsh spoken on the streets.

By this time, I was serious about Margot as she was about me and, on my visits home, I spent most of my time with her. One Saturday, I flew from Speke airport to Glasgow to attend the Western Infirmary Annual Ball, for which Margot was the organiser. It was a thoroughly enjoyable Ball and Margot was congratulated by the Hospital Matron, Mamie Miller, who presented her with a very large bouquet. I have a lovely photo of Margot holding the bouquet and leaning unsteadily against me. Apart from week-ends, my time during the weeks was taken up with studying as it was a short, intensive course lasting only about fourteen weeks. However, we did manage the occasional swim after classes. Fortunately, we all passed the examinations and received our DTM & H certificates.

On my return to Glasgow, I started a locum in the Pathology Department of the Western Infirmary. The same senior staff were still in place. I was mainly involved in slide and sample preparation and in simple microscopic diagnosis, although I occasionally assisted with post-mortem examinations.

Again, I stayed at home during this period and spent a lot of my time with Margot as she was now a staff nurse at the Western. During these years the local pub for most of the junior doctors and nurses was the "Rubaiyat", on the corner of University Avenue and Byres Road, right opposite the back entrance to the Infirmary. It was a long, narrow pub with the gantry at the entrance and the lounge taking up the rest of the establishment. This oasis was presided over by a very genial barman called Tom. Almost without fail after work at 5pm, we would meet and have a drink before going home. In the evenings, before going to our various social engagements, we would meet there again but at these times the pub would be packed with customers and very noisy, and yet there always seemed to be a seat available. Other pubs such as the Curlers and the Chancellor, on Byres Road, were also frequented but the Rubaiyat was home. In addition to the pubs, towards the middle of University Avenue, there was a small night club called the "Papingo" which kept going for quite a few years but it was not really one of our haunts.

About mid 1962, Margot's nursing year held their Final Year Dance at the Rob Roy Motel, near Aberfoyle in the Trossachs. All told, there were about 15 couples present, all of us being transported in both directions in a hired bus, which was just as well as the occasion turned out to be an uproarious and memorable one.

On 1 Aug 1962, I started work as a Senior House Officer in the Urology unit under Willie Mack, a very kind, helpful and humorous Academical. This post required me to live in the Western as I was theoretically on call for 24 hours a day, so back I moved. During this time, I became an expert at inserting various types of urinary catheters and was frequently called upon to do so by residents in the other units. It was a happy unit. The Consultants included Hamish Sutherland, a very outgoing personality, Mr. Scott, a more sedate, portly man, ably assisted by the Registrar, Murdo Turner, a tall, quiet-spoken Highlander with a subtle wit. As in all good units, the Sister in charge was indispensable—her name was Jean Dickson. With a flat nearby, Margot and I were quite regularly invited to her parties.

As my time in Urology drew to a close, I wrote my first medical article, for the British Journal of Urology entitled, "Problems associated with the diagnosis of solitary kidney: congenital or acquired?" It was published in 1964. Mr. Mack knew that I intended to work overseas and, on my departure, gave me a large textbook on operative surgery as a farewell present. I enjoyed my time in this unit very much indeed.

On a very foggy night in 1962, the 25 Nov 1992 to be precise, while walking Margot back to the Western from my home, I asked her to marry me—it took place half-way down George Street. She never actually accepted my proposal but I assume that she must have internalised it as we were married almost exactly a year later on 5 Nov 1963, a date I chose so that I would never forget our Anniversary. However, when we reached the entrance to the nurses' home at the conservatory inside the Western, we met another class mate, Eric Anderson, to whom we told our story. Margot, on the spur of the moment, invited us up to her room. Tip-toeing and scurrying like mice, the three of us hurried up to Margot's room on the first floor undetected. Here we sat and talked, but too loudly obviously, as we soon heard authoritative footsteps marching along the corridor towards the room. Margot quickly hid Eric in her wardrobe, I squeezed in between the wash-hand sink and the end of her bed, while Margot quickly jumped into bed and under the blankets fully clothed. Almost immediately, her door was opened, the light was put on and a hospital orderly poked his head around the door and, apparently not seeing anyone else, asked her, "Have you any men in here?" Margot, peering out from under the blankets, said no. That apparently satisfied the orderly who reported so to the Duty Night Sister standing behind him as the door was closed and they were heard to walk away. Eric and I then decided to make an escape but the only way to remain undetected was by window which was a not inconsiderable height above ground level as we were on the first floor. However, we did escape by window; I landed unhurt but Eric sprained his ankle on landing and hirpled away as fast as he could. Many months later, the same orderly told Margot that he actually saw my reflection in the mirror on the outside of her wardrobe. A very exciting admission!

An amusing little incident is attached to our engagement. Alastair Cochran put us in touch with a good jeweller in Glasgow from whom we bought Margot's engagement ring. Naturally, we had it inscribed with the date on which I had proposed to her, 25th. November 1962; at least, that was what we thought. A few years later, we accidentally discovered that it had been wrongly dated 25th. December 1962.

On another foggy night, we again were late in arriving back at the hospital from home. It was after 11 pm and the entrance to the Nurses' Home was now locked. So, we looked around and discovered a long wooden ladder lying against a wall; this we carried to the wing of Margot's building and laid it against the edge of her window sill. Fortunately, Margot always kept her window ajar and, very carefully while I held the ladder securely, she climbed up the ladder and into her room through the window. After a wave, I quietly and quickly removed and replaced the ladder before escaping in the fog.

Mum and Dad were very pleased with the news of our engagement, which also pleased Margot's Dad, Jack, but her Mother, Rita, said, "You're not going to marry that chap, are you?" We didn't actually get on famously, but she mellowed towards me after a while. This antipathy was due to the fact that Margot's previous fiancé, David, always brought her flowers when calling on Margot whereas I never brought her anything.

A day or two later, I told Margot that I would be working overseas, and again, she accepted this without demurring but in later years she would occasionally say that she wished that she had believed that I meant what

I had said because we remained wanderers for just over 22 years before returning to our beloved Scotland.

On 1 Feb 63, I moved from Urology to Obstetrics at Robroyston Hospital, on the eastern outskirts of Glasgow, to the unit of Dr. Bill Armstrong, another Academical. This was a relaxed unit, with John Bonner (later to become Professor at Dublin University) and Jean Strachan as the two Registrars, while Sister MacKay was in charge of the Labour/Delivery unit. My co-resident was an Aberdeen graduate called Iain Mathewson—a tall, gangling, bespectacled, long-haired and very amusing man. He soon became a very firm friend of Margot and me. However, he had two passions in life, Scotch whisky and playing the bagpipes, the former being indulged in off-duty, while the latter was always banished to the boiler-room regardless of the time. The residents always had to live in and, as can be expected, we had an occasional wild party here. Iain, dressed in a duffel coat and sandles in all weather, would visit Margot at Ruchill Hospital where she was a Theatre sister. On these occasions, the junior nurse would say to Margot that there was a "Hippy" asking to see her. It was hard to imagine that he had recently divorced an Inverness Beauty Queen. At the hospital parties he was the star attraction, especially after a few drams, because he became an india-rubber man, double-jointed in the extreme, and a most amusing spectacle when dancing. After our residency, we kept in touch for a while, then I heard that he had remarried and was in Brunei but eventually I managed to recontact him and his wife again in 1996, in Mackay, Queensland where he was a GP. At this time, I also sat my D. Obst. RCOG which I passed.

An amusing incident involving Margot occurred soon after she went to Ruchill Hospital as a Theatre Sister, and when she was relatively unknown. She had entered a competition in the Scottish Daily Express in which the prize was to be a white, mink hat. Well, she won it and when the paper 'phoned the hospital to find out if there was a Margot Stewart there, they were put in touch with an older sister called Maggie Stewart who, of course, knew nothing about it. As a result, the hat was given to the runner-up and the only remembrance we now have of this incident is a photo from the paper of the runner-up wearing the mink hat and one of Margot attending the children in the ward, which the newspaper photographer took for her as a consolation prize.

I had also started to look for jobs overseas by now. One job was in the Caribbean but I rejected this as the conditions were not very satisfactory. Another job offer came from Fiji, at this stage still a British Colony. Along with pamphlets on the conditions, I received a not inconsiderable sized book on vice-regal etiquette, how to dress for and behave in the presence of the Governor. Without further ado, I threw the idea of working in Fiji out of my thoughts and the written blurb into the waste paper basket. Sometime later in 1962, I had also applied for a Medical Officer post with the Australian Administration in the Territory of Papua New Guinea, but nothing happened and I believed that my application had gone astray.

With two-thirds of 1963 past, and having arranged for our wedding to take place on 5 Nov 63, I found that I had no work. Fortunately, I managed to arrange two spells of locum work with an excellent group of general practitioners with whom I had worked before, the Glasgow Road Practice in Paisley. As I was also to be on night-duty and do house calls, I was provided with a car. When on call, I slept on a bed in the premises. It was a very entertaining short period.

Our wedding day loomed large, so some arrangements had to be made. We decided we would only invite our parents and about 16 of our closest friends. This decision greatly annoyed all our relatives and we suffered, I suppose, because we received relatively few wedding presents—still, it was more than worth it. The Minister attached to the Western Infirmary, Mr. David Smith, of the Old Partick Parish Church was asked to officiate. Our wedding banns were also read out at Margot's home church in Saltcoats. However, Margot and I had not forgotten all our work and club mates, and so we held a really great engagement party for all of them in Margot's shared flat in Hillhead. I asked my best friend, Brian Neville, to be my best-man, while Margot asked her youngest sister, Jacqueline, to be her bridesmaid. Very sensibly, Margot decided not to have a wedding dress made and instead, on a trip to London, arranged for a lovely hired dress to be delivered to her in Glasgow, the whole transaction, I believe, only costing her £5.

As 1963 progressed, we made more definite plans for our approaching wedding on Guy Fawkes' Day. The wedding was to be consecrated at the Old Partick Parish Church and the reception held at the Grosvenor

Restaurant in Gordon Street (the restaurant was burned down years later). I also arranged for a triumphal arch of oars to be formed by members of GUBC. Apart from the snide comments of some of our relatives who were not being invited, everything went smoothly.

Two nights before the wedding, I had a "stag" night with some of my friends, mainly from the Boat Club. It was a relatively quiet affair. The big day arrived. Margot had arranged to meet her parents in town, then to go with her Mother to have her hair done, but her plans went awry and she finished up having to go alone. I had more luck with my arrangements and Brian and I experienced no difficulties.

Including our parents, there were only about twenty people at the wedding and they hardly made any impression in the Church Hall. With the service under way, Margot arrived at the entrance on the arm of her father (I learned later that it was the other way around as he had had a rather fluid lunch). Margot looked very happy and, I thought, beautiful in her simple, elegant gown. The wedding vows went without a hitch. Brian handed over the wedding ring, a very plain and simple one, (later lost in Taif, Saudi Arabia, on 5 Apr 90, my birthday, but found a month later in the carpet sweeper), which was securely placed on her finger, next to her solitaire diamond ring., which had cost me £100 at wholesale prices. That price does not seem much now but was quite considerable in 1963. (In 1990, the ring was valued at over £2000). Margot later told me that she was trying to keep her father under control as they walked down the aisle, but he kept repeating, "You would think that you were going to a bloody funeral." It was a nice, simple Church of Scotland service and when we came out of the church and were being greeted by the small crowd, we saw Aunt Mary standing there awaiting our departure. Seeing her there was our only little bit of remorse on that lovely day. Outside, we had our official photographs taken with our parents before moving into waiting cars which took us to the Grosvenor in Gordon Street. Once there, Margot and I, together with our parents, greeted our few guests as they arrived. It was now about 5.30 pm and soon we were seated at the tables for the Wedding Supper, which was wittily and advisedly interspersed by speeches and the reading of telegrammes. Everything went without a hitch. After the meal, we posed in front of our wedding cake prior to cutting it and had more photographs taken, including family groups. Once the cake had been cut, distributed and eaten, the tables were cleared away and the dancing began to a small, live band. Margot's Dad, because of the small numbers involved, had not limited the alcohol during the course of the evening and this was a big factor in making our wedding party such a great success. The dancing and merriment continued until after 11 pm and, before the last guests left, Margot and I caught a taxi to the North British Hotel, in George Square, where we spent the first night of our new life together. It was a very good and humorous night for both of us.

On 6 Nov 63, we arose early from our wedding bed, packed, washed and dressed in time to catch the train to London. Margot was the proud possessor of a new leather wallet, christened with a £50 note which her Father had given her as an extra present—but she was not to have it long. The trip to London was uneventful.

Unfortunately, the flight to Paris was an eventful one for, on entering the terminal building, Margot discovered that she had lost her new wallet on the 'plane, so she arranged to go back on board but there was no sign of the wallet; the cleaners had already been and gone. A small cloud to a silver lining. Soon, however, we were headed for our hotel, a small, private one called the Balmoral, just behind the Arc de Triomphe. It was a nice, cosy hotel and we had a fine room. By the early evening, we were quite hungry, so we went out to dinner and, in one of the al fresco cafes, we had very tasty coq au vin. After a walk, we returned to the Balmoral but it was not too long before Margot started to have painful diarrhoea, which kept both of us busy all night—she had obviously caught staphylococcal food poisoning. With a steady intake of water, the episode had almost finished by breakfast time. Fortunately, we were in Paris for another day, so we were in no hurry. Eventually, about 11am, we once again wandered out into the streets. To our surprise, while aimlessly wandering around the city centre, we met Gordon and Margaret Forrest; they had been married in Glasgow a fortnight before. Gordon had been in the Boat Club with me and was also a classmate while Margaret was a senior radiographer in the Western Infirmary. Compared to us, they were really well off and had had an "expensive" honeymoon. Although they had enjoyed themselves, they said that their fortnight had only been so-so. Margot and I continued on our walkabout just idling the time away very pleasantly.

The next day we caught the 'plane to Brest, in Brittany. If I remember correctly, it was a passenger version DC3. Unfortunately, it was not a very smooth flight and, for the first and only time in my life, I was air-sick. It was, however, a short flight. We stayed in the main hotel in Brest but we were unable to have our meals there as we were on a very strict budget. It was off-season and we appeared to have the hotel to ourselves. The staff treated us very well, especially when they learned of our surname and that the family originated in Landerneau. We were so short of cash that we shared our daily bath, for which we were charged extra, Margot going first with me following on. For all that, we enjoyed Brest with its old chateau overlooking the harbour, half full with modern warships. The weather was dull and grey with little rain and we dressed accordingly in old slacks and chunky jumpers. We usually left the hotel about 9am each morning and either caught the train or local bus to one of the surrounding areas. We, of course, paid a special visit to Landerneau, where the river flowed under houses built on a bridge. In the graveyard we saw one or two headstones inscribed "Saint-Yves". A quick visit to the parish church and a chat to the local priest gained us a search of the village records of births and deaths for the years before the French Revolution, and we were rewarded by finding records concerning the Camus/Saint-Yves wedding back in about 1720. We felt quite elated. On the other days, we visited small villages such as Brignogan and Plougastel, together with the occasional town such as Morlaix. The women in these small villages still wore their traditional Breton dresses and the villagers spoke the Breton language. One day, while strolling through Brest, we were stopped by an elderly American who asked us for directions in halting French. Margot and I were quite amused as he had obviously mistaken us for locals. Fortunately, we were able to help him in English; he was amazed that we spoke such fluent English. It turned out that he had been in charge of the American Army column which had liberated Brest from the Germans in the Second World War; in fact, he had been the first American to re-enter the city.

In Brest, we also discovered that the "original" Saint-Yves had been the patron saint of lawyers; there was now a local carving industry in which people carved small, wooden statues of the saint. We also found a Rue Saint-Yves.

For our lunches, we usually had a bistro meal, nearly always onion soup and local bread, or if travelling, cheese and bread washed down with a bottle of vin ordinaire. I remember one amusing evening meal in Brest. We were in a small bistro not far from the hotel, both of us eating omelettes. At the end of the meal I discovered that I did not have any money on me so, while Margot had a third or fourth cup of coffee, I rushed back to the hotel to pick up some money to pay for the bill. In the evenings, we always tried to have a good, solid meal, usually in a bistro, enjoying omelettes or the local seafood, which were delicious. However, we did have one special meal in our hotel before leaving and this was also of seafood; it was terrific. We were usually exhausted by the end of the day but it did not make us forget our conjugal duties which we thoroughly enjoyed on our honeymoon. The honeymoon swiftly drew to a close but I am convinced it was the sound basis upon which our marriage has been based as it showed us that we were also each others best friend.

We were soon back again in Glasgow. It was just after our return from our honeymoon that we heard of President Kennedy's assassination while we were watching TV with Mum and Dad at their flat in Cranworth Street. It numbed us all considerably. Shortly after our return, I received word from the Australian government stating that they were willing to offer me a job in Papua New Guinea, then a UN Trust Territory administered by Australia; this was well over one year after I had applied and I had actually forgotten about it. When I told my referees that I had been accepted, they admitted to me that the Australians only appeared to be interested in my political affiliations which they had checked carefully—not too difficult one would have thought as in those days I did not have any. Now, it was all to be in a rush. We were to travel out on the P & O liner "Canberra" tourist class, which I refused to do, saying that if they wanted us we would travel first class, which we did. We sailed from Tilbury in early January 1964.

Towards the end of 1963, my Aunt Marion, the wife of my Mum's oldest brother Dod, had become terminally ill. They lived in a villa, "Ruka", in the older part of Dunblane. In her well days, Margot and I occasionally visited her when all the family gathered; she was a great baker and did her guests right royally. However, when she became ill Uncle Dod was unable to cope while John and Sheila, their son and daughter-in-law, were working in London and would not return, so there was a problem as to who would look after Aunt Marion. After discussing it with Margot, we offered to look after her before our departure for the Territory of Papua New Guinea. We enjoyed our short stay there and Aunt was very grateful; however, we could not believe Uncle Dod's parsimony when he accused us of "eating" the coal for the fires although they were needed in a large, old-fashioned house. Further we were there voluntarily. Uncle Dod was never one of my favourite Uncles.

The time came for us to leave Scotland. Mum and Dad came to see us off on the overnight sleeper to London. The farewells passed without too much emotionalism and soon the train was speeding south, with Margot and I having great fun on the narrow, train bunks. Next morning, (was it from Victoria?), we caught the special boat train to Tilbury. It was all very exciting. We were even more delighted to find Aunt Mary and Uncle John, now living in Eastbourne, waiting to meet us there and see us off on the ship. There was an added bonus; the Queen Elizabeth was also tied up near the Canberra.

Our cabin was not large but was well appointed. Our cabin steward, after giving him a small token of our appreciation in advance of services, looked after us very well for the duration of the trip. Again, we almost had no money. Both of us had cashed in our government superannuation when we got married in order to pay for our honeymoon. However, the Australian government had started paying me from the day we set sail, so I was earning although I did not receive any money until reaching our initial destination, Sydney, where I was supposed to attend a course at the Australian School of Pacific Administration, ASOPA, in the sea-side suburb of Mosman. As a result of our impecunious state, we only had £5 to last us the whole voyage, we had to be very careful in our socialising. Fortunately, we became very friendly with an elderly Scottish farming couple from Harwich, the Strachans, who hailed originally from Aberdeenshire. They were on a cruise to Australia and sat at our dinner table. They invited us to all the social occasions and we had to refuse most of them initially until I explained to them that we were almost broke. Edwin Strachan said to us that we must not let that worry us and that we were to join them at any time whenever we wished; however, he asked us to promise them that when we were "comfortable" and met young people in the same straits as we were then, we would do the same for them. Margot and I have always done so since then. He also impressed upon us that we should never prostitute our professions. This reinforced what my Dad had told me many times, and again, I have always tried to follow this advice.

There were very few young people on board in the first class section, but the time passed very pleasantly with swimming during the day (the open air pool water was a constant 84F, 29C), overeating, deck games with dancing and horse racing in the evenings. I reached the heaviest weight I have ever attained in my whole life, 11 stones 4 pounds, (72 Kg), almost a stone over my usual weight and I felt truly uncomfortable. For the first time I came across, or maybe recognised, the strongly competitive nature of the Australians and their attitude to sportsmanship. It was in the deck tennis competition and somehow or other I reached the finals, overweight and all, in which I was matched against an Australian Army captain. Well, the long and the short of it all was that I beat him fairly, but he created quite a fuss over his defeat. On most evenings, dances were held. During one of these, somewhere about mid-Mediterranean, we ran into a very severe electrical storm; it was very frightening but stimulating at the same time although the dance had to be abandoned.

Our passage took us to Naples where we spent a long day. During this, we managed to arrange a trip to Pompeii, where we visited the ruins of the old Roman city destroyed by the eruption of Mt. Vesuvius. It was fascinating. Their life style, for the rich at least, included central heating in their houses and pornographic murals, not really any different from to-day really. We were also struck by the squalor of the Naples slums. Somehow or other, I recall that we also paid a flying visit to Spoleto. However, passing by Capri and through the Straits of Messina was memorable.

The passage through the Suez Canal was next. I believe that we were one of the last passenger ships to pass through before it was blocked by the British in the Suez War. Of course, we briefly went ashore at Port Said to do some shopping, but returning on board, we were more amused by the antics of the vendors on the "bum boats" alongside the ship; most of them appeared to have adopted Scottish names like Jimmy MacGregor. We stopped at Aden where we saw very many camels and met up with our old friend Eric Anderson and his wife Maureen. He was now a doctor at the RAF base there. We spent most of the day with them lying on the beach at the Officers' Club.

Our next port of call was Colombo. The Canberra anchored off-shore and we were taken ashore by ferry. Landing on the quay, we were met by a troupe of traditionally dressed, Kandy Dancers, who performed for about ten minutes on our behalf. Most of us then boarded a bus which took us through the hills, passing working elephants and crossing the river on which the film, "The Bridge on the River Kwai" starring Alec Guinness, was filmed, and so on to Kandy. This was a beautifully sited town, situated on the edge of a lake. Of course, a visit to the Temple of the Tooth, crossing a moat in which fish and turtles swam about, was mandatory and interesting, but the experience was lessened by the number of beggars although they heightened our awareness of the poverty in developing countries. Margot and I had a lovely curry lunch in the large hotel overlooking the lake. Ceylon, now Sri Lanka, was an entrancing country and one in which we first saw orchids in their profusion in the beautiful Botanical Gardens.

Our idyllic life at sea continued. We practised boat-drill in the Indian Ocean, just out of Colombo. Another excitement was to pass the islands of Minikoy, bathed in brilliant sunshine, lying low in a blue sea on our port bow at about 10.30am one memorable morning. I loved it all and took a few photos but my camera was relatively useless at that range as it did not have a telephoto lens and consequently the pictures were indistinct.

About two or three days out of Fremantle, the final social event of the voyage, a Fancy Dress Ball, was held. Many of the passengers went to inordinate lengths with their costumes. I did not enter but Margot did. I made her a "Crow's Nest" hat from a deck quoit, wrapped with some green and brown paper, to which I attached a child's rubber duck and some hard-boiled eggs. Margot won first prize, perhaps unfairly as the most popular bar on the boat was also called the "Crow's Nest". We have a happy photo of Margot receiving her prize from the Captain.

And so on to Fremantle in Western Australia. The Canberra sailed through Gage Roads, where I used to fish off the "Islander" ten to twelve years previously, and up the Swan River to the terminal. This too had not changed appreciably and still had the sign "Welcome to Western Australia" up on it. On going ashore, I was to find that Fremantle had not changed either. However, there was a lovely surprise waiting for us on the wharf. My friends from Scotch College days, with their wives, husbands and children were there to greet us as were Kath and Jim James, my parents' friends, with their son John. The welcoming party included Ross and Val Fimister (he had visited me at Stobhill one Hogmanay and had married an English girl), John Cary and his New Zealand wife Maureen (he had also visited me in Glasgow), Jenny Raison (my last girl-friend in Australia) and her husband John Walton. It was great to see them all and it was the first time that Margot had met most of them. She was delighted with our reception and their obvious friendliness. After the greetings, we went with the James family—they drove us past our old home in North Street, Swanbourne—to their lovely home in Applecross, where they had prepared a luncheon for all of us. It was a great day which passed all too rapidly and once again we were back on board by about 4.30pm. Our friends returned to wave us off on our way to Melbourne and Sydney. It had been a wonderful day for both of us but especially for Margot, on her first real visit abroad.

The journey to Port Melbourne was uneventful and the sail across the Bight had been duck-pond smooth. We arrived mid-morning and were soon on our way into Melbourne itself. We travelled by train but were appalled by the railway carriages in which we travelled; they were little better than cattle trucks and must have been about 30 to 40 years old. Melbourne seemed like any other large city and we mooned around filling in the time. We did, however, visit Captain Cook's cottage which had been transported to Australia and now occupied a nice site in Fitzroy Gardens.

The Canberra made light work of the sail to Sydney, which we reached about 6.30 am on the beautiful sunlit morning of 20 Jan 1964. Entering the harbour through Sydney Heads was one of the most memorable sights that Margot and I have ever seen—it was stunningly awe inspiring. By mid-morning, we had cleared Customs on board and were ready to disembark and collect our luggage on Circular Quay. We were met on board by an official from the Department of Territories who guided us through all the formalities. I expected to be told that I had to attend the three months course at ASOPA but instead we were told that we would be flying to the Territory of Papua New Guinea (TPNG) that night, our sparse luggage accompanying us. In the meantime we had booked into the Metropole Hotel in the heart of the city; although old-fashioned, it was friendly, comfortable and we liked it. In fact, we made it our base whenever we visited Sydney in those early years and before it closed down. Once again, we strolled about another city centre killing time. We decided that we liked Sydney even although we couldn't do too much as we had almost no money, with less than the original princely sum of £5 between us. Fortunately, before leaving for TPNG, we received some of the money owed me. Time passed quickly and soon we were on our way to the Sir Charles Kingsford Smith Airport at Mascot, passing en route a tannery from which emanated a most obnoxious smell, to catch the late flight in a Lockheed Electra to Port Moresby, via Brisbane. The flight to Brisbane was short but we were very disappointed with the terminal which, at that time, was little better than a shed; it would be many years before it would be modernised. And so on to Port Moresby.

Chapter Eleven

The Territory of Papua New Guinea (I)

LAE, MOROBE DISTRICT 1964-1965

Approaching Port Moresby, the capital of the Territory, we flew into dense, beautiful cloud which engulfed our Lockheed Electra in a blanket of cotton wool and, from that inspiring introduction, Margot and I decided illogically that we liked TPNG, and so it proved to be. It was the 21st. Jan 1964.

We were met at the dilapidated airport by a Health Department official who cleared us through Customs and the arrival formalities before whisking us off to the Boroko Hotel. Here we stayed for about a week while I was introduced to all aspects of the workings of the Public Health Department (PHD). In those days, the Boroko was an adequate hotel but still retained a colonial mentality. For example, at mealtimes, the diners were served by bare-chested, white gloved, bare-footed local men dressed in red fringed, white, skirt type, ankle-length lap-laps.

PHD Headquarters were housed in a series of low slung buildings, probably left over from the war, and were a very pitiful sight. Konedobu itself was very close to the Papuan village of Hanuabada, which stretched out over the bay on wooden stilts; while this was very picturesque from a distance, it was very dirty and smelly from close at hand.

The Director of Public Health was a tall, stern man called Roy Frederic Rhodes Scragg, a medical graduate from the University of Adelaide, who was a devout member of the Seventh Day Adventists. I also met most of the other Assistant Directors including two who were to become our very good friends—David Bowler, an Englishman in charge of Maternal and Child Health, and Vivi Bignold, an Australian who was the Director of Nursing. I understand that her brother had been Chief Justice of TPNG in the not too distant past. Most important of all, however, was the fact that I at last received my pay, so we did not feel too unhappy.

Port Moresby, we decided, had to be a second rate copy of a third rate, Australian country town, although it was attractively situated on a bay. Eventually, we were told that we were being sent to Lae, the capital of the Morobe District of New Guinea, a nice picturesque town situated on the sea. What was surprising was the fact that I was to be the Specialist Obstetrician. I said nothing to the appointment although I accepted it with trepidation as I had only very recently acquired my Diploma in Obstetrics and Gynaecology, a relatively minor qualification, and had never carried out a solo forceps delivery nor carried out a solo Caesarean Section.

And so to Lae. From the air, Lae looked lovely and once again Margot and I were captivated. The single air strip almost ran into the blue sea; at the end of the strip, there was an old war-time, bombed Japanese ship which had been beached. It was the Kota Maru and its stern just showed above the water-line. The airport terminal was once again a single storey building. On alighting, we were met by the Mainland Regional Director, Dr. John Jameson and his wife, Lesley. We had heard many stories about John in Port Moresby, but during the short period we were in contact with him in Lae, and before he became an Assistant Director of Public Health, Margot and I experienced nothing but absolute professionalism from him in his job and unstinting generosity and hospitality from him and his wife socially.

We were taken to our new house, raised on short concrete piles, with all slatted, glass windows, situated in a moderate sized garden and only about 75 metres across the main road from the airport grounds, although the airstrip was a fair distance away but still too close. Our house was one of about four which were situated on the edge of the hospital compound below a small hill, upon which was situated the township, only a few minutes walk away from our house.

The house was of asbestos but roomy and airy; Margot was pleased with it although she was worried about the noise from the 'planes coming and going on the airstrip but fortunately they were few and soon we became accustomed to the noise during the day. Luckily, there was a late flying restriction so our sleep was never disturbed. Our resident domestic family—New Guineans from Garaina—lived in a "boi-haus", a single room shed with outside cooking, but with toilet and shower facilities, sited at the bottom of our garden. The husband was called Morris Sau and he worked as a "dokta-boi" (orderly) at the hospital. His wife was Labalai, a strikingly good looking woman in her late twenties. Their family, initially, was completed with Tawai, their very pretty daughter of about seven years of age. Labalai did the general housework and washing, which was done outside by hand, using a copper boiler, while Morris generally kept the garden tidy. In addition, when we gave dinner parties, they were expected to wait and clear up after us before going to bed. We did not ask them to do the routine, daily dishwashing although that was supposed to be part of Labalai's chores. For their efforts, we paid them £A5 per month, which we thought scandalously little but were informed that that was a good wage for them. Needless to say, Margot and I, not being of the colonial mentality, did not expect too much, nor did we overwork them and, whenever possible, tried to ease things for them. They never abused our trust in return although their idea of "hurry" was not the same as ours, but we soon accepted this. We enjoyed having them and felt very secure in their company at all times.

John Jameson took me across to the hospital almost immediately. It was a new hospital of single storeyed buildings connected by open verandahs, with a capacity of about 250 beds. It had not yet been officially opened. About six weeks after our arrival in Lae, Margot and I attended the official opening which was made by the Minister of Territories, Sir Paul Hasluck, and at which he named it the ANGAU Memorial Hospital in honour of the Australian New Guinea Administrative Unit which had been operational during the war.

I was quickly introduced to the senior medical staff. The Hospital Superintendent was Jim MacKay, friendly enough but as I was to find out soon, ineffectual as an administrator. In fact, after about six months of being there, I was appointed the Hospital Administrator. Alan Shepherd was the surgeon, very good and patient. He, his wife Jill and two daughters were very good to Margot and me during our stay in Lae. The physician was John Duke—again, very good and unassuming although it was with him that I had my first quarrel at Angau concerning professional etiquette over patient care. Neville Henry, a young doctor of about my own age, was the paediatrician. Anaesthetics were a major problem and we all did some, especially Neville, although I tried to avoid them. The minor procedures, such as setting simple fractures and incising abscesses, were usually done under an anaesthetic gauze mask by the head dokta-boi of the outpatients department in a small operating room at the end of a long verandah. TPNG was also the happy hunting ground for Australian medical researchers. Two of their number were David Butterfield and Don Pryor who spent many months in and around Lae researching Iodine deficiency and the Tropical Splenomegaly Syndrome respectively. There were also, it was rumoured, some quite blatant abuses of individual rights by highly respected members of the Australian medical fraternity during these research projects. Once again, the old colonial mentality of "Do as I say and don't do as I do" was to the fore. Angau hospital was very fortunate with its senior nursing staff who were nearly all Australians and who were ably assisted by TPNG trained nurses.

I was appointed to Lae as the specialist Obstetrician/Gynaecologist on the strength of possessing a D.Obst.RCOG. This was not too surprising as the senior Obstetrician/Gynaecologist for TPNG at that particular time also only had a D.Obst. although he went on to obtain his MRCOG. On my initial visit to the hospital, I met the Obstetrics sister with whom I was to work. She was an overweight, cheerful and efficient Australian called Sheila Sim, who had been born on a plantation on Choiseul Island in the British Solomon Islands Protectorate. She introduced me to the Obstetrics staff members, all local nursing aides in their late teens and early twenties, who had been trained at Angau and who, as I very soon discovered, had been very well trained by Sheila. The Obstetrics Unit contained about 15 beds, all for the local community as expatriate patients were attended to by the local General Practitioner in the main part of the hospital. During my stay in Lae, there were about 460 deliveries in the Unit.

Naturally, I met the local GP, Bryan Todd, almost immediately. He took my breath away on our first meeting by asking me to see a pregnant expatriate who, he thought, had a Placenta praevia. So, off I went to examine the patient and, sure enough, it was one. The only solution was to carry out a Caesarean section; so, within a few hours of our arrival in Lae, I was in the operating theatre carrying out my first ever solo Caesarean section, assisted by Bryan. Fortunately, there were no complications and mother and baby did well. Eventually, I carried out about 60 sections and 40 deliveries by forceps, nearly always using the Kiellands. This was quite a high rate of interference but can be accounted for by the fact that we were admitting a considerable number of women with major obstetric problems, most of whom had never attended ante-natal clinics

Once I had to carry out a decapitation on a dead, impacted breech baby, the mother having been in labour for two to three days in a remote village before being brought into hospital. On another occasion, one very late evening, a small Kukuku woman from Menyamya, an area in the mountains behind Lae, was brought in with profound toxaemia and shock following the rupture of her uterus some days before. After dosing her massively with antibiotics and placing her on a continuous intravenous infusion, Jim MacKay decided to give her a very light nitrous oxide/oxygen anaesthetic as she was already comatose, while I carried out an emergency hysterectomy, again my first and only one. The patient was fortunate and made an excellent and rapid recovery.

The Kukuku tribes had been, until very recently, greatly feared by the coastal tribes as they had been headhunters and frequently swept down on the coastal villages to gather their "trophies". They are a small, stocky people seemingly able to put up with extreme physical pain and discomfort. I recall one woman walking for about five days to reach the Aid Post at Menyamya, after she had been hit over the head with an axe, from where she was flown to hospital in Lae. Examination of her head wound revealed that the skull had been split open with brain tissue, now riddled with fly maggots, extruding. On cleaning the wound, we were surprised how relatively little real infection was actually present;

apparently, the maggots had kept the wound "clean". Again, after surgery, she made an excellent recovery.

However, my favourite story concerns a young, pregnant Menyamya girl of about 14 years of age. She had never been out of her mountain village, did not speak any language other than her own and was, quite naturally, terrified to be in hospital. Nevertheless, with a lot of patience, the Obstetrics staff allayed her fears and she went calmly for her caesarean section. Mother and baby did well, but when it came time for her to be discharged, she refused to go immediately as she was learning Pidgin English, the lingua franca of TPNG. At her next pregnancy, we brought her in a few weeks early. She took charge of all the other Kukuku women throughout the hospital and acted as their interpreter.

I must admit that I was non-plussed when I saw my first Kukuku woman. They are all under five feet tall. This particular woman was standing over a hospital trolley cradling her baby, which was wrapped loosely in a bark tapa cloth, while she wore nothing except a "bil-arse" (a very, very short grass, fore and aft, scarcely covering her genitalia) and a long bark cloak. I also saw the most perfect human tattooing on a Papuan woman of about thirty years of age who was in hospital for her confinement. She was exquisitely tattooed from her hair-line to her toes. Tattooing was made illegal and quite rightly so when you consider the discomfort she must have endured while young and yet it was magnificent. As an Obstetrician, I never failed to be amazed by the manner in which the local women appeared to be able to relax, in most cases, while between labour pains. However, this natural ability was not enough for a newly qualified, blonde and beautiful Australian physiotherapist who breezed into Angau and blithely said that the women needed to be taught how to relax. After many heated exchanges, I finally managed to convince her that she really had little to offer them in the art of relaxation, much to the relief of all the Obstetrics staff.

I was not only involved with Obstetrics but also with Outpatients, the occasional anaesthetic and finally, the post of Hospital Superintendent. However, before finally leaving Obstetrics, there are two other amusing stories to tell. The first concerned Margot and Labalai, our house servant, who was pregnant and due to deliver at any time. One morning, Margot was urgently called to their home at the bottom of the garden. Labalai had gone into labour in her shower and had become wedged behind the door; she had been readying herself prior to hospital admission. Margot had tried to 'phone me at the hospital without success and so, without any obstetric experience, Margot squeezed into the shower and successfully helped Labalai to deliver a healthy son, later to be called Matoi. When I arrived home, I was told the whole, proud story. Everyone was well.

The other tale involved me as a consultant to an English nurse who had been referred to me from Honiara, British Solomon Islands Protectorate. She had been married for about five years and, to-date, the couple had had no family. I asked her if she and her husband had had any investigations for infertility, to which she replied that they had both been investigated in Britain and had been told that all was well. I told her that there was very little that I could do for her in Lae and, apart from advising her to try not to become too tense about it, to let things take their course. I then asked her what advice she had been given by the doctors in Honiara. With a perfectly straight face, she said that they had been advised to have sexual intercourse three times a day for ten days. After a few seconds, I could not stop myself from grinning, which she noticed and then we both burst into laughter. I never learned of the final outcome but I hoped that it was successful.

The Outpatient Department was at the end of a long corridor at the front of the hospital. During the day, it was efficiently run by three middle-aged Australian Nursing Sisters, Enid Watkins, Norrie Cahill and Jaye Smyth, ably assisted by a small team of dokta-bois. Jim de la Cruz, my next door neighbour, a mixed race Pacific islander who had trained in Suva, was the doctor in charge, assisted by myself and others as the need arose. The Unit was kept very busy dealing mainly with patients suffering from malaria, gastro-enteritis and injuries. On an average day, well over 250 patients were seen and, on a really busy day, up to 400 patients attended. Minor operative procedures and simple fractures were dealt with in the small room at the end of the verandah. Abscesses and suturing were usually dealt with by the senior dokta-boi in charge but on occasions, doctors were called in. Simple fractures requiring manipulation were also dealt with here, the patient being anaesthetised under an ether/gauze mask by the senior dokta-boi while the doctor set the fractures. It was simple and effective and I do not recall any real problems using this method. It was a good team and a very happy place to work in. I learned a lot of practical medicine and a great deal about human nature. It was the hospital's most senior dokta-boi, Bulo—a veteran of the war, who taught me to recognise tetanus. It was an interesting and exciting period.

At this time, Margot accepted a job as the first ever School Nurse, attached to the Maternal and Child Health Service, from the new Regional Director of Health, Dr. Frank Tuza, a Hungarian. He had, like many other East Europeans after the war, been allowed to practise as a medical practitioner in TPNG, as a prelude to being allowed to gain the right to practise in Australia, after a few years. Margot loved the job as it entailed travelling by Land Rover, canoe and aeroplane all over the Morobe region visiting the pupils in the village schools, sometimes having to overnight in the village itself. Occasionally, she would be accompanied by an MCH nurse. Three events remain clearly in her mind. One happened at the coastal village of Salamaua, where she stayed overnight, sleeping in a grass hut. During the very early hours of the morning, she was awakened from a deep sleep by a noise which sounded like a grunting coming from inside the tent and which seemed to be approaching her as she lay petrified inside her sleeping bag. The noise became very loud and soon she saw that it was a village hog—it came right up to her, nuzzling Margot's sleeping bag before eventually moving off, leaving her lying there relieved and unharmed. On another visit to the same village, the villagers awoke in the morning to find the tell-tale tracks of a large crocodile crossing the centre of the village to the beach.

Margot's saddest experience, however, was with a teenage boy whom she recognised as having pulmonary tuberculosis and whom she had referred to John Duke, the Physician. It was fairly early TB and readily curable by drugs. However, someone in his family had convinced him that he was going to die and, despite Margot's pleadings and John's efforts, this teenager willed himself to death in front of their eyes over a few short months.

Another time, in the company of the MCH nurse, Jean Hunt, they were being piloted by Jim Crowley in a small Cessna aeroplane when they ran into fuel problems while returning from a distant flight. Crowley was a very laid-back character and, once in the air, he appeared to do nothing but read paperbacks; however, he was an exceedingly competent and experienced pilot, as were all the pilots in TPNG in those early days. He suddenly announced that they were in trouble and may not reach Lae unless the 'plane's load was lightened. At this pronouncement, Jean, who was religious, openly started saying her prayers, and it was left to Margot to open the door, haul the heavy metal patrol boxes to it and toss them over into the jungle below, before closing the door. Needless to say, they arrived safely.

I had one sad experience. Alan Shepherd asked me to give an anaesthetic to a small, male infant on whom he was going to attempt a cleft palate/hair-lip repair. Unfortunately, the baby died during the operation. I had never enjoyed anaesthetics and after this tragedy, I vowed that I would never give another anaesthetic and I haven't.

What did we do in our spare time? We made friends with the Shepherds, the Smyths, the Riggals and the Nomensens from the hospital, the Jamesons and, when they left, the Tuzas from the regional office, and also with two plantation families, the Osbornes and the Millers, who lived out along the Wau road, and through the Horticultural Society, with the Scullys.

Alan and Jill Shepherd and their two daughters lived in town, off the hospital compound. They were a nice, genuine and very Christian family. Margot and I found their inherent goodness a strain at times, but we enjoyed their company and had occasional picnics in the bush, and lunches at home with them. Towards the end of our time, Alan had a heart attack and was off work for a few weeks. I believe that he eventually finished up as Chief surgeon at Goroka.

We had one memorable day's outing with Clem and Judith Nomensen. He was a locum surgeon and their stay in Lae coincided with one of the highlights of the annual social calendar, the Gusap Races. Gusap was quite a way from Lae and so they led in their car while we followed. The roads were unsealed and, as it had just been raining, they were very muddy. As we neared Gusap, the road became pot-holed and difficult to traverse. Needless to say, both our cars became bogged down and, while Clem and I tried to extricate ourselves, the ladies, under large sunhats, stood at the edge of the road chatting away. I have a lovely photo of the two ladies watching Clem and I struggling with the cars. Not unexpectedly, by the time we reached Gusap, most of the events were over but that did not matter as we had had a grand day and we returned home without any further mishaps.

Jaye and Ray Smyth were very good to us and remained our very good friends during our stays in TPNG and later in Australia. It was through Ray, a senior gardener at the Botanical Gardens, that we became interested in and joined the Horticultural Society. They had two daughters, Julie and Christine. We spent many evenings together sitting on their verandah listening to classical music as the cicadas chirruped. Many years later, when we lived in Sydney, we were to attend Julie's wedding to an Englishman, Tony Hillman, at Toronto near Newcastle in New South Wales. Jaye Smyth, now a widow, Tony and Julie all managed to visit us in our retirement home on Arran during 1997.

For some reason, John Jameson and I struck up a friendship and, although Margot and his wife, Lesley, were friendly enough, the real friendship was between John and me. He would occasionally say to me, at the end of a working day, to come up in the evening after dinner. I would go up by myself, and the two of us would sit in his lounge drinking good Scotch whisky, while listening to loud classical music on his hi-fi stereo console. Leslie was nowhere to be seen on these occasions. Later in 1964, he was transferred to Port Moresby as an assistant Director. I missed his great company. Before leaving, he told us a very amusing event which happened to him while he was on official business in Manila. His host had taken him to a night club one evening. On entering, he noted large notices requesting patrons to leave their firearms at the door, but he did not think any more about it. During the evening he had to go to the toilet and, while he was standing relieving himself at the urinal, he heard a gun shot and saw a bullet hole appear not too far to his right in the urinal. Needless to say, he promptly finished his business and vacated the toilet as soon as possible. John's post in Lae was taken by Frank Tuza.

John and Andrée Miller were a plantation couple although Andrée also worked at the Botanical Gardens where she was involved with orchid cultivation. John was a quiet, unassuming and well respected man. She was full of energy and was always organising something or somebody. We spent many a happy hour at their home along the Wau road despite the presence of a tame, house kangaroo which had free rein. Not long after our arrival, we joined one of Andrée's excursions to Wagau, a village in the hills behind Lae. This trip was in honour of a group of horticulturists and herpetologists from the British Museum, which included Trevor, Mick and Clive; Clive later married Alma, one of the MCH nurses. We flew into Wagau only to find that Andrée had already established the tented camp. Margot went into our tent and let out a scream. I rushed in and saw a large millipede about six inches long crawling along the bed pole. I killed it as it was capable of giving you a very severe acid burn from its secretion. In between our jaunts into the bush looking for orchids, Margot and I taught the village children how to play hop-scotch. I wonder what the anthropologists would make of that in the years to come. Some evenings, Mike, who was the herpetologist, took a few adventurous souls into the nearby bush to look for tree frogs which were in abundance and which I found strangely attractive as they were coloured a lustrous green; he also recorded their croaks. The British Museum scientists were a good crowd and, on our return to Lae, Margot and I had one or two memorable dinners with them at our home.

Sue and Ossie Osborne also made us very welcome at their plantation. Ossie, a large, bluff Aussie, was the local President of the Returned Servicemen's League and thus an important person in the local social scene. Sue, slim and very attractive, worked as a secretary at the Botanical Gardens. It was here, in Ossie's company, that I once again took up 0.303 target rifle shooting and also introduced Margot to pistol shooting. The shooting was held on a Sunday afternoon on a range Ossie had built on the end of his plantation facing onto the Busu River. We would sometimes be invited out to lunch and then go shooting. We had bought our own armaments which we kept at home, although eventually we left them with Ossie who kept them under lock and key. It was all target shooting. Margot turned out to be a very good shot and was eventually the Ladies' Champion. Ossie died a few years later, after which Sue married an Englishman and went to live in the south of England. Through them, we met Ted Henty who was a botanist and whose family members were among the very early settlers in Victoria. We liked Ted a great deal.

One evening, not long after our arrival, we were invited around to Brian and Rhonda Todds' home. He was the local GP. It turned out to be quite a large affair and was enjoyable. However, what really stuck in our minds was the supper. When Rhonda announced that it was ready, we duly took our place in the queue to serve ourselves and, when our turns came, we helped ourselves to moderate portions. When we had finished our platefuls, we were asked if we would like some more and were invited to help ourselves. On returning to the serving table, we found that it was devoid of food; the guests had piled up their plates at the first visit. We learned from this and never again made the same mistake at an Australian buffet party.

We were also very friendly with John Womersley, the Director of the Lae Botanical Gardens, and his wife, Mary. Many a good evening we had at their home, but John had a disturbing habit of stretching out his long legs after a meal and, at about 9.30 pm, fall sound asleep on his chair, while the proceedings continued without him. One of the highlights of his Directorship was the visit of Sir George Taylor, the Director of Kew Gardens. Prior to his visit, a young English assistant at the Gardens had been telling everyone how close he had been to Sir George when he had worked at Kew. On Sir George's arrival at the reception in his honour, it turned out that he was a Scot from the Glasgow area and that he hardly knew David; however, he was delighted to meet Margot and I. Most of the evening, he talked to me about football and Glasgow Rangers in particular, the team which I supported as well.

There were quite a few "characters" in Lae, such as Ma Stewart, who owned the original hotel, Bondi Becker, a Hungarian TB specialist, and his wife Sue, who later became an Australian TV exercise personality, and the Serafinis, who owned the aerated water factory. As the name suggests, he was an Italian and it was very funny to hear his local staff speaking Pidgin English with an Italian accent. His wife, Kitty, was a tireless worker for the Red Cross and was the local President.

One of the first things that we had to do when we arrived in Lae was to buy a car as there was no public transport. We bought a blue, second-hand, VW "beetle" which served us well, first in Lae and then later in Wewak, where we eventually sold it. However, Margot was still unable to drive and so, every available afternoon after work, we would drive along the Wau road for about twenty miles to the wartime, disused airstrip, once the largest in the southern hemisphere, called Nadzab. The main strip was still free of overgrowth and it was here that I taught Margot her basic driving skills.

One amusing experience occurred soon after I had bought the VW. I was driving down the hill to the house and stopped as I was entering the main road. Very shortly after, there was a slight bump at the back. Leaving the car, I was met by a tall, Australian policeman coming towards me and, together, we surveyed the damage, which was almost non-existent. He never introduced himself. A few weeks later, we were introduced to him at a social gathering and I was asked if I had met the Chief Inspector of Police. I replied Yes, I had bumped into him.

There was a recently arrived Scottish Police Inspector who had just come across from Southern Rhodesia. His name was Colin Bell. I asked him if he would brush up Margot's driving skills in town prior to her driving test, which he agreed to do. Quite unexpectedly, after a driving lesson and after they had returned to our home, he presented Margot with her driving licence. Of course, this called for a celebration and the three of us became rather jolly. Suddenly Margot remembered that she had invited David, who stayed with us for a week or two, and his Australian girl-friend, Faye, the Deputy Hospital Matron, to dinner. Colin took his leave rather unsteadily, while Margot hastily threw a chicken into the oven and set about preparing the rest of the meal. Faye was a very difficult person and acted more English than the English; she always spoke with a very "pukka" accent. Well, we sat down to dinner and managed the first course without any trauma. Then Margot brought out the chicken which David said that he wanted to carve, so we let him. He took up the carving knife and tried to skewer the bird but failed as it shot from under the fork, off the plate, across the table and onto the floor. Margot and I fell about laughing but our guests were not amused and I am afraid that the evening was not considered to be one of our successes.

When we first arrived in Lae, we bought our fresh fruit and vegetables at the local market. This market consisted of round, kraal-type buildings on stilts, open to the weather at the sides, but roofed in a conical fashion with thatch. On the raised floor of this structure sat the vendor surrounded by the fruit and vegetables, each tied in small bundles, costing one shilling each (10 p) on average, although there was occasional bargaining involved for the larger fruits such as pawpaw and pineapple. It was here that we saw our first local policeman. In 1964, the police uniform consisted of a black, red-rimmed, V-necked "dress" which reached to just above the knees, and with a broad brown belt at the waist; on his head, the policeman wore a badge-bedecked, blue beret while on his feet he wore a pair of brown, open sandals. My own working uniform during my whole stay in the South-West Pacific consisted of well tailored shorts, short-sleeved shirt and tie, with knee length stockings and stout shoes. On patrol in the bush, I dispensed with the tie and wore a soft, broad-brimmed, canvas hat. Margot, while at work, usually wore a white or pale blue, one piece belted, dress uniform.

The first addition to our family in TPNG was a youngish, stocky, moderate sized, mongrel dog of a white and reddish-brown colouring. I cannot remember how we came to own him but I think that he adopted us; we called him "Rover" and he proved to be a very loyal companion, accompanying us to Wewak and then to Port Moresby. He was an exceedingly good and discerning watch dog and would only allow those whom he recognised into the back garden. I recall Margot and I being shattered from our reverie in the lounge one late evening by a sudden loud noise as something hurtled against the side of the house, which shook, followed by a loud commotion. Running outside, we found one of Labalai's "wantoks", unknown to us and to Rover, slowly picking himself off the ground and brushing himself down, while Rover stood to the side watching him suspiciously.

Undoubtedly, one of the thrills of living in and visiting TPNG was the chance to attend either the Mt. Hagen or Goroka Show; these were held on alternate years. There were other good shows, as for example in Lae, but these two reigned supreme. Ostensibly they were Agricultural Shows but the highlight was the gathering together of thousands of tribesmen and women, in full traditional dress, adorned with natural coloured clays and Birds-of-Paradise feathered head-dresses. The tribes people would walk for many days to reach the showground, where they were accommodated in long-houses made of native materials. Saturday was the main day but most came to stay for the whole week as it was "the" social occasion and perhaps their only chance to congregate and meet their friends for the whole year. The showground itself was in a perpetual dustcloud due to the continual movement of tribal dancers gyrating to the beats of the garamut, (a hollowed out log) and kundu (a small drum covered at each end with tightly stretched lizard skins). Occasionally, one would see small groups of clay-daubed, almost naked women sitting on the ground and, if you looked closely enough, you would notice a severed, withered hand hanging around the neck by a leather thong; these were the widows and the severed hands belonged to their deceased husbands. At one of the shows, I came across Margot, wearing a broad brimmed, straw hat, standing in the midst of an advancing circle of small, squat, almost naked men who were rhythmically brandishing spears at her. She was very glad to see me. Even then, non-traditional decorations were beginning to appear in their attire but one could still photograph the participants on request without being asked for money. These were really wonderful experiences as we had the privilege of seeing true stone-age people emerging into the twentieth century. On these occasions, four or five of us would hire a plane and pilot from Crowley for the day to take us there and back. The trips were worth every penny. We also attended one or two Lae Shows but these were not as thrilling as the coastal people and islanders were a more sophisticated group and their traditional attire and dances more refined. Still, it was interesting to note the differences.

Margot and I had always wanted children and had decided on two, a boy and girl if possible. So, sometime in early December 1964, Margot came off the contraceptive pill and we both then proceeded to forget about it. About eight weeks later, Margot started to become violently sick at anytime of the day, but it still did not occur to us that this could be due to her pregnancy. Finally, she went to see Brian Todd who, of course, told her that she was pregnant, much to our embarrassment and great happiness. Unfortunately, her Hyperemesis gravidarum was severe and she hardly gained any weight during her pregnancy and, in addition, became anaemic. Eventually, she was forced to give up her job prematurely and also stopped the cooking as the smells nauseated her, so I took over the cooking. Unfortunately, I was a bit unintentionally inconsiderate as one of my first efforts was to cook a leg of ham in stout, the smell of which made

Margot even more sick as it pervaded the house. Thereafter I stuck to fillet which was readily available in rolled pieces.

The first Angau Ball was held on 17 July 1965. Margot and I went with Sue and Ossie Osborne, Phil and Rosemary Scully and John and Mary Womersley. At our table, by absorption, we also had the local Minister for Health, Mr. Dirona Abe, and a visiting Fijian Indian called Abdul Latif. Margot, although about 24 weeks pregnant, was still slim and not showing her pregnancy unduly. She wore a straight, full-length, strapped, duck-shell blue evening dress and I thought she was by far the most strikingly beautiful woman at the Ball. As a result, Margot was frequently asked to dance by Dirona and Abdul; she later told me that Dirona had made indecent suggestions to her throughout the evening. We had a good laugh about it. It was a very enjoyable evening.

The most important and welcome event that happened in our lives while we were in Lae was the birth of our first child, a son, weighing 6.5 lbs. He was born in Angau Hospital on 17 October 1965, healthy and bonny. Prior to his birth, we had decide on two names: Ruairidh, if he were to be a red-head (I had been born a red-head and my Mother was also a red-head) and Euan, if otherwise. So, he was called Euan as he was born with brown hair. It was a name we loved as it sounded gentle and peaceful. His other names brought us into conflict with my Mother because we called him in addition Stewart (Margot's maiden name) and Marie (part of the Saint-Yves family tradition) but omitted Fleming, my Mother's maiden name. We were very, very happy and, after spending a day or two in a hospital, orchid-bedecked, side-room, I brought Margot and Euan home in our VW, with Euan lying lightly wrapped in a soft blanket on his mother's knee. He was a beautiful baby, but then I suppose that all parents think that their children are beautiful. On arriving home, Rover was there to greet us. I introduced Rover to Euan immediately; Rover was never jealous of Euan, nor indeed of Michèle, our second child. Labalai and her family were also delighted. Needless to say, I also filmed them with my 8mm ciné camera.

There were two tragic events which affected the hospital staff. The first concerned a young Yorkshire nurse, Margaret Leach, who was in charge of the Blood Transfusion Service of the Australian Red Cross based in the hospital. One day, while out collecting blood from donors in the villages, and accompanied by a hospital driver, she and the driver were killed outright when their Land Rover was involved in a head-on collision. This tragedy cast a deep gloom over all members of staff for many months.

The second event concerned Margot directly. One afternoon, she was visiting Norrie Cahill, the elderly nurse from the Outpatients Department, at her home. They were both walking around the garden chatting and looking at the shrubs and flowers. As Margot continued talking, with her back momentarily to Norrie, she realised that she was not receiving a response. On looking around, she saw Norrie lying dead on the ground. She had suffered a massive heart attack. Norrie had worked at the original hospital at Malahang on the banks of the Busu River and had moved across when Angau opened. She was widely respected and loved by all members of the staff.

As Lae was the Capital for the Mainland Region, which consisted of the Morobe, Madang and Sepik Districts, we had a fairly steady stream of Head Office staff visiting the hospital. We enjoyed having many of these visitors as guests. One of the first we met socially at a dinner was the Director of Public Health, Dr. Scragg, whom I had already met in Port Moresby, although Margot had not yet had the pleasure. He had an inhibiting effect on all gatherings which he attended, especially social ones, and this proved to be no exception; all present appeared to be scared of saying anything of any interest. His attempts at social chitchat on this occasion were mainly directed at Margot and me, trying to be funny by making fun of our Scottish accents. Needless to say, we were not amused and we kept him at a distance throughout his stay in TPNG up until his retirement, when Dr. Bill Symes took over; fortunately, Bill was a very different and likeable personality.

One memorable visit was made by David Bowler, Director of Maternal and Child Health, and Vivi Bignold, Director of Nursing Services. David was a jovial Englishman who had qualified in Medicine from the University of London (MBBS) and had then specialised in Paediatrics, going onto to gain his MRCP and an MD by examination. He was married to Sally, an English lady who had been a nurse; she always gave the impression of being tense and nervy, and in her company, one always felt uncomfortable. They had a son, who later followed in Father's footsteps and entered medicine, and two daughters. Sadly, David and Sally eventually separated and, I understand, she died not long afterwards. Vivi, a spinster, had been in the Territory for quite a long time and came from a well known family. After the day's business was over, they joined us for afternoon drinks and dinner. Well, after a very fluid diet and a great dinner, we have a very vivid memory of David and Vivi crawling about our lounge floor pretending to be dogs and cats. After Euan's birth, we asked Vivi to be Euan's godmother and Brian Neville, our best-man, to be his godfather.

When we first arrived, we could not get used to the manner in which the working class, white Australian tended to treat the local Papua New Guinean. To us, it appeared contemptuous and loathsome. Fortunately, all Australians did not behave in this manner. Apart from the religiously inclined, and there were a great many, the more professional and higher administrative types did treat the locals well and, at worst, appeared to tolerate them without any obvious animosity, although their treatment was always very paternalistic. One morning, Margot was awakened by a loud Australian voice cursing and swearing. This intrusion appeared to be coming from the front garden. Looking out of the window, she saw that there was a gang of locals working on the road under the supervision of a large Australian, wearing a wide-brimmed hat, dressed in shorts and singlet, with his belt holding up a large beer belly. After a few moments listening to the abuse, for which there was no apparent reason, Margot could stand it no longer and went out to the Australian and told him that she did not appreciate his language. He told her to mind her own business, politely. Margot reported him later that day.

Even among some of our acquaintances and friends whom we invited home, there were those who swore freely. However, at one of our first dinners, Margot interrupted a conversation by distinctly saying that there would be no swearing in her home. This became a bit of a standing joke because the occasional visitor would later say jokingly, in an imitation Scottish accent, "There'll be nae swearing in ma hoose.", although Margot and I did not actually speak like that. Nevertheless, Margot's admonition had the desired effect for we never heard swearing at our social gatherings thereafter.

In those early years, Margot and I were fairly regular church-goers although we were not religious. In Lae, we attended the Lutheran Church. This was a large building, with breeze block walls about four feet high all round, supporting six feet high pillars upon which the roof rested, the space between the tops of the walls and the roof being left open to the elements, in order to allow the breezes to circulate. One Sunday evening, with a packed congregation, church services were always almost overcrowded, the Pastor was giving a good old fashioned sermon talking about winds, thunder and lightning, when there were sudden flashes of lightning, loud rolls of thunder, strong winds and a sudden, gigantic cloudburst. The rain was blown in through one whole side of the church causing the congregation on that side to hastily migrate, with great hilarity, to the other side of the hall. Everyone was very impressed. When we reached home, the rain water was about a foot deep in our front garden, so I took my shoes and socks off, rolled up my trouser legs, and carried Margot from the car into the house, all the while trying to avoid the very many frogs which were now swimming around quite happily.

Occasionally, I was able to make an official visit to other administrative centres such as Mt. Hagen, Goroka and Madang. It was on such a trip that I first met Bert Speers, the administrative officer for the Region. He was a very famous and much respected man in TPNG. One of the original Angau staff at the end of the war, he had led many of the first medical, foot patrols into the mountain villages. He became a good friend to me initially and later to Margot too. He had brought up a Menyamya boy called Maori Kiki who, when he was able, adopted the name Albert in token of his appreciation. Later, he became one of the first local Members of Parliament, and had a book written about him called "A thousand years in a lifetime"; he was later knighted. We are fortunate to have a signed copy of this book. Sadly, Albert predeceased Bert by a number of years, which caused the latter great sorrow.

Six months after my arrival, Jim MacKay, the Hospital Superintendent, stood down from this post as he was about to be transferred, so the new Regional Director, Frank Tuza, asked me to take over, which I did. This now meant that I was wearing two hats, the first as Obstetrician/Gynaecologist and the second as Superintendent; fortunately, the new duties were not too onerous and I was quite able to combine the tasks.

As an Obstetrician, I had a considerable number of surgical procedures to perform and, in addition, assisted the surgeon if required. Subsequently, I developed a severe degree of skin sensitisation, which caused blistering and weeping of the skin mainly affecting my arms, hands and face, and also causing me to become extremely irritable. Eventually, I was forced to try wearing fine cotton gloves under the surgical rubber gloves, but this was only partially successful. I put the cause of the sensitisation down to the use of Lysol for disinfection and cleaning. However, in the end I was forced to give up theatre work and was seriously thinking of returning to Scotland but fortunately, the condition was kept in abeyance. I now know that it was the use of surgical rubber gloves which was to blame and not Lysol; consequently, I then wore non—allergenic gloves for the procedures I was required to do.

It was while I was intimately involved with Obstetrics that I became interested in Family Planning and the problem of uncontrolled population growth. At this time, the main contraceptive manufacturer active in TPNG was Schering, and their representative was a small, rather forceful Queenslander called Bob Chester-Master. When I first met him I was not too impressed but as time passed he became a friend to Margot and me, and indeed, on our occasional visits to Brisbane, we were welcomed by Bob and his wife, Margaret. On one memorable occasion, we had the best seafood dinner we have ever eaten as their guests at a Brisbane restaurant. Fortunately, we were able to repay their hospitality on one or two occasions when he came to visit us in Scotland in later years.

Through our work contact, I started introducing oral contraceptives to the local women but I found that I was experiencing some difficulty in making the local nurses and the local women understand the English version of the instructions. I suggested to Bob that I have the instructions translated into Pidgin English and Police Motu, and this I did, so that on his next visit to Lae I was able to present him with the two translations. I am pleased to say that they were the forerunner of all the following formats.

Menyamya was the small administrative post in the hills above Lae, set in the heart of the Kukuku country. Apart from a hazardous airstrip, it also had a small "hospital" which served as a gathering station for patients being referred to Angau Hospital. Regular flights were made there but I had not yet managed one, so when I was asked to pick up a patient from there, I jumped at the chance. The flight was a short one and the landing uneventful. On leaving the small 'plane, we were welcomed by a few small, squat, muscular men with close cropped, almost bald, hair styles, dressed in just-above-knee length grass aprons, fore and aft, with bones through their nostrils, and standing legs apart, arms folded and smiling broadly at us in welcome. It was hard for me to imagine that these people had had the reputation of being the most feared head-hunters in all of the Territory until very recently. I could not resist this welcome and asked them if I could take their photos, to which they readily agreed. I hardly travelled anywhere in TPNG without my camera as I felt that I was very privileged to be seeing this stone-age culture before it became "civilised".

Flying in TPNG was an invigorating experience. We were very well served by excellent pilots in well maintained light aircraft, mainly Cessnas and Pipers, but it was a hazardous pastime. many of the airstrips were literally hacked out from the jungle, many were on small, hillside plateaux and one or two were approached across rivers. Not infrequently, after landing on these strips, it was necessary for the villagers to manhandle the 'plane around to the right direction for take-off as there was insufficient room. There was never any lack of willing helpers as the pilot acted as postman, gossip and taximan for all of the people in these isolated communities. Ambunti was an airstrip that fascinated me as it was approached from across the wide Sepik River, which was navigable for three hundred miles; the strip appeared to run straight into a hill. Flying from place to place, especially in hilly areas, was very exciting as the pilots flew at tree-top level and always hugged the sides of the mountains; consequently, we always had an unrivalled view of the country below and alongside us as we flew. It was a dangerous place to fly and there were quite a few fatalities. In those days the Territory must have been about the most air-minded country in the world as flying was, apart from walking and canoeing, about the only way of making contact with very remote areas on a regular basis.

About a month after Euan's birth, Frank Tuza, the Regional Director, decided to transfer me to the Sepik District as the District Medical Officer (DMO), based in Wewak. As it turned out, I would be the last DMO to be in charge of the whole Sepik from Wewak in the east to Vanimo, bordering the West Irian border, in the west. The Sepik covered an area of 30 000 square miles, an area about the size of Scotland, and had an indigenous population of 250 000 people, with a few hundred expatriates. We were very excited about the move. It was also a fateful move for me because it changed my whole career and my approach to the concept of Health and Health Care Delivery.

Margot and I had enjoyed Lae very much. It had occupied a very important period in our young lives. We look back on it with very fond memories as we made many good friends and had great fun; above all, our son, Euan, was born there.

Chapter Twelve

The Territory of Papua New Guinea (II)

THE SEPIK DISTRICT : 1965-1966

And so it was that on the 17 Nov 1965, Margot, Euan and I flew out of Lae for Wewak, the capital of the Sepik District which straddled the northern coast of TPNG, as far as the West Irian border in the west. It had a large land area of approximately 30 000 square miles, an area greater than Scotland, with a population of 250 000 people. Rover and the VW followed us later, Rover by air freight and the VW by sea.

As we approached Wewak, we could see that the area consisted of three small peninsulas along a narrow coastal strip backed by a range of low hills. The sea was beautifully blue and calm. The northern promontory was called Cape Wam and it was here that the Australian Army Command had accepted the surrender of the Japanese Forces at the end of the New Guinea campaign. The middle peninsula was the residential and administrative area of the township, with the small commercial centre lying at the neck. The southern peninsula was the home of the 2nd. Battalion Pacific Islands Regiment based at Moem Barracks. The distance between the first and last promontory was a little over four miles.

We were met at the airport by Dr. Bob Barnes, the retiring District Medical Officer, DMO, who was returning to Australia to take up a post in Industrial Health. He drove us to the DMO's house, which he had already vacated, on the hospital compound situated on a small headland, almost entirely surrounded by the sea. The house was of a similar type to the one we had just left in Lae but the site was far superior. Leaving Margot to settle in and feed Euan, we proceeded to the DMO's office. Here I was introduced to Mrs. Zen Baines, a small, middle aged widow who quite obviously was the dynamo in the office, and so it proved to be. Inspecting the Hospital, I also met Vi Quirke, a rotund, cheerful Matron and an immediate neighbour, and Barry McGarry, the Hospital Secretary, who lived in town. I was also introduced to three doctors, one an Australian, the other a German both physicians, and the third a Hungarian surgeon, Dr. Roth, who was a close friend of Frank Tuza.

Margot loved the house and its surroundings. She arranged to employ a Papuan from Samarai called "Lomi", who came highly recommended; he was indeed an excellent servant but he had his faults. In the meantime, Barry ensured that all our household entitlements were in order and arranged for Margot to do some essential shopping in town.

My first afternoon was spent in the office being briefed by Bob Barnes as he was due to fly out the next day. Zen Baines sat in on most of our discussions and it was quite obvious that she knew everything that was going on in the district. She had been in the Sepik for many years, was widely respected and unofficially known as "Mrs. DMO". I decided there and then that I would not interfere unnecessarily in the administration of the department. Although she was almost universally called Zen, I always addressed her formally as Mrs. Baines.

Our bedroom, although classified as a double, only permitted two single beds placed closely side by side and, as a result, we were unable to bring Euan's cot into the room beside us. However, we made the adjoining room Euan's. His cot was no ordinary one, but a large meat safe, a rectangular open structure covered with mosquito netting on all sides, placed on legs, each leg on casters. To stop him from breaking through the netting, there were two strong horizontal wooden struts placed on each side. It did, however, look like a cage, and when he became active and started to rock backwards and forwards on his hands and knees, it would roll across the floor, banging against the walls; nevertheless, it was cool and mosquito-proof. From this episode, Euan obtained his childhood nickname of "Tiger". We always left his room and our bedroom doors open and, before he went off to sleep for the night, Margot or I would gently rock the safe while singing him to sleep. I nearly always attended to Euan during the night and, on the slightest whimper, I would rush into his room.

All administration housing was screened with mosquito-proof netting as most areas of TPNG were highly malarious and also bestowed with a wide range of flying insects, including beetles of all types, but this protection was ineffective against some of the other pests prevalent in the country. The first night in our new home was different. On the left hand side of my bed, I had managed to squeeze in a small chair and, as I tended to lie uncovered on my right side, on top of a sheet, with my right hand thrust out, my hand and fingers hung over the chair. Some time in the night, I felt something light and cold running over my ankles, but the sensation was not enough to rouse me fully so I shook my leg and threw the thing off. A short while later, I felt a gentle nibbling of my right hand fingers so, unmoving and very quietly, I asked Margot to put on the bed light. There, sitting on the chair unconcernedly nibbling away was a small rat. Jumping out of bed frightened the rat and it quickly escaped unharmed. I was to learn the next day that the whole area was bothered by rats and that this episode was probably the result of our house having been left unoccupied for a few weeks. I asked Ernie, the District Health inspector, to try to deal with the problem, which he did. Rats were a major problem throughout the Sepik and Ernie was not infrequently called upon to deal with local plagues in the villages. The villagers blamed the increase in rats on the death of all their cats which they attributed to DDT poisoning, probably correctly, resulting from the malaria eradication spraying programme, which was then in full swing and with which I would become gradually involved.

Margot was now a full time housewife and mother. The house was ideally suited to rearing a baby. Margot and Euan spent many hours together in the garden at the back of the house, facing the sea, which illogically was actually the front entrance. Euan was nearly always bathed outside on a round, concrete garden table, set into the back lawn, or else on the ground in the front garden, in his yellow, plastic bath tub. Margot and I loved this time and the playing that went with it, as did Euan, and

Rover who was never far away. Especially memorable was the period when he was learning to sit up unaided in the tub. Euan would, of course, slide downwards into the water and, when lifted out, he would be gurgling with delight and full of smiles.

After work, when we were not doing anything in particular, we would spread a rug out on the grass in the front garden, place Euan upon it and allow him to move around, always stark naked, while Margot and I played darts and enjoyed our afternoon drinks. He was a very happy, contented and lovable child. Euan had been born with a large umbilical hernia, about the size of the old British penny, which initially caused us some concern; however, we decided that inactivity was the best policy and gradually the hernia receded.

At the week-ends, especially on Saturday afternoons, we would pack our swimming gear into a bag, place Euan's "bouncy" on the back seat of the car, allow Rover into the back, place Euan safely on Margot's knees in the front, and set off to Moem beach, with me driving. We had our favourite spot under a large tree, under which we spread out the beach towels and set Euan up securely on his bouncy facing the warm, calm, blue sea. Rover foraged about the sand dunes and scrub but never travelled far away and, every so often, would wade out into the sea and have a little paddle and swim. We had decided that we would introduce Euan to the sea as soon as possible and so, at about eight weeks of age, he had his first dip in the sea, and he loved it, even when I just held him above the surface with my right hand under his belly and gently let him float with the wave motion; immersion did not bother him at all. We loved these quiet, peaceful periods on our own.

We were in the earthquake and hurricane zone, and although we did not experience any major tremor while we were there, we did experience a moderately severe hurricane. It hit us early one evening, with the winds rising and the sea whipping up over our garden. Fortunately, I was at home and, as conditions continued to deteriorate, I decided that the safest place to be for all of us was under our beds, so I collected Euan from his room, and when Margot was safely settled, I handed Euan to her before I crawled under my own bed. I do not know how long it lasted. Next morning, we were very surprised to see that the very large tree in Vi Quirke's garden had been uprooted and had smashed down across the corner of her house; fortunately, she was uninjured.

I found my work varied and interesting as it contained an increasing amount of administration and some hospital obstetrics. The Sepik District covered a vast area and it was necesssary for me to make contact with the Health Department staff at each outstation as soon as possible. Apart from the occasional expatriate Mission doctor, mainly Catholic, the only doctors were to be found at Wewak and Maprik. At the larger administrative posts, there were "hospitals" (Haus-sik in Pidgin) staffed largely by expatriate medical assistants (lik-lik doktas or little doctors) and nurses, and in the villages the Aid Posts replaced the hospitals; these were staffed by locally trained Aid Post Orderlies (dokta-bois). It was an effective and economical system, well suited to the conditions prevailing in TPNG at that time. I did not realise it then but it was to affect my whole approach to the delivery of Primary Health Care in later years. The system was reinforced by a group of indigenous Health Educators who toured the villages and attempted to educate the communities in basic health and hygiene, and by the Malaria Eradication staff who were responsible for the spraying of all buildings with DDT at regular intervals, and finally, by the Maternal and Child Health service staff. All branches, except for the Malaria Eradication which was under the control of Dr. Jan Saave, came under my District responsibility.

Most of my visits entailed travelling by light 'plane, frequently belonging to either the Catholic Mission or to the Missionary Aviation Fellowship, or by four-wheel drive vehicle, although occasionally canoe and small boat journeys were involved. Most of the visits were for one day only, but when I visited Vanimo, I tended to stay two or three days as I visited all the outstations down the TPNG/ West Irian border, such as Amanab and Green River. Vanimo consisted of a few buildings and a small guest house clustered about the airstrip, which ran almost parallel to a beautiful beach. The proprietor of the guest house was a Mr. Campbell and he made sure that he always had fresh, locally caught lobsters on the menu for my arrival. Each border post had a small airstrip around which were scattered a few houses, with a small hospital close by. They were of considerable strategic importance being so close to territory belonging to Australia's nearest Asian neighbour, Indonesia.

There was one worrying episode which concerned myself, the Chief Health Education Officer for the District and the Regional Health Inspector. We had flown along the border posts, having set off from Vanimo, and were on our way back in a single-engined 'plane, when we ran into a severe storm with heavy cloud formations. The pilot was informed by radio that the whole of the western rim of the Sepik District was covered by a major storm and that the only way to escape it was by trying to climb above it. So gradually the'plane gained height and we soon found ourselves well above 10 000 feet, (the mountains along the border rose to about 15 000 feet at some points). This did not worry us unduly at first but then the engine started to splutter and miss and, at one stage, we actually dropped several hundred feet as the engine cut out, but it started again and we once again began to climb slowly. The four of us were quite silent until the pilot suddenly exclaimed that there was a break in the clouds, for which he immediately headed. Much to our relief, the pilot recognised that we were to the west of Vanimo, but just inside the West Irian border; this situation was speedily corrected and we were soon touching down safely at the welcome Vanimo strip.

One of my more memorable trips was to Telefomin, in the mountains along the border, and which was situated at about 7 000 feet. There was a small strip with a nearby Catholic Mission, which was ably attended by a nursing sister called Elizabeth Crouch. When I landed, I was met by a small delegation of locals, almost all of whom were almost stark naked; the young women, small but sturdily built, had bones through their noses and wore minute grass-aprons, fore and aft called "arse grass", while the men were completely naked except for wearing long penis-gourds held in place by a length of vine. There was one exception, the local policeman—he wore the regulation dress-style uniform. Their huts were of simple design and made of native materials, with a hole centrally placed in the roofing to act as a chimney; in the very cold nights, they all huddled around the open fire, including the dogs and pigs. The reason for my visit was to investigate an outbreak of medical problems in the local population; these proved to be the sequelae following smallpox vaccination. Subsequent to my visit, Sr. Crouch and I wrote an article on the outbreak which was published in the Medical Journal of Australia. While I was in Lae, I had also written an article on Malnutrition in Infants which had been accepted

135

for publication and was indeed published on 18 Mar 67, a week before the article mentioned above.

There were three interesting small events during this trip. The first concerned an Australian Army border patrol and a small family of Telefomins who both started off from the same place at approximately the same time. Not unsurprisingly, the family arrived at Telefomin within about 72 hours whereas the army patrol took almost a week to reach the outpost. The second involved the village policeman. It was at Telefomin that the last Australian Patrol Officer had been killed a few years previously and I was curious to find out about cannibalism in the area, so I spoke to the policeman about it. He assured me that there was now no more cannibalism. I asked him if he had ever tasted human flesh and he admitted that in his youth he had done so and that he liked "long pig". The third event again involved the Australian Army which was very active in this area. Late one morning, an army helicopter appeared on the scene, with the pilot and Captain Peter White, whom I had fleetingly met before. He was up to contact a tribal chief in the area, so he asked me if I would like to accompany him on his mission; this offer I readily accepted. At this height, I was told that helicopters were working at near their limit, but I took the chance and it was worth the risk. As we skimmed over the tree tops at approximately 7 000 feet, the pilot noticed a stream below us with a few gravel bars in it, and standing on one in the middle of the stream was a man. The stream was actually one of the headwaters of the Sepik River, the second largest river in the country, which flowed for six hundred miles to the sea and was navigable for about 300 miles. The pilot landed us safely on a close by gravel bar. Descending, we were greeted by an elderly man, wearing only a penis-gourd, who came across to talk to Peter. It was a one-off scene. Here was a modern military man talking to a "stone-age" man, in front of an army helicopter in the middle of one of the headwaters of the mighty Sepik; I had my camera handy as always and the resultant photo is one of my prized ones. Interestingly, Peter White left the army and was elected as a senator to the parliament in Canberra.

There is an interesting, true story of an Australian Patrol Officer working in the Telefomin area shortly after it had been brought under the administration but was still an area with much tribal fighting. This officer had an artificial eye and, just before setting out on his first patrol from the base, he called all the villagers to the front of his hut where he sat at a folding table just inside the entrance. Removing his artificial eye, which astounded the villagers, he held it up and showed it to them before placing it on a clean sheet of paper, over which he then placed his hat. As he did this, he told them that he was going on patrol and that he was leaving his eye behind so that he could see what they were doing while he was away from the village. Off he went on patrol and, when he returned, he found his hat and eye had not been touched at all and that the area had remained peaceful in his absence.

Our social life seemed to revolve around the army base at Moem Barracks. I think that this came about because the hospital anaesthetist was a Captain in the RAAMC, MacGregor Shepherd (Mac to his friends) who, although a great anaesthetist was an indifferent soldier and did not care one little bit about army discipline and rules. Nevertheless, he was an excellent friend to have. Through him, Margot and I were introduced to the Commanding Officer of the 2nd. Battalion Pacific Islands Regiment, Lt. Colonel Donald Ramsay, from Broadford on Skye. He was single then and a very heavy drinker. Nevertheless, regardless of the amount he consumed, he always managed to be on the parade ground with his troops at 6 am every morning. He became our very good friend.

Donald was housed in a small, native material donga all by himself, close to the beach, and which was known as "Castle Ramsay". Every Sunday lunch-time, the Officers' Mess held a barbecue which took place on the beach. Because I was the DMO, Margot and I were made honorary members of the Mess and were invited to the barbecue lunches. About 11 am, we would place Euan in his basket before settling ourselves into the VW Beetle for our drive to Moem Barracks and Castle Ramsay. Once there, Margot would feed and change Euan before we joined the others for pre-luncheon drinks. There was always a fine spread of good food with a liberal amount of alcohol. After the meal, the gathering would gradually disperse. Margot and I, with Euan once again comfortably settled, then sat down with Donald in his castle, chatting and drinking until about 5 pm, at which time we would drive home, somehow without mishap. This was our routine on most Sundays and we did look forward to it. Once reaching home, however, and after attending to Euan, we usually collapsed for the rest of the day in order to be fit for work the next day.

After we had been in Wewak for a few weeks, we realised that Euan had not been christened. So, through the good offices of the Lutheran Pastor, Captain Reidel, Euan was christened in a large clam shell, outside a native material church at Moem Barracks one Sunday morning, early in 1966. It was a lovely, simple service which was followed by a little celebration. We invited Brian Neville, our best-man, and Vivi Bignold, the Director of Nursing for TPNG, to be his god-parents, to which they readily agreed.

Through my official position, I was also on the District Advisory Council. This was under the chairmanship of the District Commissioner, Ted Hicks, a red-haired Australian. The other members of the Council consisted of the Assistant DC, John Wakefield (later the first DC of the newly formed West Sepik District), the Heads of the government departments, (eg. Mr. Cochrane from Education), and Donald Ramsay from the Army. We met not infrequently, and I must admit that I always received full support from Ted Hicks whenever it was needed.

On Wednesday, 18 May 66, the Governor General of Australia, Lord Casey, and his wife paid an official visit to the Sepik. Ted's wife, Shirley, had been preparing for this event, while the army had been drilling furiously as they were to be presented with their "Colours". The great day arrived. The local VIPs, Margot and I somehow were included, were lined up at the airport for his arrival, and were duly introduced to the couple on their touchdown on Sepik soil. Their entourage was not too large, but included a naval ADC, dressed in his summer whites uniform. An hour or two later, we again met the vice regal couple but this time at the DC's residence, where we had an informal get-together and some refreshments. After this, it had been arranged for Lord Casey to make an inspection by Land Rover of the immediate area, so a small fleet of such vehicles duly arrived to convey an even more select group on the official tour. Again, I was included. In my Land Rover was the ADC. Unfortunately, he proved to be a pain in the neck and he thought himself very important; however, he was justly rewarded. The small convoy moved off, but for some reason, the tail-gate of our vehicle was left down. I waved royally to the remaining guests as we moved off. For a while all went well, but we soon entered some quite difficult bush terrain which necessitated engaging the four-while drive. The passengers were seated down each side of the Land Rover, with the ADC at the end nearest the tail-gate on the right side, the driver's side. The dirt track became more difficult and undulating; suddenly, the vehicle rose sharply and the next thing we noted was the ADC sliding off the bench and out of the back of the vehicle onto the muddy track. He was a very amusing sight as he picked himself up; fortunately, his only injury was his pride.

The next official engagement, following a couple of hours respite, was the Presentation of Colours to the 2nd. Battalion, Pacific Islands Regiment, which took place at Moem Barracks, starting at 4 pm. This was Donald Ramsay's big moment and again, Margot and I were issued with an official invitation to view it. This time, we were accompanied by Matron Troy from the Hospital. It was an interesting ceremony and was very well organised. The Battalion had, of course, a good Pipe Band which led the march past of troops to their initial reviewing positions. Lord Casey was then driven on to the parade ground on the back of an open Land Rover but his appearance disappoined the many Papua New Guineans in the crowd as he wore a grey morning suit with tails and top hat instead of the more usual Governor's attire and cocked plumed hat. Slowly, he then was driven along the ranks of troops, wearing jungle greens, drawn up in review order. Descending, he then presented the new Colours to the Honour Guard, who then turned and placed them on top of a small array of piled drums. The ministers of the three main denominations, Anglican, Lutheran and Catholic, then walked together over to the Colours and each in turn blessed them. The Honour Guard raised the consecrated Colours and slow marched them in front of the troops, to the accompaniment of the bagpipes. Finally, with the CO, Donald Ramsay, at the head, with drawn sword held in front, the Pipe Band led the massed ranks with their new Colours in marching order in front of the Governor General for their final review. It had been a very interesting event and the whole vice regal visit proved to be very enjoyable and amusing.

One of the more hilarious, but potentially serious, episodes occurred as the result of an Australian Army Intelligence Report made to the District Advisory Council members. This stated that there were hundreds of rats being found dead just across the border in West Irian and that there was a plague epidemic in progress. At an emergency meeting, it was decided to place all district emergency facilities at my disposal. I immediately flew to the border area and talked to the Administrative and Health officials in each of the border posts, deciding where we would set up quarantine areas and on the quantities of different materials and drugs we would be likely to require. It was decided that we would need a considerable number of "dry-toilets" and so, on my return to Wewak, I asked if there were any available locally, only to be informed that there weren't ; the Regional store was in Lae, in the Morobe District. I contacted Lae and was told that the store in which they were normally held had been washed away when the Busu River had recently flooded and all the toilets had been lost. Dr. Tuza, the Regional Director in Lae, then arranged for the toilets to be sent up by air-freight as a priority. Not long afterwards, Dr. Charles Haszler, another Hungarian and an Assistant Director of Public Health in Port Moresby, 'phoned me to enquire about the "plague" reports, which I duly explained to him. In the midst of all this pressing activity, with dry-toilets being flown from south to north and then from east to west of the Mainland Region, official word was received from the Indonesian authorities in Sukarnopura (the capital of West Irian) that there was no plague epidemic in progress and that the few dead rats found had, on examination, been found to die from natural causes. The whole episode was rapidly brought to a close, but I still have vivid pictures in my mind of these dry-toilets flying hither and thither above the New Guinea Mainland Region.

The first faltering political steps to Independence had already been taken by the establishment of the Legislative Assembly in Port Moresby. The local representative was an Italian-Australian called John Pasquarelli, based at Angoram on the Sepik River where he was a trader. He considered himself to be the "Adonis of the Sepik". I found him abrasive and coarse. Every time we met, he would say to me, "Call me John." which, of course, I never did always calling him Mr. Pasquarelli. He never could understand why I insisted on doing so, but there was a very simple reason—I just did not like him.

There was a Seventh Day Adventist Mission staffed by sisters at Angoram and, after some correspondence, I arranged to join them on one of their regular trips up the Sepik River towards its source, to an area which had only been relatively recently been deregulated and which was now considered to be safe. I had been informed that all food would be provided for me and so I travelled light. The short flight to Angoram was uneventful and I soon found myself on the banks of the Sepik talking to the two SDA sisters. They told me that we would be travelling in their houseboat which was tied up nearby. Once everything was on board, I was surprised to find out how roomy it was and that my cabin, although small, was adequate. The ladies were pleasant and helpful but insisted that all doors and windows, fully mosquito-screened, were kept securely shut and that we start preparing our evening meal as soon as we had pushed off at about 3.30 pm. I agreed but wondered why. The meal prepared and offered was tasty and adequate in quantity but vegetarian. One thing, however, struck me as being particularly odd, all the vegetarian food was made to look like meat, as for example sausages and steak; the logic of this defeated me. The meal was soon over. The Sepik District has, in most parts, one of the highest rates of malaria transmission to be found anywhere in the world, with man-biting rates in excess of 1000 per hour being recorded, so I was not surprised to see the sisters preparing their beds and unrolling their mosquito nets, but I was surprised to see that they were actually going to be in bed by about 4.30 pm when it was still daylight. Nevertheless, I followed their example and was soon in my bunk and under the net in my cabin because the mosquitoes suddenly began to appear in large numbers, even although the quarters were supposed to be mosquito-proofed.

Meanwhile, we continued our journey down the river in the few minutes of daylight remaining, but as dusk fell, the crew tied the houseboat up alongside the bank for the night. As I lay and listened to the noises all around me, I picked up a soft, musical hum, so I shouted through to the two sisters and asked them if there was a village nearby as I could hear music and wondered if there was perhaps a "sing-sing" in progress. They laughingly replied that there was no nearby village and that the "music" was actually the hum caused by the millions of mosquitoes and other insects. I was soon fast asleep. When I awoke in the morning, I found that I had sustained quite a few mosquito bites on the parts of my body which came in contact with the net during the sleeping hours. Unfortunately, there was something wrong with the houseboat's engine and soon we were on our way back to Angoram. It had been an interesting but disappointingly short trip. I was to learn later that John Pasquarelli also ran tourist houseboat trips up the Sepik from Angoram.

Maprik was the nearest big administrative post to Wewak and it was relatively easy to reach it by road only having to cross the occasional river ford; it also had an airstrip close by. The hospital at Maprik was run by an Australian doctor, David Parkinson, who had once been a Medical Assistant. His career later paralleled my own, as he followed me as Head of the Malaria Programme, then joining the Malaria Research Unit of the RAAMC and finally by joining the World Health Organisation. I was never too struck on him as a person. Flights into Maprik were usually made with the Catholic Mission who flew single engined Dorniers. The Bishop, Bishop Arkfeld, held a pilot's licence and regularly flew. On one occasion, after a particularly heavy shower of rain, as he was obtaining traffic control advice and clearance prior to take-off, he was asked by the controller about the state of the Maprik airstrip. He replied in his slow, American drawl, "Mah-prik is wet and slippy", to which the controller laconically replied, "Oh really!".

On one occasion I had to pay a visit to a mission station just north of Wewak which I reached by Land Rover. On arrival, I was met by an agitated sister who asked me to assess immediately a woman who had been in labour for a while. This I did only to discover that she had twins and that they were not lying correctly for a normal delivery. So, after scrubbing up, I manually rotated and delivered the first child and, shortly after, I did the same for the second. Mother and babies all did well. One just did not know what medical emergency awaited you on these visits.

There was one very memorable trip that Margot, Euan and I made towards the end of our stay in the Sepik. As part of my fiefdom, the Polynesian islands of Wuvula and Aua were the most remote and I was determined to pay them a visit. The opportunity arose when a small government boat became available, so I booked it for the trip. The boat was a small one, and only had one very small, narrow cabin with two bunks one on top of the other, on the starboard side of the tiny deck-house (the galley and toilet were on the port side); towards the stern of the deckhouse was the covered hatch to the small hold. Needless to say, we had to travel light, but we did manage to take Euan's play-pen with us. We boarded the vessel in mid afternoon sunshine at Wewak and settled in as quickly as possible which wasn't difficult as the three crew members made us very welcome. After our meal, we decided to go to bed, and somehow managed to squeeze Euan into a prepared bed which lay between the two bunks and the cabin wall; there was a port hole directly above him which could not be closed properly. Not long into the night, the ship ran into a storm and soon we were being tossed around, pitching and tossing with reckless abandon; to add to our discomfort, water began to spray in through the supposedly closed door and port-hole. Euan managed to sleep through this but Margot and I were not so fortunate. When daylight arrived, we had weathered the worst of the storm but the ship was still behaving badly. We staggerd up and took Euan with us, but we two adults were unable to eat although Euan appeared to thrive. The crew members said that they would look after Euan and proceeded to put up and securely tie his playpen on the covered hatch, after which they placed him in it. He loved it and gurgled and staggerd around the play pen as the boat lurched, all under the constant watchful eyes of the crew. Needless to say, Margot and I had to go back to our bunks.

Fortunately, we arrived at Wuvulu just before mid-day and it was lovely to step ashore on such a beautiful, small, tropical island. We were met by the head-man and the Aid Post Orderly who escorted us to the village. This was one of the best kept villages I was ever to see in the South-West Pacific area, beautifully sited on golden sands, with the native material huts raised on stilts above a totally litter free village "square". We were royally welcomed and Euan was feted as many of the villagers had never seen a white toddler before; the Aid Post Orderly carried him everywhere on his shoulders. Needless to say, there were no real health problems. From Wuvulu, we made a short trip to Aua which was also another idyllic island which was a joy to visit. On our return trip to Wewak, the weather smiled on us. It had been a most enjoyable round trip.

When we first arrived in Wewak, we obtained the services of Lomi, a Papuan from the Milne Bay District. In his youth, he had been trained in household chores by sisters from the Catholic Mission and was an excellent housekeeper. He ran our house wonderfully well, even going as far as to cut pineapples decoratively for us at meal times. He had, however, one weakness—he was addicted to gambling and when the bug took hold of him, he would disappear. On one occasion, after he had been missing for a few days, we received a 'phone call from the Police station in Wewak to say that Lomi was in prison and would we please come to collect him.

On arrival there, Lomi was larger than life and was walking around the jail quite freely. Once we had him back home, he told us that the man in the next cell was being held for murdering a woman; Lomi tackled him over this saying to him that it was wrong to kill a woman as "Missus Queen" was a woman and surely he wouldn't kill Missus Queen! However, in the end, we dispensed with his services and in his place we hired Malligan and her husband, Mike, along with their two children. They were not as house trained as Lomi and nor were they as sophisticated as Labalai and Morris in Lae, but they were reliable and, as we did not make undue demands of them, they were more than adequate for our requirements as they were reliable and honest.

There was another Scot in Wewak. His name was Bruce Miller and he was the owner of the garage. A young man, he had once played the drums in a military band at the Edinburgh Festival. Needless to say, we became quite friendly. On one occasion, when our VW beetle was off the road, he lent us an old car to run about in; it was an old rust-bucket, but it worked. Margot had not long passed her driving test so she took every opportunity to drive. Well, on this fateful occasion, she was reversing, misjudged her distances and backed straight into a coconut tree. The whole of the rear part of the car crumpled. Nevertheless, she managed to drive it back to Bruce's garage where she was expecting Bruce to be rather annoyed. To her amazement, Bruce was rather amused and, after Margot had handed the car over to him, he drove it straight into the swamp. Nobody was very environmentally aware in those days.

During the days, while I was at work, Margot would frequently take Euan to our favourite spot at Moem beach, where they would laze and swim. They would very rarely have any company. One morning, she was approached by a local who verbally started to abuse her and threatened to assault her. Fortunately, Margot is a sensible and calm woman. Without showing any signs of apprehension and fear, she calmly talked her way out of the situation, the local eventually departing, leaving Margot unscathed. Unfortunately, there was a sequel to this. Soon after, an air hostess lying alone on the beach was approached by a local and assaulted; the assailant was apprehended.

We did not really have much to do with the medical and nursing staff at the hospital. There was a Hungarian surgeon, Dr. Roth, and his wife, Eva. Occasionally, he would take me out in his small boat but not too often as I was a very bad sailor. Eva was a good cook and we enjoyed one or two meals with them. There was a physician, Dr. Palme, and his wife from Hamelin in Germany. His wife had an endearing habit of inviting Margot in occasionally for morning coffee, only for Margot to discover that the "coffee" was actually a liqueur; needless to say, Margot politely refused on most occasions. Our immediate next door neighbours were a Papuan doctor, Kila Wari, his large, jovial, Fijian wife, and family. Kila was involved with the Tuberculosis campaign and was a very gentle, caring person. When his wife knew that Margot was expecting our second child, she gave her a beautiful, large Buka basket within which to carry the new baby; we still have the basket. Towards the end of our stay in the Sepik, Dr. Risto Gobius, his wife and family arrived. They were a South African family, although Risto had trained in Canada as a Paediatrician and had arrived to take up the post in the Sepik. He was a very intense, active man and although pleasant enough, I never really took to him. Prior to his arrival, I had helped to finalise the training of Aid Post Orderlies at Wewak and subsequently, years later, I was told that he had broadened the training unit by starting a nursing course also. Such is life! They are now settled somewhere in New South Wales.

Among the people we met through the Army were Di and Laurie Lewis and their two children, Judith and Ian. Laurie was an infantry major while Di was a nurse at the hospital. I believe that Laurie was second in command to Donald Ramsay. We had a lot of time for Laurie as he was a quiet, unassuming man with a good, dry sense of humour; however, we found Di a bit of a strain. She doted on her son and less so on her daughter. For some reason, one of the doctors admitted Ian, then aged about six, to hospital as an inpatient because Di had said that he was not eating. He looked perfectly healthy to Margot and me and we were quite disturbed to find out that he was unable to feed himself properly because Di, at home, helped to feed him. One morning, when there was no staff around, I went into his room and told him to stop fooling around, that he was no longer a baby and that if he did not start to feed himself immediately I would personally smack his bottom. Ian appeared to make a dramatic recovery. Laurie went off to Vietnam for a tour of duty and eventually rose to the rank of Brigadier and, on retiral, took up the post of Managing Director of Homes for the Aged in Adelaide, South Australia.

Being part of the local establishment, we were not only expected to attend the various social functions, most of them held at the District Commissioner's residence, but also to act as the hosts. The functions held by the DC were varied and nearly always interesting as the visitors were professional, usually international, people. Among the many we met was the US ambassador to Australia, a genial, overweight, 60 something Texan, who was a close personal friend of Lyndon Baines Johnson, the US President. At this particular social gathering, his most noticeable piece of sartorial adornment was a string tie, held in place at the throat by a silver "Texas longhorn "head. On our part, we were expected to entertain the many and varied senior staff who travelled north from the Head Office in Konedobu, Port Moresby. These included the various heads of departments, the Director of Public Health, Dr. Scragg, and the occasional medical advisor/consultant on secondment from Australia. The most enjoyable of these Australian visitors involved the Medical Director of a major Sydney Hospital and a Psychiatrist, Dr. Parker, from Brisbane, Queensland. After a very nice meal prepared by Margot, which had been washed down with adequate liquid refreshments, we settled down to an hilarious evening of medical anecdotes; the evening passed all too quickly. The only visitor with whom we felt at all awkward was Dr. Scragg. He was a tall, gaunt man with little sense of humour and a distinctly religious outlook, being a Seventh Day Adventist.

All through my spell in the Sepik I still had hopes of becoming a Paediatrician and had requested Head Office for study leave to attend a course at Great Ormond Street Hospital for Sick Children in London for which I had enrolled. David Bowler gave me full backing in my request. The time came for us to leave the Sepik District and we took our leave with high hopes. On the morning of our departure, Donald Ramsay came to see us off on the 'plane. With him, he brought a piper and with full ceremony, Margot and I were piped aboard all the way from the terminal. It was a very kind and thoughtful gesture. Donald eventually married the daughter of a Presbyterian minister who was working as an air hostess and, on his retiral, they settled in Sydney, where he took up the post of Registrar at Scots College.

Our plan was to go off on holiday and, on arrival in Port Moresby to receive confirmation that my study leave had been approved. Well, we started off from Wewak in high hopes that everything was in order. However, it was not to be. On landing, we were met by our friend, David Bowler, wearing his official hat this time, who told us that my request for paid study leave had not been approved. That left us rather flat and deflated; however, we quickly regained our spirits in the excitement of catching our flight connection to Sydney and home.

And so another chapter in our lives came to an end. We had thoroughly enjoyed Wewak, me professionally and both of us socially. Margot had once again been thrown back on her own resources for much of the time as I was frequently away from home on duty; unfortunate as this was, it developed a very independent spirit in her which was to stand her in good stead later, although she did resent my frequent absences. We had also happily settled into family life with all its ups and downs. It was not possible for us to leave the Sepik without ensuring that Rover joined us at a later date, wherever we should be posted; this we did, and on our return to TPNG, Rover joined us soon after.

Chapter Thirteen

Homeward Bound, 1966

Arriving in Sydney, we stayed at the old Metropole Hotel, in the centre of town. It was a friendly, old-fashioned establishment and we enjoyed being there. Much to our horror, on the morning we were due to catch the 'plane, it dawned on us that we had far too much luggage for the flight so we repacked and left one large suitcase with the hall porter asking him to arrange for its onward shipment by Gills to us in Glasgow, tipping him ten shillings (50p) for his troubles. Exceedingly generous! Margot and I thought that we would never see it again but it did arrive safely and absolutely sound about three months later. As I remember it, we must have had some time to spare before leaving for the airport because we took Euan to a barber for his first haircut, an experience which he manfully suffered without too much protest.

At Sydney Kingsford Smith airport we boarded a UTA flight, en route to Tahiti via New Caledonia. It was undoubtedly the worst flight in an airliner that Margot and I have ever experienced. We were very glad to reach Tahiti.

We landed at Tahiti quite late in the day. France was in the middle of carrying out an atomic test series at Mururoa Atoll, so there was heavy security throughout. As we stepped off the 'plane, we were greeted and garlanded by grass-skirted, comely Tahitian young women, and then herded into the terminal building where the men were separated from the women and children, before all were fully searched in separate facilities. This was the first time we had ever been searched.

Our hotel was quite a bit out of Papeete—we had chosen it because we had over 24 hours to spare—so we drove there. It was a lovely hotel, typically tropical, with many thatched cottages and palm trees. It was lovely to be able to stretch out on a bed once again and all three of us slept soundly. Next morning, we hired a taxi which took us on a tour around the island. It was everything we had imagined that Tahiti would be. An added attraction was a drive around the island taking in a visit to the Paul Gauguin museum. Papeete itself was a disappointment, a shabby, dirty and rather typical French colonial town. In the late evening, as the time approached for us to be collected from our hotel, we became rather anxious as the appointed time came and went; eventually, about 45 minutes late, our transport arrived. After a mad rush to the airport, we checked in just to be told that they had detained the 'plane especially for us. So luck was with us.

Arriving late, we changed airlines and flew on in more comfort to Acapulco where we booked into the Hilton Hotel. It was lovely, with our balcony overlooking the golden sands and the hotel's own swimming pool. Our breakfast on the small balcony was sheer heaven—even Euan enjoyed lying out in the early morning sun. We were there for a little over a day, so we spent most of it just walking around taking in the local colour. Even in those days, Acapulco was a tourist trap. From there we moved on to Tasco where we had booked in to the Hotel de la Borda, government-run and absolutely superb, with spacious, cool accommodation, superb food and service. Tasco, the old Spanish silver town, was fascinating with its old colonial style buildings and streets; again, we walked all over the place taking in the sights, sounds and smells. Time passed too quickly. I cannot recall whether we drove or flew to Mexico City, but I do remember that we did take a long drive at one stage which was memorable for the number of very poor peasants, mainly children, lining the road selling many types of birds, animals, fruit and food.

Mexico City was rather overwhelming even then. We loved it. The Mexicans thought it great that we took Euan everywhere with us. On a bus tour of the city, he was the centre of attraction for the passengers.

Time was running short and, much to our regret, we did not manage a trip to the Yucatan peninsula to see the ruins. However, the three of us did manage a visit to the Ballet Folklorico de Mexico, which was wonderful and which Euan sat through in absolute silence enjoying the bustle on stage and the rhythmic music.

One afternoon, in Mexico City, I asked Margot if she and Euan would like to go to a bullfight; she declined, so I was allowed to toddle off on my own. The stadium was filled to capacity. In the middle of the arena stood a large, fibre-glass, Coca-Cola bottle on a wheeled platform—it looked very incongruous sitting out there. Suddenly there was a loud trumpet fanfare, followed by cheering from the crowd. Then, out of the main gateway came the procession, headed, I presume, by the Patron of this particular session, closely followed by the flamboyantly dressed matadors, strutting and saluting behind; close behind them came the picadors on their quilted horses, then the arena attendants (responsible for removing the dead bulls and for sprinkling sand on the blood lying on the ground). Soon the arena was once again cleared, the Coca-Cola bottle trundled away erratically, and the first bull was allowed to charge in through the opened gate, accompanied by a huge roar from the crowd. The first two or three contests were for the novice matadors—they received a very severe jeering from the crowd if they proved to be too gauche in despatching the bull. The early contests were not particularly edifying and the poor bulls undoubtedly suffered. As each bull was given the coup-de-grace, the attendants would hurry up to it, attach chains to its hind legs and drag it out of the arena behind a horse. I understood that it was then butchered and the meat distributed to charities. Between bouts, the Coca-Cola bottle would trundle back into the centre of the arena. The main event of the afternoon was in a different class, obvious to even an ignoramus like myself. The matador taunted, pirouetted and danced before the bull, (it had previously been weakened by picadors), making passing movements with the cape and, on occasions, professionally inserting the long thin blades into the ligamentum nuchae at the back of the bull's neck. With the bull literally on its last legs, head hung low, breathing heavily, tongue hanging out and matted blood lying on its shoulders, the matador stood in front of it on his toes and with his back arched, aiming the sword accurately at the vital spot in the bull's neck, before he expertly buried it therein causing the death of the bull which slowly slumped on its front knees before rolling over on the ground dead. Then the victorious matador gathered the applause of the crowd. Although I felt great pity for the bull, the acts and movements of the matador were sheer poetry in motion, demonstrating the arts of sexual innuendo, athleticism and bravado simultaneously.

Mexico was a great experience. We said that we would make every effort to return there one day, but it was time for us to move on to Glasgow, via London.

It was nice to be home, arriving in late August, but it wasn't to be for long as I had enrolled at the Great Ormond Street Hospital for Sick Children to do the Diploma in Child Health course even although my study request had been refused. Moving south, our first priority was to find ourselves suitable accommodation and in this we were lucky as we obtained a semi-detached house for rental in Petts Wood, Kent, even although it was on the "half-crown" side of the railway line. However, this meant that I now had to travel to and from Petts Wood to London by train every week-day. Nevertheless, we enjoyed our stay here as it was here that Euan really began to get on his feet. Margot used to take him out in his stroller to the park where he would toddle, slip and slide to his heart's content, and often he would be given a swing, sitting contentedly, sitting strapped into the swing seat, contented and smiling, looking very warm and appealing in his woollen clothes as the weather was now chilly but dry. At the week-ends we would go for walks and we took advantage of the good weather.

At Great Ormond Street Hospital, I struck up a friendship with a beautiful, petite, Indian Malaysian and a tall Nigerian, both attending the same course; we managed to spend most of our course together and some of our spare time. But I soon realised after about six weeks that I was not too interested in Paediatrics at which time I decided to cut my losses and left, after discussing it with Margot. As Christmas was almost upon us, we went back up to Glasgow. Mum and Dad were still living in Cranworth street, in a large flat. This meant that Margot and I had a room to ourselves as did Euan. By this time winter was well and truly upon us, snowy and cold. Although heated, Euan still felt his room chilly during the night even although he was well wrapped up, initially at least, because he would then throw off the bedclothes, a throwback to his tropical habits when he never wore a covering in bed. Margot and I now regret putting him in a separate room, not only because we were up attending to him frequently to ensure he kept warm, but also because it must have been very miserable for him; only very rarely did we take him into our bed.

My Dad loved Euan and took him for walks whenever possible, always taking great care to wrap him up well; he would also baby-sit him on the days we were out as my Mum was also out at work. It was during these days when they were alone together that Euan would toddle through to the large kitchen, open the low set cupboard doors and systematically empty the cupboards of all the pots and pans, scattering them about the floor. Dad, a very tidy and methodical man, just could not bear to be in an untidy kitchen and almost as soon as Euan emptied the cupboards, Dad would refill them. Eventually, it became a game which they both appeared to enjoy, although it tired Dad out sooner than it did Euan. My Mum, although she was fond of Euan, never really loved him in the same way as my Dad did. Margot's parents, Rita and Jack, lived in Saltcoats, Ayrshire, and it was difficult to visit each other; consequently, they missed out in getting to know Euan very well, which was a great pity.

In the evenings in which we didn't go out, we would sit in the large sitting room after dinner talking, having our drinks and watching the programmes on the TV set which sat in one corner of the room. Euan, in his pyjamas, was allowed to stay up for about an hour before being put to bed. He was really amusing to watch as he would stand in front of the TV, gently flexing his knees and making small jumps, keeping time to the music. He was much more amusing than the shows on TV.

I had decided to try for jobs at home, and if successful to stay at home. As I had trained at the Western Infirmary, I naturally inquired there first. I still wasn't quite sure what it was I really wanted to do other than the fact that I had to avoid specialties which required me to undertake major surgical procedures (eg, surgery, obstetrics/gynaecology) in view of my allergy to surgical gloves. I attended one or two interviews in England but I cannot recall whether I was offered the posts or just did not accept them. In any case, I had started to make inquiries nearer to home, namely at the Western Infirmary. One person I spoke to was a surgical unit chief,

Mr. Clark. He recalled teaching me as a student but then said to me, "You are one of those who have deserted the sinking ship, so why should you be offered a post?" This was a typical response in those days when morale throughout the country was generally low. Returning home, I said to Margot that we didn't need to put up with that sort of response as I had a good job in TPNG and we were all happy there; so we decided to return as soon as possible.

However, we had one important social engagement during this spell at home. This was to attend the wedding of Jack Hamill, (my GUBC friend), and Ann Sudbury in Nottingham. Jack was now a chemist at Boots and he had met Ann, who was also a chemist, there. The arrangement was that Margot and I would collect Ronnie, his brother, and a lady friend (who worked in the Boots store at the corner of Argyle and Renfield streets, Glasgow), in our specially hired Mini. Well, the lady friend was a large, jovial woman and Margot had to share the back seat of the small car with her and Ronnie all the way down south. Driving down to Sudbury, Derbyshire, in an overcrowded Mini was quite exciting and humorous but very uncomfortable; nevertheless, we arrived there safely on the late afternoon before the wedding. Margot and I were billeted with Ann's parents in a large Victorian house, (Ann's father was a GP), and we were very comfortable there in all respects. In the evening, the younger wedding guests were taken to a very smart and expensive, country house hotel for a magnificent dinner. The following day was bright and crisp, perfect weather for a lovely formal wedding in the village church, attended by over 200 guests. It was a Church of England service which Margot and I found a bit strange. Jack and Ann looked very happy. Margot looked great too as she had bought a complete new outfit for the occasion although she had borrowed the hat. Because we had a long drive back, the four of us did not stay too long at the reception before starting off on our long drive north. It had been a very enjoyable break from routine.

Chapter Fourteen

The Territory of Papua New Guinea (III)

PORT MORESBY, 1967-1969

And so it was that we returned to Port Moresby early in 1967. Initially, we were accommodated in a small government flat in town, which was barely adequate for our needs, although it was close to the departmental headquarters in Konedobu. On reporting for duty, Dr. Scragg, the Director, suggested to me that I may like to consider the post of Regional Malariologist for the Papuan Region, based in Lawes Road. Although I only had the vaguest idea of what the job entailed, I thought it a worthwhile and challenging one due to my contacts with the Malaria Eradication Programme (MEP) in the Sepik, and so I accepted the offer.

Fortunately, I was able to move into a rented home in town quite soon; this house belonged to Mr. Mrs. Renwick, who were on holiday in England; Mr. Renwick was the chief government geologist. Their house was comfortable and we had the run of it, so Margot was quite happy. On their return from leave, we had to share with them for a short while, but they were a very nice couple and made us feel quite at home. Nevertheless, we were very happy when we were told that we had a semi-detached house in the newly opened Gordon Estate, a little distance out of town.

The head of the MEP was Dr. Jan Saave, a new Australian of Polish birth. Right from the start, we did not get on well; with me being

154

appointed to this post without him being consulted by the Director certainly did not help matters. Nevertheless, it was not too long before I was allowed to moved into the MEP quarters at Lawes Road, albeit grudgingly. I did not know what I was supposed to be doing initially and Dr. Saave deliberately kept me ignorant for quite a while, giving me neither instruction nor work to do. Eventually, still not knowing what I was supposed to be doing, I went out on patrol with a malaria team to areas south of Port Moresby, such as Abau, a lovely island in Marshall Lagoon. Unknown to me at the time I accepted the post, there had been a great deal of behind-the—scenes politics taking place, with Dr. Scragg trying to remove Dr. Saave; eventually, I learned that the Director had placed me in position in order to have a window into the MEP.

The staff at Lawes Road consisted of an elderly Englishman, Mr. Slater, who prepared the maps which were essential for the malaria activities, another Englishman who was the entomologist, Mr. Harry Lake, a Hungarian who acted as the chief administrative officer, an Australian, Mr. Bob Allen, who was the senior spray team manager for the MEP, and one or two senior local staff, in addition to Dr. Saave and me. It was soon apparent that the cartographer did not like Dr. Saave, that the entomologist and spray team manager just kept on equable terms with him while the administrative officer crawled to him. Needless to say, it was not a good place to work. Fortunately, I soon made good friends within head office, among them being Bert Speers, a senior administrative officer, who supported me during these difficult times. As can be imagined, my new job entailed considerable and frequent travel all over the Territory and, for study purposes, overseas to the Philippines and India.

So it was that one of my first patrols was to Abau island, which was the MEP depot for the Marshall Lagoon area. The Papuan malaria supervisor on this patrol actually lived on the island and, on arrival, he kindly invited me home to lunch. We sat down to our meal and I was looking forward to it as normally we ate tinned and packet food when on patrol. Once seated, his wife duly placed in front of us a freshly cooked, large fruit-bat intact except that it had been gutted before being cooked in banana leaves. Much to my shame, I just could not face this delicacy and after offering profuse apologies, I opened a tin of corned beef. On this particular patrol, there was quite a lot of travel by motorised canoe as we had to visit all

155

the villages in the area. Between villages, we would cast out fishing lines and on one occasion, we were lucky to catch quite a large kingfish. For the only time, I also allowed myself to grow a beard which I kept until I returned home in order to show Margot, who then promptly asked me to shave it off.

On these patrols, which could sometimes last for a few weeks, I accompanied the spraying teams, travelling being completed by foot, Land Rover or canoe, although occasionally, I would fly into an outstation and meet up with the local malaria team. The owners and inhabitants of all the houses and buildings in the area being visited were contacted prior to the team's arrival in order to enable them to prepare their dwellings (ie. removing all movable furniture and ensuring that animals, and particularly cats, were not present) for spraying with DDT, water-dispersible if made of native materials or kerosene-based if made of permanent materials. In addition, the health educator accompanying each spray-team gave talks to the villagers on the programme, prevention of malaria and simple health care. It was my responsibility to assess the effectiveness of all these activities. I enjoyed travelling around meeting the "real" Papuans and New Guineans and developed a great deal of respect for them.

Margot did not work while in Port Moresby and so, to fill her time, she became quite social. I did not realise it then but Margot did not like being left for long periods on her own and missed my company. One or two of our friends from Lae had also been transferred to Port Moresby and so Margot soon caught up with them, one couple in particular whose marriage was on the rocks. I did not object as she was always home when I was at home and I always believed that Margot should lead her own life to a large extent.

As TPNG was tropical, the weather was always warm and on occasions humidity approached 100%. I found, as did most whites, that it was most comfortable to work in shorts, short-sleeved, open-neck shirt and a good pair of shoes (or sturdy light weight boots when on patrol in the bush) with knee-length stockings (although many wore rubber slip-slops with bare legs as the way was often wet). In addition, I always wore a wide-brimmed, light canvas hat.

Eventually, we took possession of a brand new house at Gordon Estate. It was bright and cheerful and, on our arrival, we were greeted by Mike Ongulu on the doorstep. Mike was a small Chimbu with a very engaging personality; he had presented himself because he wanted a job as our servant. And so it was that Mike, his brother, Uguwa, and two other Chimbu brothers, Pius and Simbai, entered our lives. We learned later that Mike gradually infiltrated other Chimbus as servants throughout the estate. This had a very beneficial effect as it kept inter-tribal rivalry and theft away from the estate. Mike was a "bushy-tru" and Margot had to train him in household tasks from scratch but he was a very likeable, willing and quick learner, even although all communication was carried out in Pidgin English.

Chimbus appear to be natural gardeners and before long our garden was totally under control due to their tender ministrations and the advice of our neighbour, an Australian agricultural/ horticultural officer. Our neighbour in the house just behind us had problems with his garden and had been throwing his stones into our garden, until Simbai, a large, powerful man, caught him doing so and was about to assault him when I arrived home just in time to stop him. Needless to say, our neighbour never did it again. Another neighbour had employed Pius as a servant, She received a rude jolt one afternoon when she returned home and walked into her bedroom to find Pius stretched out on her bed sound asleep; she was very angry and sacked him immediately. He had just taken a rest after doing the housework. Although Mike was our only servant, all the Chimbus made our house and garden their base; they were always around and did many things for us and generally looked after us. We liked them and trusted them implicitly and were never disappointed in them.

One of the first things we did on settling in to our new home was to arrange for Rover to be flown down from Wewak. We had missed him and the whole family went down to the airport to collect him. Unfortunately, not long after his return to the family, he developed dystemper and was severely affected; however, he made a good recovery but was left with a weakness in his hind quarters. He soon settled down to his new home and remained with us the whole time we were in Port Moresby. Just before our departure, we gave Rover to a family we knew but unfortunately, for some unknown reason, Rover apparently bit their child and so they had him put down; this was a strange turn about as he had never ever shown any aggression to Euan and Michèle.

As we moved into Gordon estate, my Mother wrote asking us if she could come out for a while to help Margot look after Euan and the expected new arrival while I was away overseas. After a discussion, Margot and I agreed to her request as we felt that Margot may feel a bit lonely in this new situation without any family support. Mum arrived quite soon and all of us went down to the airport to meet her off the 'plane from Australia. Well, the moment we saw her face as she walked off the aircraft towards the terminal, we instinctively knew that it would be a difficult visit and that we had probably made the wrong decision in inviting her at all; her face showed all the signs of anger and frustration, signs that we knew so well.

Shortly after moving into our new house, our second child was due. At about the same time, it had been decided that I should attend a three months Malaria Eradication Training course run by the World Health Organisation at the Malaria Eradication Training Centre (METC) based at the San Lazaro Hospital compound in Manila, Philippines. However, our child was due on or about my intended departure date, which I kept postponing, until I was eventually told that if I didn't leave soon I would lose my place on the course. So, with great misgiving, I left for Manila. Fortunately, all went well and ten days after my departure, on 14 Jan 1968 at 6 pm., our beautiful, red-headed daughter, Michèle, was born. Mother and daughter were both well. I immediately sent a telegramme to Margot, in which I said, "Your every wish is my command" as she had so wanted to have a girl. We were all very happy. Mike was absolutely delighted with the new arrival, and although he was also very fond of Euan, Michèle was always "his" baby, He and his brother, Uguwa, spent all their spare time taking the two of them for walks and spoiling them at every opportunity. Very few New Guineans had ever seen a red-head before.

Arriving in Manila, I found that WHO had booked me into a cheap hotel near the METC. I was fortunate to make friends with a fellow participant, Seizo Sakihara, an Okinawan, a Christian and a Health Promoter. We decided to share a double room, which turned out to be a fortuitous arrangement as this hotel was more or less a brothel used by

US servicemen on Rest and Recreation (R & R) from Vietnam. However, the staff looked after us well, the room and bed linen were always spotless, and the non-stop activity and entertainment were well worth the doubtful respectability. Seizo and I would eat our main meals in Chinese and Filipino restaurants in the area in the late evenings and, on special occasions, we would spend the evening at an authentic Japanese restaurant called "Atami". On one occasion, Dr. Kila Wari, who had been our neighbour in Wewak, visited the WHO Regional Office in Manila; after his business had been completed, we took him to the Atami where we let Seizo do the honours, being very well attended by the Geishas, while we squatted on the floor barefooted, around a low-set table laden with Japanese delicacies from which we were fed.

The Dean of the METC was Dr. A.P. Ray, the internationally famous, former head of the Indian Malaria Eradication Programme; he was ably assisted by Dr. W.J.O.M. van Dijk, who had formerly worked in Indonesia and Dutch New Guinea (West Irian) as a malariologist, and two Americans, Dr. Richard Darsie, the entomologist, and Dr. Lou Schinazi, the parasitologist. It was a very interesting course and the time passed quickly. At the end of it, I knew something about Malaria Eradication, albeit not too much. At this time, the Regional WHO Director was a Filipino, Dr. Francisco Dy.

There were some interesting participants. One was Jack Graves, an American who was working in the Tennessee Valley Project, and who attended the course part-time. There were two amusing Iraqi doctors present, both of whom were rather fond of the social scene in Manila. Dr. Barzangi, who was a regional director of medical services, and Dr. Khafaji were amusing to know and certainly livened up the scene.

The course was not all work. METC arranged outings for us at the week-ends. one such outing was to Corrigedor. We reached the island on large, fast, outboard engined canoes, where we spent a fascinating afternoon visiting the various gun emplacements and the large cavernous underground storage sites cut into the hillside. We also drove along the Bataan peninsula, the infamous "Death March" route. On another outing, we also visited Baguio, up in the hills—it was lovely to rise above the dirt and humidity of Manila for a short while. As part of our field work, we also visited Dagupan City, and on the Saturday morning, we took the opportunity to visit the "Dog Market", where hundreds of the poor animals, confined in small wire cages, were on sale for purchase as human food. There were other interesting visits to San Pablo and Pangasinan. Manila, however, was a disappointing place. Apart from the small tourist area, most of it appeared to be one large slum. Away from the centre, the mega rich lived in sumptuous villas and mansions, carefully guarded by high walls and well-armed security guards. In my spare moments, I walked around the city to get a feel for Manila but it was a depressing and sad place. I was not sorry to leave but before doing so we had our farewell dinner, attended by all the students and lecturers, at which I was told that I had topped the course.

As part of the course, it had been arranged that we should go to India to see their programme in action. So it was that I flew on to Bombay, eventually finishing up in Madras, where we spent our time studying their Passive Case Detection system, reputedly the best in India. A much more interesting part of this trip was a visit to a famous Hindu temple nearby which was decorated with pornographic drawings and paintings, and lavishly adorned with sexually explicit carvings.

Dad, in the meantime, had notified me that he would be sailing into Karachi on the day I was due to leave for Port Moresby, 14 Apr 1968. He was now the Chief Engineer on the "Mustali", a ship belonging to a Pakistan company, which sailed between Karachi and Chittagong in East Pakistan (now Bangla Desh). I therefore decided that I would go to Karachi, where I booked into a double room in a large, modern hotel in the city centre. I arrived early with the intention of spending one day/ evening with my Father, but I was informed that the ship had been delayed and was now not due into the "Roads" until 5 pm. or later. It eventually dropped anchor at about 7 pm. and Dad had to catch a special fast ferry boat into Karachi, reaching the hotel by about 8.30 pm. It was wonderful to see him again as we hadn't seen each other for quite a while. Over a light meal and a couple of whisky/sodas, we talked away until about 2.30 am., talking about life in general and also taking the opportunity of pointing out to him how difficult Mum was proving to be in Port Moresby, where Margot had found her to be petty, interfering, selfish and jealous of our friends. I thought that Dad would have been upset but to my amazement, he agreed with my comments and said that he had had to put up with that for most of his married life. I have often wondered since if that was the reason he had chosen to remain at sea, a virtual bachelor, for so much of his married life. I only had four or five hours sleep as I had to catch the early flight back home, while Dad had to return to the ship. The last I ever saw of him was standing outside the hotel waving me goodbye as I left in the taxi. I was so glad later that I had made the decision to postpone returning to TPNG after the course as he was tragically killed in East Pakistan on 10 Dec 1971. Margot and I never ever felt guilt about my Mother after that. Before leaving him, however, Dad promised that he would try to arrange for Mum to join him on the ship. That was something to look forward to.

I returned to Port Moresby after about three months away to see Margot, Euan and our new, red-headed daughter, Michèle, for the first time. She was lovely but we were not the only ones to claim her as Mike proclaimed that she was "his baby". However, the overall relationship with Mum was deteriorating. She was interfering in our friendships and gradually eroding the respect for us and in particular, Margot. Fortunately, our friends kept us informed of the situation and tended to keep Mum at arms' length. However, time was passing and she had now been with us for about seven months. Eventually, Margot could stand it no longer and she said to me, "Either your Mother goes or I do." So, I urgently contacted Dad but it was another couple of months before he was able to arrange for her departure to join him in Karachi.

She eventually stayed with us for ten months. My Mum's presence, however, enabled Margot to have more frequent contact with her male friend and even more so when I was away abroad on study leave. I accepted this situation as I have always felt that, in spite of everything, Margot has always loved me just as deeply as I have always loved and trusted her. I let Margot lead her own life as a means of keeping her in the family.

In the meantime, after only one month back from Manila, misfortune befell me. On 10 May 1968, just after I had mounted my Honda 125 cc motorcycle, and was pulling away from the Regional Health Office in Port Moresby at just over 10 mph, I was hit by a car on my right side, driven by a local, civilian employee of the Pacific Islands Regiment depot. The car ran over my bike and my right ankle, leaving it almost separated from the rest of my leg. The driver had just not noticed me when he turned right. There was almost no blood loss and I felt little pain, just a sense of disbelief and numbness. Soon there was a crowd around me but I soon realised that I was the calmest person there. A man offered to take me to the hospital in the back of his open utility van; I accepted and, as I held my leg in my right hand and my almost severed foot in my left hand, I was lifted in to the back of the utility and driven to the hospital. The only times at which I felt any pain during the journey was when the utility went round corners and I found it difficult to hold the relative positions of the two pieces of my leg. The first person to greet me at the hospital was my friend, David Bowler, who directed my care from there on. After receiving a pethidine injection, I became garrulous and really didn't remember much else.

After that, David called in to see Margot at home and told her to take a seat. On seeing David's sombre face, she thought that I had been killed and was expecting the worst. When David told her that I had been involved in a road accident, had sustained a compound fracture of my right ankle and was now in hospital, Margot, much to David's surprise, laughed out aloud with relief. This was the start of a very difficult ten months of immobility, most of it spent in hospital.

With me in hospital, Margot was left even more so on her own and had to make a greater effort to secure a reasonable social life. Her friend was a senior officer in the Health Department and, to broaden her mind, gave Margot books by Sartre and Simone de Beauvoir to read during this period. In addition to the literature, he would take Margot, Euan and Michèle on picnics to the beach, and even go so far as to take my Mum out. It was a very difficult period for Margot and if it kept her reasonably content, so be it as I felt that the fault was mine due to the requirements of my job. Another couple also provided Margot with support. Rolf, a Danish engineer, and his Australian born wife of Hungarian parentage, Julie Bloch-Jorgensen, were young, full of life and great fun to be with; they cheered Margot up immensely when she was feeling blue. Margot had met Julie on Kila Beach in Port Moresby.

There were also a few men in the Health Department who proved to be very loyal and supportive to Margot; these included Reg Collins and

Albert (Bert) Speer, both former Medical Assistants who had traversed the length and breadth of New Guinea in the days of the Australia New Guinea Administrative Unit (ANGAU) at the end of the Second World War and who now occupied administrative posts at Head Office. They were particularly helpful in taking Mum off Margot's hands for long periods of time as the friction between them increased. Sad as this situation was, it was even sadder to see that Mum did not show any real interest in her grandchildren.

In the meantime, I had come under the care of Mr. Smith, the chief surgeon. However, my fracture proved very difficult to treat and after a couple of months, I was transferred to the care of Mr. Rich, a New Zealand orthopaedic surgeon. From then onwards, my rate of progress improved albeit slowly. Overall, there were three attempts at ankle fixation, the third attempt was to be the last before amputation, before a successful outcome was achieved, followed by two attempts at skin grafting. I was in a frog-like plaster of paris for many months, with my right ankle, held close to the inside of my left tibia, to enable the transfer of a full-thickness skin graft. After a long time, I was allowed out of bed and given crutches and my leg placed in a full length walking plaster; on the third day, I managed to visit, without assistance, another friend in hospital who was in a ward a considerable distance away. Eventually, after over nine months in hospital, I was allowed home, with a full length leg plaster in place. During my stay in hospital, I had continued with the administrative work of the Malaria Programme. Good news awaited my return home. Dad had managed to arrange Mum's flight to Karachi. Margot and I were now very happy and very relieved. She had been with us for almost ten very difficult months. I had realised that Margot had had a very trying time for many reasons during my hospital incarceration and I was glad that our friends gave her a great deal of support for which I was very thankful.

While in hospital, and as a result of my training in Manila, I soon became aware that the Territory's so-called Malaria Eradication Programme (MEP), as loudly proclaimed by Dr. Saave, was in fact a control programme. Consequently, I continually advised Dr. Scragg that this was the case and so upset Dr. Saave. Dr. Scragg disliked Dr. Saave and was delighted to have this additional weapon to use against him. As a result of these events,

Dr. Saave was moved "sideways" to write the history of the TPNG Health Service, while I was placed in charge of the MEP.

There were some interesting visitors to the MEP Head Office, one of the most interesting being Dr. Arnaldo Gabaldon, Director of the Venezuelan MEP and a world authority on malaria eradication; he died in 1992. Also working in the MEP was a Latvian New Australian doctor called Vincent Zigas. It was widely believed within the Health Department that he had been the first to identify Kuru (originally thought to be a slow virus, but now known to be a "prion", affecting the central nervous system and which was transmitted through eating infected brains in ritual cannibalism) in the New Guinea Highlands, but that he had been bulldozed aside by Dr. Carleton Gadjusek from the National Institute of Health, Bethesda, Maryland, USA. I cannot vouch for the veracity of this. Tony Sweeney, a graduate entomologist, and Geoff Geyer worked for the MEP but were based in Rabaul and so I only made contact with them occasionally. They were both good workers and excellent social companions. Later, Tony and I would become linked even closer.

Towards the end of my stay in hospital, the Director General of Medical Services, Royal Australian Army Medical Corps, (RAAMC), Major-General Colin Gurner, flew up from Canberra to visit me while I was still encased in plaster. Much to my surprise, he asked me if I would like to command and re-establish the 1 Malaria Research Unit, which had been disbanded at the end of the Second World War. So, without much ado, I accepted the post. Once I had been discharged from hospital, I had to start moving as I had a lot still to do for the MEP, in addition to enrolling in the RAAMC. To enrol, I visited Murray Barracks in Port Moresby and took the oath of allegiance to the Queen, before signing on. I signed on with the substantive rank of Captain, but was acting Major; however, it was not too long before I was confirmed as a substantive Major. I was one of the few soldiers in the Australian Army at that time with a Papua New Guinea regimental number, 840020.

Before leaving Scotland, I had introduced Margot to an octogenarian lady friend called Daisy Stewart who, many decades before, had been in Jamaica where she had, among other things, trained for her "Wood Badge" in the Cub/Scouting movement and for which she had maintained a hand-written diary of the training. When she learned that we were about to depart for TPNG, she gave Margot her diary and also implanted the notion that Margot may like to follow the same path. Well, Margot found that she did have some spare time and eventually decided to look into the Cubs set-up in Port Moresby and, quite soon, she joined up and went off to do her own Wood Badge course locally. We were both very pleased when she was awarded her "toggle" for her scarf and was put in charge of a newly formed troop of cubs, the troop being designated the 1st. Hohola Troop. She enjoyed this activity and was soon immersed in it. The highlight of the Scouting / Cub movement was the visit of Lord MacLean, from Duart Castle, Mull, who was then the Chief Scout for the British Commonwealth. A gathering was held for him and all the troops were drawn up. When he was told that there was a Scottish Cub leader present, he came over to Margot and asked her where she came from and, when she replied "Arran", he said, "I suppose you can call yourself a Scot", for he was a highlander. Margot was quite hurt by this snub and later had the chance to meet Lady MacLean to whom she told this story. She did not seem to be unduly surprised and as a sop, invited Margot to visit her in Duart Castle when she was next back home, but Margot never did.

In May 1969, Professor Black, who was from the Sydney University School of Tropical Medicine and Hygiene and the malaria advisor to both the TPNG MEP and the Royal Australian Army, and I were jointly responsible for organising the 4th. Inter-Territorial Malaria conference at Kundiawa, in the Highlands. This meeting brought representatives from TPNG, Indonesia, the British Solomon Islands Protectorate (BSIP), Australia and WHO (represented by Dr. van Dijk, my former teacher in Manila). At this meeting, I also met Dr. Gordon Avery, the chief government malariologist for the BSIP; our paths were also to cross again in the not too distant future.

Although we had had our trials in TPNG, Margot and I had enjoyed our almost six years in this wonderful country. Some of our most lasting and vivid impressions were gained at the Mt. Hagen and Goroka shows, which alternated annually one with the other. They were great social occasions for the local people, and, for overseas people it was indescribably brilliant and vibrant—a truly wonderful spectacle which we were privileged to witness on two or three occasions. I remember two vignettes. The first was of a small group of widows daubed in mud and very scantily dressed, sitting against a hut, each widow with the withered hand of her dead husband hung from her neck by a thin piece of vine. The second was of Margot, in bright light weight dress and large hat, being approached by a short line of tribesmen in traditional dress, rhythmically advancing, chanting and thrusting their spears at her; fortunately, it was all part of the act.

Still, we had to move on and so it was with mixed feelings that we left our flat in Gordon Estate (with its wonderful garden, which was awarded first prize a year later) and our many friends in TPNG on 26 Sep 19.

Chapter Fifteen

Australia and the Army, 1969-1973

We flew down to Sydney where we were met by an Army liaison officer who took the four of us to a hotel in King's Cross, just behind the square. King's Cross was, and still is, the tourist and red light area of Sydney. We were allocated quite a large room although it was a bit of a struggle settling in as we also had a fair amount of luggage.

These were exciting times for two reasons. The first being the Vietnam War. King's Cross was particularly busy due to the influx of US troops on R & R (rest and recreation). Our hotel was particularly popular with the local "ladies" as they were kept very busy entertaining their clients from the Cross. It has to be said that we never had any cause for complaint the whole time we were in the hotel although we were visited on the odd occasion by women asking to borrow condiments and sewing equipment. I believe that they were probably spying on us to see if Margot was similarly employed.

The second reason was the "Poseidon Mining Affair". Just before our arrival in Sydney, the Poseidon shares had been floated on the Stock Market and were available for 20 cents each. Everyone appeared to be buying them and soon the share values began to rise, being pushed up by speculators on the London exchange. We had brought $14 000 down from TPNG with the intention of putting a deposit on a house. The hotel owners kept advising us to buy shares but after long and serious consideration, we eventually decided not to do so. However, fuelled by continued London speculation, the shares eventually rose to $2.70 each relatively quickly. As the saying goes, nothing ventured nothing gained.

Before leaving TPNG, we had promised Mike, our house servant, that we would give him a fortnight's holiday in Sydney. Euan, Michèle and I picked him up at the airport and drove back to the hotel. There was no room for him at our hotel, so we booked him into one nearby, the arrangement being that he would walk round to us every morning to spend the day with us. It was a very interesting and enjoyable break for all of us as we took Mike around the town, which was equally unknown to us. There were a number of things which surprised him. He found it strange to see white men labouring and working on the roads as he had only seen his own people doing so previously. The large stores attracted Mike, not so much for the merchandise as for the escalators, which he never tired using. The biggest surprise he encountered was seeing lions when we visited Taronga Park Zoo for the first time; his comment was, "Mi likim bigpela pussycat". The activity he most enjoyed, however, was being swung round rapidly on an arm of the "Octopus" at Luna Park. There was one experience he did not enjoy during his visit, although it was repeated twice daily on leaving and returning to his hotel each day, and this was being accosted and propositioned by prostitutes. Mike would unfailingly comment, "Emi badpela missis". After his holiday in Sydney, we lost all contact with him. We had all enjoyed his visit.

It wasn't long before I started work at Sydney University, working in Professor Black's Department of Tropical Medicine, at the School of Tropical Medicine and Hygiene, even although I was in the RAAMC. My Unit, 1 Malaria Research Unit, (MRU), had been allocated a large room. Gradually, the room was filled with furniture and scientific equipment which had been ordered. However, I still had no staff and so I was delighted to learn that Tony Sweeney was coming down from TPNG to become the entomologist, with the rank of Captain. When Tony arrived, we were given another small room just along the corridor which we proceeded to convert into an insectary for the Anopheles colonies which we wished to establish. If I remember correctly, we obtained our first mosquito eggs from TPNG, carefully wrapped in moist blotting paper, and it wasn't long before the insectary was literally buzzing. It had also to be kept at a constant temperature and high humidity. In the early days, before the establishment of rodent colonies, Tony would feed the female mosquitoes, through gauze on the top of waxed paper cups, on his bare arms or abdomen. I thought it was above and beyond the call of duty but it didn't seem to bother him. He also carried out the forced mating of mosquitoes. To do this, he would lightly anaesthetise a male mosquito, place it on its back and chop off its head. Then, sucking up a female mosquito on the end of a fine pipette, he would place their genitalia together in the correct position permitting fertilisation, before returning the female to a cage. There were dozens of mosquitoes in each cage, at the corner of which was a petri dish, a shallow flat-bottomed glass dish, lined with a sheet of damp blotting paper upon which the mosquitoes laid their eggs. The blotting paper was then removed and the eggs were dusted into waxed paper cups containing water on which the eggs matured to the larval (wriggler) stage, the cups then being laid out on trays. From this stage on, the wrigglers were well fed with finely ground fish food before, after a few days, they were returned to the cages still in their cups but now at the pupal, non-feeding stage. After about 48 hours, the adult mosquito would emerge from the pupal skin which was left floating on the water.

It was decided that the MRU should be staffed by two or three science graduates who were doing their National Service. And so, we received a steady supply of these young men who were very pleased to be working outside the military environment and once again in a scientific discipline. On their arrival, they knew little or nothing about malaria or malaria research, so Tony and I had to train them first; this was beneficial for all concerned. One of the unit's first tasks was to establish rodent colonies, both rats and mice, to enable us to feed the mosquitoes and to establish drug-resistant strains of malaria parasites; in addition, we tried to establish our own pure-lines of mice and rats. Eventually we also obtained two white rabbits which were used solely to feed the mosquitoes, their abdomens being shaved. As our accommodation was very cramped, the rodents were kept in cages on top of and under benches lining the walls of our room; it was therefore essential that their cages be kept as clean as possible as the smell would otherwise soon overpower us. It was essential that we had our own malaria parasites and so it was arranged that the MRU would be sent Plasmodium berghei berghei and Plasmodium berghei yoeli by Professor Yoeli from the USA by air-freight in a vacuum flask packed in dry-ice. The rodent parasites arrived safely and were slowly brought to room temperature before being injected into the rats and mice. Over time, by gradually dosing the infected rodents with increasing concentrations of anti-malarial drugs, we were able to build up drug resistant strains of malaria parasites.

As the MRU was located within the grounds of the University of Sydney, I had been told by General Gurner to ensure that the unit members wore civilian clothes at all times so as not to draw undue attention to a military presence within the anti-war campus, as there was very considerable national unrest over Australia's participation in the Vietnam war. However, it was soon common knowledge that there was indeed an army unit within the campus and it wasn't long before we had a student deputation asking if we were involved in biological warfare. After showing the deputation around the unit and pointing out that we were involved in malaria research only, they left us in peace.

Army administration was not the unit's strong point and, as a consequence Sergeant David Cowdrey was appointed to the MRU. There wasn't really enough administration work for him to do and so it wasn't too long before he too was involved in our routine work, which he thoroughly enjoyed. David ordered our supplies from Victoria Barracks, which had then to be collected on a regular basis by two members of the unit. Their arrival at the barracks always brought howls of anguish from the regular soldiers and RSMs when they saw these long-haired, jean-clad apparitions collecting stores. Almost invariably, they were marched off for a regimental haircut. Occasionally, I would receive 'phone calls objecting to their non-military appearance; it always gave me great pleasure to inform them that we had approval to dress as civilians at all times.

Australia was heavily involved in the Vietnam War. To advise all Australian Armed Forces engaged in the conflict, the Armed Forces Malaria Advisory Board was established under the chairmanship of General Gurner. The Board's members included Professor Black, Air-Vice Marshall Trudinger, Dr. Doherty of the Queensland Institute of Medical Research and me, the meetings being convened at the Department of Tropical Medicine and Hygiene. Due to the advice formally issued by the Board, the Australian troops had a far better record of malaria prophylaxis than did their American counterparts. This was due to two main reasons—very strict supervision during the administration of the drugs and the use of a good, effective combination of two anti-malarial drugs.

I was also involved in post-graduate medical education, occasionally assisting Professor Black with his lectures on malaria and malaria control. On one occasion, Associate Professor Charles Campbell invited me to give a lecture to medical students at St. Vincent's Hospital in Sydney. At the start of the lecture, when the Professor introduced me as Major Saint-Yves of the RAAMC Malaria Research Unit, there were loud jeers and boos from the students. Eventually the noise subsided and I started to speak. I started my presentation by saying, "I don't mind you booing me at the start of my lecture but I would certainly be hurt if you considered my presentation so bad that you booed me at the end of it." I am pleased to say that they clapped me loudly at the end of my talk.

Soon after arriving in Sydney, we managed to find ourselves a nice, compact, simple, one-level house at 31 Cook Street, in the northern suburb of Forestville. Margot just had to be busy now that I was working and the children were at school. Her first job was as a salesperson for a costume jewellery company called Marcello. With her own car, a VW station wagon, she was able to travel all over the Sydney area. She proved to be an excellent salesperson as she likes people; indeed, it was her downfall, as she developed a guilty conscience selling jewellery a second time round to ladies who hadn't even sold the original purchase. She felt this was immoral and so resigned.

She had always been interested in Family Planning, so her next post was as a clinic nurse at the Glebe clinic of the Family Planning Association of Australia (FPAA). Margot thoroughly enjoyed this job and became heavily involved in the politics of it as family planning was still not widely available in 1970; she even went on street marches which was very brave of her as it was a new departure. She was also heavily involved politically, having joined the Labor Party; again, she participated in street protests against the Vietnam War, (luckily escaping arrest), and actively campaigned successfully for the Labor party against the Liberal government at election time. The Labor Party won handsomely and the new government made Family Planning respectable, injected a great deal of financial support into it, and took immediate steps to pull Australian troops out of Vietnam. It was all a bit tricky for me as I was in the Army, although I did not support the involvement in Vietnam, neither did Tony Sweeney. We used to joke that we were the only two soldiers in the army without a medal between us.

At the week-ends we made a point of doing something interesting for Euan and Michèle. Fortunately, we lived quite close to Kuringai Chase and many times we would take a walk through the Bush. The Chase was also the home of "Skippy, the Bush Kangaroo", the star of the TV series. Skippy was a female, wore a collar and lived in a special, small enclosure in which was her "home", a small kennel. The children loved going there as they not only saw Skippy but were also able to hand-feed the other tame kangaroos, rabbits and other animals.

Because the MRU now had established rodent and mosquito colonies, I took my turn with the other members of the unit to go into the unit over the week-ends to feed and water the animals and check the mosquitoes. To compensate for this overtime, a Tuesday afternoon was exchanged. During these half-days, I would meet Margot and we would drive to Palm Beach, Watson's Bay or Whale Beach for lunch.

Early in 1970, Aunt Mary and Uncle John came to Australia on holiday and resided with us for a while. It was lovely to see them again. They had one or two friends in New South Wales so they travelled around, using our house as a base. One afternoon, we all went to Palm Beach, north of Sydney. The four adults were sitting on the rocks talking and keeping a casual eye on Euan and Michèle playing in the shallows. Suddenly, I noticed that they had been swept away from the shallows and were being washed out to sea. With a startled cry, I jumped to my feet and, closely followed by Margot, ran across the sands, jumped into the sea and lunged towards Euan and Michèle who were gradually being sucked further and further away from the shoreline; luck was with us and between the two of us, we safely brought them back to the beach. It had been a very close call. Aunt and Uncle thoroughly enjoyed their visit and we enjoyed having them.

We obtained a dog shortly after we had settled into our new home. Tanya was her name and she was a lovely, large Rhodesian Ridgeback/Labrador cross. Euan and Michèle loved her and she, in turn, was great with them. On the first Guy Fawkes Day we had her, we left her out in the garden while we took Euan and Michèle to a supervised fireworks display at the Brookvale Showground. When we returned home, we found Tanya extremely agitated, and because of the noise and flashing lights from the fireworks, she had clawed a hole in our back door in desperation as she had tried to find us inside the house. Tanya loved to sit in our front garden, which was lawn to the road.

One Saturday afternoon, as we were entertaining Tony and Julie Hillman, we heard a screech of brakes and a yelp; shortly after, Tanya dragged herself through the front door into the house. She brought with her an incredibly sickening smell of "fear"; we have never smelt it again and nor do we ever wish to. We could see that she had been badly injured, so I carefully picked her up and took her to the Vet. It was soon discovered that she had suffered a crushed pelvis and the only thing to be done was to have her destroyed. We were all very, very sad about it, including the driver of the car who had swerved to avoid an untrained Alsatian (which had chased after his car) and, in so doing, had driven into our garden and hit Tanya. Shades of "Whisky"!

Just before Easter, 1970, the MRU was informed that a Lieutenant Colonel Craig Canfield, Deputy Director of the Malaria Research Unit at the Walter Read Army Institute of Research, (WRAIR), Washington DC, had arrived to see Professor Black and me. Easter in Australia was a living death, with everything closed down for days. However, I picked up Colonel Canfield from Mascot airport and booked him into his hotel, close to the University, and then drove him out to see Professor Black at his home in Hunter's Hill. We talked about the future plans for the MRU for over an hour before leaving for lunch. Professor Black then said to me quietly that I should entertain him over Easter, so I took him home to meet Margot. The three of us hit it off immediately and we had a really great time. One of the highlights for Craig was a lunch we had at the "Coachman", a smart restaurant set in a convict-built, former coaching-house. Craig was quite fascinated by it because he had never seen so many "sugar-daddies" with their dolly-birds in the same place at the same time. As a result of his successful visit, it was decided that I should visit WRAIR later in the year.

My trip to WRAIR was quickly arranged for June and, when the time came for me to leave, I bought the full quota of six bottles of Johnny Walker Black Label whisky at the airport. It proved to be a very valuable investment. I was invited to stay with Craig and his lovely wife, Bea, at their home in Silver Springs, Maryland. On my first day at WRAIR, I met the Director of the unit, Colonel Gochenour, and I gave him two bottles of whisky as a present, while Craig received another two. Well that did the trick for Colonel Gochenour said to me that he would arrange another visit for me, probably in 1972. While at WRAIR, I learned about the new anti-malarial drugs being developed and the running of mosquito colonies. My time there passed very quickly. While in Washington, Margot sent me Euan's first letter. I also received an invitation to attend the American Medical Association's Annual Meeting, which I did and which I found very stimulating.

Returning home, I was soon pitched in to preparing my paper for the 42nd. Congress of the Australian New Zealand Association for the Advancement of Science (ANZAAS) which was to be held in Port Moresby from the 17-21 August. It was nice to return to TPNG and once again meet up with some former colleagues. I gave a paper on "The methodology of malaria eradication". It was a successful and enjoyable meeting.

Early in 1971 reports were beginning to reach Professor Black that there was a possible outbreak of chloroquine-resistant Plasmodium falciparum malaria, centred on Dogura in the Milne Bay District of TPNG. It was decided that I should go to investigate it and so I flew up to Port Moresby and then down to Samarai, where I and two local malaria technicians boarded a fast Royal Australian Navy patrol boat. It was a beautiful trip on a perfectly calm, sunlit sea, zooming up the east coast of Papua at 20 knots/hour, close inshore. Arriving at Dogura station, I discovered that it was an Anglican Mission run by nursing sisters and lay teachers. However, it proved to be a very interesting place as I quickly discovered that many of the teachers were young English women who had volunteered their services to the VSO, Voluntary Service Overseas. I was given a room to myself in a large native material building, very cool and comfortable. With local help freely given, the three of us soon set about carrying out a base-line survey, then administering chloroquine under strict supervision at a given dose for a period of three consecutive days, after which the recipients were followed up with daily blood slides which were then stained and examined microscopically for the presence of malaria parasites, over a period of a few weeks. The results of my study were evaluated on my return to Sydney. No drug resistance was found at that time and I was able to publish the results. My spare time also passed very quickly as I struck up a friendship with Cilla Martenstyn, a VSO teacher. She was olive skinned, lovely, with waist length, straight, lustrous black hair, aged about 23. Like myself, she was an old colonial, Sri Lankan but of Dutch extraction. We had much in common and liked each other. We spent endless hours swimming, walking along the shore during the days and sitting on rocks under tropical skies looking out over the moon-lit Coral Sea at nights; it was very romantic but the friendship remained one of the mind alone. My time at Dogura passed very quickly. Before leaving, I invited Cilla to stay with us in January 1972 on her way back to London through Sydney.

1971 was also the year for the 5th. South-West Pacific Malaria Conference; this time it was to be held at Sydney University and I was left to organise most of it with help from the Professor and Peter Moodie, who was later to be the Professor's successor. Again, there were participants from most countries in the SW Pacific, including Dr. A. P. Ray, now the Regional WHO Malariologist based in Manila. Dr. Ray was a large, genial man who had been in charge of the largely successful Indian Malaria Eradication Programme. I liked him. I was pleased too that the Conference proved to be a success. In the evenings, after the days' meetings, we would return to Dr. Ray's hotel room for a few stiff whiskies as he too enjoyed Scotland's national beverage. Interestingly, Professor Black was tea-total. To end up the Conference, a Dinner was held in the Holme and Sutherland Room at Sydney University on 1st. October.

About this time, the Army decided that I needed some military training and I was asked to report to the Medical Training Centre at Healesville, in the Victorian hills. It was a lovely setting. Here I met other RAAMC officers coming in for refresher courses and, over the course of about three weeks, we were given a brief outline of military disciplines. However, during our stints at marching, we (about a dozen medical officers) did manage to make the drill instructors' lives difficult by deliberately marching out of step most times. This was also the first time that I had worn my army uniform. Following the training, my report stated that I was academically sound but militarily unsound—a perfect result as far as I was concerned. At the end of this period, between 24-29 October, 1971, the Director General Army Medical Services Exercise was held. At this, I gave a lecture on the role of the MRU within the RAAMC. I also met Colonel Keith Fleming briefly, already famous for raising doubts about the use of "Agent Orange" in Vietnam. Our paths were to cross later.

In November 1971, the West Pakistan/East Pakistan/Indian War had just begun. During this period, Dad and Mum (she had joined Dad on leaving TPNG) were on the "Mustali", a Karachi-registered merchant ship, sailing between its home port and the ports of the then East Pakistan. Margot and I had been writing to them over a few months telling them to return home as the situation there was rapidly deteriorating. However, they kept replying that we were only listening to Western propaganda and that everything was fine. I became quite unhappy when we hadn't heard from them for quite a while and so I asked the Australian government, through the Army, to find out what was happening to them. We received word through the diplomatic service that they were fine. And then, about two weeks later, we received word that my Father had been killed and that my Mother, although wounded, was alive. Margot broke the news to me in our back garden one sunny afternoon in mid December, on my return from work.

It was a while before we heard the full story. On the 9th. December, Mum and Dad, the Chief Officer and a few of the crew were just about to go down the gangway when they were strafed by an Indian Air Force 'plane. The Chief Officer and the crew members were killed outright, while Dad received very severe wounds to the right side of his chest, and Mum some shrapnel wounds to the scalp. Mum and Dad were brought under the care of Father Tomaselli, of the Roman Catholic Mission at Chalna. Unfortunately, there was no medical assistance available and medicines were non-existent. Gradually, Dad's condition worsened and apparently he never complained once about his obvious agony. Only towards the end of his life did he speak to Mum saying, "Rena, turn me towards the window as the light is getting dim." This was in mid-afternoon. He then died on 10 Dec 1971, eighteen hours after being fatally wounded. He was buried shortly after by Father Tomaselli in the mission grounds. My Mother was completely distraught, but somehow or other her predicament came to the notice of Mr. Ian Brodie, a reporter with the Daily Express based in Calcutta, who then took her under his wing after three weeks sheltering in the Catholic Mission. More than a week after the war had ended, she was rescued by Indian officials who had come to the village. The British Embassy in Calcutta, on hearing of her plight, did almost nothing to render her assistance but instead impounded her passport and told her that it would be returned when she had repaid the £190 air fare from Calcutta provided by the High Commission. In the interim, between being found at Chalna and returning home to Scotland, she was apparently cared for by the captain of a Danish merchant ship; for this act, we were both eternally grateful. On hearing of this sorry tale of British consular cruelty, I wrote to the Home Office but received the usual bland excuses in reply. In the meantime, Mr. Brodie had written one or two articles about her predicament in the Scottish Daily Express, which also published a leader. Mum was met at Glasgow airport by Aunt Mary and Uncle John and then taken down to Sheffield where they were living at the time. Mum still had the Cranworth Street flat which she had rented out to doctors and nurses, but she returned to find that it had been trashed. So she set about selling it and eventually went to stay with Aunt Eva, her Mother's younger sister, in Ralston, Glasgow, for a considerable period.

Back at Sydney University, Professor Black brought me into his "inner circle" of lunch-time colleagues, who met in his office during the working week. This select band included Charlie Campbell, Godfrey Scott (working on Leprosy in TPNG), Russ Hausfeld (an anthropologist / sociologist working in Aboriginal Health), and Peter Moodie (working in malaria and Aboriginal Health). Although I liked most of them individually, I was never comfortable with them as a group. I never failed to be amazed at the banality of their conversation and consequently only joined them once or twice a week for our luncheon pies and sandwiches.

Colonel Gochenour of WRAIR was true to his word and, before his retirement, arranged for me to visit malaria research units in the USA for two months, starting on 3 July 1972. A month before Margot and I were due to leave, Margot's Mum came out to Australia to look after Euan and Michèle while we were away. On the day of her arrival, we went to collect her from Mascot airport. Walking around awaiting her arrival, Margot said to me, "I know that man there walking towards us", pointing to a red-haired, stockily built figure. I looked and was pleased to recognise Alasdair Cochran, who had been my SHO in the Casualty Department of the Western Infirmary. He was now in the act of transferring from an international flight to one for Brisbane, where he was to give a lecture on malignant melanoma to an international medical gathering. We gave him our address and, on his was back to Glasgow, he spent a pleasant afternoon with us at Cook Street. He is now a Professor of Pathology at the University of California, apparently working full-time on malignant melanoma.

Margot, through her FPAA work, applied for a Bogue Fellowship on "Communication in Family Planning" at the University of Chicago. The course was to last approximately three months. Much to her surprise and delight, she was selected, the course running at much the same time as my intended study trip; she left for the USA a little before I did. When she enrolled to do the course, Professor Bogue was surprised to find that she (a) wasn't in a religious order, as he had assumed because of her professional "sister" title and (b) wasn't Australian but Scottish. Nevertheless, she was readily accepted, enjoyed the course and the company of her international class-mates. To top it all, at the end of the course, she was one of only three to be awarded an "A" grade.

A week or two later, I arrived at WRAIR to be told that I was to visit Karl Rieckmann at Joliet Penitentiary, not far from Chicago. I had known Karl vaguely from his days in TPNG. I was delighted at the opportunity to see and work with him as his research unit was now pre-eminent. Before going to join him, I spoke to Craig Canfield, who was now running the malaria programme at WRAIR, telling him that Margot was in Chicago and that we were thinking of returning to Sydney via Glasgow. He said that he would try to arrange something for us but then I forgot all about it. Off I went to Joliet where, every time I entered the complex, I was scrutinised from the guard towers, searched at the entrance house, signed in and then searched again before actually being allowed to enter the prison proper. This procedure was followed in reverse on leaving.

On my first day, I was introduced to the prison Governor by Karl. The malaria unit was within the hospital section of the prison and trusted prisoners "volunteered" for malaria service, receiving a reduction in their prison sentence as a reward. All the laboratory technicians were inmates, mainly "lifers", but trusted. It was an interesting experience. Karl took me through the research papers—how they screened the volunteers before using them in the trials, the various drugs being tested and the regimens being followed, the mosquito biting schedules and the blood testing screens. I was also interested in Karl's *in vitro* technique for testing drug-resistant Plasmodium falciparum parasites. On one or two week-ends, Margot joined me and I was able to introduce Margot to Karl and his wife, Rosemary, who then looked after her when I wasn't around.

While in Chicago, Margot and I would walk through the park at night, and used the underground. When we told this to the local inhabitants, they were aghast as both places were very unsafe. In fact, while Margot was there, another girl student was stabbed to death in the University grounds during broad daylight. One evening, after our stroll through the park, we went into a cafe. It was just like a scene from an old movie, with subdued lighting and dark-rain-coated men wearing pulled down hats perched on high stools, smoking and drinking at a long wooden bar.

One week-end, while still based in Chicago, Margot and I went to New York where we stayed at the Hilton, overlooking the famous piers. As I was the guest of the US Army Medical Corps, we were given greatly reduced rates. We didn't particularly like New York city centre as it was very dirty and run-down, with broken pavements and pot-holed streets, with the famed Broadway the most sleazy. However, we did visit the United Nations building and, one evening, had an amusing dinner at our hotel restaurant which was situated at the top of the building. The meal was duly ordered and with it a bottle of champagne. The wine waiter arrived with the bottle immersed in a full ice-bucket, placed on a small trolley. He then proceeded to take a champagne glass and fill it with ice, at which stage I said to him that we didn't wish to have champagne drowned in ice. With absolute disdain, he looked at Margot and I and said, "Sir, I am only chilling the glasses", after which he emptied out the ice, opened the bottle and poured us out the champagne. When he had left, Margot and I burst out laughing. It was a good dinner, too good as we were both happy.

Margot stayed on at the University for a short while to complete the course. In the meantime, I moved on to my next assignment in Baltimore, where I joined Professor David Clyde. He insisted that I should stay with him and so I had the chance to meet his wife and two lovely daughters. David was a Scot who had been evacuated during the war from Clydeside to Canada where he had remained and proceeded to qualify in medicine. His malaria research unit was in Baltimore Penitentiary. I arrived there one week after prisoners had rioted, severely damaging the buildings by fire. Again, we were working with "volunteers" in the hospital section of the prison, which was about the only part not damaged. David was an excellent teacher and host; the time passed very quickly. At home, David and his wife and daughters were very welcoming

Back at work, Craig had arranged the next part of my trip to visit research units at Kansas City (under Dr. John Arnold at the State penitentiary), and Atlanta (under Dr. Pete Contacos at the Federal penitentiary). At Atlanta, I stayed with Pete Contacos where I was able to meet his mother. He was a fun person to be with and, on one of our free evenings, he took me to the Atlanta Bunny Club where he bought me a Bunny Club tankard. We also visited Stone Mountain and viewed the carved faces of Confederate heroes on the side of the mountain. At the Centre for Disease Control, I was privileged to meet Dr. Bill Collins and Dr. Cochran. Bill gave me a newly published book on malaria which they all duly signed for me. As an extra, a visit had been arranged for me to fly on to Miami. At Atlanta airport, I missed my scheduled air flight. This was fortunate on two counts—first, because I was introduced to Professor P.C. Garnham who was en route to Athens, Georgia, to deliver a lecture and secondly, because my original flight had had an attempted highjack to Cuba; however, my own flight passed uneventfully. In Miami, I spent two fruitful days with Dr. Raine at his unit, which was not in a penal institute; he filled in a lot of the blanks with regard to mosquito usage and breeding. Miami, in the tourist areas, was very clean and "pretty" in an artificial man-made manner but was still impressive. From Miami, I returned to Washington DC and Margot.

There was more good news to come. On my return, Craig informed me that he had managed to arrange for me to visit the army malaria research unit in Bangkok and it would thus be possible for Margot and me to go back to Sydney via Glasgow, London, Bangkok and Hong Kong on commercial flights BUT it would cost us. I waited expectantly. Craig said it would cost $20, not each but for both of us. Margot and I could hardly believe it. So it was with great sadness that we said cheerio to Craig and Bea at Dulles airport as we boarded the 'plane for London en route to Glasgow.

Our stay at home this time was short. It was basically to see how Mum was coping with her situation and to visit Margot's parents in Saltcoats. Fortunately, her parents were well. Mum, on the other hand, was now living with Aunt Mary and Uncle John in Sheffield. She was emotionally disturbed and was receiving drug therapy for her depression, the drugs not mixing too well with the excessive amounts of alcohol which she was now consuming. It was obvious that she could not stay with Aunt and Uncle for much longer, so I arranged for her to move back to Aunt Eva in Ralston where she appeared to be happiest. That visit to my mother was the most emotionally demanding episode in my life; it left me totally drained in all respects, so much so that when I tried to drive back to Glasgow I could not do so and Margot had to complete the journey for me.

We were glad to fly on to Bangkok where we were met by Colonel Winter who was in charge of the malaria unit. Our stay was only for 24 hours. He told us that we had arrived on public holidays and consequently everything was closed down. However, while Margot remained in the beautiful hotel adorned with an artificial lake at its entrance, Colonel Winter quickly showed me around the unit which was involved in primate malaria research. All I can remember seeing were a few caged primates which appeared to be young orang-utans. Leaving the unit, I returned to collect Margot as we had decided to try to contact an ex TPNG friend, a former Czech medical assistant called Andrew Hoffman. When we showed his address to the taxi driver, he asked us if we really wished to go there as it was in one of the worst areas in the city. Arriving in the area, he was unable to find the "street" as it was really an area filled with alleys. However, luck was with us as we saw a police box at an alley junction. We asked the policeman for his help and, fortunately, it turned out that the address was almost next door. Andrew was delighted to see us. He lived in one large room which had been given to him by a Thai lady doctor but there were no sexual conditions attached as Andrew was a homosexual. After greetings, he took us round the real Bangkok, the slums and reeking streets filled with garbage, before returning us to our fancy hotel. We never saw Andrew again. During the war, he had been forced to join the Russian army as a 16 year old and had fought against the Germans. This seemed almost unbelievable as he was a slight, small and very gentle man.

We didn't particularly like Bangkok; there was too much of a contrast between the rich and the poor. It was also congested and dirty. We were more than happy to leave for Hong Kong. Hong Kong, although very congested, was quite a contrast for us even as tourists. All the usual tourist attractions were very interesting—the floating restaurants (on one of which we ate our first Peking duck), a visit to Aberdeen (totally unlike its namesake in Scotland), Victoria Peak and the panoramic view of the city below, a trip to the Han walled city (at which I took an interesting photo of Margot standing beside an elderly Han lady, dressed in black and wearing a traditional, broad-brimmed straw hat), and on to Kowloon and the New Territories. It was a short but memorable stay.

From Hong Kong, we flew on to Djakarta on a Pan-Am flight. This was quite eventful as our pilot suffered a heart attack while he was attempting to land the 'plane. Fortunately, the co-pilot coped admirably. We, the passengers, noted that it had been an unusually bumpy landing but thought no more about it until his death was announced by the Chief Steward after we had landed and his body had been removed from the 'plane. As a consequence, we were detained on the 'plane for quite a long time as we were now stranded and the airline was forced to find us emergency accommodation. Eventually, we disembarked and were transported to our respective hotels, to which we were restricted. In the meantime, the airline had to arrange for an emergency pilot to be flown out from Hong Kong; this meant that we would be detained in Djakarta for about 24 hours. Eventually, the pilot arrived and the passengers once again boarded buses for the airport where there was another delay before being permitted to board the aircraft.

Back in Sydney, we were very pleased to see our children and Margot's Mum; they were all well. Shortly after, we saw Grandma Stewart off on the 'plane back home. She had thoroughly enjoyed herself.

On her return to work, Margot's new found expertise was put to immediate use as she was made the FPAA Educator for New South Wales. At much the same time, we discussed whether or not Margot should continue using oral contraceptives; we decided that she should not and, as a consequence, I had a vasectomy done in Margot's former clinic during my lunch break, returning to work after it. It was a decision we never regretted.

I had always been interested in the "Saint-Yves" genealogy but had never really pursued it until I read a letter from a from a Colonel Richardson from San Diego, printed in Time magazine in 1971, in which he discussed France's "Ivo de Chartres" and "Saint-Yves of Brittany", who was the patron saint of lawyers and was renowned for his defence of the poor. I wrote to the colonel and a short correspondence followed which was of some help to me. Ever since, I have pursued the family tree with varying degrees of earnestness.

Through Margot and me having had a vasectomy, the FPAA put our names forward as participants in a Channel Ten, "Germaine Greer Special" TV programme on Sunday, 1 April 1973; we were accepted as the topic under discussion was supposedly "Family Planning", with special reference to vasectomies. Before going to the studio to record the programme, I had told my mates in the MRU that should I actually speak during the discussion, I would waggle my ears as I did so (an atavistic trait I have). Margot and I seated ourselves towards the back of the auditorium, dressed professionally and soberly; most of the other invited participants appeared to be rather bohemian in attire. As the programme proceeded, and Germaine moved the discussion in the desired direction, it became more and more obvious that most of the participants were trendy lefties, single mothers and women liberationists. Vasectomies were scarcely mentioned and I eventually managed to say a very few brief words about care for the elderly, not forgetting to waggle my ears at the same time. Germaine Greer's attire for the programme was rather tawdry; she had on a black skirt which was too tight for her and which was held up by a safety pin across the zip fastener at the back. The programme was broadcast and my friends noted the flapping ears. Tony made the comment that we looked so "establishment" although he thought that we would probably be the most radical of all those attending. A few months later, our friends in Western Australia told us that they had also seen the programme.

Life was not all work for us in Sydney. We had met up with some of our friends from TPNG, such as the Bloch-Jorgensens, Smyths and had made new friends locally. There were frequent dinners and lunches at which we had plenty of laughs.

The Smyths had bought a small property north of Sydney to which we were frequently invited. One of the highlights of our stay at this time was the wedding of Julie Smyth to Tony Hillman, a Londoner; we attended as a complete family and had a very memorable day. They later moved to Sydney and so we were able to see them quite frequently.

Apart from our friends, we also joined the French's Forest Gourmand Club. This was supposedly a social/learning gathering at which we were introduced to fine wines; however, the numbers gradually fell away, until there was a hard core of about a dozen members, ourselves included, who were only really interested in having a good time. At a more private level, we made friends with an English couple who were in to "swinging" parties at which the male guests threw their car keys onto a table, and from which the female guests then made their choice of a companion for the evening by picking a set of car keys. Margot and I attended one of these parties but did not participate in the partner swopping, instead talking to our friend the hostess, who also did not participate although her husband did.

Back at work, it had been decided that the MRU should be moved to Ingleburn Barracks, Campbeltown, outside Sydney. The plans were put in motion but the move could not take place until we had a laboratory to work in, so it fell to me to design this new work place, ably assisted by Tony Sweeney who advised me about the insectary requirements. The laboratory was designed to include an animal house as we intended to carry out research using monkeys, in addition to using human volunteers. The building plans were passed and the laboratory was built but unfortunately I never saw the finished building as I resigned from the army before the move to Ingleburn took place. Tony, however, worked in it until he retired and, in 1996, I was told that plans were once again afoot to move the MRU to Queensland.

Following my visit to the USA, I wrote a lengthy report on my visit, in which I outlined the research procedures currently in vogue in malariology. It had been a very worthwhile trip. Regardless of this burst of activity within the unit, I had a feeling that research was not really going to progress very far due to lack of proper funding and to the fact that human volunteer experimentation had been practically stopped in the USA due to the danger from the recently discovered "Australia antigen", now better known as the Hepatitis B virus. Then it became known that Professor Black had recommended Dr. A.P. Ray to become head of the MRU after it had moved to Ingleburn. Dr. Ray was now the WHO Regional Malaria advisor based in Manila. He was a very nice and capable man but at that stage he was trying to obtain a retiral post in Australia and to eventually settle there with his wife and daughter. Professor Black was their "way-in". I did not take at all kindly to this as I knew more about malaria research at this stage than he did and besides, he was to be given the rank of colonel while I was to remain a major. When I asked Professor Black why he had taken this step, he said that he believed I lacked enough imagination for the post. I began looking for another job and, through the good offices of Dr. Ray I was appointed to the post of WHO Malaria Epidemiologist for the British Solomon Islands Protectorate, based in Honiara, Guadalcanal. Dr. Ray and his family duly arrived just before I resigned but he did not take up his post until I had left the unit. The unit moved to Ingleburn but in reality, it did not achieve very much in the research field. Professor Black continued with the practice of placing his former, retired WHO cronies in place, I believe, because Dr. Ray was apparently replaced by Dr. Gramisci. It wasn't, however, until Dr. Karl Rieckmann returned to Australia from Joliet to take charge of the unit that some modest progress was made. As to whether or not I had enough imagination to head the unit, we shall never know as I was not given the opportunity to prove it one way or the other. On my departure from the RAAMC, General Gurner wrote me a personal, hand-written note on 13 June 1973, in which he said," I'm not sure when you move but want to wish you every success in your new venture, and to thank you for your work and achievements for the RAAMC and the Australian Army. I hope you will not lose touch with the unit or the Corps."

During this unsettling period, I was approached by Professor Charles Kerr of the School of Public Health and Tropical Medicine at Sydney University and asked if I would consider accepting the post as Director of the Family Planning Association of Australia but I declined this generous offer as I was more interested in third world problems and tropical medicine.

Before leaving Forestville for Honiara, we received the school reports for Euan and Michèle. Euan's evaluations were:"(a) Reading—fluent and expressive (b) Oral and Written expression good (c) Spelling—very good (d) Numeracy—a good knowledge and able to use this effectively (e) Attitude to learning—interested and actively involved (f) Social adjustment—In class is helpful and cooperative. (g) Muscular control—very good but writing can be hurried. (h) Overall—Euan has a great love of dancing and is very keen on role playing. He provides enjoyment to all." Michèle's Kindergarten report was: "(a) Social adjustment—well adjusted and takes part in all activities; she is very reliable. (b) Oral Communication—communicates well and talks happily about all her experiences (c) Attitude to learning—good (d) Muscular control—good (e) General—she is a keen pupil and is doing very well. She can assume quite a deal of responsibility and manages it very well. Michèle is a very positive, confident, little girl, very sympathetic towards those who have problems. We shall miss her from the school."

And so, on 20 July 1973, I took up my new post with the World Health Organisation. We left Australia with mixed feelings. Margot and the children had enjoyed their time there whereas I felt that I had been let down in my job by Professor Black although he had been supportive in other ways. His action seemed to me to reinforce the impression I had gained when I was at Scotch College.

Chapter Sixteen

The British Solomon Islands Protectorate: The World Health Organisation, 1973-1976

We flew into Honiara from Brisbane on 20 July 1973, on a hot, muggy day where we were met and routinely processed through customs. The airport, basic in design, was situated about six miles out of town. As we drove into town, along the partially sealed road, we noted the verdant foliage, the coconut trees and the humidity; it was as we had anticipated it to be.

There had been no house allocated to us as we were non-governmental and so we found ourselves temporarily installed in the Honiara Hotel, run and owned by Tommy Chan, and within easy walking distance of my new office. It was an old fashioned hotel but quite comfortable and we were well looked after by Tommy and his staff. Euan and Michèle thoroughly enjoyed themselves as there was a nice swimming pool in the breeze-way recreational area, which was decorated with palms and thatch, in which they spent most of their time. In the evenings after work and our evening meal, we would sit as a family in the palm-fringed area by the pool, sipping our drinks while watching Gilbertese dancers and singers, in traditional costumes, doing their acts. It was all very peaceful and romantic. However, we couldn't stay there forever and so we started looking around for a house.

At this stage, we were fortunate to become friendly with a Fijian couple, Oscar and Fanny Dougherty, who were about to move out of a house in Kukum to a house nearer Oscar's work, and they asked us if we would be interested in it. Kukum was a native quarter and this house belonged to a local Chinese business man called Frank Leong. Needless to say, the expatriates advised us against taking the house. However, the house was spacious, louvred, sat on a hillside overlooking the local village, with native accommodation below and to the left of us, the house of Father Fox, the New Zealand Catholic priest on our right and that of Ashley and Roz Wickham behind us (Ashley was the local politician), but most important of all, the house had a swimming pool although there was little or no shade around it and the house. We decided to take the house and never regretted doing so. Frank Leong was a good landlord and became our friend.

It was interesting being based in Honiara; Guadalcanal was, after all, one of the most famous battlegrounds in the Pacific during World War II. One could not imagine how such intense battles were fought because the sites were now so peaceful and appeared so insignificant. Red Beach was along the Guadalcanal plains, where US forces landed, and towards the town there were fortified positions (the dugout HQ of the US commanding officer, was still on the approach road into Honiara) constantly reminding one of the struggle. However, the most amazing was the Mataniko River itself, no more than about 20 metres wide, and yet it separated the US and Japanese forces and cost many lives on both sides. The sea between Guadalcanal and the Ngella islands was called the "Sound" and, during the war, it was the route used by the Japanese navy moving south towards Australia; the hills of Guadalcanal provided good vantage points for the famed "Coastwatchers" during these troubled years.

We thoroughly enjoyed our Kukum house and we were very fortunate in our choice of housekeepers. They were a married couple, Saruwe (jet-black from the Gizo area of the Western District) and Matthew, from a village on the nearby Guadalcanal plains, with a son called Ambrose who was about the same age as Euan. Matthew was the housekeeper and ran the place very well. Gradually Margot introduced him into our ways and taught him European cooking. Saruwe and Matthew loved being with Euan and Michèle, and the children all got on well together. We were one big, happy family. Matthew also did the gardening; there was no grass, the ground being very stony, and no shade. So one of his first tasks was to put in palms and shade trees around the house and pool. It was amazing how quickly the new vegetation grew and, by the end of the year, the previously bare area was quite unrecognisable. Matthew and I drained the pool, cleaned and repainted it, before filling it with fresh water. I retained control of the chlorination but Matthew kept it clean and, every so often, we would empty and thoroughly clean it before refilling it once again. The pool was in constant use. Euan, Michèle and Ambrose, together with their local friends from the village were never out of it and, when it was quiet, Margot and I would have a dip. For parties, and at Christmas and Hogmanay, we would decorate the area around the pool and the verandah which overlooked it; it was an ideal party site and we used it and enjoyed it frequently. It was a very relaxed, simple and happy lifestyle.

Across the narrow, dirt road which ran down the hill to Kukum village, Father Fox had his house. He was a Kiwi, the parish priest and, apart from us, was the only white person in the area. A very amusing and natural man, the Solomon Islanders idolised him. When we became friendly, he would come across to us after work and join us for a few drinks on the verandah. He never spoke religion to us the whole time we were his neighbours. However, he had one dislike. Our area was plagued by dogs at night and every so often he would have pot-shots at them with his air rifle. His pet hate, however, was the dog belonging to our neighbours, Roz and Ashley Wickham; this dog appeared to be the leader of the pack. Ashley was the local MP and also our friend, so it was a little tricky. Nevertheless, we hit upon a very simple plan, I obtained a few capsules of phenobarbitone from the hospital pharmacy and, one night, I spiked two sausages each with a capsule. Late at night before going to bed, I laid these sausages out on the ground near the back steps of Ashley's house as I knew their dog would soon be put out for the night. Margot wasn't too happy with the idea but we went to sleep on it. Next morning at about 5 am., we were awakened by the sound of loud human voices coming from Ashley's garden. Margot suggested that I had better make an appearance, so when I did I was greeted by a small, agitated group of people, headed by Roz and Ashley, standing around the prostrate body of Ashley's dog. I was told that someone had tried to poison it and so I made the appropriate comments and offered to have a look at it. I knew it was still alive, so I suggested that they place it under their house (which was on stilts) to keep it out of the hot sun and to cover it with wet sheets all day, after which I returned home and prepared myself for work, which began at 7.30 am. Imagine my surprise when, on returning from work, I was greeted by an upright but unsteady, still dazed dog. The drug had slightly brain-damaged the dog to our advantage as, on recovery, it became a quiet, docile, well-behaved animal. Everyone was happy in the end.

Below and to the left of our house was the village and the "Purple Parrot", the one and only night-club in Honiara. Unfortunately, it was badly sited and badly constructed as a late night place of entertainment; it was little more than a private home and, as a result, was "open" with many louvred windows which did nothing to retain the noise inside the building. We and the villagers wondered what had hit us when it first opened its doors as the noise from it was horrendous, especially at 2 am. on warm, still, balmy nights. For a while, we put up with it in order to give it a chance to settle down, but it didn't. The villagers started to throw stones on its corrugated iron roof; however, as I didn't wish them to get into trouble, I spoke to them and organised a petition and obtained over one hundred signatures from them. The petition was duly presented to the Licensing Authority but was ignored. It transpired that a few of the local MPs were share-holders in the venture and, as a result the Purple Parrot remained open. However, all was not lost. The stone throwing was renewed with increased vigour night after night and gradually the clientele lessened until eventually the night-club was forced to close. Nevertheless, we were forced to endure too many sleepless nights because of it.

Honiara was not all strife. Matthew came from a village on the Guadalcanal Plains called Komukonga. Margot, Euan, Michèle and I were invited to spend one week-end at his village. We drove out early one Saturday morning and, on our arrival, we were greeted by the whole village and made to feel very much at home. Euan and Michèle disappeared almost immediately with the other children and we scarcely saw them thereafter. For lunch, they had prepared a traditional feast for us, all laid out on tables which were covered with banana leaves. There was fish, pork, beef, yams, taro, pit-pit, sweet potato, bananas, pawpaw, mangoes, water melons and many other fruits and vegetables—it truly was a feast. As can be imagined, it lasted all afternoon. It had obviously taken the villagers many hours to prepare and had cost them a great deal of money. We were very grateful and humbled by the experience. We were then taken along to where the children were playing. We found them thoroughly enjoying themselves in a deep river pool; overlooking the pool was a hillock from which they jumped into the pool, and when tired of that, they swung on vines from an overhanging tree before dropping into the pool. They were having a wonderful time. As evening approached, we decided that we would return home as we felt that we had already put the villagers to a great deal of effort and expense. However, we agreed to let Euan and Michèle stay the full week-end. When they returned home on Monday with Saruwe and Matthew, it was easy to see that they had had a great time.

In our area, Euan and Michèle were the only white children and, as a result, they would have been very unhappy if we had tried to restrict them to the house, and besides it was against our beliefs to segregate them. This caused some comment among the expatriates but we never had any cause to regret the decision as they were well cared for and were always made to feel very welcome. In return, the local children would swim in our pool and play in the garden; the noise was horrendously happy. An added bonus was that Euan and Michèle were able to converse a little in the Malaita language as most of their friends were from that island. These were happy days for all of us.

Shortly after our arrival, we learned that the British Government was about to bring in new citizenship regulations which clearly stated your citizenship and the right to be resident in the United Kingdom. As my citizenship details were complicated in view of my previous French citizenship, I was concerned about it. Fortunately, the senior Customs and Excise Officer, a Scot, was due to leave for Suva, Fiji, the British headquarters for the South-West Pacific, and offered to take our current British passports, application forms and photographs with him. He returned about five days later with all our new passports, everything in order. It was a great relief to us.

At work, the senior WHO malaria advisor was a Korean, Dr. Paik, who was married and had two children. His family kept very much to themselves at all times. Our working relations were always cordial. The chief WHO malaria Field Officer was a Palestinian called Odeh Habash and he was the cousin of Dr. George Habash, famous for his exploits against the Israelis. He had a very attractive, intelligent and excellent hostess for a wife, called Helen. They were very social and gave magnificent parties for which Helen prepared great food. Apart from that, Odeh knew what he was doing and got along well with the locals. In addition, there was an American Sanitary Engineer, Arthur Schick, and his wife, Mattie. They became our best friends in Honiara. Not long after my arrival, I received my WHO passport (SA 30690) and then went about to have Margot, Euan and Michèle included on it.

Our counterparts in the BSIP Health Department initially were all British. The Director was Jimmy MacGregor, married to Rita with children at school at Gordonstoun in Scotland. The government malariologist was Gordon Avery, initially a bachelor, while the other senior medical officers were Dr. Baillie and Dr. Ayres. Dr. Baillie left quite soon while Dr. Ayres developed a serious illness and left for England where he died soon after. There was quite a good relationship between WHO and government staff, as there had to be if any progress was to be made with the malaria eradication programme.

Being the epidemiologist, I was also in charge of the laboratory and consequently my office was next door to the laboratory, in a building separate from both the head office and the hospital. Again, the local staff in the laboratory were excellent and required very little correction and almost no supervision the whole time I was privileged to work with them. The senior supervisor was Jathaniel Lauloafaka from Malaita; he was ably assisted by Bartholomew Riolo and Noel, also from Malaita, both being responsible for the data collection and accurate recording. Noel was wheel-chair bound but this did not stop him from enjoying his favourite pastimes, singing and playing the guitar.

Margot was also very busy at this time. She had joined the Family Planning Association. After a few months, the President, Mrs. Smith, left for home and Margot took over. She very soon realised that if Family Planning were to succeed it had to be seen to be run by local people and not by expatriates. So she set about recruiting one or two local nurses and female lay volunteers. However, much to our surprise, many from the malaria laboratory wished to join the association, chief among them being Riolo and Noel. Great store was also placed on recruiting local politicians and, in this, Margot achieved an early success with the recruitment of Roz Wickham, our neighbour and local MP's wife. Margot set about training the lay volunteers as speakers and helped the nurses to better understand the requirements for family planning. Soon, the speakers were spreading the word far and wide, and doing so very successfully.

In the meantime, Margot had contacted the International Planned Parenthood Federation (IPPF) in London for support, which they were very happy to provide, initially on a small scale. The pertinent literature had to be sent through the post throughout the islands, but much to our surprise, Margot was threatened with deportation by the Scottish acting deputy governor, Alastair Trevor Clark, for doing so as it was still against the law. However, Margot and I were invited to lunch with him and his wife Hilary (who had been a radiographer at the Western Infirmary while I was a resident there) to discuss the matter with him. Over lunch, everything was straightened out and no action was taken against Margot. I am quite sure that this was due in no small part to the behind-the-scenes efforts of Hilary.

Family Planning went from strength to strength. It was decided that the association should be renamed and so it was called "The Solomon Islands Planned Parenthood Association" (SIPPA). To accompany the new name, I designed a logo which consisted of a carved, black Nsu-Nsu female head and arms, with the hands cradling a baby's head, encircled by a black, inscribed ring inside which was printed in white "Plan a healthy family" at the top of the logo, with "SIPPA" at the bottom. At the same time, I asked Noel if he would like to write a song for SIPPA, which he promptly did. I then recorded it with him singing and playing, then forwarded the tape to the Solomon Islands Broadcasting Service. The unexpected happened. The song "S-I-P-P-A" went straight to the top of the local hit parade where it stayed for many weeks.

The plan to localise SIPPA proceeded apace. Soon all the speakers were Solomon Islanders and the clinics staffed by local nurses. A couple of the expatriate doctors from the hospital gave their services voluntarily and, as a result, SIPPA managed to cover most of the Solomon Islands with their speakers although their own clinics were restricted to Guadalcanal. Nevertheless, the stimulated demand for services put great pressure on the government to provide more extensive family planning services throughout BSIP.

It was important to put across a simple idea of family planning and the example chosen was one of spacing your children, using the example of the way in which coconut tree were widely spaced to ensure that they developed correctly. This was something every Solomon Islander understood. SIPPA not only encouraged the use of the oral contraceptive but also the intra-uterine device and the Rhythm method advocated by the Roman Catholic Church, which was very strong in the islands. It can be seen that it therefore presented a broad front to the high fertility rate then prevalent in the Solomons.

A new governor, Charles Luddington, was appointed. His wife, a Scot, was a keen Family Planner and, shortly after their arrival, Margot and I were invited to Government House to discuss the project. Mrs. Luddington must have been impressed because she agreed to become the Patron of SIPPA, which finally gave it the seal of approval. As a result, many of the local politicians threw their weight behind it although one or two from Malaita were still against it. Interestingly, one of the first local speakers was Peter Kenilorea who later, as Sir Peter, went on to become the first Governor-General of the independent Solomon Islands. Public recognition came when the Governor invited Margot and I to Government House as representatives of SIPPA on 24 February 1976.

There was a great feeling of cameraderie among the SIPPA staff and everyone worked as a team; this was surprising as nearly all activities were undertaken after routine working hours. One Sunday afternoon, a SIPPA Walkathon was held. The participants were asked to walk at their own pace from the town office to the King George V School Sports Ground, a relatively short distance. At the completion of the walk, a small celebration was held there. As our family meandered along the route, we spotted a tiny, brown puppy which was obviously lost. Euan and Michèle decided that they would like to keep it, which they did, and which was then called, quite appropriately "Sippa". It turned out to be a nice dog and, on our departure from the Solomons, we gave Sippa to Matthew and his family.

Almost every year, A Solomon Islands Fair was held in Honiara, in the park opposite Government House. This was a very popular event for, in addition to choosing Miss Solomon Islands (all contestants had to wear traditional costumes), SIPPA put on a "Family Planning Play" in which the actors wore papier-mache "heads", which they had made themselves. These plays proved to be very popular.

Because of SIPPA's success, Margot became such a "hot" topic of interest that a skit about her was put on at a Guadalcanal Club social night in which she was referred to as "Mrs. Pill". So, when it eventually came time for us to leave the Solomons, Margot had the great satisfaction of knowing that SIPPA had been totally localised, that it would not collapse, that it was supported by all the churches and that it had, as its President, Edward Kingmele, a man who firmly believed in its principles. It was nice to learn that her efforts had been appreciated because, on 18 March 1976, she received an official letter from the new Chief Executive Officer of SIPPA, Edward Kingmele, stating that she had been elected as a Patron of SIPPA; in the letter, SIPPA also thanked me for my help.

The WHO Regional Director for the South-West Pacific, Dr. Francisco Dy, flew from Manila to pay the Malaria Programme and staff an official visit. He was accompanied by Dr. Hirshman, the Australian area director, based in Sydney. Margot, as president of SIPPA, asked me to invite the two of them to a SIPPA Dinner Party which Margot had previously arranged and which was to be held in our house. This I did. Dr. Hirshman became quite annoyed and said that I had no right to invite Dr. Dy to our home for dinner. I told him that it was really none of his business as I only relayed a message from the President of SIPPA. Dr. Dy was delighted to accept the invitation and we noted that Dr. Hirshman accompanied him. The dinner was a great success and Dr. Dy was delighted to meet the SIPPA committee and staff. The next day, Dr. Dy gave me a Philippine handbag and a warm letter of thanks for Margot, as a token of appreciation for her hospitality. Unfortunately, the Hirshman incident was not too atypical of the pettiness within WHO both at the local and other levels.

Meanwhile the Malaria Eradication Programme had its ups and downs. In the Western District, total eradication of malaria had almost been achieved, but Guadalcanal proved a very difficult problem with all the other islands—Choiseul, Malaita, Santa Cruz etc.—lying somewhere in between. To cover these other islands, I usually had to (a) fly to Gizo in the Western District before catching a small boat to Wagina and Choiseul. Occasionally, travel was by outboard canoe to some of the smaller, local islands. On arrival, travel was then either by foot or Land Rover, depending on the terrain. (b) fly to Malaita, and then by Land Rover and foot (c) by boat to Santa Cruz and the Ngellas. I enjoyed all the travel although I wasn't a very good sailor and the small government boats were not noted for their comfort.

The Guadalcanal Club was the centre of the social scene but even at this late stage of colonialism it was still almost exclusively a "Whites Only" club. We didn't frequent it socially very much although we did enjoy the occasional swim at their large outdoor pool, while Margot also played tennis there. In fact, she played in a tennis tournament just before our departure and, by some miracle she won it. As a prize, she was presented with a lovely hand-painted, ceramic statue of a Japanese Geisha girl, standing about ten inches high. The Club was also a hotbed of extra-marital affairs and most couples appeared to be either about to separate or be divorced. The expatriate scene was not one to be admired. The ones most to suffer in such a scenario were the children, who sat around the pool all day bored out of their tiny minds, almost abandoned by their carousing parents.

Among our few friends in Honiara were a west country Englishman and his Finnish wife, Lisa. Geoff taught mechanics at the High School while Lisa worked part-time in the Honiara Newsagent shop. The first time I saw her there, I was struck by her beauty—small, blonde, blue-eyed, beautiful face and nice appearance, all topped off with a soft, broken-English accent. They became our bridge partners and, on wet week-ends, we would go round to each others houses and play bridge.

Apart for being responsible for the supervision of the laboratory and the accurate preparation of the programme's statistical data, I also had to keep a close eye on the effectiveness of the anti-malaria methods used in the field, the spraying, drug-administration, blood sampling and health education. To do this, I accompanied a spraying team into an area, reaching there by 'plane, boat, canoe, Land Rover or on foot. Once reaching the "local" base, all the travelling to reach the villages in the area was on foot. This could be very difficult as many villages were inland and on mountain ranges. Consequently, to move from one village to another could mean walking for five to six hours over very rough, bush tracks. On such journeys, I suffered a great deal of pain in my "frozen" ankle and I usually found it necessary to have a complete rest the following day in the village, just doing the necessary paperwork and helping with the blood sampling. Such trips could last up to ten days and it was necessary to carry your own provisions and personal belongings, although the villagers were very generous in providing fresh fruit and local vegetables.

One particularly difficult area was the "Weather" or south coast of Guadalcanal, where the villages were strung along a very difficult and relatively inaccessible coast line. This area was also the territory of a local leader called "Moro". Unfortunately, he had a son aged about ten who was severely spastic and for whom little or nothing could be done except to provide good care. Every time I visited the area, I went to see Moro and every time he would ask me what I could do for his son. It was very sad. An interesting follow-up to all of this was the visit of David Attenborough to the Weather Coast, where he filmed for his television series. One evening, the family went down to our local cinema and saw the film he had made there. It started with him climbing out of a canoe, clad only in a G-string, and walking up the beach. The locals fell about helpless with laughter. He then proceeded to say that this part of the country was very primitive and that he was almost the first white man to visit it. After that, I was never able to take David Attenborough seriously.

At the other end of the Solomons, on one of the islands in the New Georgia group, there was another leader who was head of a community which ran a modified cargo / religious cult. He, however, set himself up as some sort of messianic figure and walked around in flowing robes, and wore heavy make-up on his face, topping it all with a round, flat hat on his head. In addition, he ensured that all the young maidens of the village were made readily available to serve as "Vestal Virgins" in his church. The village was called "Paradise" and I must admit that it was one of the cleanest in the whole of the Solomons. His religion must also have been a profitable one as I understand that he had his son schooled in one of the best Australian schools.

Frank Leong, our landlord and friend, became increasingly concerned about the place of the Chinese community in an independent Solomon Islands and consequently set about applying for Australian citizenship for himself and family, which was granted. He accompanied them down to Australia, where they decided to buy a house in Brisbane to settle. Frank returned to Honiara to carry on with the business. On his return, we invited Frank up for dinner; however, he insisted that he would only accept if he were allowed to prepare the meal. Margot readily agreed to this. Frank duly arrived with all the necessary stuff and set about both preparing and instructing Margot in the intricacies of Chinese food. Needless to say, it was delicious. It was the first of three or four meals which Frank prepared and we all enjoyed.

Margot and I thought long and hard about our future and, in particular, what was the best thing to do for Euan and Michèle, particularly with regard to education. They were both still at Woodford School in Honiara, a preparatory school, and if they had stayed in Honiara, they would have progressed to King George V School locally. We were also worried that, if they stayed, they would turn out to be typical "colonial kids"—usually brash, spoiled and bad-mannered in our experience. Above all, we felt that they should have a sense of "belonging". At home in Scotland, we had Margot's parents and my Mum. However, sending them home would mean boarding schools for both of them. Margot was not at all keen to send them off to boarding-school, especially as they would have to go to different ones. We were also influenced by my own good experience as a boarder at Glasgow Academy, in a small, boarding-house run on family lines. And so we eventually decided, much against Margot's better judgement and with very heavy hearts, to send Euan and Michèle back to school in Scotland and to the holiday care of our parents. On our short holiday home, Euan sat the entrance test to Dollar Academy in Clackmannanshire, and he was accepted by letter on 7 March 1975. Michèle was accepted for Butterstone House, a small, private school near Dunkeld, in Perthshire on 29 April 1975. Margot and I can recall vividly taking them to the airport one August morning to put them on the 'plane for Glasgow, as they were travelling home by themselves in the care of the flight staff. School for both of them started in September. We have a photograph of them standing outside the terminal building. Euan, ten years of age, was very quiet and subdued, but Michèle, two years younger, was excited and bubbly. So, with very sad and heavy hearts, we said cheerio to them as they boarded the 'plane. A year or two later, Michèle told Margot that Euan had cried nearly all the way home—he felt, he told us later, that we had cast them out of the family to punish them, and that we did not want them. In hindsight, it was the worst decision we have ever made as it had further repercussions but it was made with the very best of intentions and with their best interests at heart. At this time too, my future with WHO was uncertain as I had been offered a post in Onchocerciasis control in the Upper Volta, but we were not particularly keen to go there. So altogether, we thought that we had made the correct and best decision but it was the wrong decision and one for which I accept all the blame. However, it taught us belatedly that we must treat everyone as individuals and that what is good for one is not necessarily good for someone else.

My fortieth birthday was a very memorable one. Margot took me to the Mendana Hotel for dinner and, about three-quarters of the way through it, we received an urgent telephone call requesting us to return home promptly, which we did. On arrival, I was very surprised to see so many cars lined up nearby but I was even more surprised when I entered the house as it was a "Surprise Party". All our friends were there, somewhere in excess of forty. Needless to say the party was a great success. Perhaps the highlight of it was when I "streaked" from the bedroom through the assembled guests gathered in the lounge into the swimming pool; actually, I was wearing a pair of Margot's flesh-coloured pantyhose. That was the signal for almost everyone else to start discarding bits of clothing, scattering the pieces all over the verandah and garden, before jumping into the pool. Margot and I were particularly amused by the participation of the Guides Commissioner, particularly partial to brandy, who discarded her outer garments and jumped into the pool in her large bra and bloomers. It was a great night.

The Queen and the Duke of Edinburgh arrived in the Solomons on board the "Britannia" for a short visit. The locals were delighted and the wharf was packed with flag waving locals, as they stepped ashore. There was to be a royal reception on board that evening but invitations for this were severely restricted and expatriates moved hell and high water to obtain one. Margot, as the head of SIPPA, received an invitation for both of us but decided that SIPPA should be represented by a Solomon Islander, so she gave the two invitations to Roz and Ashley Wickham. However, she did receive a further invitation for herself to attend a reception for Prince Phillip at Government House the next day which she attended. Margot's invitations annoyed the wife of the English Harbour Master. They had not been issued with an invitation initially but by using every avenue of approach, she was eventually successful in obtaining two for the reception on the Britannia.

On one occasion, this couple very pointedly excluded us from one of their parties. As it happened, their house sat on a ridge almost directly behind our house. As their party progressed, the noise became louder and louder as the hour became later and later, until about 1.30 am, when Margot and I decided that we had had enough, so we anonymously telephoned the police and made a complaint. Shortly after, they arrived at their door and brought the party to an end. They never knew for sure who had complained about the noise but I think that they suspected that we had. Relations were even more strained after that.

Time passed and the Solomon Islands headed towards independence. At work, local medical officers were eased into the top administrative posts, supported by their British counterparts. The first local Director of Public Health was Peter Beck who, if I remember correctly, moved over to become the first Minister of Health. This was also the time for some civil unrest which was short-lived and relatively non-violent. I remember driving into Honiara from Kukum to find the town deserted apart from a few youths moving furtively about, and most of the stores boarded up—those which weren't had broken windows, while the streets were lightly littered with stones and debris. Fortunately, it didn't last long and I found it chilling although it was a mild disturbance.

Occasionally, overseas medical specialists visited the Solomons to do a short spell as a locum. One such visitor was Ed Passarro, a surgeon from the Veterans Administration based in Los Angeles. Near the end of his locum, I was able to take him with me on an inspection tour with a malaria team around one of the islands in a government work-boat. The weather was kind and Ed thoroughly enjoyed himself. He thought that it was the highlight of his whole trip.

Towards the end of our stay, I managed to arrange for Margot to accompany me on a working trip around the Ngellas, which was to last about a week. We picked up the malaria team on the government work-boat. It was a tiny little boat almost totally open to the weather and, apart from Margot and me, there were four malaria workers on board. Fortunately, we didn't sleep on board but in rest houses in the villages at which we stopped each night. The weather was very kind to us and we had a truly wonderful week visiting the villages, checking on the spraying and drug treatments and speaking to the people. The malaria team looked after the two of us very well and we had a lot of fun.

In April 1975, the WHO Malaria Assessment Team, consisting of my old friend Dr. van Dijk and Dr. Khalid, the Director of Medical Services for Sabah, arrived. They were well pleased with the progress the programme was making. On Thursday, 10th. April, Margot and I were invited to Cocktails at the residence of the Chief Minister, the Honourable Mr. Solomon Mamalone, to welcome the guests. Fortunately, their visit was a successful and happy one which paved the way for continuing WHO input.

Life was not all fun and malaria for the two of us. We also entered into print. Jointly, in 1974, we wrote a little pocket book called "Questions and Answers on Family Planning" which was published by Rigby Ltd. of South Australia. It was put on sale for 50 cents and was so popular that more were being stolen from bookshops than were being sold. Margot was also involved in a joint effort with James Sulimae, the senior Health Educator, and a representative from the Catholic Church, in writing and publishing a simple family planning book for the Solomons. Again jointly, Margot and I wrote another family planning book called "Family Planning for Doctors and Nurses" which we submitted to the FPAA in Sydney. We were told that it would have been accepted except for the fact that one of their senior medical advisors, Professor Llewellyn, was currently writing one. So, we had the book printed privately in Manila but it was not made available to the public.

In addition to Family Planning, I was also busy writing articles on malariology. Quite unexpectedly, I received a letter from a Dr. Ivan Goldberg, the editor of the Drug Therapy Tape Library in New York, on

10 May 1974, prior to leaving the MRU, asking me to prepare tapes on topics of interest to me. Once in the Solomons, I followed this up, WHO permitting me to proceed so long as I received no royalties or remuneration, and it did not jeopardise my position with WHO, which it didn't. So, I went ahead and prepared the tapes for the SIGMA Information Inc., which were officially released in 1976. I had prepared six tapes, each of one hour, the whole costing $48. The subjects for each tape were as follows: (a) the History of Malaria (b) the parasitological aspects of malaria (c) the entomological aspects of malaria (d) the clinical aspects of malaria (e) the chemotherapy and prophylaxis of malaria and (f) Malaria control and eradication. Unfortunately, I never received an author's copy of these tapes. In July 1975, I had an article on drug therapy for Plasmodium vivax malaria published in the WHO/MAL series. Later, on the 10 February 1976, I received a letter from Dr. G Buckle, the co-editor of a proposed 4th. edition of the Australian National Health and Medical Research Council's book, "Chemotherapy with Antibiotics and Allied Drugs", asking me to write a chapter on the chemotherapy and prophylaxis of malaria, which I did. This book was duly published and a copy was made available to all medical students in Australia and to medical practitioners who requested it. I also wrote two more articles while in the BSIP, the first on malaria chemotherapy and the second on Splenectomy, both of which were published in the Papua New Guinea Medical Journal in 1977.

There was a very active St. Andrew's Society in Honiara which Margot and I joined. We enjoyed one or two excellent Hogmanay and Burns' Night Balls, usually held at the Honiara Hotel. One year, I was elected Chieftain. One of the first members was a young Polynesian called Charles from Lord Howe Island; he was the club's best Scottish Country Dancer, having been taught at school by one of his teachers. Margot and I promised him that we would bring him back a kilt, sporran and stockings when we returned from holiday. At home, Brian, our best-man, remembered that he had an old kilt etc. belonging to his Father, which he duly looked out and handed to us. On returning to Honiara, we gave Charles his present—he was delighted and quite obviously the proudest man in the Solomons. He wore it at all the special occasions.

One of the last things I did before leaving was to write an MD thesis. For my subject I chose, "Population Dynamics in relation to the progress of the Malaria Eradication Programme in the British Solomon Islands Protectorate, 1973-1976". The whole thing took me about three months of quite hard work collecting data, most of it from the departmental records but some of it my own. I had it printed in Honiara, a total of 56 pages, including the bibliography and, on a visit home towards the end of 1975, I submitted it to the Post-Graduate Dean at Glasgow University. A few days later, he asked me to come back and see him, which I did. He said that the subject was good but he felt that the presentation was too brief, in fact it was the shortest he had ever received, so he advised me to pad it out. I replied that I had no more of value to say and wished it to be considered as it stood. Margot and I returned to Honiara. Two or three months later, I received word that I had been awarded the MD for my thesis and that the Graduation Ceremony would take place in the Great Hall on Saturday, 10 July 1976. Needless to say, we made the necessary arrangements to be there. Margot and Michèle both had nice new dresses, Michèle's dress was orange and green in colour. As luck would have it, this particular Saturday was also the day on which the Orange Walk took place, a march celebrating the victory of William of Orange, the Protestant king, at the Battle of the Boyne over Catholic forces of King James in Ireland. As we walked along Byres Road to the University, an elderly man stopped us and, looking at Michèle's dress, said "Playing safe !" and walked on. On arrival at the University, I separated from the family to join the other graduands, to be kitted out with scarlet academic gowns and mortar boards. I was pleased to see that Ross Lorimer and Alasdair Spence, both in the same undergraduate year as myself, were also being awarded an MD; I hadn't seen them for abour 16 years. The four MD graduands were seated in the front row and indeed our degrees were the first ones conferred that afternoon. I was delighted to see that Margot, Euan and Michèle had been allocated good seats near the front of the hall. After the ceremony, we had official photographs taken by a photographer based in Belfast, Ian Long by name. It was a very pleasant afternoon, even the sun was shining. I mention the photographer because even after we had left the Solomons and returned home in November, we still had not received the photographs. So, I wrote to the Chief Constable in Belfast setting out the details. The police were very helpful and, after a week or two, the photographs duly appeared.

Before coming home for my graduation, I had applied for eight jobs, seven in Britain (six in England, one in Scotland) and one in Hong Kong. I was offered interviews for all of the jobs. The post in Hong Kong was as the Asian Manager for Pfizer, the drug company, another was as the European Manager for Fisons (drugs), the makers of "Intal", based in Copenhagen, while another was as an International Medical Health Officer with the Department of Health, based at Alexander Fleming House, London, (I was interviewed by Sir Henry Yellowlees, the Chief Medical Officer for England and Wales), another was as a Medical Specialist with the Public Health Laboratory Service at Colinton, London, and the final one as a General Practitioner in a group practice in Alva, Clackmannanshire, Scotland. I rejected the post in Hong Kong as I really wished us all to return to Britain as a family. Of the remainder, I was offered six of the seven and chose the one in General Practice. This may seem to have been a strange decision but I didn't really want to live anywhere but in Scotland, to live all together under one roof and to bring the children up as Scots. My overseas experience had made me a fervent Scottish Nationalist, which I have remained ever since. Was it the right decision? Professionally, probably not, for the family, again uncertainty. However, that is life but there is one thing that I am certain of—I would seriously reconsider doing the same again.

While home on holiday for my graduation, Margot and I made a little trip to visit Mel and Fini who, by now, had left the Solomons and were once again back home in Holland. We flew to Schipol airport, Amsterdam, where we were met by Mel and driven to their home in a small village. The three days we spent with them passed very quickly and pleasantly. It was crowned by a small party on the second night, when another two couples were also invited. Again, after a well fortified meal, it became a heavy drinking affair. Margot and Fini eventually retired from the scene, while the three Dutchmen began to talk more and more among themselves. Consequently, I was left to entertain the two wives, who were sitting on either side of me on the settee. The were both attractive, but one of them was more voluptuous than the other. In actual fact, we began to entertain each other as the three men totally ignored us being more interested in alcohol.

From Holland, we took the train to Denmark, visiting my old friend from Aarhus days, Mogens Kirketerp, and his Norwegian wife, Anna, and their children. Mogens was now a general practitioner with special interest in dermatology. They had not met Margot before, so it was nice that they all got on well together. They were a loving, gentle family and we had a caring, restful few days in their home before we returned to Glasgow to say our farewells before returning to Honiara for the last time.

There was confirmation awaiting me that the Upper Volta post was mine should I want it. However, I was becoming a bit disenchanted with WHO and, in any case, Margot and I had already decided that we would return to Britain in order to have a real family life.

Before leaving the BSIP, the local staff of the Malaria Eradication Programme, many of whom were active Family Planners, gave Margot and me a Farewell Party in the laboratory building. For this, they prepared a massive amount of varied and tasty local food in the traditional ways beautifully presented on banana leaves bedecked trestle tables in the middle of the room. The room itself had been lavishly and beautifully decorated with palm fronds, hibiscus and allamanders. After the meal, there was, unfortunately, some unnecessary unpleasantness, as one of the staff, in advance of the "official" programme, presented Margot and I with a large, but rather ugly, hand-painted, turtle shell from himself. He knew the rest of the staff were also about to present us with a smaller, but beautifully hand-painted turtle shell, depicting the Solomon Islands, the logos of the MEP and SIPPA and our names. So there was considerable embarrassment when Jathaniel presented us with this superior shell, which we profusely praised in our final speech of thanks and farewell. To end it all, we had a photo taken, with Jathaniel presenting us the shell, outside the laboratory, in front of the assembled staff. Unfortunately, we didn't like to tell them that we disapproved of killing turtles, but then, turtles and their eggs have always been eaten by south sea islanders.

We could not leave Honiara without giving a Farewell Party of our own. Over sixty friends from SIPPA, the MEP, Health Department and other parts of the local community attended. It was a great success and continued on into the "wee sma' oors". Perhaps the highlight of the party was when we were all on the verandah chatting, eating and dancing. Suddenly Jathaniel, who was standing at the far corner of the verandah, saw a large brown snake gradually lowering itself from the roof of the house. It was our "pet" house snake which lived in the rafters and kept the rats under control—we had often heard it during the nights; even it had joined in the party. I suppose that the noise had attracted it.

It was time to leave the Solomons and Honiara. We had enjoyed our stay and we felt that we had been able to help the local people. However, the decisions we had made contained the seed of problems we encountered after we had returned to Scotland.

We did not fly straight home but stopped off in Manila as Margot wished to see her friend Nery whom she had met in Chicago. The two or three days we spent there passed very quickly and Nery looked after us very well. Although I had been to Manila before, this was Margot's first visit. Marcos was in power and the city was under martial law. As we landed, we saw the Concorde on the airstrip; it was apparently on a proving flight. Nery treated us as tourists and took us everywhere, the most memorable site being Lake Taal, set in a volcano crater. Of the hotels in Manila, we were most impressed by the Manila Hotel. It was a great visit and, shortly after, Nery married an American, and moved to the USA to stay.

WHO had not forgotten me either. While signing off at the Regional Office, I was given a personal letter from Dr. Dy, dated the 2nd. November 1976, the Regional Director, thanking me for my contribution to the MEP.

Chapter Seventeen

Scotland and General Practice, 1976-1984

Our flight home was quite memorable as we were to land at London airport on 5th. November 1976, our thirteenth wedding anniversary. Sometime during the flight, I had casually mentioned to the air hostess that it was our anniversary and then forgot about it. Imagine our surprise when, on being given our breakfast, the hostess also opened up a small bottle of champagne and proceeded to fill glasses for Margot and me, to the accompaniment of cries of congratulations from the other passengers. It was a lovely touch.

We were fortunate that we still had our luxury flat in High Pines, Blanefield, on returning home in the middle of November, 1976, as we were able to move into it straight away. There were problems living there as my new post as a General Practitioner (GP) was in Alva, about 20 miles away. Nevertheless, it allowed us a bit of time to look around.

Euan and Michèle were delighted to see us home, as we were to see them. For Euan, the boarding experience at Parkfield House, Dollar Academy, had not been a pleasant one. Although he never said anything about it, Margot and I gained the impression that he had been bullied. In addition, all boarders were forbidden to visit friends' homes at the week-ends when invited; there were other petty restrictions as well, which tended to force the boarders into all types of unnecessary mischief and consequently break school rules. The Housemaster and his wife, Mr. and

Mrs. Galbraith, were a nice caring couple but, at the week-ends, they would leave Parkfield House for their own home in the nearby village of Muckhart. We never did find out who was in charge (if anyone) when they were away. It was an unsatisfactory and strange environment.

Michèle, on the other hand, thrived at Butterstone House School, Dunkeld. The school was set in beautiful countryside, near the Loch of the Lowes, the home of the Ospreys. It was a small, private school catering for about 40 girls for the ages 8-13 years approximately. On visiting it, we realised that the girls were largely the daughters of the local landed gentry, and included the daughters of the Earl of Mansfield and the MacNab of MacNab. How Michèle was accepted we will never know but we were delighted she had been, not because it was a select school but because it was an excellent school, with a good academic record, taught social skills and encouraged the arts and the love of nature. The Headmistress, Mrs. Langlands, was a lovely person. Teachers, parents and pupils adored her.

One of the first things we did was to go on a short break to London. Through genealogical correspondence, I had made contact with Patrick Saint-Yves, who was the European agent for Avon Cosmetics based in London. He invited us to call on him and his wife, which we did. Later, Margot said that she received quite a surprise when he opened the door to greet us as he appeared to be a younger version, by about ten years, of me, although we were not related. Once we had settled down and after having something to eat, Patrick insisted on going through the Paris telephone directory looking for the numbers of other Saint-Yves, whom he then 'phoned; this carried on until about midnight as he managed to find out two or three who were not related to himself. From them, he obtained their addresses which he passed on to me. It had been a very entertaining night. During the day or two we spent in London, we took Euan and Michèle around all the usual tourist haunts, which they appeared to enjoy.

I settled quickly into the Practice. The senior Partners were two brothers, Vincent and Kenneth Gordon, both just on retiring age. The other active partner was Michael Illingworth, whose father was Sir Charles Illingworth, my former teacher and Professor of Surgery at Glasgow University. Interestingly enough, Mike had been at Glasgow Academy at the same time as myself but a few years ahead. The Gordon brothers were straight forward, helpful and friendly, particularly Vincent. Fortunately, the support staff were good and included office staff, nurses and health visitors, all of whom were fun, helpful and efficient.

It was, however, quite a long drive from Blanefield to Dollar and return, on the one day. All through the first winter of 1976, from 1st. December (when I started at Alva) through to April 1977, I drove to work in my VW Beetle daily. Fortunately, I enjoyed the drive as it took me along the back road into Stirling, past Stirling castle. The problems started when I was on call at nights and over week-ends. Fortunately, Mike soon arranged for me to stay with Dan and Edith Hamilton, an elderly farming couple, in Tillicoultry, the next village to Alva. This was an excellent arrangement as we soon became very good friends; they were always very generous and helpful and I was soon made to feel like one of the family.

However, living in Blanefield was unsatisfactory, so we decided that we would live nearer my work as it would also enable us to bring Euan and Michèle home from their boarding schools. We started looking for houses along the "Hillfoots", the Ochil hills, in Clackmannanshire. Quite soon, I was able to ask Margot to come and see one in Menstrie, the next village to Alva nearer to Stirling. The house was called "Laurel Bank", a late 19th. century bungalow, originally built for the manager of the local distillery. It was on the outskirts of the village, on the Tullibody crossroad, and stood in one-third of an acre of walled gardens, surrounded by fields on three sides, with Broomhall (a 19th. century ruin later converted into a nursing home) and the Ochils behind. Margot loved it although it was large; we moved quickly to purchase it, which we did for £ 26 000. Finally, we moved into Laurel Bank in April 1977.

One of the first things that we did was to buy two pups, one a West Highland Terrier whose kennel name was "Laurel Minima", but which we called "Minnie", and the other an Aberdeen (Scotch) Terrier, whose kennel name was "Fozzy Whisky" but which we called "Whisky"; as they were white and black respectively, they were a good advertisement for my favourite tipple. Minnie was a few weeks older than Whisky.

Our new home needed to be redecorated to suit our tastes and so, in all our available spare time, over a period of about six weeks, we set about redecorating the house; indeed, we had almost completed the redecoration, when disaster struck us. The lead flashings on the roof had needed to be replaced and we had called in the appropriate workmen. This particular morning, 17th. June 1977, Margot was in Glasgow visiting her Arran childhood friend, Jean Currie, while I was at work. Apparently, my partner, Kenneth Gordon, was driving down Tullibody road towards our house, while returning from a house call at about 11 am. on a bright, sunlit day, when he noticed smoke billowing from the roof of the house. He called the Fire Brigade and then made efforts to contact me. Our receptionist eventually found me at a house in Tillicoultry, about six miles away. At the time I received the 'phone call I was in the act of examining an elderly female patient's abdomen. When I explained the situation to her, she said, "Son, your need is greater than mine." So, I excused myself and made my way back home. As I hit the main road, which ran almost straight through Alva to Menstrie, I could see a thick plume of smoke rising into the clear blue sky. (When I finally returned to see the patient, I was pleased to find that it was an easily cured condition she was suffering from).

When I approached the crossroads at our house, the Police had already restricted the approaches and fire-brigade vehicles were in place with their hoses running into the house and operational. It was then that I noticed a tall, middle-aged Police Inspector directing the proceedings. His name was Sam Middler, an Aberdonian, and unknown to Margot and me, lived with his wife, Ivy, in the bungalow behind us, nestling at the foot of the Ochils. He introduced himself and I expressed my heartfelt thanks to him for all that everyone present had done to-date. There was still no way I could contact Margot in Glasgow as she was going shopping in town. After a few hours of frantic, expert work by the firemen, the fire was eventually doused and the house made safe. Sam had also arranged for heavy tarpaulins to be placed securely across the gaping hole in the roof in an effort to make the house watertight.

Apparently the fire had been caused by an unnoticed spark from the workmens' blow torches as they repaired the flashings, which proceeded to slowly ignite old birds' nests under the eaves of the house. Although the flashings had been inspected by the workmen on completion of the job, it had taken another hour before the smouldering nests burst into flames and the fire noticed. The fire had started in the guest bedroom, upstairs, at the front of the house, and to the left of our bedroom. This room was directly over our lounge, which had an ornately decorated, late Victorian frieze running around the junction between the wall and the ceiling; this frieze was a cause for concern as there was only one company able to replace it should it be destroyed. Strenuous efforts were made to prevent the ceiling from collapsing, including the placement of strong wooden supports from floor to ceiling; fortunately, all the efforts were successful. Needless to say, most of the house was badly water and smoke damaged, necessitating a complete repair, redecoration and refurbishment of the whole house. The insurance assessor placed the damage at £ 17 500.

In the midst of this upheaval, I suddenly remembered that I had not seen Minnie and Whisky at all, so I started searching and asking, but nobody seemed to know what had happened to them A lady then appeared at our garden gate and said that she had come down to the back garden at the start of the commotion because she had heard the pups barking. Seeing their predicament, she had gathered them up and she now had them safe and sound up at her house She offered to keep them for the night, which I gratefully accepted.

Margot did not return home until about 10.30 pm. the same evening. She couldn't believe her eyes; hoses were still left running into the house, over the garden wall, and needless to say, she was very upset by it. We decided that we would not evacuate the house during repairs as it would have left it open to vandals. Unfortunately, we were unable to sleep in our bedroom due to the strong, persistent smell of smoke, and so we each slept in a bath-tub in our two bathrooms. Everyone rallied round quickly and soon Marshalls, the contractors, were at work on the house. All this time, Sam kept a friendly eye on all the proceedings. Fortunately, we had not yet taken Euan and Michèle out of their boarding houses; however, when they did come home for their summer holidays, they were unable to use their own bedrooms, and both had to sleep in the downstairs cloakroom. I think they thought it rather an adventure. The gods were kind to us as the summer of 1977 was a long, dry, hot one. After the roof had been repaired, Bill Crawford, the painter, arrived to paper and paint the house. We became firm friends and he did a great job of redecoration. Lunch-times became a social event when he was around. His boss, John Marshall, asked him if he was also sleeping at Laurel Bank as he thought

Bill was taking too long to complete the job—which he probably was. Eventually, however, everything was finally completed and, in November, we gave a big combined, "Thank You and Housewarming Party" to all who had been involved with the house up to that time. It had been a traumatic event, especially for Margot as it had left her depressed, but it was now all behind us. Still, probably as a result of that, we never felt a complete empathy with Laurel Bank during our stay there.

Our next big decision was when to withdraw Euan from Parkfield House, Dollar Academy, and Michèle from Butterstone House School, as we had managed to arrange Michele's admission to Dollar Academy as a day-pupil.

We were now all safely ensconsed in Laurel Bank. Margot and I occupied one of the two front bedrooms while Euan and Michèle had a back bedroom each. Whisky and Minnie slept downstairs in the laundry. The cottage also contained a large, front-facing, ground floor living-room, a porch and large entrance hall with a fine wooden staircase at two levels leading up to the bedrooms (at the split-level, there were two bathrooms), a front-facing, large lounge which was connected through an archway with a large dining room looking onto the back garden and the Ochils; in addition, there was a large, modern kitchen towards the rear in which we ate most of our meals and did most of our correspondence, with a large cloakroom and toilet off the rear of the hall. It was gas-fired, centrally heated and appeared to maintain an ambient temperature of about 60F all year round. Another added attraction was its walled gardens, a small one to the front and a large one, with an additional vegetable garden fenced off, to the rear. In addition to a large greenhouse, there were herbaceous borders, rose bushes and trees, with a mass of tulips and daffodils. It was a lovely house.

Margot had always been interested in politics, so I was not surprised, and indeed I encouraged her, when she said she was going to enrol as a mature student at the nearby Stirling University to read Political Science and Sociology. She was accepted and initially all went well both with her studies and at home. However, I suppose that it was inevitable, knowing her gregarious nature that she should join up with a crowd of social, male, mature students. Strangely, on starting in general practice, my not-so-heavy drinking lessened until I became a very moderate drinker. Margot, once she joined this group at University, continued with her social pattern.

She is a very bright, outgoing, generous, gregarious and intelligent person and, to be quite honest she appeared to find the course too restrictive and easy. Almost without fail, she would be awarded an A or B+ for each of her assignments, although she seemed to do very little study at any time during the week. Therefore, it was not surprising that she was one of only two students to be asked to proceed to an Honours degree; after a great deal of thought and discussion, she declined the offer, but her decision came back to haunt her later. I felt that she had made the correct decision. Margot had always said that the course had not extended her intellectually and, by and large, she felt that it was inadequate. Margot graduated BA on Friday, 27th. June 1980. It was a lovely sunny afternoon and Margot had bought a nice light lilac/blue dress and matching hat; she looked lovely. The graduation was held in the Stirling Town Hall after which we all moved over to the University grounds for a quite quiet social gathering. In the evening, we went to the Graduation Ball by ourselves as none of her cronies wished to attend; this was held in the Golden Lion Hotel in Stirling. We both felt it was a flat ending to a nice day.

Nor was life a bed of roses on our parental front. My Mother had originally stayed with her aunt in Ralston, between Glasgow and Paisley, on returning to Scotland, but it was an unsatisfactory arrangement as Mum was difficult in her manner while Aunt Eva was quite elderly. So, one of my first duties was to find Mum somewhere to stay. She did not have much money and had received almost no compensation for my Dad's death, so any accommodation would have to be modest by necessity; fortunately, we found her a small, ground floor flat in Ibrox, Glasgow. We visited her regularly and tried to keep everything running smoothly.

Mum was understandably very lonely and depressed. For her depression, she was receiving prescribed medication but in addition to this, she too had started heavy gin drinking. In an effort to alleviate her boredom and isolation, she started attending "Swinging Singles" clubs two or three times per week and invariably staggered home. Her situation progressively worsened and it was quite amazing that she was never assaulted or robbed while she was in this state. Then one evening, she fell and fractured the neck of her right humerus, which necessitated her admission to hospital for treatment and physiotherapy. It was realised that she was now quite incapable of looking after herself. Margot, after her previous experience, refused to have her stay with us, a decision I agreed with. After a long search, the Social Welfare Department managed to secure her a place in Leslie House, Leslie Road, Pollokshields, which was run by a Mrs. Elizabeth Parkins. This was a very fortunate placement as it was a very well run and happy Home, into which Mum quickly settled, and which she later considered to be the best move she could have made under the circumstances. The staff were very good to her and put up with all her idiosyncratic and belligerent ways. She stayed there until her death in September 1997, in her ninety-second year, contented to the end.

Margot's parents, Jack and Rita, were also a worry to us. We knew that they were never really very happy together but we were still very surprised when they decided to divorce in their late sixties. Jack coped very well, buying himself a wee flat in Saltcoats and busying himself by helping his friends, Jeanette and John, in their boarding house on the Ardrossan sea-front. In return, Jeanette fed and kept an eye on him. He did very well.

Rita proved to be a sad case. She moved into a small council flat by herself. However, she soon started to leave her flat with the door left open, visiting friends and neighbours unannounced and staying for many days. In addition, she was a great danger to herself as she would leave her cooking stove on and forget all about it. Margot and I contacted her GP and the local Social Works Department repeatedly until they eventually did something for her, but not until they had realised that she was suffering from early Alzheimer's Disease. After a great deal of manipulation, she was admitted to a small nursing home in Stirling so as to be near us. However, her dementia increased in severity and she was finally admitted to the Psychiatric Hospital, Larbert, so as to be relatively close to us. She stayed there for many years until she was nothing but a walking skeleton, who failed to recognise us and who never spoke.

I still had to go to work and give an appearance of normality to all and sundry. For the first nine months in general practice I was quite contented and the atmosphere in the surgery was fine. Kenneth Gordon retired and was replaced by a very nice, quiet and considerate married, young doctor called John Young. Not long after, Vincent Gordon retired and a young, single lady doctor called Janet Scott joined the team. Mike Illingworth was now the senior partner; he was also a staunch member of the BMA and was a senior member on the local committee. I had long resigned from the BMA because of its then existing racial discrimination (on first returning from TPNG, I had applied to the Glasgow office of the BMA for BMA-sponsored, cheaper car insurance, only to be told that I was ineligible as I had been born in India). I also did not consider that it supported general practitioners adequately and was too sycophantic towards the government. Mike was also on the local GP committee and had been its chairman. For a while, I was also on this committee but I found it stultifying and all talk, so I resigned from it.

Soon, I was unhappy with the manner in which general practice appeared to function. I felt that, in the light of my overseas experience with suitably trained Aid Post Orderlies and Medical Assistants, a similar system would prove ideal for general practice for the type of illnesses and problems encountered therein. I set about to write an article called "Patient Care in Time and Space" for the Royal Society of Health Journal, in which it was published in the October 1978 edition (vol. 98., 5., 239). In this article I described a whole new system of Primary Health Care (PHC) for general practice and suggested that GPs may not be necessary for the provision of care at the point of first contact. To achieve this, I suggested that there should be three grades of "suitably trained "paramedical staff (a) the Clinical Associate (CA) who would hold surgeries, be trained in diagnosis, make house calls, be "on call", be able to refer patients to hospital and prescribe from a restricted list of drugs. Training would include the ability to recognise and treat / deal with the commonly occurring illnesses and conditions encountered in practice; any conditions encountered which lay outside of the sphere of training were to be referred to the General Practitioner acting in a capacity of "Specialist Generalist". (b) the Community Nurse (CN) who would carry out the normal nursing duties, but excluding the routine, physical care of house-bound patients. The CN would also be allocated an area of the practice to care for; within this area, the CN would be required to visit every household (the "Space" concept) at pre-determined, fixed intervals (the "Time" concept) to check on the presence of illness, to give advice and to provide health education.

(c) the Nursing Aide, who would be responsible for the physical care (eg. bed bathing, mobilisation, nail-cutting etc.) of housebound patients. For the General Practitioner, I suggested the role of the "Specialist Generalist", (which would add lustre to the newly introduced MRCGP qualification). The GP would still carry out surgeries although they would tend to be for patients referred by the CA, though patients would still have the choice to choose the GP in the first instance; Specialist clinics would be of increasing relevance and would remain the sole province of the GP. In addition, the GP would provide a back-up service for all house calls, including out-of-hours calls. This system not only would provide a totally comprehensive, caring PHC service but also a much more cost-effective and efficient one as it would make far better use of suitably trained staff.

I set about making my views known in the medical journals and through the letter columns of the newspapers. The responses were amazing, ranging from anger to interest and support. All of the respondents grasped the significance of the grades of staff to some degree but none grasped that they were a part of a whole new system of PHC, based on the Malaria Eradication concept of "Patient Care in Time and Space". Because it was a new concept for the National Health Service in Britain, I chose to give the name Clinical Associate to a new category of staff; in hindsight, this was an error of judgement and I should have retained a familiar sounding name and chosen "Nurse Practitioner" (copied from the Americans) instead, as this was the title used when a similar grade of paramedical staff was eventually introduced towards the end of the 1980s. Consequently, although I was the first one in Britain to introduce this heretical concept, I was eventually never fully recognised as having done so.

This new concept split our practice. The Nurses and Health Visitors attached to the practice became enthusiastic supporters, whereas Mike was totally opposed although my other partners remained non-committal and, by and large, sat on the fence over the whole issue. Mike was so opposed to my proposals that he wrote a long letter in the "Pulse" medical newspaper on 20th. September 1980 in which he said that I should cease commenting in the medical press and push for an investigation in depth and that his other colleagues in the practice had agreed that the Alva practice was not going to be the guinea pig. However, he did concede that I had managed to reduce the number of trivialities being dealt with by the doctors as many were now being delegated to Nurses and Health Visitors. Mike's opposition was not the only one I experienced; there were comments from senior officials of the BMA and of the Nursing profession. However, there were many letters of support, one of the most pertinent being from Ms. Barbara Stilwell who wrote in the October 1980 edition of the Journal of Community Nursing that she was stirred by my article "The dilemma of Primary Health Care" in the August edition, as she and Dr. A. Bird had just submitted a research proposal for funding which envisaged making use of a Health Visitor as an alternative point of contact for the patient both in the surgery and at home. Not long after, Ms. Stilwell visited Margot and I at our home in Menstrie to discuss this concept further; since then, she has risen high in the Royal College of Nursing and is now the expert on the role of the Nurse Practitioner within the NHS, but fails to make reference to my original work in her writings.

This article was only the beginning as I went on to develop the theme by comparing costs in training GPs and the proposed grades of paramedics, expert "Team Work" within PHC, as well as outlining clearly training schedules for each new category proposed. I continued to take every opportunity to attack the current system. Slowly, things began to move in my direction and I was being listened to with more attention. On the 10th. October 1980, Mr. A. W. Jarvie of the Glasgow Herald, wrote a leading article entitled "Is the Family Doctor Service due for change?" in which he clearly propounded my ideas favourably. My friend, Mogens in Aalborg, also sent me a cutting of an article which appeared in the Danish magazine "Nolk" in 1980 in which my article in the Practitioner of September 1979 had been precised. In the February 1981 issue of "Primary Care", Mr. J.P. Stephenson wrote an article entitled "Rethinking the Primary Health Care Team" in which he too expounded my views favourably. In September 1983, my article "The changing role of the Practice Nurse" was published in Current Practice where I once again clearly enunciated my proposals.

Needless to say, the comments were fast and furious. Pulse magazine ran an article written by Jane Cameron, "The heretical challenge to GP's principal role" in the Analysis section of the paper on 30th. August 1980. In it, she briefly outlined my proposed system and also printed comments obtained from (a) Dr. John Fry, Chairman of the General

Services Committee, who categorised the CA as an analogue of the barefoot doctors of the third world and thought little of my proposals (b) Dr. John Hasler, the Secretary of the Royal College of General Practice, said that although the College had not commented on the matter, he admitted that there were many things that nurses could do in general practice and that it happens (c) Dr. John Ball considered the proposals "third world" (d) Dr. John Weston Smith in Tamworth said his practice were already using practice nurses in a limited manner but he would not agree to nurse prescribing nor being able to refer patients to GPs and (e) both the Royal College of Nursing and the General Nursing Council said that if a nurse is not trained to do a specific task, she should refuse to do it—with which I agreed wholeheartedly. I always believed that the opposition to my proposals by the medical establishment had more to do with loss of prestige, financial clout and a real failure to understand the proposals than with an overall concern for patient care. As I said repeatedly, the future would be dictated by economics and, as we enter the new millennium, this has proved to be correct. Any mention of the extended role of paramedics in PHC in this period of time was met with cries from the medical profession of "Barefoot Doctors", but as I always asked what was wrong with that honourable term, especially as they were providing a good service, whereas the system of PHC in operation, run by well shod and well-heeled GPs, was failing to provide a satisfactory service. I am glad to say that, in the last year or two of the twentieth century, many of my ideas are now in place, although there is still quite a way to go before they are all implemented and operational.

Our life was not all conflict and frustration. Margot, when she was not overloaded with social appointments, was a very good hostess. With our large home, we were able to entertain our guests, mainly from overseas, in some comfort. One of our first visitors were Edward and Ruth Kingmele. Edward had taken over from Margot at SIPPA, and was now in Britain to do a course in Wales; however, as it was now Christmas / New Year, they were asked to come up to stay with us, which they did. That particular winter, 1979, was a particularly severe one with plenty of snow and ice and, unfortunately, Edward and Ruth found it a bit too cold; however, they enjoyed their short stay with us and we were very pleased to see them. On another occasion, we had Mogens and Anna Kirketerp with their twins, Mads and Bente, over to stay for a few days. Their stay coincided with the day of the Men's Final in tennis at Wimbledon, in which Bjorn Borg defeated John McEnroe; needless to say we were all supporting Borg, while eating strawberries and cream as we watched the game on TV. Arthur and Mattie Schick, whom we were friendly with in Honiara, also paid us a visit. This was the last time we saw Mattie as she died a few years later from lung cancer; we did, however, see Arthur again. Towards the end of our stay in Laurel Bank, Mogen's elder daughter, Mette, paid us a visit staying for about a week.

Not long after we had settled down in Laurel Bank, I joined the local (Menstrie) branch of the Scottish National Party (SNP). I had become progressively more nationalistic the more I had come into contact with English people abroad, especially the so-called establishment figures who, almost without exception, equated all things "British" with England, purposely ignoring the fact that Britain was composed of Scotland, Wales, Northern Ireland and England. I had nothing against the English as individuals, only against the establishment. I threw myself wholeheartedly into the activities of the local branch. Margot was not so sure about nationalism and tended to keep on the fringes of my activities; she was more inclined to Labour. The local committee was small in number and consisted of John MacDonald, Sheena Fraser, David Manson, Iain McKillop, Jim Campbell, Willie Miller and myself; we kept quite busy and, on a regular basis, the branch held a Bingo session for fund-raising purposes. At local and national election times, we were all busy doing leaflet drops and knocking on doors. Margot and I also acted as the Branch representatives at the Annual Meetings held in Arbroath, Perth and Fort William. During the 1979 referendum on Devolution, the SNP was very active in supporting this initiative and, although the Labour Party in Scotland officially supported this line, there were very many Labour supporters and candidates openly advocating a "No" vote. In addition, a Scottish MP, Mr. Cunningham, representing an English constituency, had introduced a bill in parliament which required 40% the total electorate to vote in favour of the motion. This was the first and last time that such an obvious block was used in British politics. It is interesting to note that if this 40% had been standard procedure for parliamentary elections also, only one MP in the whole of parliament would have been elected and that, ironically enough, was our own SNP MP, George Reid. Needless to say, the Devolution Bill was defeated. Since then, Margot and I have despised the Labour Party and consider it to be without principle.

Not long after joining the local SNP, I received a letter from Mr. James Ferguson, the Chairman of the Clackmannan and East Stirlingshire Conservative Association, dated 17th. December 1977, asking me to lead the Alva Committee. He had apparently been incorrectly informed by our friend, Mr. James Thomson, that I held Tory ideals and may be interested in joining. I wrote to Mr. Ferguson thanking him for the doubtful honour of asking me to join the Tories and pointed out to him that I was a card-carrying member of the SNP. He, in turn, wrote me an amusing letter in which he said that he hoped I would soon see the error of my ways.

In addition to my local branch activities, I also wrote two political pamphlets which I had distributed to all SNP branches in Scotland. The first, published in March 1981, called "Community Politics and Scottish Independence", called upon the SNP to work from the bottom up in framing their policies and to adopt Conflict as opposed to Consensual politics. The second, published in May 1981, called "The Way Ahead", in which the political education of the Scottish electorate was shown to be the key to Scottish independence; the SNP must win the hearts and minds of the people of Scotland to succeed. There can be no stability and hope of independence in a country which does not know itself.

In February 1983, the Menstrie branch put me forward as a prospective parliamentary candidate for the forthcoming general election in the seat previously held by George Reid for the SNP, Clackmannan and East Stirling, but now held by Martin O'Neil for Labour. I enjoyed full support from the Tullibody and Menstrie branches, but mixed and openly hostile support from the Alva, Alloa, Tillicoultry and Dollar branches. Tales were spread around the constituency about all the personal problems affecting our family. These, however, were not the major factors against me. Originally unknown to me was the fact that another prospective candidate was Jeanette Jones, who was not only on the national executive, but was also, I believe, the mother in law of a Tillicoultry branch officer. Nevertheless, three of us were put forward for selection, the third candidate being Alan MacArtney. I gave a good speech which apparently was considered too intellectual by quite a few present (at least, Margot told me so). I also pointed out forcibly that Jeanette Jones had lost on two or three previous occasions and that, if re-selected, she would be beaten again; I told the members that the choice was between Alan and me if they wanted the SNP to win this seat and that I was their best hope as I was widely known and respected through the area because of my GP work. Needless to say, Jeanette Jones won beating me into second place and, needless to say, the SNP were soundly beaten into third place, their worst showing ever in this constituency. So, this constituency remained in Labour's hands right through until the new millennium as Mr. O'Neil once again defeated Mr. Reid in the 1st May 1997 General Election, at which the Labour Party gained a 178 seats majority, in the process removing the Tory Party from the Scottish and Welsh electorates.

There were other official and social occasions which kept Margot and I reasonably busy during our period at Laurel Bank. I was invited to attend the Official Opening of the Maegraith Wing at the Liverpool School of Tropical Medicine on 5th. May 1978 by the Minister for Overseas Development, Judith Hart MP, but I was unable to attend. On the 14th. March 1980, Margot and I spent a few days in Basle, where I attended the joint meeting of the Royal Society of Tropical Medicine and Hygiene and the Swiss Tropical Medicine and Parasitological Institute. We were accommodated in a top class hotel on the banks of the river. During the day time meetings, the wives of participants were very well entertained by their hostesses. Of particular importance to us was the reunion with Craig Canfield whom we had last seen in Sydney about ten years previously. Needless to say, we spent most of our spare time in the evenings together. Unfortunately, we haven't had the chance to meet Craig since then although we are still keeping in touch through E-mails. One evening, when we were in the hotel's lounge bar, we became involved in conversation with Prinz Alexander Liechtenstein who gave Margot and I his visiting card and issued us an open invitation to visit him, which we never did. The next morning, we were introduced to his mother, a small, impressive woman at breakfast. On 10 Sep 2010, I came across the visiting card and thought I should write him a letter which I did but to which I did not receive a reply.

I received a letter from Dr. R. J. Donaldson of the London School of Hygiene and Tropical Medicine dated 5th. October 1979 in which he asked me to be a guest speaker at the Annual Medical Conference of the St. John Ambulance which was to be held at Nottingham University between the 18-20th. April 1980, taking as my subject, "Teamwork in Primary Care." I accepted the invitation and drove down the day before my talk; I found that I was part of a panel of four speakers, if I remember correctly. I gave my speech which was favourably received, especially by the nursing participants. In the evening there was a very enjoyable social evening consisting of a lively dance and buffet supper which was held in a University Hall. At about 2am. I staggered off to the room allocated to me although the celebrations continued. The next morning, after breakfast, I thanked the hosts before driving off to Welwyn Garden City to stay with Geoff and Lisa Edwards, our friends from the Solomon Islands, for the evening before returning home.

At the end of 1979, I wrote a letter to the Prime Minister in which I enclosed copies of my most pertinent articles on Primary Health Care. I don't really know if I was expecting anything to happen as a result, but I did receive a letter from 10 Downing Street, dated 15th. January 1980, thanking me for my communication.

Margot, as well as attending University, had also joined the local Community Council and had become involved with the local youth. She enjoyed both of these activities. She had also taken up golf in a big way and, in addition, joined the Menstrie Tennis Club the members of which played on the DCL courts in the village. The highlight of her membership of the Tennis Club was when she was asked to present the prizes to the winners at the end of November 1983, just before we moved house. At a more intellectual level, she became more interested in bridge through her association with Margo Webster and joined the Alloa Club as well as playing at Dollar and Stirling. In spite of all her pursuits, she also managed to join up with the Scottish Education in Action (SEAD) group, a network of volunteers who organised discussion groups and other educational activities in support of a series of weekly programmes, "Common Interest" which started on Channel 4 TV on 20th. January 1983.

The longer I worked in the Alva Practice, the more frustrated and unhappy I became. I told Margot that I would love to do something else and so I started looking around once again. One job which came up was as a ships' chandler business in Uig on Skye; in addition to the chandlery, the job also entailed the sale of fuel to the ferries which plied from the small harbour. An added attraction was the provision of quite a large, modern bungalow almost adjacent to the business, on the waterfront. One week-end, the whole family took off for Skye going across on the ferry from Kyleakin to Broadford, and then driving up to Uig. We thoroughly enjoyed our outing but very soon decided that business was not our forte.

The second attempt at escape was to a single-handed practice at Canisbay, the most northerly practice on the Scottish mainland. When I 'phoned up to find out about it, I was very surprised to find myself speaking to Dr. Bill Pyle from the Orkneys, whom I had last met as a student on one of the Boat Club Outings to Aberdeen; he was vacating the practice to emigrate to Australia. The drive up was completed in wonderful sunny weather; however, on the next day as we visited the practice, a dense "haar" enveloped the area. This put Margot and I off the notion of moving up there. On the drive down south, we ran into heavy snowstorms and driving winds. Looking back on it, the weather saved us from making a grave mistake.

Margot and I drove down to King's College, Cambridge, on the 24th. September 1982 as I wished to attend the 75th. Anniversary Dinner of the Royal Society of Tropical Medicine and Hygiene the next day. On our arrival, we were allocated a small student apartment in the college, basic and wooden but quite adequate and charmingly quaint. As we had most of the after noon to spare, we had a look around King's College and the town itself; we found it all fascinating, even more so as we enjoyed good weather. Cambridge really is a place of "glittering spires". There was a Sherry / White Wine Reception in Chetwynd Court at 6.30 pm. followed by the Dinner at 7pm. We were very fortunate in our seat allocation as we enjoyed good company with Dr. and Mrs. Nomura from Japan, Dr. Goodwin, Dr. Christine Duggan and Dr. John Macarthur, his wife and daughter. Dr. Macarthur was Glasgow born, and was famous for inventing the portable, pocket microscope; he only died in 1995. In addition to the interesting diners, I am pleased to say that the meal was also good. Margot and I thoroughly enjoyed the ambience, being particularly impressed with the Dining Hall.

We had another little holiday to ourselves in France, this time with the family. Through a cheap week-end package, we booked into a fairly humble hotel in the old carpet-making area of Paris. The clientele was varied to say the least; however, it was clean and the staff were good to us, which were the most important factors. The weather was also kind and we were able to show Euan and Michèle all the usual tourist sites. While eating at a roadside cafe, at which Michèle happily practised her grasp of French, we met a French couple who offered to take us out that evening. I was not too keen to attach ourselves to perfect strangers but in the end I agreed. In the same evening, we met them and they took us to a discreet night-club at which we had to knock on a heavy door and be scrutinised before being allowed admission. Once inside, it was all subdued lighting, deep red decor and soft dance music, with a few couples dancing on a very tiny circular floor. Euan and Michèle loved it and, I must admit, so did we not leaving for our hotel until late. We met the lady next morning at her shop—she owned her own hairdressing salon.

We had two more family holidays. The first was a short break in April when we drove down to Devon and Cornwall. It was my birthday and we had a nice little dinner together at a restaurant in Exeter. Driving down into Cornwall, we stayed in a bed and breakfast, as we wanted to do a bit of sightseeing. We enjoyed visiting St. Ives, Penzance, Mousehole and Land's End, all places we had previously only read about and seen on TV and films.

The next family holiday was in Southern Ireland. We drove down to Anglesey and took the ferry across to Dun Laoghaire. En route to our farm-house base in Clonakilte, we spent the afternoon in Dublin. The farm house we stayed at was like a home from home, although we weren't the only guests. We were well looked after and were fed like fighting cocks. There was an Anglo-Irish family present also, the Browns from Dublin, who had a son and daughter about the same ages as Euan and Michèle. They were a nice family and we all got on well together. However, most of the time we did our own thing, although we did join forces for a trip into Cork one day, where we enjoyed a good meal at a high class restaurant. We visited Bantry, Killarney, Kinsale and Blarney Castle. Euan and Michèle enjoyed Blarney Castle as they were able to kiss the Blarney Stone, as indeed we all did, having to bend over the parapet to do so, in a fine drizzle. Still, we have a certificate each and photos to prove it. The Irish pubs we found especially appealing as they were not just drinking dens, but places of family entertainment, where many customers enjoyed the entertainment provided over cups of coffee only. One evening, we went to a Ceilidh, the main attraction being a famous Irish lady Harpist and singer; she was far superior to the much more famous Mary O'Hara in my view. Another singer asked the audience to suggest a song; an English visitor requested "It's a long way to Tiperary". This was greetd by a stony silence lasting a few moments, after which the singer said that he refused to sing that song as it was an "English" song associated with the Irish War of Independence. Fortunately, the rest of the evening passed happily without further incident. Our Irish holiday was wonderful on all counts except for the weather, although it did not deter us.

Castles have always fascinated me so that when the Stirling Branch of the National Trust for Scotland ran a bus tour to the "Castles of Mar" over the 23rd.-25th. July week-end in 1983, Margot and I eagerly joined it. We were not disappointed as these castle are, by and large, fortified tower houses and in a beautiful state of preservation. Our tour covered Crathes Castle, Craigievar Castle, Castle Fraser, Drum Castle in addition to visiting Pitmedden Garden and Haddo House on our way back home.

In October 1982, the Duke of Edinburgh made comments expressing concern about the Solomon Islands population growth rate and appeared to lay the blame at the feet of the new government. Margot had a letter published in the Glasgow Herald of 23rd. October 1982 in which she pointed out all the problems that SIPPA had encountered, and in which she laid the blame for the current rate squarely at the feet of the British Administrations in Honiara and London for failing to heed the warning I had given them in my MD thesis, in which I had pointed out that the growth rate was 3.9 per cent per annum. I also wrote a letter to the Guardian on 31st. October saying much the same thing. In addition, I wrote directly to the Duke of Edinburgh at Buckingham Palace clearly outlining the situation there. I received a letter dated 26th. November 1982 from Major, the Hon. Andrew Wigram, on behalf of the Duke, thanking me for my letter, stating that he had just been informed of the birth rate there and that "under the circumstances, it struck him that a little self-restraint might be in the best interest of future generations."

At work, I was becoming progressively more disillusioned. There was more and more discord within the practice and I was disenchanted with the direction in which general practice appeared to be heading. Towards the end of 1983, we interviewed one or two doctors with a view to offering one a partnership; the doctor chosen, an Aberdeen graduate, was chosen against my advice. At about the same time, I wrote to Professor Black in Sydney, unknown to Margot, asking him if he knew of any posts which were available and would suit my experience and training. There was a deathly silence.

There was more to follow. We had thought about leaving Laurel Bank, although Margot was initially not too keen on the idea. However, I eventually went to look at a modern, detached villa, set beside the stream which flowed through Dollar, and I liked it; although Margot also liked it she did not really want to leave Laurel Bank. However, we did so in October 1983, moving into 2 Park Place, and called the house "Tigh an t'Srutha", Gaelic for the "House of the Stream". It badly needed re-decorated and we once again called on our friend Bill Crawford to do it. It was an ideal family house, as the downstairs section was self-contained with its own toilet and kitchen; this we gave to Euan. The upstairs section had two bedrooms, a kitchen, bathroom and lounge/dinette with a small verandah. The rest of us occupied the top part. Margot liked her new house, and I busied myself by replanting the many bulbs which I had brought with us from Laurel Bank. I never saw my finished handiwork but the rest did and they said it was lovely.

Early in 1984, I received a letter from Dr. J.K.A. (Keith) Fleming, the Secretary for Health of the Northern Territory Department of Health offering me a post. I told Margot and said I would think about it; by lunch time of the same day, I had decided and had telegrammed him accepting the post without consulting Margot further. Margot was, quite rightly, very angry with me, and this rash move threatened our already precarious relationship even further. Things then began to move rapidly. We were asked to come and see the Australian Consul in Edinburgh as a family, which we did. It was quite amazing to learn that they actually knew very little about life in Darwin and the Northern Territory. Euan and Michèle were keen to go to Australia but Margot wasn't and she had said previously that I could go on my own. The lady Consul sensed this and said that we had to go as a family or not at all; this, we later discovered, was quite untrue. Margot remained non-committal. The upshot of our visit was that I would go out first, the family following on although Margot had still not agreed to the move. For the next couple of months, I was kept very busy preparing for my move.

I knew Margot was angry with me but there was more to it than just my rash decision. I had always loved Margot, literally from the first moment I saw her on the playing fields of Balshagray, and even now, during her present crisis and almost total rejection of me, I always knew that deep down I truly loved her. I had always found her to be a warm, generous, gregarious, giving and intelligent person, much more interested in men than in women. It was, therefore, with increasing concern that I noticed her friend playing an increasingly important role in her life. The more I commented upon it, the more estranged Margot and I became. I really did not know what to do as I did not want us to separate although I did consider it, for the first time, this being an appropriate stage to do so. In the end, I didn't.

The other members of our family deserve some comment. Minnie and Whisky were still with us. When Whisky was just over a year old, and having her first "season", we decided that she should be mated. This was arranged and Whisky duly became pregnant. She had an uneventful pregnancy and delivered four or five pups. Unfortunately, she rejected them and, despite my attempts to hand feed them, they died one by one; I buried them in the garden together at Laurel Bank and planted a bush over them. Whisky was just not mature enough to deal with pups. We were all very saddened with the episode and never attempted the exercise again. As they grew older, Minnie developed quite severe dermatitis which I was only able to keep under control by treating her with steroids, while Whisky developed grand mal epilepsy, which I controlled with phenobarbitone. Now that I had decided to go to Darwin, I realised that we could not really ask anyone to look after them as they required constant medical attention. So, it was with the greatest regret that I took them in the car, with their tails wagging, to the Vet and had them put down. We had all loved them. In addition to the two dogs, I had also kept a pet rabbit, which I let loose on the Ochils one sunny afternoon, and tried to breed both budgerigars and canaries with varying degrees of success.

Soon it was time for me to leave for Australia. Personally, our stay in Scotland, and especially the period spent at Laurel Bank, I had found very traumatic in very many instances. It had not been a good time for us individually nor as a family; however, we had surprisingly remained together through it all. Perhaps that was what it was all about, to strengthen the family through adversity. I have always loved Margot, Euan and Michèle and I always will come what may.

.

Chapter Eighteen

Australia:
The Northern Territory (1984-1987)

The Pilbara, Western Australia (1987-1988)

I arrived at Darwin airport on 27 Mar 1984, at the unearthly hour of approximately 4 am. I had been told that there would be someone there to meet me, so I whisked quickly through Immigration Control and Customs. About half an hour after most of the passengers had departed, there was still nobody there to greet me. At this stage, even the taxis had disappeared, so I asked one of the male staff who appeared just about ready to depart for home if he would mind taking me into town and dropping me off at a motel; this he did very agreeably and I was deposited at one which I later discovered was almost next door to the Health Department HQ. After signing in and unpacking, I dropped off to sleep not awakening until about 10.30 am. Following a quick shower and dressing, I took a taxi into the Royal Darwin Hospital in the suburb of Casuarina, where I presented myself to the Hospital Superintendent's secretary. After sitting in the corridor for about half an hour, I was introduced to the Hospital Superintendent, Dr. Pauline Wilson. Laughingly, she said that she was the one who was supposed to have met me but didn't because she had slept in; further, she had not expected me to report in so soon. Needless to say, I had not been impressed with my welcome and nor was I impressed with

Pauline Wilson; I had no reason to change my impression of her the whole time I was in Darwin.

The first thing to be done was for me to be given some temporary accommodation. This didn't present too much of a problem and I was soon settled in a single officer's unit on the hospital grounds. However, this was quite a way from the Health Department HQ, which I understood was to be my base. Fortunately, there was another doctor who was also based in town, so he took me into work every morning and brought me back in the evening. However, this could not continue for long, so it was not too long before I bought myself a second hand, 1981 model, Ford Laser, a small, compact car. This car lasted me the whole time we were in Darwin and, on our departure, we gave it to our daughter Michèle.

While living in the hospital unit, I met a doctor called Aileen Plant who was also living in one of the units. I found her difficult to fathom and we never reached a decent level of rapport; I must admit that I thought that she was always looking out for the main chance and appeared to be a highly ambitious woman. So, I was not surprised to read, a few years later, that she was well up in the hierarchy of the Australian Faculty of Public Health Medicine.

Dr. Fleming, the Secretary for Health, was a tall, engaging Queenslander. Promptly on my arrival at Head Office, he asked to see me and, over a period of about an hour, we had a long discussion, as he found out about my experience and what I could do in the Public Health field. He said that he remembered me from Healesville, (RAAMC), and had also received good reports about me from Professor Black. My first suggestions to him he said were quite alright but could I not go ahead and do something a bit more challenging, asking me to come back and make him a firm proposal, virtually drafting my own job description. Settling into my office, I started to make some enquiries about the department and what the staff felt was needed. It soon became apparent that there was really little or no epidemiological work being done and that the statistical data collection left a lot to be desired. Quickly, I drew up a brief job description and presented it to Dr. Fleming. He was delighted and gave me a free hand to get things moving. My title was to be the Director of the Epidemiology and Assessment Branch, the first in the Territory. Very gradually, I built up a small unit consisting of a secretary, Penny Wooley, and a computer programmer, Les Reif, but was also able to tap into other units within the department. I received full backing from Penny and Les, who became my good friends also. Penny was a very cheerful lady, humorous and also very efficient, while Les was a bit blustering, but fun with it and also competent. In those days, I was not very knowledgeable about computers, which were becoming more and more invaluable at work, so I had to learn quickly and rely on Les both to teach me and to do the unit's computing. We were a happy small team and I settled in quickly.

I was in constant touch with the family, so I was not surprised when Euan said that he would like to come out to join me. So that he would not be unemployed, I hunted around the good hotels in Darwin and managed to arrange a job for him in Travelodge. He duly arrived and it was good to see him. However, this now meant that there were two of us living in a single officer's accommodation, a situation not to our liking. Margot was still very uncertain whether or not she would join Euan and I in Darwin. She told me later that what decided her was a strange experience she had in her sleep—she heard my voice calling her to join me. So, still undecided, she asked Michèle if she wanted to go as she was just about to enter her final year at Dollar Academy; Michèle said yes although Margot was still not happy about the idea. Margot contacted me with the great news but it left me with a lot of work to do as I had to hastily arrange a house for us. As we were bringing a complete household out from Scotland, it was essential that I should initially rent a house with lots of storage space. This I managed to do. It was a typical Darwin house, built on stilts, with the living accommodation on top, and the ground level part enclosed as a large garage. Most of the living area was wood-panelled and, looking back on it, I should have realised that Margot would find it too depressingly dark.

Fortunately, Margot and Michèle arrived quite soon and we were once again a family unit, living under the one roof. Euan and I collected them at the airport, took them to our new house and allowed them to rest and recuperate. I had arranged to take the family out to dinner that evening to a hotel restaurant but had failed to reconnoitre it before hand. On arrival, we found it to be little better than a bistro with cramped tables, poor service and inadequate food. Altogether, the evening was a disaster. Nor did Margot like the house from the start as it proved too depressing and dark for her, although the storage area was very adequate. Our new life in Australia was already off to a dreadful start.

There was also the task of setting Michèle up in school as soon as possible. In this we had more luck and she was quickly and happily enrolled at Dripstone High School, not far from our house. The longer we stayed in the rented house, the more angry Margot became; it was imperative that we obtained our own house as soon as possible. Again, we were very lucky and soon managed to buy a bungalow, consisting of a kitchen at the end of a large lounge which ran the whole length of the house and to the side of which, at a slightly higher level were three bedrooms, the largest one (ours) being at the end, with Euan and Michèle having the other two. In addition, it had a mosquito-proofed breezeway, a large area accessed from the lounge and opening at one end onto a nice enclosed garden containing a lovely swimming pool. One of the first tasks done in our new home was to tile the breezeway and thereafter we spent almost all our home hours in it. The house had an interesting history as it had been built just prior to the devastating "Cyclone Tracy" which hit Darwin one Christmas Eve a few years before; it was one of the very few houses which had remained intact. The swimming pool was a terrific bonus as the summer temperature of Darwin was an almost constant 31 C, with humidity approaching 100% on most days.

At work, I set about straightening out the data collections and ensuring that the systems in operation were as efficient, complete and accurate as possible. This proved to be a major task as the data collections had burgeoned haphazardly. Quite soon after settling in, Keith Fleming (we were soon on first name terms) introduced me to a small, vivacious, highly intelligent lady of Arab extraction called Mariam Smith, married to an Englishman, schooled in England but who had trained in Computer Systems engineering in the USA. She would be joining our unit. This proved to be an excellent move. The Department desperately needed a comprehensive computerised health system in place so, from scratch, Mariam and Les, with me providing the medical input, started to develop the "Total Health Information System" (THIS); at a later stage, and after considerable ongoing consultations with all levels of staff, a commercial computer company, DATEC, was also brought into the development. It became an all-absorbing task.

Shortly before Margot and Michèle arrived in Darwin, I received an invitation for Margot and me to attend the Official Opening of the Menzies School of Health Research by the Governor General of Australia, Sir Ninian Stephens, on the 23rd. June 1984, in the grounds of the hospital. As Margot was in Scotland, I took Mariam instead. It was a straightforward affair and quite enjoyable. Shortly after, on the 16th. October 1984, I was invited to join the Research Committee of the School. The founding Professor was John Matthews with whom I enjoyed a good, professional relationship.

On the home front, Euan moved into a flat in town and once again started his old habits, changing from job to job although he did manage to keep out of trouble. I tried to get Euan interested in wind-surfing, which he did try once but gave it up. On his own initiative, through a girl friend, he tried his hand, for a short while, as a male fashion model for the House of Vogue, his picture appearing in the NT News of 10th. July 1984.

Margot lead a mixed life. She soon found herself a job as she could not bear being idle. Her first job was as a clinic nurse with the Commonwealth Department of Health in town, where she dealt with vaccinations and assisted with employment examinations. She was still socialising and life was not all roses. We often went with Jan and Ray Anderson to the new casino in the evenings and spent a couple of hours there having a drink or two and spending a few dollars on the gambling machines. Ray also decided to buy into a greyhound which he raced regularly at the Dog Track; on one or two occasions, Margot and I joined them for a meal in the Owners' pavilion before spending an enjoyable couple of hours wasting a little of our money betting on the dogs. Michèle settled in very well at school and enjoyed her new environment, continuing to do well scholastically and making nice friends.

I had quite forgotten just how large Australia was. In my job, I was responsible for all aspects of epidemiology and data collection throughout the NT and was therefore required to travel widely. Nevertheless, I was relatively surprised that it took about two hours flying time from Darwin to Alice Springs in a large passenger jet aircraft. I was equally surprised at the impressiveness of the MacDonnell range on the approach to Alice Springs. Alice Springs was not a very inspiring place although it was the "capital"

233

of the eponymous region, whose Director of Public Health was Kerry Kirke. He had been there for many years and had built up an efficient, comprehensive health service. As in the other regions, I travelled widely, visiting bush hospitals and almost all of the aboriginal settlements such as Yuendumu. In the Darwin region, most of the travelling was done by road. I had to fly to the Arnhem Region, where Ernie Lindfield, a former English nurse, was the Director of Public Health, based at Nhulunbuy. South of Darwin was the Katherine Region where the Medical Director was Fred McConnell and the Director of Public Health was another Englishman called John Popper, who later transferred to Darwin. Between Katherine and Alice Springs was the Central region, run by another Englishman based at Tennent Creek. The NT covered a vast area.

Not long after Margot's arrival, we were invited by the Deputy Chief Minister / Minister for Health, Nick Dondas, on Friday, 7th. December 1984, to attend the unveiling of a plaque commemorating the fiftieth anniversary of the opening of Katherine Hospital, which was then followed by a reception at the Katherine Hotel. We had driven to Katherine with Age Dyrting, a Scandinavian doctor who had done some of his training in Scotland and who was now responsible for the Sexually Transmissible Diseases (STD) programme, and Margaret Dougherty, the NT Director of Nursing. We enjoyed the company and the outing.

AIDS was becoming a major problem in Australia and there was the very real fear that a major epidemic was a distinct possibility among the Aboriginal communities due to their initiation ceremonies and promiscuity. This was of especial concern to the NT Health Department as approximately 21% of the population was Aboriginal. As a result, when the Commonwealth Health Department decided to hold its initial AIDS meeting, the NT was also asked to participate; Keith Fleming and I flew down to the meeting in Sydney towards the end of 1984. It was a straightforward meeting and Keith, after it, more or less handed me the whole task of putting the NT programme into gear on our return. After the meeting, he took me out to a Chinese lunch at a smart restaurant, before moving on to see "Dune" at a cinema.

Setting up the Northern Territory AIDS Committee was quite a task as it had to be representative of the population. Consequently, I not only invited one or two medical and nursing staff to join, but also a representative of the local homosexual community, a minister of religion, a member from the education department, a local newspaper reporter and a member of the constabulary. The committee met regularly and advised on the long-term plans for the programme. In addition, Age Dyrting and John Law, a contact tracer in Age's unit, helped me to prepare a video on STDs and AIDS which we distributed to all Health Centres throughout the Territory. Much of my time was also spent in preparing information leaflets, giving public talks on the subject and setting up branch committees in the regions. A major concern was the screening of blood donors and the committee moved quickly in this direction setting up an efficient screening procedure, and a confidential register of HIV-positive patients. Controversially, all criminals in detention were also screened for the HIV. Throughout, great emphasis was placed on prevention, and the use of condoms, safe-sex and suitable protective clothing were widely advertised and recommended. All in all, everyone cooperated and the programme ran effectively. When the first Australian AIDS Conference was held for all involved in the nation-wide campaign, I attended as the NT representative.

There were one or two very good restaurants in Darwin. One, attached to the NT Museum, overlooked the sea. Margot and I not infrequently went there for lunch. It was to this Museum that we donated a six foot square, hand painted Tongan tapa (bark) cloth which had been given to us by a Swedish nurse attached to WHO whom we had looked after in Honiara when she had taken ill. We had had it framed and hung on the wall at both the Menstrie and Dollar houses, but we did not want it to deteriorate and so we thought that it should be returned to the south Pacific area. It was given the registration number NGE 1292. Margot also involved herself a little, through her friendship with Jan Anderson, in the Red Cross Society, and at a special "Twilight Cocktail Party" held at Government House on Friday, 24 May 85, we accompanied Jan and Ray.

There was a growing Scottish community in the Darwin area which supported two Pipe Bands. Not surprisingly, it didn't take long before it was decided to hold a Highland Ball. The inaugural one was held on Friday, 14 Jun 85, in the Foskey Pavilion at the Darwin Showground.

Once again, Jan and Ray accompanied us. We had a great time although the venue was not too wonderful. The following year, the venue was changed to the newly opened Casuarina Shopping Mall, the Ball actually being held in the central foyer, which was large and ideally suited for the occasion. This was the best of the three balls which we attended; the following one, although held in the same venue, was not so successful.

Things developed apace with the AIDS programme. Professor David Pennington, accompanied by his wife, Dr. Sonay Pennington, arrived in Darwin to assess the NT's programme. He was Head of the Australian AIDS Programme and Professor of Medicine at the University of Melbourne. To mark their visit, the Hon. Jim Robertson, MLA, the Special Minister for Constitutional Development, gave a luncheon for selected guests at the Holtze Cottage Restaurant on Tuesday, 25 Feb 86, to which I was invited as Head of the NT's Programme. Dr. John Quinn, the Deputy Secretary for Health, also attended. During his visit, he inspected all aspects of our programme and made visits to one or two centres. So, it was with some trepidation that I awaited his report on his return to Melbourne. He wrote directly to John Quinn on 10 Mar 86, saying how much they had enjoyed their visit, and that he had been very impressed by all aspects of the Territory's programme. In a hand-written PS, he wrote "Many thanks also to Ian Saint-Yves. He is a very able person and I much enjoyed chatting with him about the AIDS problem and other things."

I was not only involved with my epidemiology and AIDS. I also was a member of the Child Accident Prevention Committee which was chaired by Dr. John Edgar, a colleague in the department. Through this, Margot and I were invited to a Civic Reception given by the Lord Mayor, Mr. Alec Fong Lim, on Thursday, 13 Mar 86, at the Civic Centre. I quite enjoyed this committee as it was interesting to see what types of toys and other articles could prove to be of danger to young children.

In the meantime, there were minor upheavals within the Health Department. Keith Fleming was moved to a new, larger, non-health department, his job as Secretary for Health being taken by Dr. Ella Stack. Ella had been Lord Mayor of Darwin at about the time of the cyclone, and was also a well known medical personality. A small, rotund woman of Irish-Spanish extraction, she was sharp-witted and witty; however, I felt that she was not really a public health doctor and consequently never really came to grips with the problems in the community, especially those affecting the aborigines. Ella did not like the continued progress being made in the THIS computer development; I suspect that this was due to the fact that it was not her "baby". Although we were well along the path, she gradually reduced the funding and eventually stopped the programme. In its place, the department introduced an American commercial system.

There were other things which we did not see eye to eye about. My major concern in the health field was the type of health service being supplied to the aboriginal communities throughout the Territory. I was utterly amazed to find out that I was almost invariably the first "Head Office" official to visit them; consequently, it was not surprising that their views on the problems facing their communities were not known accurately within the department although there was a senior doctor supposedly in charge of Aboriginal Health. Further, the type of service being provided to the more remote communities was a "fire-brigade, band-aid" service, in which a doctor and nurse would fly in, spend a couple of hours looking at acutely ill patients, and fly out again, returning every two to four weeks. It failed totally to address the public health problems to which they were subject. When I wrote reports after visiting these settlements, I emphasised that the system was not solving any problems due to the fact that it was not reaching the people at the community level. I suggested that a doctor and nurse should be based on a rotating basis in an area to serve several aboriginal communities. Unfortunately, largely on the advice of the Head of Aboriginal Health, Dr. Dyalan Devanesan, ('DD' within the department), an Indian graduate, my reports were not acted upon because they were thought to be too "political". Ella did, however, have one saving grace; she had a keen sense of humour.

DD was good at talking and mouthing all the medically appropriate and politically correct platitudes into the ears of the hierarchy both medical and political, but poor in effective action. He boasted that he had a great relationship with all the Aboriginal communities in the NT and yet, while I was investigating their community problems with the aim of writing actionable reports, I was invariably told that I was the first Head Office doctor to visit them. So, I was not unduly surprised when my community reports were rejected by Ella Stack as being 'too political'. There was no love lost between DD and me as Margot unfortunately discovered while attending a dinner party hosted by Kerry and Barbara Kirke during Margot's holiday in Australia towards the end of 1992-early 1993 at which DD was present and at which he criticised me for most of the evening, so much so, in fact, that Margot threatened to leave apparently. Nor did it surprise me to learn in 1997 that DD had been awarded the 'Order of Australia', for his obvious talents, no doubt.

We had two or three visits from our European friends. One of the first to arrive was Margo Webster. I think that she stayed about six weeks and, for a part of that time, the two of them went to the luxury hotel at Yulara, Ayres Rock, for a holiday. Quite unexpectedly, Mel and Fini from Honiara appeared on the scene. We took them a way for a few days to show them around Darwin and the Katherine area; we had a mutually enjoyable time. Very sadly, their teenage daughter had recently died of leukaemia. Our next amusing visitors were Chris and Mette Gede from Denmark. They arrived in the wet season and just loved sitting in our breeze-way in the evenings, drinking whisky, chatting and listening to the deafening roar of the bull-frogs all around. Quite frequently, we sat in the swimming pool drinking and, rather dangerously, watched the forked lightning during tropical thunder storms. Darwin is the world's record holder for the intensity and number of electrical thunder storms. After they left us, they took a bus across the top of Australia to Queensland before flying back home.

Margot had changed jobs by now and was now working as a School Nurse at Darwin High School. She thoroughly enjoyed this work as it brought her into contact with the young people. She also enjoyed her colleagues as they were a hard-partying and drinking group. Her particular friends were Jill Adair, a small, pert blonde, and Steve Steiger, a tall Sagittarian just like Margot who also had the same birth date but was a good ten years younger. I accompanied Margot on one or two drinking parties but didn't really participate in or enjoy them. There were many and Margot went to quite a few by herself. In the evenings, she would accompany Jill to either the Darwin Casino or the Beaufort Hotel in the evenings and yet was fit to go to work the next morning.

Steve was not too much of a drinker. A married man, we had only met his wife once but we were not too impressed and I said to Margot that all was not going too well for them but she didn't believe me. They invited us out to dinner one evening. We arrived at the proper time to be greeted by Steve alone. His wife had not yet arrived back from playing tennis; time passed and at 11pm. we took our leave without a meal. On arriving home, we 'phoned him again to see what had happened to her. She still had not arrived home, so we advised him to contact the police and the hospital. Fortunately, injury was not the problem; unfortunately, they divorced soon after. He later married a Danish girl, Lisa, and now lives in Denmark with his wife and three children, leading a happy family life on his farm.

Life was not all fun and games for Margot; she did actually manage to do one good bit of basic research. She decided to follow the Year 8 pupils for a period recording the types of illnesses they suffered and the periods spent absent from school. I helped her in analysing the data before she set about writing it all up in an article which she successfully submitted for publication. For a number of years "First Year Health Activities in a Northern Territory of Australia High School: Role of the School Nurse" appeared to have been the only article written on the topic in Australia.

There were once again minor upheavals in the Health Department. Keith Fleming was brought back and, on the day he arrived for the hand-over, Ella Stack called a meeting so that new members would have the opportunity to meet the new Secretary. Keith also brought a team of his own from his previous department and set about reorganising the whole Head Office. The department was renamed the Department of Health and Social Welfare. Strangely enough, the Epidemiology Branch was brought into a larger unit headed by Jack Smith, Mariam's husband. This did not prove to be a very smart move as the new unit appeared to lose direction. Keith did not last long, however, and once again Ella was brought back in. A meeting of senior staff was called to meet her. For this occasion, I wore a long sleeved shirt, long trousers and tie and sat with my fellow medical colleague, Max Chalmers, in the front row. Max had also placed a row of ash-trays in an obvious position so that Ella could clearly see them at first glance (she was a heavy smoker). The entourage duly entered the room. Ella almost immediately asked me why I was all dressed up, to which I replied that I always dressed up when I went to a funeral. She also made a comment about the ash-trays. The rest of the meeting passed off quietly. However, that was not the end and finally Ella was replaced by Mr. Norman, the former Health Promotion chief, as head of the Department, while she was left in charge of the Health unit. The Department was not a happy place.

In the meantime, our joint social life continued. We attended the first official function at the newly opened Beaufort Hotel on 22 Mar 86, a cabaret dinner being held in the Hotel Ballroom, on behalf of "The Friends of the Duke" Awards. For some unknown reason, we were not happy at attending and, to worsen matters, we were given a poor table allocation. Margot and I fortunately managed to extricate ourselves from the ballroom without too much difficulty or embarrassment; however, as we were descending the curved stairway just behind John Quinn, she tripped and fell down part of the way. Fortunately, she did not hurt herself and nor did John Quinn see her fall.

Shortly after Jack Smith arrived at the department, we invited Penny Wooley (my secretary), her husband, Les Reif, his wife, Jack, Mariam and their small son, to a luncheon in the breezeway. Things started off quite well but, as the afternoon progressed, the conversation became more heated and Jack started making more and more anti-Scottish comments. I did not let him away with it.

St. Andrew's Day, 30th. November, is also Margot's birthday. One year, we gave a fancy dress party which we held in our breezeway and garden. It started in the early evening, and as the guests arrived we became more and more amazed with the range of costumes. The party went with a swing right from the beginning as most of the guests were from Margot's school; it continued well on into the wee small hours without anyone becoming too obnoxious. Everyone reckoned that it was one of the best local parties for a considerable while

One of the lady teachers at the school held a pilot's licence. She very kindly offered to take Margot, Michèle and me to Kakadu National Park along with a young male friend. We excitedly gathered at Darwin airport and then packed ourselves into a small aircraft, before heading off to

Kakadu. We decided that we would have lunch first and this we duly did. After lunch, we took off again this time heading for the Twin Falls. She managed to take the 'plane in close and we all enjoyed great views; in my opinion, the views of the plains and the Arnhem Land escarpment were equally impressive. All told, we had a thoroughly enjoyable day.

I was asked to present a paper at the 8th. National Conference of the College of Nursing, Australia, which was to be held in Darwin on 29/30 May 86. The theme of the Conference was "Nurses in Transition". I accepted the offer and presented a paper entitled "Some Health problems in the Territory." as I felt that Australian nurses should be made aware of the so-called "tropical" diseases which already existed, or had the potential to exist, in Australia. Just prior to the opening of the Conference, Margot and I were invited to a Reception given by the Administrator of the NT and his wife, Mr. and Mrs. Johnston, for the Councillors of the Australian College of Nursing which was held on 27 May 1986 on the Terrace of Government House in Darwin; as usual, it was an enjoyable evening as Jan and Ray Anderson also accompanied us.

In the meantime, Michèle had done very well at school and had decided to try her luck living away from home. After some discussion with us, she moved in with her boy-friend, Steve. We were not too happy with the idea but did not stop her. Unfortunately, I don't think she found it a happy relationship. She applied for a place to do Art at Adelaide University. When she went down to the campus, she found that she had arrived too late and that all places had been filled, so she followed in her mother's footsteps and enrolled for Political Science, which she thoroughly enjoyed and for which she gained a good degree.

Euan once again tried his luck at academia and decided to go back to school as a mature student. He enrolled at Casuarina High School and for a while, he seemed to be quite interested. He even managed to sit the final examinations and did quite well gaining four subjects. He went ahead and applied to study Psychology at the newly opened Darwin Institute and, amazingly, was accepted. However, once again his old failing reasserted itself—he found it too boring, and only stayed six weeks. After that, he returned to the hotel trade in Darwin, working in the Beaufort Hotel in charge of a section. Once again, it seemed to emphasise what Euan has always maintained, that studying was a waste of time for him.

On the social front, he was not idle either. At the end of November 1986, the Trash Ball was held at the Diamond Beach Casino nightclub, Crystal's. The concept of a Trash Ball originated in New York in the mid-1960s; emphasis was on an outrageous, unrestrained glamour but with plenty of style. Euan entered and won the "Most Outrageous Costume" title; he was in drag, and wore a black, lacy dress, long black net gloves, a small black pill box hat, long ear-rings, black high-heeled shoes, and smoked a cigarette held in a long black holder. For this, he won a prize holiday to Bali and his photo appeared in the NT News on 2 Dec 86.

One of the last social engagements Margot and I attended in Darwin was a Reception to launch the International "Polio Plus" campaign hosted by the Administrator and his wife on the Terrace at Government House. This was held on 21 Jul 1987 and, once again, Ray and Jan Anderson accompanied us on another successful social outing.

At work, I was not happy with the scene in the Health Department. In any case, I felt that I had done as much as I could at that particular stage of development. It may have been personal relationship problems but whatever it was, I had decided that enough was enough. Margot had always said that I got on well with my subordinates but less so with equals and superiors. My superiors always found me difficult to come to terms with as I was straight talking, knew what I was about and was a quick, accurate worker. Strangely enough, although Australians have a reputation for straight-talking I have never ever found this to be the case; they preferred to beat about the bush and consequently found my directness off-putting. Unfortunately, at about this time, Margot, having second thoughts about school health, had successfully applied for a job as a lecturer in Sociology at the Darwin Institute and was awaiting final acceptance. Euan was now away from home while Michèle was down in Adelaide attending the University. So, Margot was not at all happy when I said that I had applied for a job as a Consultant in Public Health Medicine based at Port Hedland, (South Hedland), in the Pilbara Region of Western Australia. She decided to go back home for a holiday. In the meantime, I accepted the new job over the telephone without ever being interviewed (looking back on it, I must have been the only applicant) and began to put everything in order before handing over. Dr. Dianne Houghton took over the AIDS programme while the Epidemiology Branch went to an American statistician called "Gypsy" Dyrling. I visited him on one occasion at about 4pm on a Friday afternoon. He had his feet up on the table and sitting around were two or three of his cronies helping him to drink alcohol. Changed days! Still, I liked Gypsy as he was a character.

As Head of the Epidemiology Branch, I was the Department's representative on quite a few local and national Committees. These included: NT Maternal and Child Health Committee (Chairman), NT AIDS Committee, the National Committee on Health and Vital Statistics, NT Statistical Liaison Committee, NT Cancer Advisory Group, National Association of Cancer Registries, NT Child Accident Prevention Committee. Belonging to these meant that I had to travel considerably within Australia; I even managed a visit to Hobart.

I wasn't really sorry to leave Darwin although Margot was, once she had managed to settle. We had made one or two good friends socially such as the Andersons, the Henrys, the Flemings and Steve Steiger, and also a few at work such as Penny Woolley, Les Reif and Age Dyrting. Margot had also made a few good friends through her tennis and golf, and was a member of both the Winnellie Lawn Tennis Club (founded by Audrey Kennet) and the Darwin Golf Club.

At about this time, the NT government opened an inquiry into Aboriginal social problems following the relatively high number of aboriginal deaths occurring in police custody, the inquiry being headed by Justice Muirhead, noted as the judge who presided over the infamous 'Chamberlain Dingo trial'. He had asked for appropriate written submissions from Territory residents to aid him in his inquiries; I sent him information concerning all the reports I had written on aboriginal communities for the Health Department. These were gratefully acknowledged and used.

I resigned from the NT Department of Health and Community Services (as it was now called if I remember correctly) on 31 August 1987 and flew via Alice Springs (flying over Ayres Rock on a gloriously sunny day) to Perth where I met the retiring Director of Public Health, a Glasgow graduate like myself. Everything was straight forward and the preliminaries were soon over. Fortunately, I still had our good friends John and Maureen James to stay with in Perth and they made my overnight stay very enjoyable. I hadn't seen them and their two sons for about seven years.

Next morning I was up early and away to the airport to catch the "milk-run" flight to Port Hedland. The flight itself was uneventful and the scenery from the air absolutely dreadful with vast areas of nothingness except a reddish soil and a few scattered trees. I was met at the airport by the Administrative Officer, Geoff, and taken to the Regional Office in South Hedland. Port Hedland, (including South Hedland a couple of miles along the road), was a dreadful township, with low grade buildings, almost no amenities and only one main road which led from north to south. To worsen matters, everything was covered with a fine reddish brown dust from the iron-ore which was shipped from the port. On the landward side of the road between Port and South Hedland, you drove past the highest point for miles around—a vast salt pile, which gleamed white in the strong sunlight. It was a depressing place and, by and large, the local community was equally depressing.

Arriving at the Regional Office, I was met by Dr. Andrew Penman, the Regional Medical Officer, a man slightly younger than myself. He seemed quite pleasant at first meeting as indeed he had over the telephone. The next person I met was the Regional Director of Nursing, another obese youngish woman called Bronwyn Scott. I was then introduced to the remainder of the central office staff, a male administrative officer, a white Australian, and a female Aboriginal secretary, both of whom were very pleasant. My own office was situated in the Regional Community Health unit situated just below the Regional Hospital in Port Hedland. The whole set-up was rather depressing and quite inadequate, and my office was rather dingy and cramped. Fortunately, the Community Health staff were quite refreshing and cheerful, interested in their work and very helpful.

The staff members consisted of five white, female nurses (of whom two were English, one Welsh, one American and the last Australian), three Aboriginal Health workers, two of whom were females. My particular contacts, and friends, were Mari Sutherland (she had been married to a Scot but was Welsh) and Joan Stewart (English but married to an Englishman of Ulster extraction, Dr. Rob Stewart). We all got on well together right from the word go.

Accommodation was limited but I was given a detached bungalow set in a run-down part of South Hedland, with a garden which had not been tended for some time. It was a dingy, depressing house with two dark bedrooms, a lounge-dining room, small kitchen and bathroom, with an attached car-port; the small back garden, almost totally devoid of grass and any greenery, was enclosed in a high fence, just like a prison yard. It was truly depressing.

On the first evening in Port Hedland, Andrew Penman invited me to dinner. He picked me up and drove me to his house, of a superior quality to mine, in Port Hedland. We were greeted by his wife, a quiet, subdued, little woman who scarcely said another word apart from the initial greeting for the rest of the social gathering. The other guests were the Harbour Master and his lady-friend, both Scots, and Dr. Rob and Joan Stewart. I must admit that I was not too impressed with the two Scots and neither Margot nor I became friendly with them at any time. Rob and Joan were quite another kettle of fish. Rob was the Regional Medical Consultant at the Hospital; a slightly younger man, he was about my height but slightly more rotund, and of a very cheerful nature. Joan was very thin and full of nervous energy, but like Rob, was of a very cheerful nature. I have to admit that if it had not been for the presence of Rob and Joan, the evening would have been a total disaster for me. That was the first and last private social gathering I ever attended with the Penmans.

There was one good thing, however; I was provided with a nice large, air-conditioned, four-door, Ford station-wagon, which I was also allowed to use personally so long as it was not excessive. Such a large car was essential in order to enable me to cover the vast distances which I did in order to reach the various Health centres, Schools and Clinics scattered throughout the Pilbara. Most of the roads were only partially sealed, dead straight and seemingly never-ending, with the carcasses of kangaroos edging the road on both sides. The scenery, to me, was relatively uninteresting being dead flat in most part, with stunted trees and shrubs scattered about, and an ochre red soil stretching endlessly to the horizon. Off the sealed roads, you were able to tell of the approach of a vehicle miles away because of the dust rising up into the air. I occasionally had to visit Onslow, about 540 kilometres south of Hedland and situated on the sea. These trips I quite enjoyed as the road was quiet and, although I had to leave early, I always reached there before lunch-time taking approximately five hours for the journey, and being made most welcome by the Australian nurse and her husband in their home. It was also an historic area with some convict buildings and settlements nearby.

As soon as I was reasonably settled, I contacted Margot in Scotland and arranged for her to join me in *Shangrila*'. Well, she duly arrived and hated the place at first sight. Part of this was undoubtedly due to the fact that she was angry with me for having forced her to leave Darwin but the main reason was the fact that the whole place was depressing. When she saw our house, she almost blew her top—she hated it. I must admit that I did not blame her at all. Nevertheless, this was now home for a while so we both tried, with great difficulty, to make the best of a bad lot.

My work was a mixed one. Part of it was acting as a GP for the mainly Aboriginal population in the township at a clinic held two or three times a week, another part was going out to one of the Aboriginal settlements on the outskirts with Mari and the female Aboriginal Health worker and trying to improve their conditions while the two ladies ran a medical clinic, a third part was to do with education of the Aboriginal Health Workers, a fourth part acting as a "flying doctor" leaving Port Hedland in a Nomad 'plane and flying into Aboriginal settlements in the interior for a few hours to run a clinic before flying home, while the last part consisted of visiting Regional schools throughout the Pilbara by road. It was a varied and interesting job but I was once again exceedingly disappointed to find that the same pattern of Health Service for remote Aboriginal communities was being implemented by the West Australian government.

About four months after my arrival, Andrew Penman and Bronwyn Scott had arranged the annual conference for Public Health staff. There was quite a gathering, almost all of them nursing staff with a sprinkling of Aboriginal Health workers. I was asked to make a presentation and I accepted the offer. I chose as my topic the system of Aboriginal Health care I had advocated in the Northern Territory. On the first day of the

Conference, when my time was approaching, Bronwyn asked me to make it a short speech as time was running out. Not long after she appeared again and asked me not to make a speech at all. To this I refused but said that it would only last a few minutes. Well, I was the last speaker and my speech did last only a few minutes but it caused ructions, with Andrew and Bronwyn almost jumping up and down in rage, while the nurses were almost equally split for and against me. Interestingly, my colleagues at the Community Health unit supported me totally as did the Aboriginal Health workers, while the other nurses expressed mixed reactions.

That night was the Conference Dinner. Margot had newly arrived and did not know anyone so she was quite looking forward to meeting some new acquaintances. The pre-Dinner drink session was enjoyable and passed without incident. However after the dinner was over and the speeches started, it was quite a different story. As the few invited old-guard got up and made their speeches, they kept referring to my talk and asking who did I think I was to tell them what to do. Margot, naturally, was most upset and asked me what I had said and so I repeated the story she already knew. My friends among the diners were very upset and felt that it should have not been raised at a social gathering. Anyway, the next afternoon, I demanded that I be permitted to speak to the participants for a few moments before the end, and this was grudgingly accepted. On speaking, I said that I thought that it was exceedingly bad taste to bring differences in professional opinions to a social dinner, and that I would tell them who I thought I was, telling them of my overall experience, emphasising that I had roughed it in New Guinea and the Solomon Islands on foot and that I had had considerable dealings with Aboriginal Health provision in the Northern Territory. I may have been wrong but I did not spare them because all I had done was to suggest a system of Health Care. Again, I was widely applauded and condemned in turns; Bronwyn and Andrew, from then on, scarcely spoke to me for the rest of my stay in the Pilbara, for which I was truly thankful. Needless to say, all this was quickly relayed to Perth and it was not long before I was asked down to see the boss, a Glasgow graduate, who was due to retire shortly. Strangely enough, I was welcomed and was tentatively offered the post of Regional Director for the Kimberly Region. While there, I met an old colleague from the Solomon Islands, Bill Beresford, now an Assistant Director. So, I returned to the Pilbara popular in Perth but detested by the Regional Directors of Public Health and Nursing. It was a difficult atmosphere to work in. I never had much time or respect for either of them and so, I was quite amazed to learn later that Andrew Penman had first moved to Perth as an Assistant Director of Public Health, and later to Sydney as Director of Public Health for New South Wales; I just found it quite beyond belief.

Margot was still socialising. Nevertheless, she applied for a job at the Hospital and started work as a nurse in one of the wards; however, she hated it and only lasted there about six weeks. One good thing was that she eventually had her varicose veins attended to and, fortunately, has had no trouble with them since. Socially, we tended to stick with Joan and Rob, visiting them, their daughter and Joan's mother at their home in Port Hedland. We enjoyed their company very much. In an effort to improve our social life, we joined the "Port Hedland Wine and Dine Society". On New Year's Eve 1987/1988 we attended the Society's Masquerade Ball at the Civic Centre, but it was rather a poor affair and we left soon after seeing in the New Year. Strangely enough, there was a Chinese restaurant locally which prepared the best roast duck we have ever tasted anywhere, to which we regularly went; the one good spot in a social desert.

Shopping in the area was adequate. Fortunately, the main supermarket was in South Hedland not far from home. There was only one drawback. The area has a large Aboriginal population and unfortunately a very high proportion of them were alcoholics. At the entrances to the supermarket, there would be groups of drunken aborigines, men and women, lying on the ground, yelling, screaming, vomiting and doing more indecent things. The treatment of the Aborigines in Australia is a study in itself, suffice it to say that I believe that they have been demoralised and degraded, their culture broken and their needs and aspirations left unknown through a lack of worthwhile governmental communication. If Margot and I wanted a change of venue, we would drive down to Karrattha, two fast hours down the road, do our shopping and have a nice meal, before returning home.

Margot could not take Port Hedland and me for too long and I was not surprised when she said that she was returning to Scotland to consider her future, with a view to a possible separation. This she did, returning to the Ochils, and Tillicoultry initially, where she rented a room in a cottage in a run-down area, before signing on with the Social Security, as she strongly believed that she was going to leave me. It always puzzled me why she chose to return the Hillfoots and many years later she told me that it was because Margo Webster, her best friend lived in the area. Anyway, I kept in touch with her and she eventually moved into a rented, small, modern, semi-detached house in a private estate at Arns Grove, Alloa. Nevertheless, she was still very angry with me. I also kept in constant touch with Euan and Michèle who were still in the NT and South Australia respectively.

Late in 1987, my very good friend Tom Smart from Tain suffered a heart attack but fortunately made a good recovery. When Margot returned to the Hillfoots in early 1988, she contacted Tom who then said to her that there was one thing that he wanted to do as soon as possible in case he died soon and that was to go and see me in Port Hedland. So, I was very happy to hear from him and to learn that he would be bringing his grandson, Gordon, then aged about twelve years, with him. This was no problem as I had a spare bedroom at my house in 4, Parker Street. Tom and Gordon duly arrived on 29 Jun 1988 and left me on 8 Jul 1988. During this time, we explored locally as well as hiring a car and driving up to Broome, the former pearling centre in the Kimberly region, for a couple of days. Broome was a small but interesting place although there was relatively little to do socially in the evenings except drink, which most of the local inhabitants appeared to do. An interesting spot was the cemetery for the Japanese pearlers who had died over the years. I couldn't come to Broome without buying some jewellery for Margot so, without too much hesitation I bought her a pair of lovely gold and pearl ear-rings, together with a magnificent necklace made up of a strand of large, pink coral beads. Another place we went to was Wittenoom, the asbestos mining centre, but also more famous for its gorges. We spent a lovely day there meandering about the rocks but ran into a spot of bother on the way back when the fan belt of my car broke; it was only through the kindness of another motorist who gave me one which we had to adapt that we managed to find our way back home. The township itself is only a shadow of its former self but there are still miners there digging for semi-precious stones; both Tom and I bought a few. Returning home, I gave a small dinner party to which I invited Rob and Joan Stewart and Mari Sutherland. It was a thoroughly enjoyable evening. Just before Tom and Gordon left for Darwin on their way back home, Rob and Joan gave Gordon an Akubra hat, which he cherishes to this day. As they left me, I contacted my friends Angus and

Puka Henry in Darwin and asked them to look after the two of them which, I am pleased to say, they did right royally. They arrived home safely and said that they had thoroughly enjoyed their holiday. I am glad to say that Tom never had another heart attack for over ten years, but eventually succumbed in 1997.

There was one thing that I made sure I did before leaving Australia and that was to visit my old Professor, friend and mentor, Robert Black and his wife, Gail, at their home in Sydney. He was then in the terminal stages of lung cancer but still alert and witty. It was a nice visit and one that I was glad I had made because he died shortly after it on 17 Mar 1988.

The Pilbara had been a relative disaster for Margot and me on nearly all counts. So, I was not at all sorry to resign on 12 Sept 1988 but not before I had secured a job in Saudi Arabia. From Port Hedland, I again flew south to Perth and stayed overnight with John and Maureen before catching the 'plane home to Margot.

I was not sorry to be leaving Australia as I did not enjoy the society and although I found the work in the Northern Territory (NT) and the Pilbara (WA) interesting and challenging, I felt that I did not receive the support I should have from the health departments.

In both of these posts, I dealt almost exclusively with Aboriginal problems and visited practically every settlement in both areas. My most disturbing finding on visiting these settlements was to find that almost invariably I had been the first "Head Office" doctor to visit them let alone find time to sit down and talk to them (even in Pidgin English as far down as the Katherine region of the NT). It was repeatedly brought home to me that the governments of the NT and WA were following a policy of "Do as I say, don't do as I do"; there was little or no worthwhile discourse on health and social matters and so the Aboriginal viewpoint on their own health problems was unknown.

I also felt that the type of health service provided to the outlying communities was inappropriate and ineffective; it was based on a short, flying visit by a doctor/nurse team at regular fortnightly/monthly intervals.

I reality, this only provided a "band-aid" service. In those days, there was little or no restriction on entering these Aboriginal areas. Glue and petrol sniffing were major problems which did not receive much attention, as were sexually transmitted diseases and alcoholism. I was also strongly advised not to make it known that some of the local Aboriginal population in the Alice springs region may have already contracted the HIV.

I wrote comprehensive reports on each visit I made in both the NT and WA, outlining the problems and suggesting possible solutions. In both situations, my reports were always met with the same reply, "You don't expect to act on these; they are far too political." In such a climate of political fear, medical laissez-faire and almost total lack of communication, is it any wonder that Aboriginal society and health are in such dire straits? Even John Howard, the Australian Prime Minister, in 2005 refused to make a full apology to the Aborigines for their horrendous treatment at the hands of white settlers.

Chapter Nineteen

Al Hada Hospital, Taif, Saudi Arabia: 21 Sep 88-22 Oct 90

I arrived home to be greeted by Margot at Edinburgh airport. It was good to see her again and I felt that our Australian upsets were well and truly behind us. We were both very sorry to leave Euan and Michèle in Australia but they were now quite adult and were leading separate and independent lives. This time, I was only to be home for a matter of about three weeks before flying off to Saudi Arabia.

Margot had bought a small Metro car and it was a bit of a struggle fitting in my large suitcase but we managed. She had moved from her rented room in Tillicoultry into a—rented semi-detached in Arns Grove, Alloa, modern but very cramped. Once back home things quickly returned to normal fortunately, as I only had about another week or two at home before I was due to fly out from London once again on the Saudia flight to Saudi Arabia. The time passed all too quickly and soon Margot was dropping me off at Edinburgh airport for me to catch the shuttle flight to London Heath Row.

I made all the connections without any difficulty. However, for some inexplicable reason I had been booked to go to Taif via Riyadh instead of via Jeddah. The six and a half hours flight was boring and uneventful and the first touchdown was at Jeddah, on a Friday, at about 5.30 am, just in time for the first "prayer call". All the passengers were off-loaded and asked to go through Immigration and Customs; however, we couldn't be processed because all the Saudis were busy kneeling and bowing saying their prayers, which lasted for about half-an-hour. Separate from the male Saudis was a small group of females dressed in long, black, loose-fitting robes (the abaya) from head to ankles It was a most inauspicious introduction to the country. Eventually, formalities were completed and the on-going passengers reboarded the aircraft for Riyadh. I arrived in Riyadh in late morning and found that I had about three to four hours to kill, before I could catch the connecting flight back to Jeddah. So, I walked out of the airport and caught a taxi into town, about 40 kilometres away, and which cost me SR 50. This part of Riyadh did not impress me too much as it was a vast impersonal city of almost three million people, of whom over half were Asians who had been allowed in to do all the menial tasks which Saudis felt disinclined to do.

It was only later that I discovered I had broken the law as free travel within the country, even between cities, is very strictly controlled and is only permitted if the traveller has a valid travel permit which specifies the places and dates of travel. Anyway, I arrived back at the airport safely and caught the connecting flight to Jeddah where I was met by a hospital driver who helped me with my luggage before setting off on the two and a half hour drive to Taif up in the mountains. I found the drive quite interesting. The desert was everywhere and it was interesting to see the herds of camels and goats being shepherded as we drove past. It defied belief to see the number of mosques along the way. Every tiny hamlet had at least one and sometimes it seemed as if there was a mosque every half-mile along the road. It was a desolate landscape and not at all appealing. Gradually, we left the desert plain and started to climb up towards Taif, up a wonderful, twisting, Italian-built road which climbed to about 6000 feet, providing panoramic views all around. Friday in Islamic countries is equivalent to the Sabbath or Sunday in Christian countries, so when we arrived at our destination, Al Hada Hospital, a Ministry of Defense and Aviation (MODA) Hospital, we found almost no activity. The driver showed me into a single officer's quarter which was quite comfortable and modern, but small and with shared facilities. It was adequate for the first few days but I had signed a married officer's contract and was entitled to married quarters.

The hospital was situated almost at the top of a mountain and commanded fine views, and was within a large compound which contained the hospital and all the accommodation and leisure facilities. Taif had formerly been the "summer" capital of the Saudi Royal family but had fallen out of favour with King Fahd. Nevertheless, it still boasted magnificent palaces of various sizes perched on the pinnacles surrounding the hospital, and an under-used Hilton Hotel nearby. The town itself was about half-an hours drive down a windy road and had a population of about 250 000 inhabitants. It was an unprepossessing place with scattered but adequate shopping facilities, although it did have one good international hotel out on the periphery.

Although the hospital had been up for a few years, I was still amazed at how opulent it was. All the surfaces of the building were lined with marble veneer, and in the two main entrance foyers there were fountains and glass chandeliers. As this was a MODA hospital, the Director was a military officer, a Major General Lenjawi, who must have been near retiral age and, in his earlier years, had been a surgeon. He was in fact the Administrator. Interestingly enough, the Medical Director, a civilian, was his younger brother, Dr. Essam Lenjawi, an Obstetrician/Gynaecologist. They were of Pakistani extraction. On a professional and personal level, General Lenjawi treated me very well and supported me in everything that I tried to do in the Hospital. Dr. Essam was another kettle of fish and could be rather prickly and, on occasion, lose his temper which he did with me once. Nevertheless, he treated me courteously and professionally, providing me with as much help as he was able. This was realised by the other expatriate medical staff who, if they wished to raise anything with Dr. Essam which might prove difficult, usually asked me to approach him. There was one Saudi failing which irked me at all times in the Kingdom. If I had to call in at any Saudi official, I would be politely asked to sit down along with the others but, instead of being taken in turn, any Saudi who entered after would be attended to first. There was little I could do about it so gradually I came to accept it and, as a consequence, spent an awful lot of time sitting around needlessly.

All the administrators were Saudi, some military and some civilian. Regardless of their seniority, they all occupied large plush offices filled with expensive, large furniture. It appeared to me that very few of them appeared to do much work as they either sat around all working hours drinking Arab coffee and talking or closing up and disappearing at any old time. There appeared to be very little direction. There were quite a few European, American, Canadian and Australian medical specialists, who occupied the top clinical posts, together with senior expatriate nursing staff, nearly all of whom were female, although there were a few male and female Saudi nurses. There were quite a few doctors from Arab countries, mainly Egypt, while the junior nursing posts, kitchen and cleaning staff were largely from the Philippines. The lesser jobs, such as security, were filled by Saudi soldiers.

I was quickly introduced to the General and to Dr. Essam. They seemed to be genuinely pleased to have me on the team. It turned out that I was to take charge of the Preventative Medicine Department within the Hospital; this suited me fine. I was also allocated two young Saudi soldiers whom I was to train in Public Health. They were both called Ali, intelligent but not altogether hard working. The smaller of the two, when he left the Army, wanted to take up religion; he had recently been married. They were a nice couple of young men and we got on well together. My Administrative Officer, and unofficial boss, was a youngish, slim, Saudi called Mohammed Al-Refaie, who, like most of the professional Saudis had been trained in an American University, having completed a course in Public Health. He was excitable and was keen to actually do things, working much harder tham most of his colleagues and taking a keen interest in the workings of the Preventative Medicine Department. Unfortunately, my Arabic was non-existent, and his English was not good although we managed to communicate very well, considering. We became very good friends and he always called me "Dr. Ian". Through him, I managed to secure a small, but comfortable office, the only expatriate to have one, even although it was situated on a corridor leading to the hospital mosque. This led to a standing joke between us. Every afternoon prayer-time, as Mohammed passed my office to go to the mosque, he would knock on my door if I were in, poke his head around the door and say, "Prayer time, Dr. Ian" and I would reply, "Not to-day, Mohammed."

My duties in my new job were quite varied. I soon discovered that there were no policy documents in place for most of the commonly occurring communicable diseases so, without too much trouble, I managed to get

Dr. Essam to approve them after I had written them. I was also responsible for advising on cleanliness and sterile procedures within the hospital, especially in the Operating theatres. In this, I was very ably assisted by a tall, bespectacled Australian nurse called Patricia Wells. Once again, I was fortunate to make a good friend of her in my time there. All fresh meat and vegetables entering the hospital were also inspected by me on a regular basis. With the Housing Administrator, I was responsible for ensuring that the accommodation for all expatriate staff was kept up to scratch; this entailed regular inspections of the quarters and facilities and sometimes it proved to be quite hair-raising. In addition, the leisure facilities, which included an indoor sports complex with a full-size, fresh-water pool, bowling alley and gymnasium, had to be strictly supervised There was also an outdoor swimming pool for expatriate "family" members, which permitted mixed bathing. Within the compound, there were also two food stores which we inspected unannounced at least monthly.

Down in the town, I was also responsible for similar activities at the Rehabilitation Hospital, a smaller but depressing hospital almost totally filled with young Saudi males with severe spinal cord and head injuries resulting from road traffic accidents. A third hospital, the Prince Sultan Hospital, situated a bit out of town and to which I drove (having obtained a local licence) was also within my ambit. These other two hospitals were visited about once a month. In addition to these duties, I also carried out formal lectures for staff on Communicable Diseases, trained my two staff members, and with the help of the Scottish medical secretary and the Director of Health Education, Dr. Al-Harthy, I wrote and had printed a manual on Preventative Medicine for use within the hospitals. Still, this was a military hospital and there were 14 military establishments within the Taif area and so, I was not surprised to find out that I was also allocated a large modern, furnished flat in Building 3, half-way up a small hill, overlooking another hill and the road into Taif. It was a lovely airy flat with a balcony and modern fittings, with two bedrooms, lounge-dining area, kitchen and bathroom.

Staff facilities for shopping were quite limited within the hospital, so once a week, a large bus was provided in the evening to take those of us who wished to go shopping into town, permitting us a couple of hours there before bringing us back up to the hospital. We usually arrived there just on "prayer-time", and it never failed to amaze me to see the religious police browbeating the Muslims to enter the mosques; of course, the shops had to close but many shopkeepers could be seen hiding behind their shutters keeping out of the way until they were permitted to open for business again. Saudi women, I felt, were very much treated as second class citizens. They could be seen trailing after their husbands clothed from head to toe in their black abayas and, if left by themselves, seated on the ground. Nevertheless, they seemed to do a lot of shopping and to be able to spend a lot of money, especially on gold jewellery. I must admit that I thought the way all women were treated in Saudi Arabia was poor, as all were required to wear the black abaya in nearly all instances in public, although certain areas were more liberal, (in Jeddah, expatriate women were allowed in public without the abaya, and did not require the eyes to be covered).

When we became really fed-up with Taif, we obtained a permit to travel to Jeddah, the hospital providing us with a bus for the journey. In Jeddah, there was a medium quality hotel which most of us used on our week-ends. It was nice to get away as Jeddah was quite "liberal" in comparison to Taif which was a fundamentalist area. It was a large, thriving, modern city with beautiful, Arab style buildings, fine shops and good restaurants and was a joy to visit. It was also situated on the Red Sea and enjoyed a natural beauty. Along the shore line, the municipality had built a very long and splendid esplanade, "The Corniche" which stretched for miles and is reputed to be the world's longest; along it are statues, sculptures and mosques. It provided a very enjoyable drive. The more adventurous among us would disappear to a hotel further north of Jeddah and spend time snorkelling and sub-aquaing.

Jeddah is also a great port and naval base. However, perhaps its most important role is as the main point of entry for pilgrims making the annual Hajj pilgrimage to Mecca. At this time, over two million people enter the Kingdom. To simplify their arrival by 'plane, a gigantic terminal had been specially built for arriving pilgrims, who are then transported away in buses kept only for the annual Hajj. It is a mammoth undertaking which is, unfortunately, not infrequently attended by disaster on a grand scale. However, for expatriates visiting the city, a far greater danger was the traffic. Saudis are bad drivers and, although there are road rules, most

Saudis choose to ignore them and, consequently, a driver takes his life in his hands literally on every occasion. I say "His" hands for the sole reason that women are forbidden to drive. I even saw a motorist going against the traffic on a major roundabout and survive miraculously. The hospitals are full of severely road-traumatised citizens, mainly young men.

About a month before each Hajj, I was involved in their preparations. First, I personally had to go to the household of the local Prince, one of King Abdullah's many grandsons, and vaccinate all those going to Hajj against Meningococcal Meningitis. He lived in a palatial palace close to the hospital and, while there, I was very well treated. Back at the hospital, I was indirectly involved with immunisation of the other pilgrims and was responsible for advising the Hajj authorities on water purification carried in the water tankers used for supplying the pilgrims on site. It was quite interesting. During Hajj, the hospital almost closed down for the whole month and it was pleasant taking things easy in an almost empty hospital.

My domestic routine was simple. I did almost all of my shopping at the larger of the two stores in the compound. At the week-end, (half-day Thursday, full-day Friday) I cooked two separate meals, and split them up into seven portions which I then placed in the deep-freeze; on alternate days, I defrosted a different meal. I had corn flakes and fruit for breakfast, while I had a light snack at the cafeteria during the working days at lunch-time. On a Thursday evening, I usually ate at the cafeteria with the other expatriate doctors, and it gave us a chance to have a chat. I did the washing on a Friday, drying it all off in the tumble dryer. In my spare time in the evenings and at the week-ends, I read, (ever since we first went to New Guinea, I have always subscribed to the Guardian as it provides a weekly air mail edition with good world news coverage), indulged in my hobby of painting (although I failed to do any decent paintings there) and listened to CDs on my Walkman through two small speakers. Of course, I did a lot of writing, mainly to Margot, Euan and Michèle.

I made a few friends there, all being colleagues on site. There were quite a few Europeans, a few Australians and a couple of Americans, so it was reasonably cosmopolitan. My colleague and first friend I made was Peter Wyman, a tall, blond Englishman married to an Irish nurse, who was in charge of the "Housekeeping Department". I learned a lot from Peter, and from his excellent Pakistani, Philippino and Sudanese supervisors, about the use of detergents and correct cleaning procedures throughout the hospital. There was an added attraction; for any festivities, the Filipinas in his unit would prepare very varied and delicious meals to which I was always invited. Peter and his wife left about nine months after my arrival, to be replaced by a Scot.

The Chief Surgeon was an Englishman called John Bolwell. He was an amusing character and we hit it off quite well. When he felt he had time to spare, he would wander down to my small office for a chat, which sometimes could last for quite a while. He had been at Taif for a number of years and I really doubted if he would ever be able to leave. Although married, his wife never appeared on the scene during my sojourn at Al Hada.

Again I was very fortunate with my work associates. My close associate in the nursing field was Patricia Wells, who had been well trained in Infection Control procedures in hospitals, for which I was truly thankful. Once again, we got on well together and worked as a team, without stamping on each other's toes. For a short while, I was fortunate to meet up with Hans, a Norwegian physician who, unfortunately, did not stay too long.

Peter's replacement was a slightly overweight Scot of average height. His wife was also on site working as a nurse. Again, he got on well with his staff and with me, which was very fortunate for all concerned. Unfortunately, he came to a sticky end. Like quite a few people on site, he brewed his own alcohol at home illicitly; the Saudis knew it was going on but so long as it was kept hidden, they tended to turn a blind eye to it. My friend John Bolwell became involved in this tale. As Chief Surgeon, he was intimately involved with the visits of Specialist Surgical Teams from abroad. One such team came from a prestigious English hospital to perform cardiac surgery on pre-selected patients. Of course, there had to be an "expatriate" party to welcome them to the hospital and for this, alcohol was needed. It was rumoured that the team brought their own along with the surgical equipment, but John felt that more was needed, so he tapped all the known sources around the hospital, our friend being one of them. His wife was against him giving any of their alcohol to John in case things got out of hand, but eventually he decided to do so. Well, the party must have been a great success for next morning a German nurse who had attended the party was found staggering around the hospital compound very drunk. Needless to say, she was picked up by the security guards, allowed to sober up and then questioned. The trail lead to John, but thereafter the story became very confused. Suffice to say that one English maintenance engineer was immediately sent back home, while our friend was grilled for a few days before he and his wife were also sent packing home to Scotland. For a considerable time thereafter, John was distinctly persona non grata, although he totally denied involving our friend at all in supplying some alcohol.

About six months after my arrival, another Scot appeared on the scene. Tommy Burgess came to take over the Catering Department. Married, he was a typical wee Glaswegian, knew his job and was exceedingly funny. Once he got started, he kept all around in stitches with his stories, especially the ones relating to his National Service experiences in Cyprus. His wife joined him shortly after. Being in charge of Infection Control, I was quite intimately involved with the workings of both the Housekeeping and Catering Departments and, fortunately, I could not have asked for better colleagues in both departments.

One of the Consultant Dermatologists was an Australian, Peter. He was a quaint, older man but quite amusing in a dry style. We became quite friendly, especially when he knew that Margot and I had been in Australia and were also Australian citizens. His wife, Margaret, paid one or two short visits to Al Hada. I found it quite strange that both John and Peter had great difficulty in diagnosing measles.

I was fortunate to become friendly with a few of the senior Saudi hospital staff. My Administrator, Mohamed Refaie, proved to be a very good friend in all respects; he was helpful, humorous, interested and loyal and, above all, had a good sense of humour. I didn't have so much to do with Dr. Essam but I always found him approachable, willing to hear whatever it was I had to say and to support me whenever necessary. I must have been accepted as I was one of the few Europeans to be invited to Arab dinners on special occasions. Another very knowledgeable and helpful colleague was the Army major in charge of the laboratory; he was assisted by a tall Army captain who was also a "matawa", although he never appeared to let his religious duties interfere with his work. The specialist Pathologist was a very tall, thin Swede and between them, they made a good team. For some reason, I was allowed to enter their working environment and was always made to feel welcome. Before I resigned from the hospital, the Major gave me a beautiful, very expensive Parker pen as a parting gift, which I have scarcely used.

I had always been interested in medical statistics and soon found my way down to the Medical Records section. Here, I was very fortunate with my colleagues as the unit consisted of three, and for a short while, four expatriate female coders. The boss was a small, lively Canadian, ably assisted by an Australian, and one English coder. They were a cheerful bunch and very helpful. Whenever I felt like some light relief, I would go down to their unit for a coffee and have a good laugh. Anything I asked for from the records, I was promptly given. In the secretarial field, I was also very fortunate. The first secretary was a small Scottish lady called Linda who hailed from Stonehaven; she was married to a Filipino and had a small child. Needless to say, we got on like a house on fire. On her departure, she was replaced by another Scottish secretary, who was equally helpful to me. In fact, at one stage, we were called the Scottish mafia by my friend Mohammed, as there were four of us there at the one time.

There were one or two other Europeans who caused some amusement. One was a very senior Canadian nurse who went missing for a number of days. Nobody in the hospital knew where she was although it was known that she had headed in the direction of Jeddah. Enquiries were therefore made in that city and she was eventually discovered in jail; she had been a passenger along with five Sudanese in a car which had been stopped by the police—all were drunk. Such was life in the fast lane!

An Australian physician was the next one to attract a bit of notoreity, although he did not do so until after he had left Al Hada hospital. It was rumoured that he moved to another hospital in the Riyadh area. Like most of the expatriates, he enjoyed an alcoholic tipple and this was to prove his undoing. It was reported that one evening, after he had had too much alcohol to drink, he somehow gained access to the minaret of the hospital mosque and then turned on the loud speaker, after which he began to make a mockery of the Islamic prayer call by singing "Waltzing Matilda". Needless to say, he was quickly silenced and placed under strict supervision. The next day, he was on a 'plane back to Australia.

I had signed a married contract and so Margot was entitled to come out and stay with me once my three months probationary period had been satisfactorily completed. The time passed without any problems and I soon started to put the wheels in motion to enable her to come out to Taif. It was exciting to drive into Jeddah knowing that I was going to meet Margot once again. The London 'plane arrived at about 11.30 pm, but Customs and Immigration formalities meant that passengers were not through for about another forty-five minutes. As I expected, she bounced through the gates and looked as cheeky as ever. It was great to see her again. That first visit, I only booked ourselves into the hotel which the staff used routinely when visiting Jeddah; it was clean and cheap. Margot was tired and so we had a quiet night in the hotel. The next day, we went into town and walked around, visiting one or two of the many, opulent shopping malls and enjoying the exoticism of a modern, Arab city. There were many excellent hotels from which to choose and, for our first lunch, we chose the Red Sea Palace Hotel; the ambience and the food were excellent. It was soon time for us to be collected by the hospital transport driver for our long, two and a half hours trip back to Al Hada. The early part of the drive was through flat, desert type country and was markedly uninteresting except for noting the occasional camel and goat herds by the side of the road. Margot was particularly amused to see camels being transported in the backs of small, open Nissan trucks; they appeared to enjoy the drive, contentedly chewing away. Eventually, we approached the foot of the great escarpment, about 6000 feet high, upon which the hospital was situated. The drive up the windy road, still not fully completed, was exhilirating and provided us with inspiring views. Eventually, we entered the compound and were driven up to our block of flats. Margot loved our flat and soon felt completely at home in it.

Life in such a restrictive social environment is particularly hard on Western expatriate women, as women in general, to our eyes, lead a very confined and second-class existence. All were expected to wear the long black abaya, even within the hospital compound, when outside their own accommodation; to travel on their own on public transport, and indeed to drive, were both forbidden. Nor were they allowed to enter hotels and restaurants on their own. I pointed all these out to Margot but she was soon able to see it in operation herself. Taif was in a relatively fundamentalist area but fortunately, the hospital administration was relatively liberal in its outlook. There was a "family" open-air swimmimng pool for expatriates in which mixed-sex bathing was permitted during the summer; however, this pool area was well screened to prevent the Muslims from seeing too much "flesh". There was, however, a large indoor pool in the Recreation Centre but here there were special periods allocated during the day for single sex bathing. In addition, there was a ten-pin bowling alley and a small gymnasium, again for segregated use. There were also two, open-air, tennis courts which were also segregated, one being solely for female use (it was screened) and the other for family, expatriate use. It was a totally artificial and, to my mind demeaning, situation for women.

Margot soon settled in, however. I managed to introduce her to one or two bridge players, and soon she had joined the small group which played weekly in the American compound in town; she had to be driven there discreetly as she was not travelling with her husband to these meetings. Among the female staff members, there was also a social environment, albeit limited. Margot managed to play a few games of tennis and bowls with a few of the nurses, as well as going swimming with me in the family pool and on her own during the Ladies' sessions. She adapted very well.

Margot was present on my birthday, 5th. April, and so we decided to have a small dinner party. I invited my good friend, Hans, a Norwegian physician who was just about to return home, and Patricia Wells. Margot prepared a nice meal, with no alcohol available. Nevertheless, we enjoyed the meal and had a good chat and laugh together.

Still, being cooped up in a hospital compound was not much fun and so, on one or two occasions, we escaped to Jeddah, which was far less restrictive in its social standards. In the meantime, I had found a very lovely, top class hotel to stay in, the Al Fau. From then onwards, on the three or four times we visited Jeddah, we always stayed there. It offered us a taste of luxury, and, amazingly, appeared very reasonable in price. The hotel meals, as befitted a top hotel, were fabulous. Margot and I well remember the first dinner we had there. It was a buffet and the spread and variety of food available were mind-boggling. Particularly noteworthy, for me at any rate, was the sea-food which was based on large lobster-tails; I had one helping and then the waiter returned to offer me another lobster-tail; this he did on two more occasions, so that I finished up eating four scrumptious lobster tails before moving on to the cold meats selection. It was a stupendous spread. However, we didn't eat all our meals in hotels. On the sea front, not far from the royal palace and almost opposite the high spraying fountain, we found an open air fish restaurant, which we frequented and in which we enjoyed lovely fish dishes.

Margot had been bothered with upper abdominal discomfort ever since her Menstrie days, but it only occurred very occasionally. Fortunately, it occurred at Al Hada, and so I arranged for her to see John Bolwell, who had her examined and X'Rayed, only to discover that she had gall stones. The next day she was taken to theatre and had a cholecystectomy, before being installed in a VIP suite. She made a quick and uneventful recovery, In particular, she was very well looked after by John and by the nursing staff. Margot was well pleased by it all. I gave her collection of gallstones to Patrick, an Irish dental mechanic, who placed them in a heart-shaped acrylic creation and presented it to Margot.

Still, we both knew that Margot would soon find this situation claustrophobic and after about three months, I made plans for her to return home. I was still in my first year of a two-years contract and this meant that she would only be allowed one more, company-paid visit in my second year. Margot is a very active and social person and I knew that she was missing her friends at home, especially Margo, with whom she seemed to spend some of her time. It was with a heavy heart that I accompanied Margot once more to Jeddah to put her on the 'plane for home. Fortunately, the employing company allowed her to come and go on a British Airways flight, which meant that she was able to enjoy a gin and tonic or two on her flight home. Soon after arriving home, she bought a small, former council flat at 7 Mitchell Crescent, Alloa.

For me, life continued as before once Margot had left, although I tried to vary things a bit. Fortunately, I was occasionally asked to visit the army bases around Taif to advise on a variety of public health topics, so I was never bored. I also became quite friendly with Dr. Al Harthy, the Director of Health Promotion, through the preparation of lectures which I had to present. He had his own block of offices separate from the hospital but within the compound. To establish a base-line, I decided to start writing a manual on Public Health for use as a training tool within the hospital; this took me into my second year to complete and, with the help of the Scottish secretaries and Dr. Al Harthy, who arranged for it to be photocopied and bound, I was able to leave it for the staff in Al Hada on my departure.

On the social scene, I was fortunately able to get on quite well with the Saudi administrators; the group in Al Hada had a sense of humour, which I found to be their saving grace. On one or two occasions, Dr. Essam invited me to a feast. These were all male affairs and, at the most, there would only be about two or three expatriates present. On entering the hall, your shoes had to be removed, and the first thing to be noticed was the almost total absence of chairs; consequently, all the guests either stood or sat about in small groups on the carpeted floor. Most of the small groups were busy playing cards for a Saudi meal is a leisurely affair and you have to spend the time somehow. Eventually, the kitchen staff would start to bring in the food laid on large, round silver salvers, which they would place on table cloths laid out on the floor. The food was almost always the same—hot, very succulent lamb, placed on savoury rice, with a selection of vegetables; around the salver, were placed bowls of fresh fruit and bottles or cans of soft, aerated drinks. The lamb was always delicious, but one had to move quickly and grab a seat on the floor near a salver, and start eating promptly with your hands as there was no ceremony involved, if you wished to satisfy your hunger. When you had finished the meal, there did not appear to be any formal ending to the occasion as the diners just rose and drifted away home. I found it strange but interesting, but always made a point of thanking the host before leaving the hall.

The holy month of Ramadan was the month in which Muslims are forbidden to eat and drink between sunrise and sunset. As far as I observed, it was also the month in which they ate to excess, the eating starting early in the evening and continuing for several hours, during which they ate enormous quantities. This appeared to be the pattern every evening. Expatriates were not allowed to be seen eating, drinking or smoking in public, while their offices were curtained off to allow them to do so. At the end of Ramadan, there was the Eid Holiday, which lasted for a few days. On the first day, Dr. Essam always arranged for a decorated table laden with sweets, sweetmeats and cool drinks to be set up in the main entrance hall for everyone to help themselves on entering the hospital, while he personally wished each one. It was a nice gesture.

When the end of my first year arrived, I was glad to be leaving; it was a draining environment, quite artificial and just not of the real world outside Saudi Arabia. Again, I was fortunate to be flying British Airways. As soon as we had left the ground, the chief steward came around all the passengers and, without asking, offered us all "doubles" of the alcohol of our choice; I chose Scotch and soda. The six and a half hours flight passed quickly.

Margot was waiting for me at Edinburgh airport. It was great to see her again and wonderful to be home in Scotland. She was still living in the same area but our new flat, although not large, was modern and well appointed; we were also able to have all our belongings about us once again. It was an upstairs flat but had quite a large garden. Of more importance, our new neighbours were very nice. An old man, Willie Wright, lived immediately below us, while Stefan and Leila Nasczk, and Ann Docherty were our other neighbours in the block. This was a special holiday as we had arranged to take all three weeks at our timeshare so that we could celebrate Michèle's 21st. birthday on 14 January 1989 for which she was coming home from Australia. To make it a truly family occasion, I had also invited Euan from Australia against Margot's advice. Anyway, Michèle arrived with a large female friend in tow. This put a considerable damper on proceedings as it turned out that Michèle did not like her too much either. Then Euan appeared in time for the party dinner which we had arranged with the management. All our old family friends and two of Michèle's Dollar Academy girlfriends arrived on time and everything appeared to be going well. Sam Middler took great pains to video the whole evening. In fact, the dinner/dance was a great success apart from the fact that the Aussie friend had somehow managed to injure her ankle. Afterwards however, things were different. Euan eventually drifted back to the hotel while the rest of us went to bed. About two in the morning, Michèle appeared at our bedroom door crying, saying that Euan was being terrible towards her, so I went downstairs to the lounge to find a party in full swing, with Euan having brought over the younger hotel staff. I felt that I had to ask them all to leave, which I did. In the morning, Margot insisted that Euan should leave and so, with a very heavy and sad heart, I took him to the bus stop in Aberfoyle with his suitcase. He travelled down to London on the bus but en route, someone stole his case and with it his passport. As a result, he had to obtain emergency documentation to enable him to catch the 'plane back to Australia. It was one of the saddest days of my life.

Later on the same day, Margo and Bob Webster returned for a meal but the injured ankle was causing Michèle's friend a lot of trouble, so I drove her into the Casualty Department at Stirling Royal Infirmary, where it was X'rayed, found to be broken and put in a plaster. Altogether, I felt that poor Michèle's birthday was a sad affair because of Euan's behaviour although Michèle appreciated our effort on her behalf. It wasn't long before the two returned to Australia. I was only home for a little over two weeks, so the time passed very quickly and soon I was being driven back to Edinburgh airport by Margot, en route to Taif via London and Jeddah.

I have always realised that it must have been difficult for Margot to be on her own for such long periods of time while I was overseas. I was pleased that Margo at least kept Margot busy in one way or another, such as hill-walking, golfing and social outings. Margot has always been more of a man's woman than a woman's woman; I have always known this and have never objected to it. I knew that she had male friends with whom she went out to lunches and the occasional dinner. Neil remained one of her close associates and frequently invited her through to Edinburgh to stay. She had others, though, closer at hand. The two main ones were local, married business men. I was not really too surprised as loneliness and excessive partying (with its accompanying depressive state) are very potent and dangerous.

Once more back in Taif, I continued to keep myself busy. I was involved in helping to set up the new 50-bed hospital near the military air-base; it was called the Prince Sultan Hospital. It also came within my jurisdiction and, once opened, I regularly drove out there to keep an eye on things. I tried to obtain a Saudi car licence and, with the help of some locals, I managed to do so without any testing or bother. I did this because I had been told that I could occasionally use a hospital car for my own purposes as well as for official business. I did use it but not very often as I felt that it was really too dangerous to drive a lot. This was unfortunately borne out by the death of one of our doctors being killed in a road accident. A collection was held for his wife and family before they returned to France.

The prince also asked me to return at Hajj time to vaccinate all the members of his family and staff, to which I agreed as it was a nice change from the hospital. I did, however, receive quite a surprise when he asked m if I would care to be his personal and family physician which would mean having to give up my job. After a little thought, I declined his very generous offer as I did not want to be at their beck and call 24 hours a day although I am sure that I would have been well treated at all times, even on their overseas travels. In addition, I was not sure how this would affect Margot. Looking back at it, I do not regret the decision I made.

Once again, I arranged for Margot to come out and join me. She arrived safely and she felt slightly more at home this time, as she now knew one or two people socially. Since her last visit, Peter's wife, Margaret, had arrived. We all became quite good friends. Margot played tennis and went swimming with Margaret, and occasionally we invited them over in the evenings. Things had, however, changed slightly since Margot's last visit. I had introduced her to Tommy Burgess and his wife, and on one or two occasions, we had gone across to their flat, where he had the local alcohol, "sadiq" (friend) available. On one visit to their flat, fortunately in the rainy season, Margot became slightly tipsy The problem was that they did not live in the same block of flats. However, it was dark, with the rain pouring down, when Tom and I steered Margot out of the flat to the top of the concrete steps leading down to our own block of flats. Here, she placed a large brown paper bag over her head and started yelling loudly. From the top of the steps, I was on my own with Margot and, amazingly, we safely reached our own flat without meeting anyone and without apparently attracting any attention. Needless to say, she collapsed on to her bed.

When my second birthday came around, we invited a few more friends, but this time there was alcohol present, although this was only given to a selected few, among them being Margaret, Peter and I refusing to take any at all. All the guests except the Hoares eventually left. Peter tried valiantly to get Margaret to accompany him back to their flat but she refused and eventually he left on his own quite disgusted, while Margot went to bed shortly after. In the meantime, Margaret continued to drink, while I sat on the armchair trying to humour her to go home; she did move, but only to sit on the floor beside my left leg, resting her arms and head on my lap, rambling on. After a considerable time, I managed to persuade her that I should take her home and again, luckily, I got her down the lift, walked her along the path to her own building and took her up on the lift to her flat without being seen. Such was life in Al Hada hospital behind the veneer of respectability. Margaret returned to Sydney shortly after.

Margot still participated in the evening bridge sessions and played tennis and bowls, even taking part in a fancy dress party organised by the nurses, in which she dressed up as a clown. With my driving licence, I borrowed a hospital car and we drove down to Jeddah on one or two occasions, once again staying at the Al Fau. We thoroughly enjoyed these outings. Margot's visit soon came to an end, and once again I saw her off on the'plane for London from Jeddah.

Time passed reasonably quickly but there were dark clouds on the horizon as we neared the end of 1990. Iraq attacked Kuwait and their troops over-ran the country. Saudi Arabia was immediately drawn into the affray along with the Americans, British and sundry other nations. Those of us who listened to the BBC World Service daily were well aware of the situation but the Saudi national media kept all news of the invasion off their air-waves for many days after the war had started. Quite unbelievably, the Air Force Commander at the Saudi military air base in Taif did not even know of the attack and had to be kept up to-date on the situation by an expatriate friend. Eventually, however, they could not hide it any longer and consternation broke out. The soldiers within the hospital were put on standby and the major in charge of the laboratory was transferred to a military hospital in the eastern district. Taif was a reasonable distance away from the Iraq border and the scene of conflict and apparently out of range of the Iraqi Scud missiles, so we felt quite safe. As is well known, an American led task force was put in place and proceeded to tidy up the situation. Socially, the presence of

American forces appearing in number throughout Saudi Arabia caused considerable upset as, within their ranks, were women soldiers who did not restrict themselves to Saudi dress and social conventions at any time. In one reported incident, a female driver was forcibly stopped and told to stop driving the military vehicle by a Saudi policeman (women were not permitted to drive); she refused outright but he persisted, so she got down from her truck and punched him squarely on the jaw knocking him to the ground before climbing back in and driving off. For a flickering moment, the more educated Saudi women thought that they might receive more freedom but after the war had been concluded, the social and moral screws were applied even more tightly.

At about the same time, I was beginning to think that I had achieved as much as I could at Al Hada so, when my time came for my end of contract vacation, I had more or less decided that I would leave. To this end, I packed up my few belongings and had then air-freighted home. However, I did not resign when I flew home on holiday at the end of September.

Once home, I told Margot of my intentions and she agreed as she was more worried about the state of war in the region. I looked around for suitable jobs in Scotland and was fortunate to be given an interview for an environmental health post in Glasgow. I was unsuccessful at the interview but only partially because, although I did not get that particular job, it did lead to another. On the interview panel, I recognised an old school friend from Glasgow Academy, Jim Donald, whom I had not seen for about forty years; he also recognised me but apart from the interview conversation, we never talked personally and so I never thought any more about it. In the meantime, my holiday was rapidly drawing to a close so I 'phoned Dr. Essam and asked if I could extend my holiday until the end of October, to which he agreed. About the middle of the month, I received a 'phone call from a Miss Ann Marron at Trinity Park House in Edinburgh asking me to come to see her. This I did and, after meeting Miss Marron, I was introduced to Dr. John Clarke. Both of them asked me about my experience and I told them that I had been the Epidemiologist in the Northern Territory and was familiar with coding and ICD9. Much to my surprise, they asked if I would be interested in working with them, but the offer would have to receive official approval in the first instance. That was fine with me, so I went back home happy. However, time was passing and my deadline to return to Taif was fast approaching; now into my last week, I still had not heard from them, Friday being the last day as I would have had to return to Saudi on the Sunday. Friday dawned and I was quite prepared to return when, at about 10 am., I received a call from Ann Marron saying that my job had been approved and that I was expected to start on 1 Dec 1990. Margot and I breathed a sigh of relief and I lost no time in letting Dr. Essam know that I would not be returning.

My time at Al Hada had been quite an experience but it was, to me, a quite artificial and totally unnecessarily restrictive environment. I have never really been religious but my experience of Islam had quite definitely put me off religion in all its forms although I remain a believer in Einstein's "god" (responsible for all things we know nothing about). I was glad to leave but was also glad that I had had the chance to meet Saudis and, I must say, that those I met in Taif treated me very fairly and well; above all, as far as I was concerned, they also had a sense of humour.

Chapter Twenty

Scotland: Alloa and Trinity Park House. 3
Dec 1990-9 Feb 1994

It felt wonderful to be back home again and to lose the sense of being restricted in your activities. We were well settled in our wee flat in Alloa and I took the opportunity to get to know our immediate neighbours. As I had a bit of spare time, Margot asked me to redecorate the lounge and this I did, making it lighter in colour. The rest of the house did not require much.

I was excited at the thought of starting work again in Edinburgh but was a bit worried about the transport situation as we only had the small Metro to share between us. The first thing I had to do was to lease a Crown car through my new job, which I did, finishing up with a diesel Peugeot 206. I was not at all sure of my way to Trinity Park House (TPH) as I did not know Edinburgh very well. So, on the last Sunday in November, a lovely sunny day, we drove into the outskirts, had a nice walk along the banks of the river to the waterfront at Granton, before having lunch outdoors at a restaurant overlooking the Firth. After this, we found our way to TPH. Fortunately, it was not too difficult a journey and we timed ourselves on the way back home; it only took about fifty minutes, much of it on the motorway.

She had always been male-oriented in her social life and this had never bothered me unduly. She met nice women, through bridge and golf, but these only occupied a peripheral part of her life on the whole. She did, however, meet a very nice elderly lady, recently widowed, called Connie Young, whose husband had been the mayor of Alloa. I think that she became a mother-figure to Margot and this was good for her as her own Mother was now in Larbert Mental Hospital, confined there because of severe Alzheimer's disease.

Margot did try to work and for a while she went back to nursing elderly patients at Sauchie Hospital. This was hard work and she found the staff difficult to get on with. Eventually and inevitably, she gave it up. Her social life became more important and we scarcely saw each other during the day and did very little socialising in the evenings. I must admit though that, through Margo, she did lead a much more active, outdoor life playing golf and hill-walking, between bouts of heavy socialising. There were one or two other ladies who became her friends. Hilde Axien was a German who lived close by and, together with Jean Robertson, who lived in Tullibody, Margot occasionally enjoyed other company. Through all her travails, her lady friends stood by and supported her, both figuratively and literally.

However, she had not given up her male friends altogether. She made contact with Neil and with one or two other friends, going out to lunches and other social functions with them. Her male friends seemed to confuse her lady friends, so they began to be called by their initials instead of by their names. This became a permanent fixture and in-joke. I still did not mind at this stage.

Well, Monday 3rd. December duly arrived and I set off in the Metro at 8am. as work started at 9am. The drive was uneventful and I arrived safely. After an initial chat with Ann Marron, I completed the administrative formalities and was told that I was on a rolling contract. I then went back to Ann Marron who, by this time, had been joined by John Clarke. Together they outlined my new post. I was to be the Head of a new unit, the Scottish Clinical Coding Centre, (SCCC), which was about to be formed, based in TPH. This unit would be responsible for implementing the Read Codes for medical classification and coding which had been accepted by the National Health Service in Scotland as the coding system to be used routinely throughout the hospital and primary health care services; in addition, the unit would be responsible for liaising with the NHS (UK) over the introduction of ICD 10 for use in national data for World Health Organisation and UK requirements, the Read Codes being cross-compatible with both ICD 9 and ICD 10. In addition, the Unit would be responsible for dealing with Read, ICD and OPCS 4 (for operations and surgical procedures) coding queries from throughout Scotland. As I only knew a bit about ICD 9, I had quite a lot to learn about coding and about the computer systems in use, in a very short time.

Apart from myself, the unit had no staff. My immediate superior was to be Ann Marron who had overall responsibility for quality control of all coding data throughout the NHS in Scotland. Her own unit consisted of six staff, four of whom were women, all working together in one large room. Initially, I was squeezed into this room and worked away on my own learning as rapidly as possible. Ann Marron was very supportive and her staff were helpful and good company, so time passed quite rapidly. John Clarke was peripherally involved with us as his unit was responsible for the collection of quite a large swathe of Scottish Morbidity Records (SMR). Also involved, but to a lesser degree, was Susan Cole, her unit being responsible for the collection of SMRs dealing with Obstetrics/ Gynaecology and Mental Health. All of these units came under the immediate jurisdiction of Mr. David Adams Jones, Director of the Information and Statistics Division of the Directorate of Information Services, which was headed by Mr. Charles Knox.

It was still a mystery to me how I was offered this job in the first place but it wasn't too long before the penny dropped. The Information and Statistics Division was based in TPH under the general umbrella of the Common Services Agency, whose Director proved to be Jim Donald. Apparently, knowing that it was intended to establish the SCCC, he had spoken to Mr. Adams Jones about me being a likely candidate.

I was now the Head of a Unit in name only as I did not have any staff. However, things were in hand. I learned on the grapevine that a Mrs. Betty Lomax, from John Clarke's unit had requested to be transferred and that she was well known for her direct approach to life. Betty duly arrived, a woman of the same age as myself whose birthday was on the 3rd. March, the same day as my Father's (Strangely enough, Ann Ward, also in Ann's unit, had the same birthday too). She was married, about my height and with silver grey hair and, quite correctly, she was very direct and blunt. The most important thing, however, was that she was efficient, knew TPH inside out and was a trade union representative; right from the start, we got on famously together. With two of us, we now needed somewhere to work, so we were shifted upstairs to a small room for a while. A little while later, our unit was enlarged by the arrival of Maria Dunlop, a married, small Glaswegian. She was an excellent ICD9 coder and was brought in to provide support to the unit. It amazed me just how close Betty and Maria became because they were quite the opposite in nature; fortunately, the three of us gelled and we developed into a close, friendly, supportive, efficient and productive unit.

Margot and I once again made contact with our mutual friends, the Nevilles, Middlers and Smarts. Brian (my best-man) and Elspeth had moved from Killearn back into Scotstoun, Glasgow, Sam and Ivy Middler had moved up to Arbroath while Tom and Lynn had remained in Tain. We visited them all occasionally and they us. It was nice to renew our old, mutual friends. In Alloa, almost all of our social engagements were undertaken with Bob and Margo; fortunately, I liked Bob and, at these social occasions we all enjoyed the food, the excess alcohol and the good company.

Fortunately, we had good neighbours. Immediately below us, there was Willie Wright, a retired gardener who suffered considerably from ill-health and a fondness for alcohol. He was very fond of Margot and not infrequently, they would drink together. Initially, he helped us considerably with our garden but in the end, I cut his grass and kept his small lawn tidy. Next door to him, there were Leila and Stefan Naczk. She was a local lass who had married Stefan, a former Polish military policeman. Leila was a very talkative and inquisitive wee woman with a heart of gold, while Stefan was a tall, quiet, obliging, helpful and domesticated man who spent a lot of the time in his workshop and appeared to do most of the housework and cooking. Above them, was Ann Docherty and her husband, with whom we had less dealings. Altogether, we were a very supportive group. When Willie began to decline in health in late 1995, Stefan and I kept a general eye on him, while later, when he was more or less housebound,

Stefan did his shopping and tidied up his house in between visits from the home help. Willie died peacefully in his armchair early in 1997, not long after we had moved.

As the end of 1990 approached, I heard that Susan Cole, as the NHS in Scotland representative for the implementation of ICD 10, was to represent Britain at the WHO conference to be held in Sao Paulo, Brazil, in April 1991. The next thing was that she had to withdraw because she was unable to leave her aged mother, so John Clarke was asked but he too was unable to go so, much to my surprise and delight, I was asked to go; needless to say, I accepted. Fortunately, early in 1991, Susan and I went down to London to meet and talk to Dr. John Ashley, the Deputy Chief Statistician, Office of Populations Census and Statistics, London, who was nominally in charge of ICD affairs within the UK but who hated aeroplane travel and so very rarely went on long journeys. He was a pleasant man and managed to fill me in with the details and provided me with the gist of a paper which I was to present at the Sao Paulo meeting.

In the meantime, Margot had applied for a job as Matron/Manager of a Nursing Home in Dunblane. On the 13th. February 1991, she was offered the post and started work there on the 4th. March. For some obscure reason, she was not shown around the Home before starting with the result that she had a rude awakening on her arrival there. The whole place was very, very dirty and unkempt, the worst place being the kitchen. Margot 'phoned me up to come and see the place, so I went across at lunch-time just to see the kitchen and I must admit that it was a disgrace. Margot felt that she could not remain at the Nursing Home, with which I agreed, and so she resigned after one day.

At TPH, flexi-time was in operation and so I made use of it, leaving the house at 7am. every week-day morning to avoid the worst of the traffic, starting at 8 am and leaving at 4pm. One of the first things I needed to do was to learn something about the Read Codes, so off I went down to the Computer Aided Medical Services (CAMS) Centre at Loughborough, where Dr. James Read, the originator of the codes, had established the headquarters. Over a period of about two days, I attended a course on the codes along with coders from the English NHS. I met James Read, but I cannot say that I was particularly impressed by him. At a later date, Maria also went down to Loughborough to attend a training course. When there, I met Dr. Paul Amos and Martin Strange, Paul being responsible for code implementation while Martin was responsible for computer affairs. At all times, I found them friendly and helpful, which was just as well as we had a lot of contact with one another., both coming up at regular intervals to Scotland. James Read had also installed his brother, Robert, as Manager of the Centre. Again, I was not too impressed.

The date of my departure for Brazil was the 5th. April, my birthday. I had to fly down to London and then catch the national Brazil flight to Sao Paulo. I was met at the airport and taken to the Lorena apartments where I had been allocated one. All the participants had been booked into the 'Lorena'. The flat was small, clean and adequate. Every day, we were collected and brought back after the meetings and any group social outings. The actual conference was under the auspices of the WHO/ PAHO with the local Brazil delegate, Dr. Laurenti, a Professor at the University of Sao Paulo, acting as host. The conference lasted from the 7th. to the 15th. April and the workings days were concentrated and quite long, as delegates from around the world discussed the implementation of the new ICD 10, with its attendant difficulties. Fortunately for me, my short paper passed without comment. It was very interesting to meet these interesting international figures. The biggest delegation was from the USA and among them was Connie Percy, an internationally renowned oncology coding expert and joint editor of the WHO ICO 2 manual (with Dr. Calum Muir of TPH), and Edna Roberts, a Statistician with PAHO based in Washington DC.

It has to be said that Professor Laurenti, his local committee and members of the WHO Secretariat at the Meeting, looked after us socially very well indeed. On the Saturday, we were taken to Professor Laurenti's home for a lovely buffet lunch, where we also had the chance to meet his family before visiting an agricultural college well out in the country, followed by a most interesting visit to the world's largest orchidarium which I found fascinating as I had always been interested in them ever since our days in TPNG. During this trip, I sat next to Edna, a small, grey-haired, lady of Margot's age, married to another statistician, and who hailed from Puerto Rico. We got on very well and thereafter usually sat together on our social outings. On Sunday, we were picked up again and taken to an old colonial town where we had a lovely lunch in a beautiful colonial setting. Much to my surprise and delight, I was asked to sit at the top table. After lunch, we were let loose to wander around and do some shopping. The University also has an excellent art collection and we were permitted to view it privately, a truly privileged experience as there were a few Modgliani paintings on show.

In addition to the outside trips, the WHO Secretariat gave the participants a Cocktail evening in the Lorena Hotel on the 10th. This was the first time I had actually met Edna as she had arrived late on the previous day. After the cocktails, a small group, which included Edna and me, settled in the Hotel bar and drank and talked until about 2 am. before staggering off to bed. Strangely enough, I also met Dr. Smith, whom I had known in Australia, at the gathering, and the two of us spent quite a lot of time together. Another evening, the local Brazilian unit took us all to a private dinner in a Japanese /Brazilian restaurant where we not only had a lovely meal but were entertained by young dancers who introduced us to some Brazilian dances, including the "*Lambada*" in which we were asked to participate; some did. Another evening, Edna and I decided to go to a so-called Arabic restaurant where we ate the usual kebabs. Apart from ourselves, there was only one other full table, the main attraction being the belly-dancer who gyrated in front of the tables while the diners stuffed paper money down her bra and into the waist-band of her diaphanous, skimpy dress. As can be imagined, the food wasn't too good and altogether it wasn't too exciting. On our last evening, I suggested to Connie and Edna that we should go out and have a good meal. After some enquiries, we decided on a Spanish style restaurant where the three of us settled down to the biggest and best paella I have ever tasted.

Like all good things, it had to come to an end. It had been a very enjoyable visit and well worthwhile in every respect. Before saying cheerio, I invited Edna and her husband, Charles, to visit us at our Timeshare in Aberfoyle over the Hogmanay period at the end of the year.

The Clinical Coding Centre in Loughborough was brand new and had not yet been officially opened. It was nice to receive an invitation to attend the opening, which was held on Monday, 17 June 1991, the Parliamentary Under Secretary of State for Health (also the local MP, I believe), Mr. Stephen Dorrell, officiating. On meeting him, I thought him to be a typical politician. Still, it was an interesting and important visit as I made contact with other interesting and useful people.

Back at work, I came into contact with more consultants at the head office of the NHS Information Services based at Keith House. These included Mr. Charles Knox, the Director, who had apparently been there ever since he had qualified from the Open University, and Mr. Len Douglas. Together with Ann Marron and John Clarke, Len had apparently made up the team which provided the NHS Scotland requirements for the Read codes Version 2 Encoder (Readscan) to be incorporated into the computing system to be used within the NHS and being developed by Computer Projects Ltd. This was a whole new ball-game for me and for a long time I went along with the flow, taking the opportunity to learn as much about the system as possible. Fortunately, a new Computer consultant was appointed to TPH to deal with Read and ICD computer problems; he was John Jamieson and, on his own volition, attached himself loosely to our small unit, where he provided us with expert computer information and advice as well as helping us to sort out the many problems associated with the implementation of the Read codes which we were starting to find progressively on an increasingly broad front.

Increasingly, bridge, golf, hill-walking, luncheons, days-out with Margo took up much of her waking moments. Further, she occasionally came home tipsy from these outings and, when she did stay at home, she had a drink or two in the evenings, sitting in the armchair beside the music centre, while listening to Barbra Streisand. I found this life style hard to bear as I had to arise at about 6.15 am. in order to leave for work at 7am. Whatever, I was beginning to find it difficult to cope with the situation. Margot and I talked about it frequently (through it all, we never stopped talking to one another and this was undoubtedly the major factor which kept us together) and consideration was given to her attending counselling, which she did on two or three occasions, but which always ended after a short period as she said that she already knew it all. I had experienced similar problems in my eight year period in general practice; in this whole period of time, I believe that I only had success with such a patient. Still, it was very difficult to accept when it was your own wife and

I knew that there would be no improvement until Margot internalised the basic fact that she had a serious problem.

However, she had amazing powers of recovery and, every mid-morning she would arise and look fresh. I put this resilience down to two things, her genes and to the fact that she never stopped eating well. In spite of it all, she again applied for jobs. Later, she applied for, and was accepted, the post of Administrator for a community education programmed called "Living and Learning in Clackmannanshire" (LALIC); this job lasted a few months before she packed it in. On one unfortunate, but memorable occasion, she visited an old lady friend in a Hospice after a luncheon and asked the nurse if she could take the friend for a stroll in the gardens, which she did; after a few minutes, the matron approached them and said that the friend should not be out strolling. Margot thought that this was ridiculous as the friend was not distressed and was obviously enjoying the gentle stroll. Margot turned to the Matron and said, "You're nothing but the Angel of Death." then turned to her friend and said cheerio. Her friend died ten days later.

In the late summer of 1992, Michele and her girl-friend, Donna, came home for a short holiday. It was great to see Michèle again—she looked well and was obviously enjoying life. Fortunately, the weather was fine and I was able to take them up to Dunkeld to show Michele's old school, Butterstone House School, to Donna. It was a bit sad for, on our arrival, we only met a caretaker who pointed out to us that the school had actually closed and that the new Butterstone House School had moved to a new site close by and was to become a "special" school. Nevertheless, Michèle was happy to see it again. Their visit was all too brief and soon they were wending their way back to Australia. At least, Margot and I felt happier having seen her, however briefly, after a period of three years.

Apart from answering all the ICD9 and OPCS4 coding queries, most of which was done over the telephone, the Unit was also responsible for running training courses for coders in ICD9, OPCS4 and Read Codes version 2. These were done on site at hospitals, Regional offices and TPH. For these training sessions, Maria and I were responsible for preparing the programmes and delivering the presentations, which usually took two days. We both enjoyed this as it gave us the opportunity to travel around

Scotland. Not only did we instruct in coding, but as time progressed we took it upon ourselves to involve ourselves in the actual implementation of the Readscan encoder in hospitals' computing systems. This was where we discovered considerable problems throughout almost all of the sites we visited.

In my investigation, I found problems in four major areas of development. After each visit to a site, I wrote a formal report which was submitted up through the correct channels. With the computing details, John kept me correct. In the light of my previous experience of government departments, I was not at all surprised that the reports appeared to cause little or no comment, and certainly no apparent action. More of this situation will appear later, suffice it to say, that everything was well documented and forwarded through the correct channels at all times.

As more and more sites made plans to move over to Read codes, the more busy the unit became. Fortunately, Betty was very efficient and, whenever possible, I would take both Betty and Maria to sites if necessary. We travelled quite widely and, on my own, I also visited Lerwick, Kirkwall and Stornoway. The more and more we travelled, the more we discovered that the whole system, in our opinion, was in a considerable mess.

To try to keep things running, fairly regular meetings were held at which representatives from CAMS (usually Paul Amos and Martin Strange), Keith House, TPH and the Regional Health Boards staff attended to discuss problems and review progress. At these meetings there was a considerable amount of talk and, in reality I felt, little true progress. At one such meeting, it was decided that the unit should prepare a comprehensive policy document outlining the philosophy behind the Read codes, and the need for their introduction. So, I set about writing this document, with a little input from Ann Marron. After each draft was completed by me and approved by Ann, it was submitted to Len Douglas and Charles Knox at Keith House; very few changes were made to each draft. Eventually, it was considered ready and no more changes were contemplated, so Ann asked me to go ahead and print 300 copies of the policy document for distribution throughout the NHS. The report was printed but not distributed before I submitted it to a full meeting of the above representatives. Imagine my surprise when Len Douglas said that it was unacceptable and must not be distributed. At the end of the meeting, I asked Tom Divers, the Chairman, if I may say a few words, to which he agreed. I then said that I was extremely angry with Len Douglas and Keith House officials for their rejection of the document as it had been cleared by them at every step of the way and that it was not only a gross waste of money but also of time and effort. I then watched the participants as they squirmed, embarrassed in their seats for they knew that what I had said was true. The document was never distributed and another was never prepared; the original copies lay in a cupboard in our office ever after.

I had gradually begun to realise that a medical practitioner was not needed for the job I was doing and that the main service I was providing was as the "icing on the cake", with one medical practitioner talking to other medical practitioners at hospital level; in other words, I was doing a public relations job trying to sell the system by interesting the future users. I was also peripherally involved with general practitioner implementation, and occasionally visited the GPASS head office in Hillington. Some practices were already using Read codes, version 1, in GPASS but there appeared to be some major problems in compatibility with the proposed hospital system.

There was a further academic gain for me. Early in 1991, I wrote to the Faculty of Public Health Medicine in London asking if I may have reciprocal Fellowship with the College as I was a Fellow of the Australian College. The reply was that I would require to be assessed before I could be granted exemption from the MFPHM examination. I did not object and, so it was that towards the end of the year, I received word that I was to be assessed by Professor James MacEwan, Glasgow University, (whom I had previously met at my interview in Stornoway), and Dr. Maria Dlugecka of Edinburgh, in Edinburgh. For the assessment, I took along my CV and copies of all my publications. They were both very considerate and attentive and the interview passed without difficulty; just before my departure, they informed me that they would be recommending my exemption from the examination. This was confirmed in a letter written to me on 31 Jan 1992.

At the end of December 1991, it was time for us to welcome Edna Roberts and her husband, Charles. I drove down to Glasgow airport and collected them off their flight from Washington DC, where they lived. It was good to see Edna again but, as I had never met Charles and had no idea what he looked like, I was very surprised to see that he was very tall, 6ft. 5in. The drive home was uneventful and it gave them time to readjust slightly. Charles was an easy going, humorous, gentle man and, like Edna, was also a statistician. There was no sense of diffidence between us. Margot was all prepared to meet us on our arrival. As we had arranged for us to spend Hogmanay at our timeshare, we would only be spending one night in our flat so, after wash-up and a light snack, we took them to see some of the surrounding beauty spots, among them Dollar Glen and Castle Campbell. After a lovely dinner in the evening, we all had an early night and went off to bed.

The next morning we prepared the car for our trip to Kinlochard and the timeshare. On our arrival there, we quickly settled in and allocated our visitors the guest double-bedroom. All went well. It was a reasonable day, so I decided to take our guests for a long day out. Margot thought that this was a good idea as it would give her a chance to tidy up. When I have guests from abroad, I always try to take them up the west coast to Wester Ross if possible so, as we had left quite early, I managed to take them up through Fort William, past Ben Nevis and the Commando Memorial at Spean Bridge before striking west to Loch Duich and Eilean Donan Castle, my favourite Castle. Although exhausted by the time we reached our base, they had thoroughly enjoyed the outing and the scenery, being especially entranced by the number of lochs. After a nice meal prepared by Margot we all retired to bed early after a short chat.

It was now Hogmanay and we had booked a table for six as Sam and Ivy were coming down from Arbroath to join us. They arrived safely, Sam resplendent in his kilt. Margot and Edna had also dressed themselves up, while Charles wore a relatively casual jacket and tie, and I my kilt. But things were not perfect. Our table was fine, set quite close to the band but the band was not a Scottish Country Dance or Ceilidh band but a pseudo-American jazz band. Unknown to us, the new female manager of the timeshare had hired the band of which her husband was the leader. Consequently, for the whole night we did not have one piece of Scottish music, which totally destroyed the whole atmosphere. I even spoke to the band to play at least one or two Scottish selections but they appeared unable to do so. Nevertheless, the meal was quite good, everyone behaved and Sam managed to take his video recording for posterity, so it was a moderate success and our little group got on well together. Just before midnight, the silly manageress ushered everyone out of the dining hall into the foyer to mingle with the other guests, so that we were all left standing like clothes poles idly waiting for midnight to strike at which stage a piper marched through the foyer. It was a disappointment and not at all traditional as we had failed to sing the traditional "Auld Lang Syne" while joining hands. Later, I learned that the other diners were also grossly disappointed and many of us, myself included, wrote letters of complaint against her. Since then, all Hogmanay Balls have been traditional.

Sam and Ivy only stayed until the afternoon of the 1st. January before returning to Arbroath. The next day, Margot's old lady friend, Connie Young, came to stay overnight. Charles and Edna thought she was lovely and they all got on well together, so that was a relief. As Connie left for home, Bob and Margo Webster arrived for the afternoon and dinner. Once again, we had a pleasant time and the Websters liked our American guests, so all was well. And so, the week at the timeshare passed off well in the end. In any case, we returned home to Alloa for one complete day before it was time for me to take them back to Glasgow airport to catch their flight home. Such was Life!

Back at work, the decision was taken to hold a large conference for all senior NHS staff in Scotland who wished to attend The theme of the conference was to be "The Read Clinical Classification in Health Care Records". Once again our unit was responsible for the organisation, the administrative aspects being dealt with by Betty Lomax, ably assisted by Maria Dunlop. I arranged for the guest speakers, who included James Read, Bill Dodd (Scottish Home and Health Department), Dr. Young (Deputy Chief Medical Officer), John Ashley (OPCS, London), Paul Amos (CAMS), Ms. J. Witty (Resource Management, Pontefract), and other guest speakers from within Scotland, with one or two from TPH and Keith House, including Charles Knox, John Clarke and me. It was held in the Walton Suite of the Southern General Hospital, Glasgow, on the 4 Jun 1992 and lasted all day. It was considered to have been very successful.

Through all our problems, Margot and I never stopped loving each other although at times our relationship was put under great stress. Margot made great efforts on our behalf at such important personal events such as birthdays and wedding anniversaries., and arranged for us to go away for a few days at these times. One such occasion, we spent a few lovely peaceful days at Dunoon in a comfortable hotel, which provided good food and which provided us with a base for doing a little touring in the Cowal peninsula. It must have been for our wedding anniversary for the autumn colours were superb and we enjoyed quite bright, dry weather. On another occasion, for my birthday, we spent a couple of days at a luxury hotel in Oban, which had formerly been the summer lodge of the Dukes of Argyll. Here, the food was superb and the time passed all too quickly. For Margot's birthdays, I always arranged for us to go out for a good dinner at a quality restaurant as she enjoyed that more than anything else.

Early in July 1992, Margot joined Margo for a ten days hill-walking holiday in the highlands. During this time, I too had a holiday and went up to my favourite part of the country, Wester Ross and Sutherland, where I stayed in B & Bs, returning home through Skye and Oban. The weather was dry but dull and I thoroughly enjoyed myself.

However, Margot was still having problems and was obviously unhappy and unsettled. I was very concerned with the fact that she was still spending little time with me and more time with her male admirers, not infrequently out overnight in Edinburgh. I was becoming more and more saddened and frustrated and was unsure what steps to take, although I seriously considered every option.

In about the middle of the year, we were given very disturbing news. Very fortunately, Margot had always gone for regular breast and cervical screenings and she once again attended for her regular cervical screening; this time, however, the very worrying news came back that she had been diagnosed as having cervical cancer, CIN 11. Very quickly, it was arranged that she be admitted to the Gynaecological unit at Stirling Royal Infirmary and, within the week, she had a very successful hystero-salpingo-oophorectomy performed. Very quickly, Margot recovered from the operation and quickly regained her own composure although we were all still very concerned. Regular check-ups have followed and, thank

Ian F.M. Saint-Yves

goodness, these have all been clear. This very serious episode concentrated Margot's mind as to her future, especially in her relationships with Euan, Michèle, Margo Webster and me.

After a considerable degree of thought, it was suggested by one of us that perhaps a trip out to Australia to see Euan and Michèle might turn out to be a good idea. Eventually, we both agreed to this and so everything was arranged quickly at both ends. She left just before her birthday at the end of November 1992 and flew to Perth, Western Australia, initially, where she stayed with Euan. As she had a "progressive" ticket, she was able to travel around Australia without any extra cost, which allowed her to visit Michele in Adelaide and most of her other friends in New South Wales and the Northern Territory. She did not return until March 1993. Although she had enjoyed the visit, she admitted that she was glad to be back.

During a part of this time, I took another ten days holiday, in January, but this time I went to Argyll and spent about ten days exploring the Kintyre and Cowal peninsulas, paying special attention to the castles. By and large, the weather was agreeably mild and dry although on the day I visited the Mull of Kintyre, it was fog bound with gale force winds driving the snow; it was so wild that I had to lean at almost 45 degrees into the wind to walk. I also failed to see the point of land. Nevertheless, I enjoyed it all as an experience.

We both still had our parents alive. My Mum was well settled and happy in Leslie House, a private Old Folks' Home in Pollokshields, Glasgow. Margot's Mum now had well established Alzheimer's Disease and was in care in the Larbert Mental Hospital. It was heartbreaking for Margot as her Mother's condition almost worsened before her eyes; her two sisters could not bear to visit her because of the grief it apparently caused them. So, it was with a great sense of relief that Rita, Margot's Mum, died in July 1993. Her Dad, Jack, since his divorce many years before, had been living in a small flat in Saltcoats, Ayrshire, where he was well settled and happy. With the two remaining parents happily settled, we breathed a sigh of relief. All that remained for Margot and me to do was to keep an eye on them both, which we were pleased to do.

The 5th. November 1993 was our 30th. Wedding Anniversary and for this, we went to Dunoon, where we booked in to the Enmore Hotel at Kirn for the 5th. and 6th. The dinner was a specially created one for a total of eight guests and it was delicious. We took the opportunity to look around the area for housing as we had decided that we did not wish to remain in Alloa. Margot knew that I favoured the Torridon and Argyll areas and, although she liked both, she ruled Torridon out as too remote (especially in winter) and although she liked Argyll, she said what was the point as she would always be looking over towards Arran, where she wanted to go, if she lived on the Kintyre peninsula. So, we decided not to look any further. We had, in February 1991, made our first effort to sell our flat but withdrew it from sale as things were unsettled.

The situation was changing at work. There were great reorganisations taking place and I felt that it would soon be our turn at the Coding Centre. A new system of data collection and vetting was introduced and given the acronym "COPPISH". Units were amalgamated and staff were given their notices. So, I was not at all surprised when I was asked to call upon David Adams Jones, the Director, early in November 1993 and told that, due to the setting-up of COPPISH, my post within the Clinical Coding Centre was redundant. I received the confirmatory letter, with three months notice of termination, on 9 Nov 1993. It upset Margot and me as I was hoping that this job would see me out until I retired, but I was not disheartened. Within the unit, Betty decided to retire and that she did, while Maria decided to stay on within another unit. Fortunately, I received a reasonable lump-sum payment and a moderate pension for my relatively few years within the NHS, the payment enabling us to pay off our mortgage on the flat.

Still, it was now a new ball game as I had to look for a job, so during this period of notice, I applied for one or two jobs, one as a GP in the south of England and two others as a Consultant in Public Health Medicine, one in the Newcastle area, and the other in Powys, Wales. It was only when I applied for these jobs that I discovered that I had to be accredited by the Faculty of Public Health Medicine, although I had never been told this when I had been granted the membership. I must admit that I felt this was unfair as I probably had more experience in Public Health and Infectious Diseases than 90% of the practising consultants, although I did not know much about the new NHS set-up nor the legislative requirements. Needless to say, I was unsuccessful. In addition, I had applied for a consultant post in Dubbo, New South Wales, and to our surprise, I was asked to participate in a telephone interview, which I did, but once again I was unsuccessful. I had already realised that I was really too old to be starting up in a new career within the NHS, so I was not altogether surprised when I failed to be appointed to other posts within Scotland for which I had applied.

I still had to do one or two things requiring attention. Maria and I had visited many of the proposed sites throughout Scotland in early 1993, and I had prepared a paper stating our findings. On 21 Jul 1993, a meeting was held at Keith House at which the senior members of ISD and DIS involved with the Read Codes were present. The Read Codes were discussed generally as usual, after which I presented my report on Sites' visits; this was very briefly considered. The reaction was mixed, one or two saying that my findings were immaterial, another saying that they were important, while a third said later that she wished that she had taken my comments more seriously, although no decisions were taken in the end.

Before leaving, I asked to see an old friend, in a senior NHS position, in order to obtain his advice as to what I should do in view of what I considered to be a serious situation. I said that I thought I should write to Mr. G. Scaife, the Chief Executive of the NHS in Scotland informing him of the difficulties; he thought that this was a good idea. I also discussed my intention with Bob Webster and he agreed. So, on 12 Nov 1993, I wrote to Mr. Scaife highlighting the areas of concern which I had mentioned previously, and attached copies of important memoranda which I had forwarded up the tree. I received a polite letter of acknowledgement but no action was taken.

I cannot say that I was sorry to leave TPH on the 9 Feb 1994 as the job was now a non-job; I did loosen my ties with Betty, Maria and John as a result, but not before we had an enjoyable farewell luncheon together in Edinburgh, which Margot and Dr. Angela Anderson also attended. Still, I was now unemployed and the future did not look at all promising.

About the middle of February 1994, I unexpectedly received a 'phone call from a recruiting agency in England asking me if I would be interested in taking a post as Consultant Epidemiologist in a hospital in Saudi Arabia. After a quick discussion with Margot, I said yes but also pointed out that I did not have a "letter of no objection" from the government; however, this was apparently immaterial as it was now over two years since I had last been in the country. I duly received the details and found out that the post was in the King Fahd Specialist Hospital, Buraydah, Al Qassim Region, 400 kilometres north of Riyadh.; I was expected to start on 13 March. From then on, it was all go.

Chapter Twenty-One

King Fahd Specialist Hospital, Buraydah: 13 Mar 1994-24 Jun 1996

Once again I was winging my way back to Saudi Arabia, only this time to a quite large desert township in Al Qassim province called Buraydah, situated about 400 kilometres north of Riyadh. After an uneventful flight to Riyadh, I had to sit around the airport for a few hours while awaiting the connecting flight to Buraydah, a flying time of less than one hour. Riyadh airport is of opulent design but as with most things in Saudi Arabia, there was a distinct lack of attention to the basic needs of passenger comfort as, for example, the maintenance of chairs which were nearly all trashed and almost totally useless. Further, there were few of the other passenger comforts such as a decent restaurant and a decent shopping concourse to while away the boring hours of waiting. Consequently, transit passengers just had to sit and, if they were fortunate to find usable chairs, have a doze. However, the time for my connection eventually arrived and I boarded the Saudia flight to Buraydah. The female flight attendants were Filipinas, the male ones Arabs, while most of the passengers were from the Indian sub-continent returning to their jobs in the region. The flight lasted about 45 minutes. The landscape appeared to be almost all desert and was most uninteresting.

After a safe landing, I was pleased to move quickly through the arrival lounge and meet the vehicle driver from the company running the hospital. He was a Sinhalese, friendly and helpful. In fact, I found all the drivers working for this company to be friendly and cooperative, most of them coming from the Indian sub-continent and Sri Lanka. It was about a forty minutes drive into Buraydah. I was struck by the barrennesss of the countryside and by the number of mosques along the road side; there appeared to be a small mosque every half mile at one particular stretch of highway. It wasn't long before I discovered the reason for this apparent excess of religiosity—just outside of Buraydah, there was a major religious teaching and training centre for Matawas and other religious clerics. In fact, Al Qassim turned out to be a particularly fundamentalist area and, it was reported, relatively anti-House of Saud, the ruling family.

The approach drive up to the hospital took me briefly through the town itself. It appeared to be quite large and spread out but it was little more than a long main street in the "town centre", lined with small shops, most of which were selling electronic equipment such as TVs and VCRs. It was not a particularly appealing city. Driving up to the hospital was quite imposing as it was enclosed by a wall and, once through the gates (guarded by security officers), the size and relative modernity of the building became apparent. It held approximately 350 beds and was about nine years old. I was taken to meet the local director of the managing Company, an Indian called Pilar. After a short chat, and having signed my contractual papers, he handed me a parcel of food for my use as I had arrived on Friday, the Muslim sabbath, and the main shops were closed. I was then taken across to my new "home", a small cramped flat on the first floor of a prison-block type of flats given over to males and married families.

I doubt if the flat had been refurbished since it had first been built. All the equipment supplied originally, such as cutlery, crockery and cooking utensils, was grossly deficient. There were no actual carpets on the floors just the felt underlay which was badly stained. My dining room table had a large iron scorch mark on it and the walls were all marked with the remains of sticky adhesive tapes. My so-called armchairs were broken and of the cheapest quality. Such were the pleasures of working in a Ministry of Health Hospital as compared to a MODA one. I made representation to the housing department but it was like whistling in the wind. There were four Saudis in it but they did absolutely nothing except sit around smoking and drinking coffee. In fact, they felt that they were so over-worked that, between them, they employed a Filipino clerk to do all their work although they still turned up at the office and deigned to collect their pay each month.

Anyway, I had to make the best of it. On Saturday, I turned up to work and was called up to see the Regional Director, Dr. Talat Al Beyari, and the recently appointed Hospital Director, Dr. Hisham Mohammed Nadrah. I found that I took an instant distrust to the Regional Director as he was small, dumpy and shifty-eyed. Apparently, he had been the preceding Hospital Director and still interfered in the running of the Hospital and maintained an office in the hospital, much to the anger of Dr. Hisham; there was no love lost between them and this was heightened by the fact that Dr. Hisham did not came from this region but had been brought in specially. Dr. Hisham was about my own height, 5ft. 8in. with a small beard and a lively looking face. They talked to me about what they would like me to do. Their biggest problem seemed to be the almost total lack of control of infection in the hospital, so they asked me to try to rectify the situation as well as doing some training and education. To this I readily agreed. I was told that I was to report directly to Dr. Hisham and that I would be on the Infection Control Committee.

I was then taken across to meet my new staff in the Infection Control Unit. The Unit was situated in a separate building, No.3, across the compound on the top storey in a floor otherwise given over to the Medical Education and Research Committee (MERC). The Infection Control team consisted of Abel Alonge, a Nigerian who had obtained his M.Sc in London and had also trained at the Centres for Disease Control in Atlanta, Evangelista (Gee) Angeles, a Filipina nurse who had done a course in Infection Control in Riyadh, and Agnes Waz, an Indian nurse. I liked them instantly as I felt that they were keen on doing their jobs. Abel was a short, stocky man, very knowledgable and amusing, while the other two were good workers. However, I was unhappy with their accommodation as they were cramped into two very small rooms along with all their office equipment; what was worse, I was expected to move in with them. I refused and went to see Dr. Hisham who, although not directly involved with MERC (which came under the jurisdiction of Dr. Al Beyari) still had control over the hospital. MERC had two or three rooms unused, so he insisted that I be given one of them, which I was; it was quite a nice office with good carpeting and a Parker Knoll arm chair. I settled down quietly and quickly.

It was amazing to discover just how little basic Infection Control procedures doctors and nurses actually put into practice, even if they knew them. The most important procedure of all, the correct and full procedure of hand washing was unknown to them; nor did they wash their hands at the correct times. Consequently, I was not surprised about the monthly infection rates. I immediately made contact with the Head of the Bacteriology laboratory, Dr. Talal Othman, a genial, helpful and knowledgable Egyptian who ran a good laboratory service and was, in fact, Chairman of the Hospital Infection Control Committee. In Egypt, he was the Professor of Microbiology and Immunology at Mansourah University, but had obtained leave of absence for a few years to come to Saudi Arabia. He was very pleased that I had been put in charge of Infection Control. My first task within the unit was to make my three colleagues feel that we were a team, with primary responsibility to ourselves, and that I was always available to them at any time should a problem arise. My next task was to look at the recording system which I found to be inadequate, so I set about redesigning the forms, so that all units could be clearly identified. Abel brought the isolation cards up-to-date; these were hung up outside wards in which there were patients with transmissible diseases. All these basic steps were readily approved by Dr. Hisham. One day, Dr. Talal and I drove to Riyadh to visit the American sister in charge of the Infection Control Unit at a large teaching hospital. This was a very instructive meeting and Mary-Lou, the sister, continued to give me support whenever it was needed.

There were very few white staff in the hospital. Dr. Ernst Hens was the ENT surgeon, a very good one and his unit had an almost negligible infection rate. A quite, unobtrusive man, he had a sense of humour and gradually grew on me. The Nursing Director, Patricia Breasley, was a small, rotund American who had been in the hospital for about six years. Quiet and efficient, she stood up for her nursing staff and was idolised by them. She was also helpful when the need arose. Terence Evans was an English technician in charge of the laboratory staff, efficient but difficult and who had been there for a number of years. I never really took to him. John Keogh, a Scotto-Irishman, former SAS, was ostensibly a nurse but

I never actually worked out what he did; he had an office opposite to the Infection Control Unit in MERC. I liked John as he had a great sense of humour. Slightly later, a young Australian, David Dodridge arrived to take over as Chief Radiology technician. He fitted in well but was soon disillusioned with the place. Later, there was one other, Jay Baecker, a Scot of German parentage, who arrived as a nurse. He was a tall chap with died blond hair and, when I first saw him, was wearing a light grey suit with a light pink shirt. According to him, he was a Ph.D. in Oceanography, in addition to his nursing qualifications, had written two or three books and owned flats in two or three cities throughout the world. Needless to say, we all believed him. However, it was true that in his youth he had played in a rock band in Glasgow. Probably the one person on whom the whole hospital revolved was a tall American who was the Hospital Secretary, called Mark Brown. He had been there for a number of years and was in with the bricks and thought himself indispensible and rather wonderful. As befitting his position, he was a mine of local information and gossip although he was also amusing and helpful when he wished to be. There were one or two lady Finnish doctors and nurses who stayed for a short while but they kept very much to themselves.

As the unit became more active, it became quite apparent that we were a bit short of staff and so I approached Dr. Hisham who, in turn, approached Pat Breasley. After a bit of a struggle, Gloria Salvador, a Filipina nurse, joined our unit. Our clerical facilities were totally inadequate as we had to share a secretary with the Obstetrics unit, our needs being very much second best. The secretary progressively objected as we supplied her with a continually increasing number of reports; eventually, she developed Repetitive Strain Injury and we were shunted over to the typing pool, but this was even worse. Once again I approached Dr. Hisham who agreed to find us a secretary. In this we were very fortunate as Estela Agreda Bahr joined our unit. I am certain that she was the best one in the hospital. A Filipina librarian she was married to an Egyptian doctor who was responsible for the Hospital Museum, which seemed a very easy job as he was hardly ever in it. I found it interesting that Estela and Gloria had converted to Islam, as had Agnes, (Agnes' husband was an Indian Muslim who worked as a driver for the hospital company, Al Mutabagani) all of them originally being Catholics. Abel, an Anglican, was distinctly anti-Islam, no doubt from his experiences in Nigeria. Almost voluntarily included in our unit was the secretary of MERC, a tall christian from Southern India called Ebenezer (Ebe) Fenn. He was grossly under appreciated in his own unit and was glad to have me to talk to at any time. He did a lot of little things for us and we helped out by letting Estela do some of our typing whenever possible. MERC came under the jurisdiction of Dr. Al Beyari and he made considerable efforts to have me vacate my office but Dr. Hisham stuck by me and I remained there until I resigned in June 1996.

The medical staff did not appreciate my professional intrusion into their cosy little world as I gradually pointed out to them in official memoranda signed by the Hospital Director exactly what they were supposed to be doing but weren't. Quite obviously, they also did not like the fact that I appeared to have jurisdiction over all their units. However, fate was moving in my direction. Quite unexpectedly, there was a major outbreak of Methicillin Resistant Staphylococcus Aureus (MRSA) infections in a few units throughout the hospital. This organism is resistant to all antibiotics except Vancomycin (although I now believe there are resistant strains). I immediately approached Dr. Hisham, told him that this was a true emergency and that the first thing to be done was to call an emergency meeting at which I would lay down all the things requiring to be done; I also pointed out that immediate plans would have to be made to set up an isolation unit to which all positive MRSA patients could be transferred. In addition, I suggested that an emergency MRSA committee be set-up to monitor the situation as required. To these suggestions, he agreed. At the first meeting of all the hospital nursing and medical staff, and after Dr. Hisham had made the introduction, I pointed out to them that they were not even following the first principles of Infection Control and that from now onwards, these principles would be rigorously enforced. In addition, extra measures would be enforced immediately to contain the MRSA outbreak, including the setting-up of an Isolation Unit. Dr. Hisham rose to make a rather embarrassed, apologetic response as it was quite obvious that the staff were angry, and then asked for questions from the floor. For a moment there was total silence, then Dr. Salim Akhtar, a senior physician, stood up and said that that had been the most unethical speech he had ever heard. He was followed by the Chief of Surgery, Dr. Salem, who said much the same. I then thanked them for their comments but refused to retract any of my speech.

Nevertheless, Dr. Hisham did what he promised and structural alterations were soon under way to transform one wing of the medical unit in to an isolation ward. Dedicated nurses and doctors were appointed to work in it and strict infection control procedures were enforced for all requiring entrance and for those working in the unit. Further, specific at-risk groups were identified, screened immediately and transferred to the unit if any were found to be positive. As a referral hospital, all transferees were also screened., as it was found that a considerable number of positive patients came from these hospitals, where patients were not routinely screened for MRSA. Shortly after, Dr. Hisham asked me to give another talk on MRSA, which I did only this time pointing out the progress being made and the procedures which still had to be followed.

The MRSA Committee appointed consisted of the heads of the Laboratory service, Medical and Surgical Departments, the Intensive Care Unit, and the Nursing Director, with one or two senior administrative staff, together with Abel and me. To our surprise, Dr. Hisham appointed Dr. Al Salahin, a newly arrived Ophthalmogist, as Chairman of the Committe, for the sole reason that some 20 years before he had done something in Infection Control. The first one or two meetings went off quite smoothly as the members began to understand the problems but it soon became obvious to me that the Chairman was out of touch and was leading the committee members up the wrong path. In one crucial decision which he disagreed with, he managed to swing almost the entire committee to his way of thinking. To me that was the last straw. I said that I could no longer participate in a committee in which the members did not follow internationally recognised criteria and that I believed the suggestions made to be stupid, then rose and left the meeting. After cajoling, I returned to the next meeting. Dr. Al Sahalin then came up to speak to me after the meeting and said that he objected to being called stupid. I replied that I did not say that he was stupid, I only said that his suggestion was stupid and in any case, it was all past and the subject was closed as far as I was concerned. Fortunately, he returned to Riyadh shortly afterwards. As part of the MRSA process, I immediately wrote a suitable policy and, learning by our own experience, I updated it into a small booklet, which was distributed to each ward and unit throughout the hospital, and to the Regional Health Office in Al Qassim.

As the Epidemiologist and Infection Control consultant for the regional Specialist Hospital, I was also invited to join the Regional Infection Control Committee. These were pretty unintersting meetings which seemed to achieve little and were initially under the chairmanship of Dr. Al Beyari. Much to my surprise, he presented my MRSA policy to the meeting and said that it was to be introduced throughout the Region, and that those hospital which were not screening for MRSA should take immediate steps to do so. A few months later, the national Ministry of Health issued an MRSA policy which was, in fact, a slightly modified version of my own.

After about six weeks, the number of MRSA patients in isolation fell from 38 to six, at which time it was suggested that the isolation unit could be closed and that the positive patients be returned to single rooms and placed under strict isolation conditions. After this MRSA episode, although many of the doctors still held a dislike of me, my stock improved within the hospital. I gave unit lectures on various aspects of infection and transmissible diseases, and carried out small epidemiological studies for individual units. Gradually, I was invited to look into perceived problems within units by the Heads of the units. Finally, they seemed to realise that I was actually trying to be helpful, although there were one or two who never seemd to understand the basic procedures. Even Dr. Salem, the Head of Surgery, became a friend of mine and used me to improve awareness within his unit. Taking advantage of this new partnership, I joined with two other senior members of his department, to produce a small manual on basic surgical procedures to accompany a video which demonstrated the procedures described; this was distributed within the hospital and proved successful.

The units which gave the Infection Control Unit the most problems were the Neonatal Intensive Care Unit, headed by Dr. Rodney Aguiar from India, and the Intensive Care Unit, headed by Dr. Mohamed Takriti from Syria. Dr. Rodney was very dynamic and up-to-date and he welcomed my attentions right from the start. It was quite obvious that his unit suffered from two major problems, gross over-crowding and a chronic, serious understaffing and, as a result, it was not always possible to carry out basic control procedures satisfactorily. This unit could optimally deal with 26 babies but at most times was running with 36+ babies, being cared for by seven nurses per shift. Between us, we managed to obtain a considerable improvement but not really enough. There were similar problems in the Intensive Care Unit, although these were aggravated by staff entering the unit failing to follow correct procedures. Again, after quite a struggle, this situation also improved somewhat. Perhaps the biggest problem in all Saudi hospitals is the visitors; they absolutely refuse to follow simple instructions when visiting patients and argue with nurses and doctors at all times. There is a total failure of community education about hospital requirements and consequently all things suffer. In addition, other patients visit patients supposedly in isolation because they refuse to listen to the Filipina nurses and sometimes to the doctors. It is a very difficult social environment to work in.

If Taif was restricted for social life, Buraydah was even worse. Even within the hospital compound, we were not permitted to gather in the open in a small group and talk to members of the opposite sex. In the "whites" accommodation, in which males and females stayed, the balconies running around the three levels were bricked up at each entrance, so that males and families could enter at one side and single females at the other. As I pointed out to the Hospital Director, this was a distinct fire hazard as the means of escape were blocked off at each end of the building but it didn't make any difference. Over the Christmas/ New Year period, an official hospital circular was issued saying that no parties were to be held to celebrate the occasion. I have to admit that Buraydah turned me against Islam as it showed me how intolerant it is always expecting people of other faiths to accede to their religious demands but not willing to make any concessions in return. In addition, I felt that they treated their women folk as second class citizens.

Exactly what social life did we enjoy as men. On my arrival, I found that Terry and John had taken to having a Dinner every Friday, the week-end, alternating between flats, each taking turns at cooking. To this group I was duly invited to attend and, when David arrived, he was too. It was nice not to have to do your own cooking every night of the week, and the meals were usually quite tasty, being washed down with liberal supplies of non-alcoholic beer. The talk usually started off with local gossip but inevitably finished up by discussing Islam and how restrictive a religion it was. Terry was usually the most critical in this. John was usually the most amusing while I listened to their words of wisdom on the local scene. Suddenly Terry stopped coming to our gatherings and the next thing we knew he had converted to Islam, and immediately became more Arab than the Arabs by wearing the thobe and ghoutra to work. He almost shunned us and mixed instead with the locals. Later, I asked him what made him convert and he said that he was driving along one night when he suddenly saw "*The Light*"; as someone said later, he probably did as there was a large illumination on that particular road. He became decidedly more unapproachable so we left him in his new religious isolation. We often wondered what happened when he returned home on his first holiday to his wife and children after his conversion. Jay arrived shortly after, and to fill the void, we invited him along although I was against this but John eventually persuaded me. Our first dinner with Jay was also our last of the group, as John had applied for another job in the Eastern Province with the same company. Jay turned up in black leather, almost-skin tight pants, obviouly wearing a protective over his private parts as the area was very prominent, and cowboy boots. The dinner party, held in my flat, was different but later David and I decided that it was definitely the last. Soon it was time for David to go on leave and he came to see me saying how frustrated he was in the job, so I suggested that he should go on holiday and just not return. He agreed that was a good idea and that was what he did eventually.

In my first year, I arranged for Margot to come out for six weeks. It was great to see her again. She was quite surprised at the place, so unlike Taif and Al Hada and she began to commiserate with my predicament. There was very little for her to do except to go swimming in the lovely indoor pool, and join the occasional shopping expedition into Buraydah. I knew six weeks was too long for her to stay in the hospital compound so I arranged for a ten days holiday in Dubai over the 1994 Christmas period.

Arriving in Dubai was like arriving on a different planet; it felt free and "civilised". At the airport, there was a car awaitng for us from the Chicago Beach Hotel. This turned out to be a lovely hotel, with nice rooms, restaurants, friendly and unobtrusive staff and excellent service, situated on a beautiful sandy beach but also with its own swimming pool. With additional shopping and gastronomic visits to the city itself, and the ready availability of alcohol, we both thoroughly enjoyed ourselves. The Christmas Dinner at the hotel was stupendous, highlighted by a cabaret and an exhibition of belly dancing. Strangely enough, after about eight days, it began to pall and, at the end, we felt that ten days were a bit too long. Although we thought Dubai was a very modern and up-to-date place, it was still nothing but a concrete jungle with very little natural beauty. Returning to Buraydah, Margot only had another ten days to go and these passed very quickly. Soon I was seeing her off at the airport.

There were a few of the senior female nursing staff whom I became quite friendly with in the wards. Among the original arrivals at the hospital was a small group of Nursing Supervisors who hailed from Nigeria and Uganda; they were great fun, British trained and knowledgeable. Within the hospital, there was a small Quality Improvement Unit which was always headed by an American nurse, assisted by four Filipina secretarial staff. The first one I encountered was a black, Cuban American called Julie; she was too frenetic and although she tried hard, she was not taken seriously and achieved relatively little. She did not stay for long and, oddly but unknown to us, had booked to take her holiday at the same time as we did at the Chicago Beach Hotel, much to our amazement. The next Head, Bobbie Ward, was a quiet, white, early-60s, lady, unassuming but strong-willed and focussed. She did not antagonise anyone and managed to achieve a great deal. We became good friends. The overall supervisor for Quality Improvement (QI) for the six specially chosen, pilot hospitals (of which King Fahd was one) was a jovial, grossly obese, black American lady from Chicago who visited the hospital approximately every two months, at which time she convened a meeting for the Heads of the pilot units within the Hospital; the Infection Control unit was one and, I am pleased to say, one of the very few which was up-to-date with QI requirements.

One of the nicest things about having these expatriate ladies was the fact that they were always baking and invariably, they would hand me a plateful of their wares to sample. I enjoyed these tidbits very much indeed. When a senior member of a Unit was due to leave, a small unit party was held at which the nurses usually provided the fare; this was mainly Filipino food, very tasty and varied. I was quite often invited to these, usually by the nursing staff needless to say.

A major calamity hit the hospital during the wet season. The ground upon which the hospital had been built was low lying with a high water-table; strangely enough, no drainage had been put in at the hospital nor along most of the roads so that when any rain did fall, it lay in sheets around the hospital compound and on the road edges, disappearing mainly by evaporation, as the high water-table prevented seepage. A routine consequence was the emergence of vast hordes of mosquitoes which were a major nuisance to the residents and, although I worked hand-in-hand with the staff of the maintenance department, our efforts did not solve the problem as mosquitoes have an approximate flight range of one mile (without wind assistance) from their breeding sites. One day the heavy rains started and soon the hospital compound was flooded, with some of the buildings becoming isolated; then the roads flooded and the rain water poured into the hospital compound resulting in the flooding of the basement of the actual hospital where all the electric and air conditioning machines were located. As a consequence, the whole electrical system of the hospital and compound failed. There was water everywhere and the rain continued to fall. An emergency meeting was called by Dr. Hisham at which Dr. Al Beyari acted as Chairman. It was decided to stop admitting patients and to evacuate as many of the patients as possible to the neighbouring hospitals. This was done quickly and efficiently. Emergency water pumps were brought in from the municipal depots and the surface water gradually siphoned off into water tankers over a couple of days; in addition, emergency electrical power supply and telephone systems were installed. Laundry proved to be a major problem as it could not be dealt with correctly; in fact, it lay around in large laundry bags in the side-rooms of the wards and became progressively more pungent. After two to three days another meeting was called, at which I raised the question of the laundry. Amazingly, Dr. Al Beyari wanted to retain this very badly soiled and heavily contaminated linen to have it washed ready for reuse. I dug me heels in and insisted that all the contaminated linen be disposed of by burning and this was eventually acceded to. Gradually the essential services returned although the telephone service never returned to its previous coverage within the hospital. My major work after this episode was to put all the infection control procedures in place and to ensure that operating theatres, delivery rooms and intensive care units were back to their original, uncontaminated states. As usual, there was a flurry of building at the basement level of the hospital with walls and ramps being built in an effort to prevent water flow, while on the road piles of coarse sand were laid along the side of the roads leading to the hospital. There were rumours that proper drainage was to be installed but nothing had been done up to the time I left.

I had never been a close confidant of Dr. Al Beyari and it was quite obvious that he only tolerated me because Dr. Hisham gave me his full support. Still, I was very surprised to be told by Dr. Hisham that Dr. Al Beyari had requested the Head Office at the Ministry of Health in Riyadh to send a doctor to investigate our unit as he was unhappy with our performance. Dr. Hisham was also rather upset but I assured him that there was nothing to worry about as our unit was actually an efficient one. About one month later, the Chief of the MOH Infection Control Department arrived at the hospital to begin his inspection, which lasted one day. I was happy to see that he was a very polite and quiet, unassuming Sudanese man; there was a good rapport between him and the members of the unit. We had everything laid out and ready for him and also guided him around the hospital so that he could meet and speak to anyone he wished. He followed the unit nurses around the wards on their routine rounds, read our policies, investigated our data collection and recording, noted our training and education schedules and generally overviewed our efforts. Late in the afternoon, he had a meeting with Dr. Hisham to tell him about his findings and impressions. He said that it was a good unit but he would send a written report on his return to Riyadh. This he did and in it, he said that not only was it an efficient and up-to-date unit but also probably the best unit of its kind in the whole of Saudi Arabia. We were delighted when Dr. Hisham showed us the report; Dr. Hisham congratulated the unit. There was silence from Dr. Al Beyari. Shortly afterwards, he was transferred to Riyadh.

Margot once again came out to Buraydah, but this time we stayed put and did not go anywhere except for the occasional jaunt into Riyadh. It must have been even more boring for her this time but still, we were happy to be together. There was one amusing episode. Our friend invited us down to "tea" in his flat one Thursday afternoon, the week-end. We duly arrived and after the introductions we sat down and chatted while he provided us with tea/coffee which he had himself. Gradually, we noted that he was becoming more and more garrulous and soon it was quite obvious that he was drunk as he had been spiking his coffee. At this stage, we took our departure. It wasn't long after this that he left the hospital. Once again, it was time for Margot to return home, and I accompanied her into Riyadh where we stayed in a suite at the Marriott before parting at the airport.

There was a great need for an Infection Control Manual which would cover all the departments within the hospital. So, over a period of about five months, I wrote a large manual; in this, I was assisted by Abel who wrote the chapter covering the Radiology department. It was beautifully typed by Estela and the original was given to Dr. Hisham, after it had been approved by the Heads of Departments, for his approval and signature. Mark Brown was then asked to order 50 copies for distribution to the regional office and to all the hospital departments. Much to our amazement, the first 25 copies arrived promptly and were delivered to the regional office and the main hospital units; however, the rest never appeared. I later received word that the Manual had been accepted as the standard reference for all hospitals in Saudi Arabia, although I was not able to confirm this.

I also wrote a short politco-economics book which I called "The State-Us Quo? (a private view of a public spectacle)" which once again was well-typed by Estela. On returning home I submitted it to about three publishers but all rejected it.

Towards the end of my stay at the hospital, I developed severe backache and also discovered that I was having problems with micturition. I contacted the orthopaedic surgeon who gave me a thorough examination, which included X'raying my spine. I was pleased to learn, in view of the serious injury to my right ankle in 1968, that my spinal column was correctly aligned, that there was no narrowing of my disc spaces and that there was very little osteophyte formation. He arranged physiotherapy and told me to change my chair in my flat, which I did bringing across the Parker Knoll armchair from my office. I next asked my friend, Dr. Shaukat Menon, a Pakistani urologist to assess my urinary symptoms. He found that I had a small nodule in the right lobe of my prostate gland. This I already knew and I told him it was as a result of a badly directed injection of sclerosing fluid to treat my haemorrhoids while I was at Al Hada Hospital in 1989.

Nevertheless, he arranged an ultrasound examination for me; this showed a small iso-echoic nodule in the right lobe, which appeared to be benign in nature. A blood sample was also tested for Prostate Specific Antigen, the result being within normal limits. It was decided that the nodule was benign. Indeed, all my symptoms began to improve once I started using the armchair from my office. On the strength of this, Dr. Shaukat and I decided to write a short article about my case which we submitted to the British Journal of Urology but it was rejected unfortunately. The title of the article was "Multiple clinico-pathological symptomatology presenting as a urinary problem."

Back at the OK Corral, indeed throughout many of the hospitals in Saudi Arabia, things were going from bad to worse. The government stopped paying the companies employing the staff. The worst affected group in King Fahd Hospital was the maintenance staff; it wasn't long before their salary was stopped completely and eventually their company had to provide them with a subsistence allowance just to buy food. Indeed, one of their workers collapsed from hunger and was admitted to hospital suffering from malnutrition. In their case, they suffered severe pay restrictions for almost a year. In our own case, we were first placed on half-pay and then for one month, we were not paid at all. At this, there was a big outcry and representation was made to Dr. Hisham who in turn officially approached the local Prince, the regional governor, to no avail. To Dr. Hisham's credit, he became more and more embarrassed as the situation continued. Meetings were held by the medical and nursing staff and various options were put forward, one being the formation of a small representative group to act on our behalf; the group was duly formed but proved to be ineffectual.

In the meantime, Pat Breasley had decided to retire. The nurses were greatly saddened by this and gave her a very emotional farewell party. She was their surrogate "Mother" and fought for them at all times. In the interim between the two Nursing Directors, Florence, a mature English nursing sister, was the acting director. The new Nursing Director was a white, young, buxom American, so-called whizz-kid from Alabama called Lawanda Nall. Unfortunately, she did not appear to endear herself to the staff at all and apparently left the hospital soon after I did. Florence did not like the new set-up and very soon after Lawanda's arrival tendered her resignation and applied for the post of Nursing Director at a nearby hospital, which surprised us all.

In the meantime, the financial situation continued. We were once again on half-pay. More meetings were held at which company representatives, and on one occasion the Finance minister, were present. But it was all hot air. I wrote personally to the company owner, Mr. Al Mutabagani, pointing out to him that the company were in breach of their contract. To this, I received a letter from the company manager, Mr. Hopper, stating that this was not the case. I then approached the British Embassy and was put in touch with their legal advisor, Michael Dark, who worked for the Saudi law firm, Al Hejailan. It was a great pleasure to be able to confide in him as he was exceedingly helpful and active on my behalf. He agreed wholeheartedly with me that the company was in breach of their contract and indeed of Saudi labour laws. He notified them accordingly and received a lot of legal waffle in reply. Mr. Dark then told me that the only option left was to take them to court but that this was probably take a number of years to resolve. However, by this stage, I had decided to resign as the company had promised that they would pay all outstanding salaries, but not pro-rata bonuses, to those who wished to leave. I again pointed out to the company that they had broken the contract by not paying us and that on resignation, I was entitled to the payment of my pro-rata bonus. Again they refused. By this time, I was sick to death of all things to do with the company, the hospital and Saudi Arabia so I tendered my resignation. By the time I resigned, we had been in financial strife for a period of about nine months and the situation had still not been resolved. The reason given for this financial mess by the Saudi Finance ministry was that the government did not have enough money because they were paying off their 1990 Iraqi War debts. During this strife, I even went as far as writing to the Prime Minister, John Major, seeking government assistance but only received a polite, unhelpful reply. However, I have to admit that our local MP, Martin O'Neil, whom I would have stood against had I been chosen, went out of his way to be of assistance, albeit unsuccessfully.

As the time came for me to leave, I was very agreeably surprised at the complimentary comments I began to receive from the most unlikely people. The saddest group was undoubtedly our own little unit; we had all got on very well together. Abel and I had managed to have all our nurses trained in Infection Control procedures in Riyadh, and we had provided them with our own tutorial sessions throughout my spell there. We were an efficient, knowledgeable and respected team. Interestingly, just before I put in my resignation, I was invited to join the national Infection Control Committee in Riyadh; I managed to attend one meeting where I told the chairman, the same doctor who had come to investigate our unit a few months before, that I had resigned. He was very sorry indeed to hear that.

Over the last few days, I was the guest of honour at a few ward parties, the most memorable one being our own unit's, although I enjoyed them all. I received one or two farewell presents. The present from Abel consisted of two black, wooden carvings of an Ibo chief and his wife—I have placed them in a prominent position in our retirement home. No matter how bad the posting, I have always found it sad to leave a place as I always manage to make one or two good friends and Buraydah was no exception. However, when the day came for me to leave, I was ready and happy to do so.

Chapter Twenty-Two

Home, 26 Jun 1996, the last attempt and Arran retirement.

Once again, it was great to be home. Margot was at Edinburgh airport to meet me. The wee flat was in good shape and the neighbours were very pleased to see me back.

My immediate concern was what was I going to do next. Fortunately, Margot had been active on my behalf. While I was still in Buraydah, she saw an advertisement in the paper for a locum Public Health post for the month of July at the Fife Health Board head office in Cupar, so she contacted the office and managed to arrange for the necessary application form to be sent out to me for completion. Duly completed, I returned it. On my arrival home, Margot told me that I had been accepted and that I was expected to start work on the 1st. July.

Once again, the week-end before I was due to start, Margot and I drove out to the head office to locate it, having a nice lunch on the way. It was about an hour away, part of the drive being on the motorway. The head office building itself was set in the fields surrounding a mental hospital; many rabbits could be seen quietly nibbling away, all very bucolic.

There was no difficulty on my first day at work. I met the Director of Public Health, an Englishman called Eric Baijal. He was welcoming and pointed out what he would like me to do; it turned out that he wished me to look at a new method of administration and to look into the problems facing the Health Board in psychiatry. I had also applied for a permanent post with the Health Board and had been chosen for interview at the end of the month; again, this permanent post related to psychiatry and I was not at all happy with the thought as I was not au fait with the NHS set-up, nor indeed the local situation. Nevertheless, I thought that the month within the department might stand me in good stead.

I was not really impressed with the set-up within the Health Board. Each doctor was allocated a small, dingy office. Once I started work in this dingy cell, I never saw another soul except for the secretary occasionally. Further, as I did everything that was given to me, I realised quite soon and forcibly that if this was what public health was like within the NHS, I didn't really want to do it. Fortunately and unfortunately, on the day of the interview, I discovered that the other interviewee was an English lady doctor who worked in psychiatry and she, quite correctly, was offered the post. That was the fortunate part; the unfortunate part was that I now had no job.

On the last day at the Fife Health Board, I left work early and quite tired. Such was the start of my move into retirement. At a later discussion with Margot, I decided there and then, the writing had already been on the wall before I went to Buraydah, that I would no longer try for permanent posts within the NHS as I was now too old and not in touch with the workings of the NHS. It was especially hard to accept financially as our financial state was not good and we were hoping that I would be able to work in a permanent post until retirement at 65.

Returning from Buraydah, I had not realised just how socially dependent Margot had become, but I soon found out during my first month back home. Quite amazingly, she was still working part-time with Medifit and was involved in the Health Screening of Scottish Office staff in Edinburgh and elsewhere. her powers of recovery after a night out were quite amazing and she was able to do her work, driving to the places of examination, without any obvious interference.

I had to do something as we needed an income, so I looked around for locum jobs in the Stirling area and I was successful in finding a few in Stirling, Callander, and Cumbernauld. I was not happy returning to general practice but beggars can't be choosers and, as it turned out, they were not too onerous.

Margot paid the occasional visit to Arran looking for a suitable plot or house as we had decided that, as there was no permanent employment for me locally, we may as well make our retirement move sooner (although it was sooner than we had intended) than later. So it was that, in mid-August 1996, we went across to Arran for the week-end and luck was with us for once. We visited the estate agent in Brodick and had a look at a few houses but they were either unsatisfactory or too expensive; as a result, we did our own scouting and were told that there was a block of land for sale in Whiting Bay, Margot's own village, near the Nursing Home for the Elderly, "Cooriedoon". Margot couldn't believe her luck, so off we went. The plot was very small and appeared as if it would be hemmed in and overpowered by the two houses being built by the owner of the land and "Cooriedoon". Nevertheless, Margot wanted it and went to speak to the owner's daughter to find out the cost and to say that she was interested. The cost was £10,000, which I thought rather expensive. In addition, when the daughter found out that Margot was a nurse, she offered her a job in the Home, which Margot accepted as she was also offered single accommodation there until our house was built and ready for occupancy.

Having accepted the Arran offer, Margot resigned from the Medifit job at the end of August, although it was the one that she had enjoyed most of all. Margot started work at Cooriedoon early in September and moved in, while I put our Alloa flat on the market. At the week-ends, I came across to Whiting Bay and stayed with Margot in her room. The more I saw of the plot of land, the less I liked it and told Margot so. Fortunately, one of the solicitors was on holiday at this crucial time and the intent to purchase was not established before I was able to change Margot's mind. Belatedly, she told me that she had seen another modern, compact bungalow nearby but didn't think I would like it as there was a large garden attached. Anyway, we went to look at it. I loved it at first sight. It lay behind the Royal Hotel, on the ground formerly occupied by the hotel's tennis courts, and was the middle and smallest one of three, but it lay in a lovely open, uncluttered garden of 0.7 acres, with a lovely view of the sea. The house itself was modern and barely required anything to be done to it apart from some redecoration and updating of the heating system which was all-electric; in addition, it had a wooden porch at the entrance which was to prove invaluable. Without more ado, we withdrew definitely from the purchase of the plot of land and took steps to buy this house, which was called "Dunvegan".

Once we had made the decision, Margot was very happy indeed. I had always said that she would have the last decision as to where we would retire. She promised me solemnly that it would herald in a completely new beginning and life-style for her as she realised that we would now be living in a very small, gold-fish bowl community. Further, she was already known on Arran, especially in Whiting Bay, as Jack Stewart's daughter; in addition, she had also gone to the old primary school in Whiting bay (the new school was on the same site at the foot of "School Brae" which led up to our new home) and attended the school in Lamlash before moving on to Rothesay Academy. She was well known.

The sale of our Alloa house didn't go too smoothly. We only had two inquiries. The first group found that the garden would have been too much for the elderly woman it was intended for although they liked the flat. Our second inquiry was from a young couple, the wife expecting a child reasonably soon; they liked the house and especially the garden as it was "safe". Contracts were exchanged but at the last moment their solicitor insisted that we comply with some recent local authority window safety regulations before sale, or else reduce the price. As there was now no time left for us, we reduced the price by £2000, the house eventually selling for £32000; they got a bargain.

Fortunately, I managed to continue my locum work on a regular basis at Cumbernauld. I usually did a full day every Friday, but also filled in on holidays and the occasional half-day on Saturdays. However, this meant that I had to leave home on the Thursday evening and return on the last ferry on Friday night during the summer months, or the afternoon ferry on the Saturday. If I did the whole week, I left on the Sunday and usually returned on the Friday or Saturday afternoon. Most of the year, the ferry service ran efficiently and without interruption; however, during one month in the winter, the regular large ferry, "Caledonian Isles", is taken out of service for its annual service and replaced by the smaller "Isle of Arran". Unfortunately, this change usually coincides with the worst weather and very occasionally, the ferry would either be cancelled or diverted from Ardrossan to Gourock; this added almost two hours to the journey from Brodick. Fortunately, these were very rare occurrences. By and large, I enjoyed the sails backwards and forwards, especially coming home.

Margot settled down quickly into her job and the new routine at Whiting Bay. At work, she took on three nights a week, although she not infrequently found it too demanding. She joined both Whiting Bay and Brodick Golf Clubs, but preferred the Brodick club. In the winter, she joined a bridge club in Lamlash. So, she was quite happy

I carried on with my locum work. During my nights away, I stayed with Margot's Dad, Jack, at his wee flat in Saltcoats. We got on well together and I was glad of his company and he of mine. Whenever necessary, I helped him with his business as he was becoming progressively more incapacitated by arthritis in his knees and by loss of sight. Still, he was always cheerful.

Fortunately, Margot had relatives on Arran. Andy and Jean MacCormick lived in Lamlash; he was Margot's uncle on her mother's side of the family. They were a cheerful couple and we always had a good time when we visited each other. Andy worked at the gate entrance taking tickets from visitors entering the Brodick Castle grounds during the summer season, while Jean served food the lunches at the Lamlash High School. Andy was very helpful in a variety of ways and we always felt that were able to rely on them.

We were very fortunate to have very good immediate neighbours. Brian and Brenda Wilson were the English owners of the Royal Hotel and had been there for a number of years. From time to time, Brenda would bring us up pieces of home baking. To our right, William Watson looked after his mother. He could never stop working and transformed his garden with excellent pieces of decorative woodwork. We had decided not to buy a lawn-mower for our first year, so Wiiliam kindly cut our grass for us and assisted me with any odd jobs which we required done. To our left were Rob and Margaret Stewart, originally from Uddingston. They had retired and kept themselves very busy in their immaculate garden. Again, they were very helpful and friendly. An added advantage was that Rob played golf so, every so often, he would have a game with Margot. If he was not too busy gardening and golfing, he would go for a sail in his dinghy. Very luckily, all the neighbours were also friends.

Margot had joined Brodick and Whiting Bay Golf Clubs. Slowly, she began to make a few new acquaintances; however, she had decided not to rush into setting up friendships. As the first winter was almost upon us, Margot also decided to join a Bridge club, where she again made some new acquaintances.

From her schooldays in Whiting Bay, she still had her best friend, Margaret "Binnie" Haddow, and her husband, Robert, living in the village. They were in business on the island initially but over the years, Robert had expanded the business to include the setting-up of water purification plants and this took him on many trips to countries in the Middle and far East. Margaret gave Margot quiet support and friendship.

There were still a few things requiring attention in the house, the chief among them being to update the heating system, which was all electric and based on storage heaters in the main parts of the house with booster heaters in the two bedrooms. This took longer than anticipated and for a couple of months we were either too cold or too hot and consequently ran up quite horrendous electricity bills until we learned how to adapt to the wonders of electricity after the simplicity of gas central heating. We also experienced problems with the installation of our BT telephone, first being given a Brodick number, then a number already allocated to another and finally having difficulty with our house name. I can never understand why all Scottish business appears to be transacted through an English office, especially when the operators dealing with the queries have absolutely little or no idea of Scottish geography, place names and accents. It most certainly is not consumer friendly but then again, Scotland is probably considered to be a region of north Britain.

Eventually, everything had been completed and we were comfortably settled in for the winter. On one of my spells at work, Margot had a house-warming to which she invited a few of her lady friends.

For my part, I decided that I would write my autobiography which I started in October and also attempt some serious painting once again. It was here that I found our porch most useful. My computer occupied one corner and, when sitting at it, I could look towards the sea. I had never really been too involved at a personal level with computers but once I started my book, I really began to enjoy the experience. When I ran into problems, I was very fortunate to be able to fall back on Jackie, Margot's sister, who taught computing skills. One thing I also revived was poetry writing as I had written one or two verses earlier. I had first written some poetry in about 1991 but had let my versifying lapse; however, with more spare time, I put my thoughts to paper once again. While living in Alloa, I had done some painting but had also let it lapse for a while. This again I revived but instead of working with my usual water and oil paints, I tried acrylics. When painting, I set up my table in the middle of the porch, again facing the sea, and worked away from photographs I had taken, each painting taking me about four hours to complete. Acrylics I found difficult initially as they were quick drying, but I liked the brightness of the colours. Strangely, once the winter gave way to the spring and summer, I found that I was less in the mood to paint and so I rested for about four months. I tried to sell my paintings, even going so far as to take a stall for a couple of days at the weekly Whiting Bay summer sales in the village hall, place an advertisement in the Arran Banner for six weeks and to hang paintings in a tourist cafe, but all to no avail. The trouble is that there are too many artistic people on Arran. Margot said that she would act as my agent; her spirit was willing but the flesh was weak.

As our first festive season on Arran approached, we were happy that we had made the move from Alloa although it had occurred a few years earlier than we had intended. Whiting Bay was a nice spot to be in as it never became too busy in the tourist season and was always blessed by a lovely view of Holy Isle and the varying moods of the sea and the sky. On the island itself there was always quite a lot to do in one way or another. There were picture shows in Brodick, concerts both classical and modern, ceilidhs and dances, many of which we attended as the winter set in. If one wished, it was possible to lead a very social life indeed. Margot and I attended the Bridge Club annual dinner, where I met her fellow players and, as Christmas approached, we had a quiet dinner together at the Argentine in Whiting Bay which we both enjoyed. Margot continued her usual custom of having a party on New Year's Day, to which we invited all the neighbours and our friends, many of whom Margot had met over the years; even Jackie, her husband, Kenny, and their dog, Lady, came up from Billinge in Lancashire to join us. It was a great party and everyone enjoyed themselves without any fuss. Jackie even managed to sort out one or two computer problems I was experiencing. Telephone calls to Euan and Michèle in Alice Springs and Adelaide respectively put the icing on the cake; they were both well, happy and enjoying life.

The first winter had been a relatively mild one and I only missed my locum job once due to ferry cancellation although, on two or three occasions, the ferry was diverted from Ardrossan to Gourock.

At the beginning of the summer, 1997, I heard on the grapevine that the Read Codes implementation had not made much progress within the NHS in Scotland. The "New" Labour government had just been elected with a massive majority and Scotland now had a new Minister for Health, the Rt. Hon. Sam Galbraith, himself a former neuro-surgeon. After discussion with Margot, she agreed that I should once again forward a letter, with the same attachments which I had submitted to Mr. Scaife, to the Minister for Health; this I did and, once again, received a polite note of confirmation. Again, there does not appear that much action has been taken. Such is life in government and politics but these are early days yet.

The summer was a lovely hot one, adequately interspersed with the odd days of rain so that the garden never actually appeared dry. Margot and I went a few walks, relatively short, as I was inconvenienced by my old fractured ankle. Golf kept Margot fairly busy, while I gardened, wrote my book, did my locum work and continued with my books and poetry. In between, we had visitors to stay for a few days. During these visits, the weather was always perfect. Brian, our best man, had not been on Arran since a youth, while Elspeth, his wife, had never visited the island; they liked our wee home and were entranced with Arran. On another sad occasion, Betty, Maria and Dorothy, my old work-mates from Trinity Park House, visited Arran for a couple of days. Margot and I invited them out to a lovely dinner. Later, Tony and Julie Hillman, friends from Australia, visited us for a few days. Again, the weather was perfect, Margot was fine and the guests thoroughly enjoyed their visit. Early in July, we were able to bring Jack, Margot's father, across for a week and, although he enjoyed his visit, he was adamant that he did not want to move across to Cooriedoon. Again the weather was perfect.

I continued to take an interest in Primary Health Care once again and made comments at every opportunity in the medical papers and newspapers as the occasions arose and, in addition, forwarded copies of a few of my papers on Primary Health Care to Frank Dobson, the Health Minister, for his consideration. A Health Administrator writing a thesis on manpower usage approached me about the use of suitably trained paramedical staff in PHC; I was able to send him copies of my previous articles.

Similarly, my interest in politics and, in particular, my belief in Scottish independence, still occupied my attention and again I wrote to the newspapers expressing my opinions. The Referendum on Scottish Devolution on 11 September 1997 gave every one considerable scope for thought and, although I did not want devolution within the union, I supported it as independence was not an option on the referendum ballot paper and I believed that it was an inevitable step towards independence for Scotland. For the Referendum, the Herald ran a poetry competition in which contributors were asked to submit a verse of not more than twenty lines which was not to be anti-English in tone. I wrote and submitted one of twenty lines entitled "The 11th. September 1997". Earlier in the year, I also wrote two poems, "Materialism" and "Life" which I submitted for publication. Both were accepted, the first in the "Age of Enchantment" and the second in the "Star Laden Sky".

My computer allowed me to indulge in my other pastime, genealogy. Through the post, I received from "Burke's Peerage" a book on the "SAINTYVES" which contained about seventy addresses of those with the surname (most of the families spelt their name as above, while the Canadians had the hyphenated surname, the same as our own) scattered throughout France, the bulk of them, Canada and Scotland (my own family). I worked my way through the book, writing to each person mentioned. The replies from France were few and far between, but I was able to recontact Gabrielle and two other apparently separate families, although I think Gabrielle's family has a distant connection with one of the other two. My efforts here are almost at an end and I am hoping that I shall be able to send my

Canadian and some of my french eponymous friends floppy disc copies very soon. I have found it very interesting as I originally started it to provide Euan and Michèle information about their ancestry.

In mid-August, Margot received a sad 'phone call while I was away at my locum; Tom Smart, my old friend from Tain who had gone out to Western Australia to see me, had died of a heart attack. I had spoken to him only about ten days before after he had returned home from hospital after having had a knee operation; he was feeling very well. I immediately 'phoned Lynn, his wife, on my return to convey our condolences and to find out the funeral arrangements. So it was that I drove up to Tain from Saltcoats on 20 August 97 to attend his funeral and then return on the same day. We had lost a very good friend. Lynn and Tom always made us very welcome and considered us members of the family. Coincidentally, Jack, Margot's Dad, was admitted to Crosshouse Hospital on 18 Aug 97 to undergo a similar operation on his knees but fortunately he made a good recovery.

Towards the end of August, we received a very sad and worrying letter from our old friend Julie Bloch-Jorgensen in Australia. She had had a serious operation and had only just been discharged from hospital, this being the second major operation withion a few years. Julie and Rolf had visited Margot while I was in Saudi Arabia and, one week-end, they had come across to Arran. While here, they had gone across to the Buddhist Retreat on the Holy Isle. They both felt physically and spiritually rejuvenated by their short visit.

The long week-end beginning Thursday, 11 Sep 1997, proved to be a memorable one for Scotland and for Margot and me. It was the Devolution Referendum Day, held on the 700th. anniversary of the battle of Stirling Bridge at which the Scots, under William Wallace and Andrew Murray, defeated the English at the start of the wars of independence. The Scottish electorate did not falter and returned a resounding YES both for Devolution and Tax-raising powers. Margot and I were delighted as we believe that it will be the first step to independence.

Towards the end of September, I received word from Mrs. Parkins at Leslie House, where my Mother had been resident for over 15 years, that she was dying. For the two days prior to her death on Saturday, 27 September 1997 at 00.10 am, I visited her during my lunch-breaks and sat beside her for over an hour, holding her hand, unspeaking and unrecognised as she was semi-comatose. I though long and hard as to whether or not I truly loved my Mother and, I am sorry to say, that in the end I came to the conclusion that I did not, and that everything I did, and had done, was through a sense of filial duty. Strangely, as I sat there looking at her face, now quite free of wrinkles, I recognised the resemblance for the first time in my life. Her funeral was delayed due to a public holiday, so it gave me time to complete all the administrative and legal requirements. In the end, her funeral was arranged for Friday, 3 October 1997, 12.30pm, at Craigton Crematorium, Glasgow. Mum has asked for no hymns to be sung, so the funeral service was very short and uncomplicated There were ten mourners present, Margot and I, three family members, Brian (our best man), and four of the ladies from Leslie House who had looked after Mum so well for all these years. In the end, it once again brought home to me the unanswered question, "What is the point of living?"

My Mother was, in many ways, a difficult woman and had few real friends throughout her life. She was obsessed about her age of which I was never really sure about until I obtained a copy of her birth certificate about one month before her death, an act quite unrelated to her eventual death. She was actually born on 21 August 1906. When I was twelve, she kept telling everyone I was her younger brother. At the same time, she told me that I was born when she was 19 years of age, but in fact, she would have been about 30 years of age. Later, she went so far as to alter her passport so as to falsify her true age. She hated the fact of growing old.

In mid-July, 1998, we were greatly saddened to learn of the devastating tidal wave, a 'tsunami', which followed three submarine earthquakes in the Bismarck Sea, and which killed an estimated three thousand people and destroyed the lives of thousands more in the Aitape region of the West Sepik province in Papua New Guinea. It was especially popignant for me as I had been the last DMO to be in charge of the whole 'Sepik District' as it was then. In fact, on my last visit to Aitape, I had to perform an emergency, natural delivery of breech-presentation twins at the Catholic Mission Hospital there. The Sepik will always hold fond memories for Margot and me.

Looking back on my life, I realise that I have followed a very similar path to that taken by my Father but thanks to Margot's insistence that I should not go abroad again to work, I am alive, in good health and looking forward to a happy retirement with Margot. It was only after my Father's death that I realised how much I loved and missed him as he was a "gentle" man in all aspects of the word. My Mother was a difficult woman to love because I felt that she had never really loved me, although she may have done in her own fashion. She certainly did not show too much interest in Euan and Michèle. Probably I am a typical product of the boarding school—distant, not outwardly affectionate and very self-reliant. Margot always said of me that my early Jesuit schooling showed in my character. Undoubtedly, I feel that my school years in Western Australia had the most impact on me and I was deeply upset when we returned to Scotland. However, on entering Glasgow University and learning about Scotland, participating in its culture and way of life, I became a confirmed Scot, a conviction that was to remain with me for the rest of my life, and indeed was further strengthened by my years working overseas before finally returning to Arran. I now have no desire to return to Australia other than to visit our children, if that will be possible.

It has always been the one major question I have asked myself, "Should I have done medicine?" My original wish was to be a journalist but parental pressure and the relative ease with which I entered the University, saw me take up medicine instead, a choice with which I have never been completely happy. Perhaps it was the correct choice for someone who was once said to have little imagination. Even as a doctor, I have always dabbled in writing, sometimes medical, sometimes political and sometimes literary—was it to escape from the confines of practical medicine? Fortunately, medicine encompasses a vast field and I was able to practise in quite a few specialties; I only hope that I was able to make a worthwhile contribution to each specialty I worked in and that the patients and persons with whom I came in contact benefited from my efforts.

There is no question that my decision to marry Margot was the only one I could have made considering the life style which we both later followed. Indeed, our friends have said that no one else would have accepted me, and no one else would have accepted Margot. We have always been "twinnies" and although we have had, at times, a very stormy marriage, we have, at rock bottom, always known that we have loved each other and that is what has carried us through it all. We have been very privileged to have seen and done things together which relatively few have had the opportunity to see or do. Fortunately, we worked in allied professions and, in the Solomon Islands, I was able to help Margot a little in setting up SIPPA.

After all these years together, Margot still occasionally states that I took these overseas jobs because, at heart, I wanted to run away from her and the children. I can honestly say that this was never the reason and, in fact, never ever entered my thoughts. The one and only reason was that the jobs in my particular branch of medicine (Public Health) were much more varied and interesting overseas.

Margot has often asked me why I did not stay in one specialty as she considers that I could have reached professorial grade. I have thought about my reply on many occasions. My nature was against a static post as I liked challenge. Further, I always seemed to be able to come to grips very quickly with any post I was in and, once I had, I found that the challenge of the post no longer existed. Although I am a person of routine, I cannot bear to have a routine and unchallenging job. In addition, I adapt very quickly to any situation I find myself in, indeed, so does Margot. As to why I never remained permanently in Scotland, I feel the answer to that lies in my family background and upbringing and to the fact, that, once having worked abroad, I found the jobs far more stimulating, more hands-on and more constructively helpful at the individual level, person to person; nearly all of these jobs were divorced from the red-tape which is rife within the NHS, thereby allowing me almost untrammelled scope for individual thought and action to suit each situation. To work in England never really appealed to me although I did apply for the occasional post there when I tried intermittently and half-heartedly to return to Britain.

When I first broached the subject of marriage to Margot I warned her that I would be working overseas for most of my life and although she heard what I was saying, I do not believe that she had actually internalised it for, in later years, as the constant travel and change took their toll of her, she would say that she wished that she had believed me. Undoubtedly, especially after the births of Euan and Michèle, this constant change did affect our family as a whole and, although it did provide us with hidden strengths, it also adversely affected our family life which it most certainly was not intended to do. Without any doubt, every decision Margot and I made concerning the family, in particular decisions concerning Euan and Michèle, were made with love and the very best of intentions but, as Rabbie Burns said, "the best laid schemes of mice and men gang aft agley". Frequently, we have regretted many of the decisions we made, in hindsight.

Although Margot was able to accompany me to all of my postings, she chose not to do so permanently in Saudi Arabia and, in many of the others, she found that she was left either with Euan and Michèle or by herself for relatively long periods on many occasions due to the requirements of my work; consequently, she had to develop self-reliance and to learn to lead a semi-independent life although this pattern may have been a factor in her social problems. She had to develop a sense of independence which has continued throughout our marriage, much to the amazement of our friends; she may enjoy a sense of independence but we remain together in love and this type of relationship, born of necessity, tends to confound many of them.

Euan and Michèle were greatly affected by our lifestyle and undoubtedly suffered unduly, especially from the decision to send them to boarding school. In this, I was influenced by my own experience as a boarder and Margot, although intuitively against the decision, was guided by that also. However, in hindsight, it was the wrong decision and it was one we have regretted ever since; of our two children, Euan was the more adversely affected as he felt that we had abandoned him. It is only relatively recently that they have begun to realise that we did not abandon them and that we took the decision because we loved them. Still, it was the wrong decision.

It was only when we returned from the Solomon Islands that I became interested in politics. My experience of the British, but in reality English, establishment attitude both abroad and at home had coloured my perception of the so-called "British" unionist state. Repeatedly, it was driven home to me that the English establishment considered Britain and everything British to be England and English, an attitude which I found to be increasingly unacceptable and patronising. The Scottish establishment, by and large, appeared to condone this. So, it was inevitable that I should join the Scottish National Party and even attempt unsuccessfully to become an MP. I did this not because I was anti-English but because I felt, and still do, that Scotland should know itself before it can take its place on the world stage and that the only way to achieve this is through independence. The Referendum on 11 September 1997 did not offer the Scottish electorate the choice of independence but it did offer Devolution within the unionist system of government, which we supported as we believe that Devolution will inevitably lead to independence after almost three hundred years of unionist, English dominated and anglo-centric politics.

I have always felt a sense of frustration in my work due to the fact that I believed that my efforts were not appreciated by my superiors. Although I did achieve relatively high positions within the various hierarchies, I felt that I always came up against a brick wall at the last hurdle. Margot has always said that although I get on very well with my equals and subordinates, I tend to antagonise my superiors because I am too straightforward and forthright, do not suffer fools gladly and cannot stand delays. Futher, as our friend Stan Struthers once said to Margot, "Unfortunately, Ian is almost always right in what he says." This may or may not be true and, if true, does not endear me to superiors. I have experienced this obstacle in all of the jobs I have held in Australia and Scotland and if I had not, would I have changed our life-style? I daresay not. Interestingly, I had my handwriting analysed anonymously in TPNG. This analysis suggested that I was honest, loyal, sincere, peace loving but secretive, with self-control, and lacking in spontaneous emotion due to total head control. In addition, it stated I had keen judgement and an excellent mind, was a good organiser, was economical and practical, reliable, generous, tactful, logical and prudent, with a sense of pride, self-respect and had poetic tastes, with a doubtful simple, child-like personality and exaggerated ego. Others who know me can make up their minds on the analysis but it is nevertheless interesting.

Now that we are on Arran, Margot and I can sense that we are more at peace within ourselves and with each other. The calmness, the unhurried lifestyle and the few good friends we have, both on Arran and on the mainland, give us great happiness although we sometimes worry about the "goldfish bowl" environment which living in a small community entails. Margot has her golf, bridge and tennis to keep her happy and occupied in "Our major regret is that Michele is in Adelaide, South Australia, but she does come back regularly to visit us. Our son Euan returned to Arran and is now a restaurant manager in Brodick. He is thoroughly enjoying it."to her home and garden while I enjoy painting, computing, writing letters to the Herald and poetry and together, we enjoy our visitors, the occasional meal out, the local concerts, ceilidhs and other social events. Our one major regret is that Euan and Michèle are so far away and that we are not able to see them too frequently. Still, we are very happy that they are well settled in Australia and are in jobs which they enjoy but above all, we are most happy with the fact that we are a family once again and that we love each other although widely separated. We will always have their visits to look forward to.

The more leisurely lifestyle on Arran has given me ample time to consider the most important question concerning life, namely "What is the point of living?" I cannot truthfully say that I have come up with a good reason and, overall, I tend to come to the conclusion that there is no real point to life although I have led a varied, interesting, exciting and basically happy life which I have enjoyed overall. But enjoyment is not a good enough reason for living as it depends too much on circumstance. If I were religious, I would say that religion would provide the answer to any doubts I may harbour; however, I consider that all religions to be man-made, hierarchical systems of thought and social control, although many people undoubtedly receive great succour from them. As a consequence, I find it strange that the government should condone denominational schools and the continuation of religious education within schools, for religion is certainly divisive if not destructive, and such religious institutionalisation unwittingly helps to maintain the already existing prejudices in society. Yet, mankind tends to look after the unfit and, by so doing, is sewing the seeds of self-destruction in the long-term. This makes it very hard for me to accept a logical reason for the purpose of living for we are still animals and we will survive or fall, by our animal efforts. To-date, mankind is not making a good job of surviving. Procreation and the overall continuation of life may be the most important beliefs held by many people as the reasons for life on earth, but if there is an in-built self-destruct mechanism, it is also an invalid one. There is little else to consider. Nevertheless, I have enjoyed my life but I still do not consider it an adequate reason for living. Not surprisingly, Margot gives this as her main intellectual reason for her wish to commit suicide and, I must admit, I cannot really disagree with it. As Margot's father said, "Life is a struggle from the womb to the tomb."

So here in Whiting Bay, on the Isle of Arran, off the west coast of Scotland, all our paths have come together and our journey has finally brought us to our lovely retirement bungalow and to a peaceful, contented retirement. With visits from our daughter and our son returning home to Scotland, we are happy. In my spare time I write letters to the Scottish newspaper, The Herald. The various paths have brought Margot home at last and for this I am very happy. We will enjoy ourselves here because we will make it happen.

At last, we have arrived Home.